Thinking Planning and Urbanism

BETH MOORE MILROY

Thinking Planning and Urbanism

UBCPress · Vancouver · Toronto

© UBC Press 2009

All rights reserved. No part of this publication may be reproduced, stored in a retrieval system, or transmitted, in any form or by any means, without prior written permission of the publisher, or, in Canada, in the case of photocopying or other reprographic copying, a licence from Access Copyright (Canadian Copyright Licensing Agency), www.accesscopyright.ca.

17 16 15 14 13 12 11 10 09   5 4 3 2 1

Printed in Canada with vegetable-based inks on paper that is processed chlorine- and acid-free.

Library and Archives Canada Cataloguing in Publication

Milroy, Beth Moore, 1940-
   Thinking, planning and urbanism / Beth Moore Milroy.

Includes bibliographical references and index.
ISBN 978-0-7748-1614-4 (bound); ISBN 978-0-7748-1615-1 (pbk.);
ISBN 978-0-7748-1616-8 (e-book)

   1. City planning – Ontario – Toronto. 2. Sociology, Urban – Ontario – Toronto. I. Title.

HT178.C22T67 2009   307.1'21609713541   C2009-902736-4

Canadä

UBC Press gratefully acknowledges the financial support for our publishing program of the Government of Canada through the Book Publishing Industry Development Program (BPIDP), and of the Canada Council for the Arts, and the British Columbia Arts Council.

This book has been published with the help of a grant from the Canadian Federation for the Humanities and Social Sciences, through the Aid to Scholarly Publications Programme, using funds provided by the Social Sciences and Humanities Research Council of Canada.

UBC Press
The University of British Columbia
2029 West Mall
Vancouver, BC V6T 1Z2
604-822-5959 / Fax: 604-822-6083
www.ubcpress.ca

The true story lies
among the other stories ...

MARGARET ATWOOD,
"TRUE STORIES"

Contents

List of Illustrations / ix

Acknowledgments / xi

Abbreviations / xiii

1 Opening / 1

2 History / 42
(*with Nik Luka*)

3 Regenerating / 67

4 Redeveloping / 98

5 Defending / 138

6 Implementing / 180

7 Closing / 217

    Appendix 1   Selected elements of the planning framework / 238

    Appendix 2   Chronology / 250

    Appendix 3   Basic characteristics of the planning area / 254

    Appendix 4   Socioeconomic information about the planning area / 257

Appendix 5 Seven development options, Yonge and Dundas area, December 1996 / 260

Appendix 6 Financial plan and costing scenarios, Yonge and Dundas area, December 1996 / 262

Appendix 7 Issues raised at public meetings and via correspondence regarding the redevelopment scheme, spring 1997 / 266

Appendix 8 Bylaws before the Joint Board / 269

Appendix 9 Decision of the Joint Board: Jurisdiction, conclusions and findings, decision and conditions, and obiter dicta / 271

Appendix 10 Sample calendar of events at Nathan Phillips Square January to July 2000 / 280

Notes / 282

References / 293

Index / 308

List of Illustrations

Figures

1.1 Toronto in its North American context / 3
1.2 Toronto in its regional context / 4
1.3 Selected subareas of the City of Toronto's core / 5
1.4 Southeast corner of Yonge and Dundas, 1998 / 6
1.5 Northeast corner of Yonge and Dundas, 1998 / 6
1.6 Looking southeast down Yonge Street, 1998 / 7
1.7 Yonge and Dundas' new image, 2007 / 7
1.8 Dundas Square, formally named Toronto Life Square, 2008 / 8
2.1 The Toronto Plant of the T. Eaton Co., c. 1919 / 48
2.2 Yonge Street as a boulevard in front of Eaton's College Street store, c. 2008 / 48
2.3 Yonge Street Strip, 1975 / 53
2.4 Yonge Street as pedestrian mall, 1974 / 54
2.5 Toronto Eaton Centre interior, 2008 / 58
2.6 Plan to connect Dundas Street West and East / 63
3.1 HMV's "urban box" form, 2005 / 72
3.2 Looking south on Yonge Street, 1999 / 78
3.3 Reinvestment area and larger community improvement area / 80
3.4 Yonge Street's built-form context, 1996 / 83
4.1 Development parcels, Yonge Dundas Redevelopment Project / 108
4.2 Original illustration for the redevelopment of the Yonge-Dundas area, 1998 / 109

4.3 Conceptual drawing of the future square and surroundings, 1997 / 110
5.1 Looking south down Yonge Street to Lake Ontario / 147
6.1 Salvation Army building and the Senator, 1998 / 185
6.2 Original design of the Torch, 1999 / 187
6.3 The Torch, 2008 / 188
6.4 Dundas Square, winning design, 1998 / 191
6.5 Triangular sidewalk outside the Eaton Centre, 1999 / 200
6.6 Reduced sidewalk outside the Eaton Centre, 2008 / 200
6.7 Downtown Yonge Business Improvement Area boundaries, 2001 / 202
6.8 Chess players on Gould Street, 1999 / 211

Tables

4.1 Number of police "contact events," 1995-97 / 132
4.2 Drug, prostitution, and total criminal offences, 1996 and 1997 / 133
6.1 Changing management of Dundas Square / 193

Acknowledgments

At the beginning of this project, Nik Luka was as deeply immersed in the Yonge-Dundas material as I was. I thank him for many hours of discussion and research devoted to trying to decide what to make of the transformation that was taking place quite literally outside the doors of the Ryerson University planning school. We met at Ryerson, where I was the director of the planning school. I had recently arrived in Toronto and was digging myself into the local culture, while he, a Toronto-born young graduate of the planning program, was preparing to leave town. There was a fruitful period of overlap. He subsequently went on to other intellectual pursuits, and, in the fullness of time, the project evolved into something quite different from where we had started. I gratefully acknowledge his early collaboration, which was a pleasure to have had, and expressly add that he bears no responsibility whatever for any judgments, errors, or omissions in the final text.

It was a great help to have been invited to discuss the project with undergraduate and master's students in several programs at Ryerson University and the University of Toronto and in doctoral seminars at the University of Toronto and the Università di Roma Tre. As I prepared for each of these events, my rising level of anxiety about how I would be able to simply and succinctly say what seemed only complicated and unyielding to abbreviation had a way of focusing the mind, as the expression goes. I thank all who participated in debating *why* with me at these events. My ideas were also sharpened along the way thanks to exchanges with Heather Campbell, Philippa Campsie, Brendan Cormier, Frances Frisken, Neil Harris, Michael Neuman, Lucia Nucci, Giorgio Piccinato, Katharine Rankin, Scott Rodgers, Yvonne Rydin, Huw Thomas, and several anonymous referees who critically read versions of the manuscript. I sincerely thank them all for their insightful comments. A special thank you also goes to Luigi Mazza for several conversations that contributed to this project, all of which took place during delightful periodic walkabouts in various European and North American cities.

Because of the location and nature of the project, it needed little funding. However, I was glad to have received several small grants that I used to hire occasional research assistants and specialized professional services and to travel to academic meetings in France, England, and the United States to discuss the work as it progressed. For this most welcome assistance, I thank Ryerson University and, in particular, the Faculty of Community Services.

I was often given assistance in timely and important ways by friends, colleagues, assistants, and strangers regarding materials used in the writing of this book. Many thanks go to all of them, including, but not limited to, the following: Judith Bell, Louise Berthiaume, Scéno Plus, Montreal; Carys Craig; Elizabeth Cuthbertson, City of Toronto; Paula Gallo; Carolyn Gray, senior copyright advisor, Service Ontario Publications; Gordon Grice, Gordon Grice and Associates, Toronto; Sherrill Rand Harrison, Mahone Bay, Nova Scotia; Ian Lord, Weir & Foulds, Toronto; James Robinson, Downtown Yonge Business Improvement Area; Zack Taylor; Cheryn Toun, City of Toronto; Stephen Waqué, Toronto, for permission to quote from "Notes on argument in chief by the City of Toronto," 1998; and Richard White.

Finally, my very special appreciation goes to Barbara, Louis, and Jessica, who lovingly and continuously share so much with me, including their appetite for ideas and learning.

Abbreviations

BIA	business improvement area
BID	business improvement district
CCTV	closed circuit television
CIP	community improvement project
DYBIA	Downtown Yonge Business Improvement Area
DTYS	Downtown Yonge Street
GDRA	Garden District Residents Association
OMB	Ontario Municipal Board
OPA	official plan amendment
PPP	public-private partnership
RFP	request for proposals
RFQ	request for qualifications
TEDNA	Toronto East Downtown Neighbourhood Association; Toronto East Downtown Neighbourhood Alliance
TEDRA	Toronto East Downtown Residents Association
TTC	Toronto Transit Commission
UDC	urban development corporation
UDP	urban development project
UEC	urban entertainment centre
YSBRA	Yonge Street Business and Residents Association
YSM	Yonge Street Mission

Thinking Planning and Urbanism

CHAPTER 1

Opening

On one level, this book is about how planners and others puzzled over what to do with a small downtown area in Toronto and the eventual outcome, a redevelopment intended to mimic New York's Times Square and London's Leicester Square. It is a story of planners at work on a difficult issue in perplexing times, and it is described in detail from conceptualization to implementation to show precisely how planning was practised. On another level, this case is paradigmatic of planning problems encountered in a broad spectrum of urban areas where pressures of contemporary urbanism are felt. These pressures include the problem of how to pump new value into small areas when conventional assumptions about the relationship between an urban core and its periphery no longer obtain. For example, one outdated assumption is that the core provides essential services for its periphery; another is that "urbanness" is measured by population density rather than electronic and other exchanges. At this second level, the book grapples with the adequacy of the theories planners use to inform their work on a planned intervention such as this.

The powers and forces configuring urban areas today are considerably different from those associated with the industrial revolution of the mid-nineteenth to mid-twentieth centuries. Many attribute current changes primarily to globalizing economies and concomitant social conditions. While these forces are undoubtedly major contributors, the context in which this case study unfolds points at least as much to technology as a driver of contemporary urban form. The urban and regional planning field has tended to be less cognizant of technology's significance to the evolution of urban form, except as a derivative of economic and social revolutions.[1] Transportation and communications technology in particular add specific capacities to urban development, such as being able to spread out over enormous areas while still enabling people to be connected at any time to anywhere else. How to deal with the diffuse settlement patterns made possible by the combination of technological, social, and economic changes is a major question. A complementary question is how to treat the holes that are left, or made, in contemporary urban space by expansive development. Together, these questions call for a new form of urbanity, of conviviality, and for a reciprocal readjustment between the form of the urban tissue and the forms of engaging with each other.[2]

The story is about a specific type of small core area space and the arguments for conceptualizing the space in particular ways. Throughout city history, such debates have been common. In this instance, there is an unusual opportunity to examine the discussions in detail because the city's planning department put forward two proposed solutions concerning the same site, each of which was dominated by a dramatically different conceptualization of space. In the first proposal, the aesthetics of space, such as perspective and proportionality, and its technical features, such as sunlight and relative location of things, carried considerable weight. In the second proposal, space was conceptualized as nothing in and of itself but instead as what can be created out of it by people who seek to use the space to advance their goals, be they economic, social, or political. That is, the dominant conceptualization of the second proposal is that space is produced through social relations. Seeing the two proposals side by side sharpens the distinction between technical-aesthetic and socioeconomic conceptions of space and prompts questions about how the two inform theories and practices of planning.

As a point of departure, I accept that both the technical-aesthetic and socioeconomic conceptualizations of space are properly part of urbanism and urban planning. This study explores a case in which the tension between the two understandings of space was lost. When the second proposal was implemented, a model from elsewhere that was expected to solve social and economic problems was set down in the city core in a location defined as a suitable receptacle for the proposed treatment. Scholars have analyzed comparable projects, using social science–based urban theories to uncover how and why such projects were developed. While recognizing their insights, I have approached this case differently, immersing myself in its dense detail to see what questions it raised about planning and urbanism. The manner of conceptualizing space emerged as a central issue. It shaped the proposals of planning practitioners, and it either opened up or closed down the potential for innovation. The proposals are classic illustrations of how to treat space, each with centuries of urbanistic practice behind them. I consider the implications of these conceptualizations of urban space for theorizing planning.

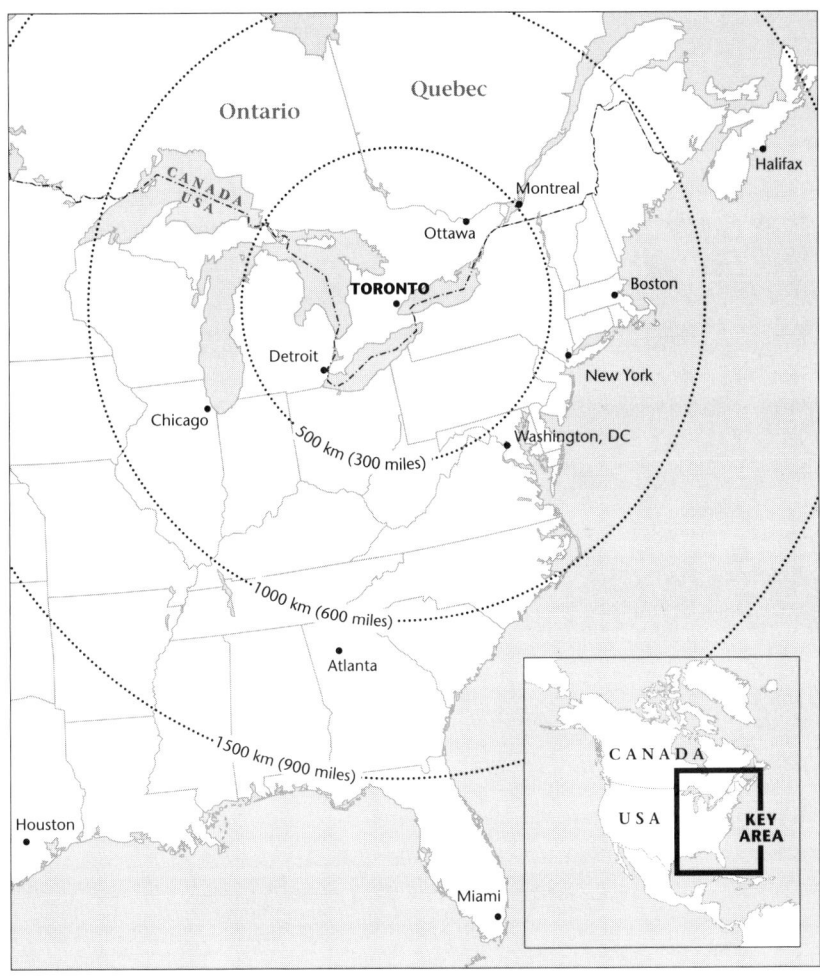

1.1 Toronto in its North American context. | Adapted from Toronto (1992, 113).

The Story in a Nutshell

The area in question is in the vicinity of the intersection of Yonge and Dundas streets in downtown Toronto. (See Figures 1.1 and 1.2 to locate Toronto in its North American and regional contexts and Figure 1.3 for selected subareas of the city's core, which is where the case takes place. See Appendix 3 for a written description of the area.) For years people had noted the absence of redevelopment money going into the ten or so blocks in the vicinity of the intersection. Some said redevelopment was not happening because the area

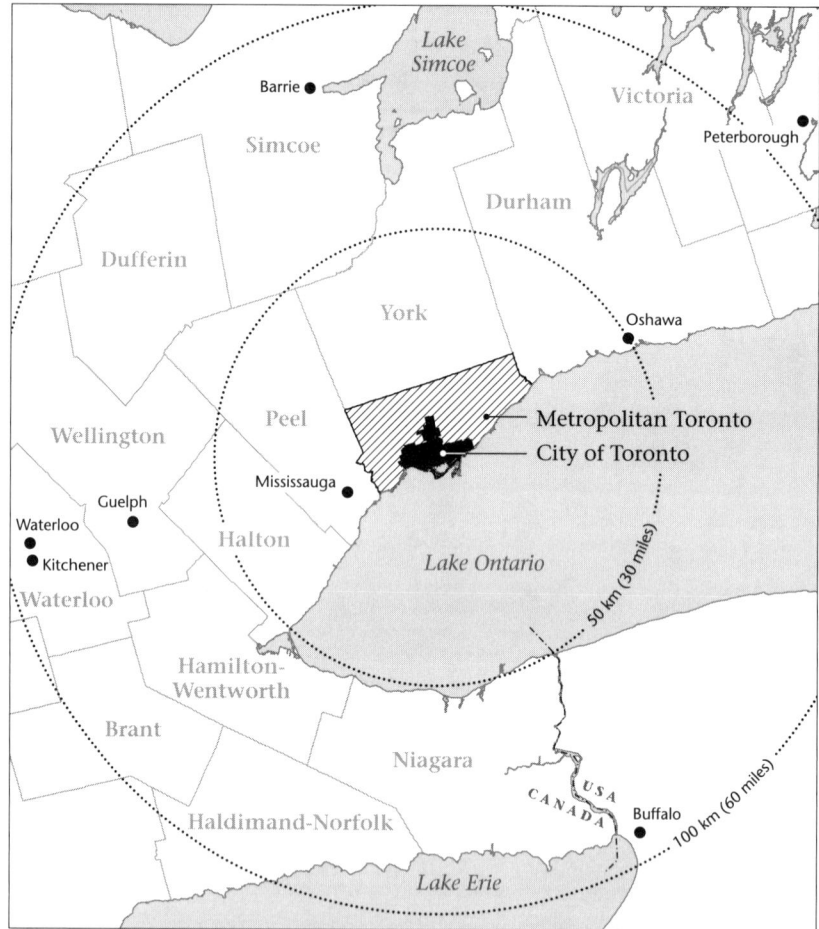

1.2 Toronto in its regional context. Aside from the City of Toronto, only upper-tier municipal boundaries – counties and regional municipalities prior to amalgamation – are shown. | Adapted from Toronto (1992, 113).

was so down-at-the-heel; others argued the reverse – that it was down-at-the-heel because the land use restrictions in the city's official plan discouraged redevelopment. Whatever the cause, the area was in poorer condition than civic authorities and a wide range of other people thought appropriate. After all, this was reputedly the busiest corner in the country and the location of the main door of the Eaton Centre shopping mall, which is said to have the highest turnover retail sales space in Canada. It was widely agreed that a planned solution was needed. Efforts made to fix up the area over more than two decades were judged to have had little effect.

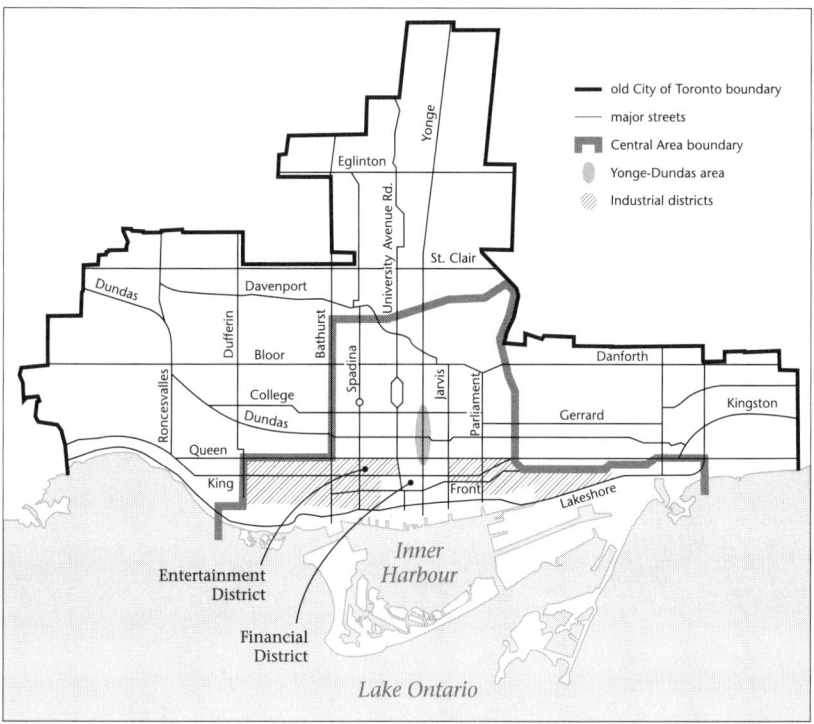

1.3 Selected subareas of the City of Toronto's core. | Adapted from Toronto (1990b, 16) and Toronto (1994c, Map M.2)

For decades there has been hand wringing over the Yonge Street Strip. Older adults have worried about its influence on their children at least since hippie youths hung out there in the 1970s, followed by punk youths in the 1980s and hip-hop youths in the 1990s, always with a certain amount of drug use and trade happening. From the early '90s, the picture also included increased numbers of students at Ryerson University a block away; two youth shelters and a shelter for homeless men within two blocks of the intersection; increased numbers of psychiatrically disturbed people wandering around because deinstitutionalization policies were not matched by community care; more homeless people because senior government funding for all social housing programs had been stopped; and more panhandling and loitering than had likely been seen in Toronto since the 1930s because welfare provisions had been cut by more than 20 percent on top of a deep five-year recession, which brought high unemployment rates, particularly for young people. By the mid-1990s Yonge-Dundas looked very stressed, certainly to middle-class eyes. (See Figures 1.4 to 1.8 for before and after views of the Yonge-Dundas area.)

1.4 The World's Biggest Jean Store on the southeast corner of Yonge and Dundas, 1998. | Author's collection.

1.5 Stores on the northeast corner of Yonge and Dundas, 1998. | Author's collection.

1.6 Looking southeast down Yonge Street, 1998. Dundas Square Street is to the left; Eaton Centre is on the extreme right. | Author's collection.

1.7 Yonge and Dundas' new image, 2007. Dundas Square, looking west from the bandstand to Eaton Centre with its media tower. | Author's collection.

1.8 Looking south over Dundas Square, formally named Toronto Life Square, on a sunny Sunday afternoon in May 2008. Hard Rock Cafe is just off the square on the right. Financial district towers are in the background. | Courtesy of Sherrill Rand Harrison.

In 1996 two solutions were proposed: a gentle regeneration-style solution was approved but was superseded nine months later by a dramatic expropriate-and-redevelop proposal. The latter has been in the process of implementation ever since and is the proposal that receives all of the attention. No one seems to remember the regeneration plan. Politics had a great deal to do with the switch from one plan to the other. Because there were two plans from the same planning department and from some of the same planners for the same geographic space in overlapping time periods, their foci and rationales can be compared. In the transition from one to the other, we see the position in which the planning department (the Planning and Development Department, which was renamed Urban Development Services in September 1996) found itself after having been politically forced to reassess its first, gentler strategy. The routes open to the planning department seemed to be as follows: (1) to refuse the new, more aggressive model and be sidelined while the planning framework was operated without the planning department; (2) to strongly make a case for why the new approach was wrong and then, if the city council still insisted on going ahead, to do the best planning job possible by trying to avoid the worst outcomes; or (3) to be persuaded to go ahead with it, either because the department saw no alternative or because the second proposal was the better strategy. Regardless of whether it was in its better judgment, the planning department took the third route, at least publicly. Because it chose the third alternative, the planning department had to formally defend it when an appeal was launched.

Planning was central in this case and, indeed, a battleground for political struggles. In one struggle, planners were pitted against planners: the city used in-house and contract planners and a coalition of area business interests to oppose another set of business interests equipped with its own contract planners, economists, and land evaluation experts. In another struggle, certain interests were trying to shift the role of planning in Toronto. The justifications the city gave for its change from regeneration to redevelopment, and for its preference for its own plans over those proposed by opponents, provide some evidence for the hypothesis that planning in Toronto was being nudged toward an entrepreneurial approach, that is, to inviting the private sector to lead redevelopment initiatives and reap the rewards of property value increases.[3] This contrasted sharply with conventional planning approaches in Toronto, including the predecessor plan for Yonge-Dundas. Using Brindley, Rydin, and Stoker's (1989, 11) terms of analysis, the regeneration plan could be described as a mix of regulative and trend approaches, that is, managing urban development in the public interest while using a few tools to entice the market to deliver what it was more or less ready to offer anyway. As for the redevelopment approach, the term "entrepreneurial" does indeed describe it. The project site was turned over to private-sector redevelopment interests to make Toronto more competitive in comparison to other cities; processes were largely kept away from public scrutiny, and the so-called public square ended up promoting private consumption. A decade later we can see that entrepreneurial planning like this has not taken over in Toronto but, like elsewhere, has become one style among several that a city may employ. As an approach, entrepreneurial planning is likely to produce repetitious rather than distinctive environments (see Hall 2002, chap. 11; Loukaitou-Sideris and Banerjee 1998, 292) and, thus, less competitiveness (Hanna and Walton-Roberts 2004). However, beyond the matter of planning styles, there is now an overall greater propensity than there was in the mid-1990s to use more entrepreneurial attitudes, actions, and language (Courchene and Telmer 1998; Laxer 1995); to seek to criminalize or ostracize poverty (Gordon 2004; Kipfer and Keil 2002); and to use mixed public-private ventures to carry out a variety of municipal activities by various means, as has been seen in many other cities (e.g., DeFilippis 1997; Eisinger 2000; Gómez 1998; Gómez and González 2001; Hagen Hodgson 1997; Hoyt 2003; McGuirk and MacLaran 2001; Plaza 1999, 2008; Waitt 1999; Williams 2003; Winter and Brooke 1993).

What kind of reasoning went into justifying the second project? Some of it was sound and appropriate, but much was fallacious (appeals to emotion were used, symptoms and root problems were elided, solutions used elsewhere were parroted), and much was post hoc rationalizing with a view to obtaining approval for a project that proponents wanted, regardless of whether there was evidence to support it. As was the case in Bent Flyvbjerg's (1998) Danish example, rationality took the form of *Realrationalität*, that is, rationality practised in the face of power.

One of the fallouts from this entrepreneurial example concerned the commons, which shrank because public space was turned over for private interests to shape. The use of the term "public space" assumes that it is useful to define space along a public-private axis, even though meanings will be specific to cultures and historical periods (Lofland 1998, 8). Not all public spaces have the same level of publicness. The most public of spaces are owned by governments and are expected to remain open for public discussion and political expression; traditionally, these are streets, sidewalks, parks, and squares. Other forums, such as community centres, libraries, universities, subways, and airports, may have constraints on their use that do not apply to traditional public spaces. Dina Graser's (2000, 70) assessment of a government's relationship to public space in the Canadian legal framework is that it is quasi-fiduciary, which means that governments "have a responsibility not to unduly restrict freedom of speech in public spaces" and "a corresponding obligation ... to ensure a right of access for this purpose as an essential part of a functioning democracy." In this view, traditional public spaces are places where political activity may be expected, not places to be protected from politics (Deutsche 1996, 283). They are places where those people whose behaviour – sleeping on the street or panhandling – may disrupt a notion of urban order have a rightful place, along with anyone else who may, when encountering them on the street, be reminded of the political fact that their government appears to be failing some of its citizens.[4] In the Yonge-Dundas area, some of the merchants set up a so-called public-private partnership with the city to mastermind redevelopment of the street. Subsequently, the city created a board dominated by active proponents of the redevelopment to run the square, and a new privately managed Business Improvement Area was established in accordance with provincial regulations to look after the surroundings. It treats the street rather like a mall, so the street's character changed from political to economic (Graser 2000, 68-69). The actual street, not simply its uses, was commercialized with the assistance of the city and the province. The conventional idea of a street was challenged, as was the idea of the city square. Private security services were procured for the square, and the new board sought to sell the "public" square to paying users. The administrative set-up of the square is, therefore, contrary to the grounds upon which the city approved the development and defended it in a legal wrangle. The degree to which this development increased cynicism about the commons cannot be gauged.

The unstated goal of the Yonge-Dundas redevelopment was to increase consumer spending in the area. All imagery was directed to that aim via spectacularization – passive watching and being in the presence of spectacles. Huge lighted screens hang on almost every surface around the square, advertising products, services, and lifestyles. Spectacular events periodically fill the square to boost consumption: Sir Richard Branson sliding down a wire from the Olympic Torch into the square to launch his newest Virgin product; the World's Biggest Stir Fry to promote Arctic Gardens food products; a world-record-seeking, chocolate-milk-chugging contest to advertise Grab, Gulp, and Go from Nestlé.[5] Consumption is an individualized activity for the consumer and a privatized activity for the provider. When streets and squares are designed to serve individual and private activities, the conventional assumptions of the public-private axis are completely altered. Part of the unwritten social contract has been revised – without taking a vote. This is why it is important to pay attention to the transformation that occurred with the help of the planning framework.[6] Civic place making, as Peter Rowe (1997) describes it, requires both publicness for democratic reasons and aesthetic appeal for a wide range of people. Together, the socioeconomic and technical-aesthetic can make a civic place. Torontonians learned not to take for granted that their civic government would use its property to make a civic place.

A stated goal of the redevelopment phase was to increase the variety of people using the area; however, the mix was already astonishing. In fact, the project was designed to flatten the mix to a particular consumer stratum. It is difficult to avoid the conclusion that the stated goal was code for increasing the number of people with disposable incomes and discouraging the presence of loiterers, indigents, and those working in the underground economy.[7] Since no survey was done of who was using the area, the outcome of this large intervention can never be evaluated from the point of view of its often-stated goal. Indeed, despite all the money spent on costly contract planners, expropriation lawyers, land economists, disturbance damage experts, quantity surveyors, tax experts, signage rights specialists, and square naming experts, no one asked what that goal meant and whether physical redevelopment would achieve it, let alone whether it was the best way to achieve it. The opponents' counsel in a quasi-judicial hearing into the need for expropriations to accommodate this project was the only person who tried to show why that goal was not achievable via the chosen means.

It is unclear how success should be measured in this case. Were planners guided by public or private interests? When it comes to planning actions on the ground, is the putative division of public and private interests even useful? If the area attracts new international chain retail outlets as was expressly desired by the project planners, along with family shoppers whom the ward councillor wanted to see there, and tourists who were the hope of businesses in the area, then some will take those results as signs that the redevelopment worked. And if the dollar stores, drugs, and homeless people move elsewhere in the downtown area, by what measure would these city-owned issues have been solved? Has the public interest been served?[8] Or, how does one measure Torontonians' sense of having been duped when it is found that the public square is managed first and foremost for commercial interests? How can this venture be evaluated when the cost to the city can never be known, at least from outside the bureaucracy? Many of the documents necessary to make that assessment were purged from public files on the ground of confidentiality. The idea of planning as an activity that serves the public interest is severely tested in this case. To what extent was society improved by these activities?

In my view, this case is not unusual. This is a study of decision making and action as planners often experience them – as struggles over who controls decisions, investment opportunities, and symbols in a city's core. Planners were working on a difficult problem and, in this instance, in a very difficult context. The planning of Yonge-Dundas took place at a time when the city was emerging from a deep recession that had lasted five years, from 1989 to the end of 1994. In mid-1995 a newly elected provincial government came to power on a platform – the common sense revolution – that had all the earmarks of neoconservatism. It promised to fix Ontario's economy via huge tax cuts, the reduction of social programs, and the introduction of workfare and law-and-order measures. In the course of this "revolution," the new government sought to reduce the number of local governments and their range of activities, including subsidized housing and libraries (Courchene and Telmer 1998; Ibbitson 1997). By the end of 1996, the city of Toronto was trying to stave off legislation to force its own amalgamation with five adjacent cities and the eradication of the metropolitan level of government, which had been in place for forty-five years and was a model of success. The metropolitan government had been credited with contributing to the Toronto region's incorporation of rapid population growth while maintaining a healthy city core, unlike many US cities (Frisken 2008, chap. 1; Lemon 1996, chap. 7; Sharpe 1996). For a few months in 1997, during the later planning period for Yonge-Dundas, the attention of city officials and Torontonians was on trying to convince the provincial government to reverse its amalgamation plans and a confusing series of moves designed to alter the financial responsibilities of the municipalities and the province. Once the Toronto amalgamation was certain to go ahead, politicians and bureaucrats began to position themselves as best they could, because it was obvious many would lose their jobs by the end of the year in the next civic election, when the number of elected officials would be cut in half.

It was in the midst of unprecedented pressure by the province to amalgamate voluntarily or be forcibly amalgamated, and the subsequent reorganization of local government departments, that those involved in the Yonge-Dundas project laboured (Frisken 2008, chap. 6; Sancton 2000). Although it was a busy time and, consequently, there may have been some inattention, the area around this intersection was not so different that the lessons of the case are inapplicable to other times and places. Local government is more often than not a tremendously busy arena, and many who, in the best of all possible worlds, would want to give individual issues more attention are actually too busy to do so.

Situating Contemporary Urbanized Space

In order to situate contemporary urbanized space, a quick trip through time is necessary. Simplifying excessively, Western city formation can be envisaged as having taken three forms, albeit with many variations, since antiquity. The first phase is represented by the classic city, in which a person's place of residence and citizenship were closely correlated so that a citizen belonged to a place. City spaces were distinguishable from rural spaces, and activities in the two were mainly complementary. The building of cities was planned and managed through various means, including civic governments of administrators and councils. From at least Roman times, dense population and diverse activities have been defining features of cities.

The second phase is represented by the city of the Industrial Revolution, which emerged with massive migrations of people from the countryside as well as from one country to another. Out of that period of urbanization came the new word "urbanism," which refers to reflections on and the shaping and managing of densely populated and dynamic urban areas. Urbanism is one name for practices that today include urban and regional planning. The complementarity of urban and rural ways of life changed gradually as "work" came to be identified with employment in the cities of the new industrial capitalism. The identification of work with the city reinforced a core-periphery relationship in which the city centre was the service site for its hinterland. Built-form changes included trying to bring, for health and safety reasons, the country into the city via gardens and open spaces and the city to the country via low-density new towns. Although explanations for the rise of industrial cities tend to focus on the economic and social revolutions of the time, the argument can be made that an ongoing technological revolution in transportation, communications, electrification, and building techniques was just as responsible for making the industrial city possible (Ascher 2001; Choay 1994, 27-28).

The third phase – which was also spurred by the ongoing technological revolution, especially in communications, and associated with new possibilities for economic production and management, and for urban form – was felt by the 1960s. Dispersion was added to urban sprawl. As in the previous phase, settlement continued in suburbs, but it expanded well beyond them into hinterlands that were not contiguous with urban regions. For example, in Canada from the early 1990s a growing number of "amenity movers" chose places that offered pleasure over economic opportunities – perhaps a slower pace of life, ski hills, hiking trails, beaches, sailing, splendid views, or clean air – even when these were in isolated locations (Chipeniuk 2005). The city centre no longer provided essential services for those in the vast periphery. The complementarity of urban and rural ways of life ceased to be the norm. The correlation between place of residence, work, and citizenship weakened so much that a person might live in one location, work in another, and be a citizen elsewhere. In this "hyperurbanité," the density of movement is more significant than population density (Bordreuil 2000, 169). If footloose industries showed a marked increase in the earlier decades of this phase, footloose workers – people who can choose where they work and live – have become more common in its later decades.

There is no consensus on what to call the contemporary phase of urbanization, which affects people on five continents, or the type of urban form that is being generated. The phase and the form are not separable. Regardless of whether people live in villages or large cities, their experiences are increasingly shaped by "the urban," a kind of generalized, global urbanness. Louis Wirth's phrase "urbanism as a way of life" seems apt, even if his analysis does not apply today ([1938] 1969). Names for the phase include the information age, the network society (Castells 1996), *l'urbain, l'ère de l'aménagement reticulée* (the era of networked land-use planning) (Choay 1994, 1999), and *société hypertexte* (Ascher 2001). On the unanswered question of what to call the urban areas that are situated within the broader urbanness that shapes our way of life, Kenza Benali (2006) gives a helpful overview of the issues. One issue is that the larger urban areas are less reliant on the state than had been typical in the industrializing period, and they function increasingly as cities linked together in defined ways. Eclipsing conventional metropolitan and regional forms, terms such as *système métapolis* (Ascher 2001), "city-region," "super-region" (Courchene and Telmer 1998; Jonas and Ward 2007; Scott and Storper 2003), "polycentric metropolis," "mega-city region," "polyopolis" (Hall and Pain 2006), or "network" refer to urbanized areas that are not necessarily contiguous and may even cross national boundaries but link up to create a competitive edge for some product or service. Sometimes "postindustrial city" is used, but the term has drawbacks. First, it implies a counteraction to the industrial city. It draws attention to economic activity rather than to the opportunities that these areas generate to innovatively combine a range of activities across various spaces, and it hides new technological evolution. Second, the term retains the word "city," which is a problem given that the complementarity of city-not city has been severed, as has the connection between territory and citizenship that was a hallmark of the classic city. "Urban" is more dynamic, less bounded than "city." To be sure, "city" will continue to be used, but its users are on notice that the term can obscure as much as it reveals. In effect, the meaning of centrality as it concerns urban space is being redefined (Sassen 2001).

Analyses of contemporary urban areas show that the geographic expansiveness made possible by technological innovations and the ability to plug in more or less anywhere and anytime have had disparate effects on core areas. Some urban areas – the larger, more globally connected – thrive more than ever but with disparities in income and opportunities that are alarming in some cases, less so in others (Fainstein 2001b). Middle-scale cities (population about 100,000 to 500,000) struggle against the odds to keep a vibrant core (Filion et al. 2004), while the cores of smaller cities may be emptied of retail and other economic activities that disappear or relocate to the outskirts, where taxes are lower and access by private vehicles is simpler. All of these developments require finding ways to reuse city cores because the newly emerging urbanity brings different conditions but does not annihilate all physical signs of previous ones. The centres of older cities, some of which predate the Industrial Revolution, concretely propose forms for living and working in close proximity. There are lessons to be learned about built form in those spaces. What techniques can be used to adapt these spaces while opening the city to innovative activities? What techniques can be applied to ensure the pleasure of face-to-face communication and built form that respects the physical features of proportionality, patterns, coherence, and so on, continues? How can one best use existing patterns, generate extensions, fill holes, or bridge the space between A and B? Retrofitting is essential because the use of the core must change when a centre is no longer the service centre to its periphery. Ongoing innovation and ingenuity are demanded in the practices of urbanism.

This description of contemporary urban form connects to the book's case study in the next chapter, which describes the development of the core during the industrializing period and the onset of uncertainty when the effects of rapid suburbanization begin to alter the core in the late 1950s. Later chapters describe the two proposed treatments that were developed in the mid-1990s. By that decade, the proposals represented different responses to how Toronto's core had gradually changed in relationship to the rest of the region and, more immediately, was changing under the pressure of economic recession and increased social problems. These changes were associated with broader international conditions affecting Canada's economy that had specific effects in downtown Toronto via national, provincial, regional, and metropolitan policies, as would be the case in any location (see Donald 2002a, 2002b; Gertler 2001; Gertler et al. 2000).

Structure of Planning: Activities, Planners, and Frameworks

Planning is often called an art, a science, or a discipline. In my view, planning is a field of practice in which people reflect on and suggest how to shape and manage an area that is jurisdictionally defined. Urban areas are prime examples. A field of practice brings knowledge and skills together with ideas about better and worse ways to act, given the conditions the practitioner faces. Planning is but one of the fields of practice engaged in urbanism. A field of practice differs from a "discipline," which is a term applied mainly by people in educational circles to the sciences (social, physical, and biological) and humanities. A discipline is an area of investigation, the purpose of which is to better understand the subject matter, not to try to treat it. For instance, geomorphology is a discipline devoted to studying the earth's surface. The discipline's scholars seek to better understand the origins and transformations of the surface of the earth to better predict outcomes or explain effects, not to change the earth's surface.

Brendan Gleeson's (2003, 765) straightforward view of public planning activity is that it takes three forms:

1. development control centring on the regulation of land uses and built environments at the local scale;
2. assessment of environmental and social impacts of proposed development activity at the local and regional scales;
3. strategic planning involving the coordination of public and private investment and of government regulation within particular spatial frames.

Strategic planning includes generating planning policies that may appear in various forms such as in official, strategic, and subarea plans. These policies are future-oriented, spelling out actions needed in the short to medium term to serve needs but simultaneously safeguarding opportunities for the long term. Planning is more than land use regulation: it is more akin to intentional interventions to influence land and building development (see, e.g., Brindley, Rydin, and Stoker 1989; Tiesdell and Allmendinger 2005). These planning activities are carried out by conducting studies and having discussions with those concerned about matters relevant to land and building development.

To put some boundaries around planning, it is useful to note that not all urban development outcomes are the results of formal planning. In some cases planners recommend X, but Y is done; in others, no recommendation is made using the accoutrements of planning – action comes out of someone's, or some group's, sheer power to act.

The people I call planners fit either or both of the following criteria: (1) they use the legal and other instruments of planning and are trained as planners or work in municipal or regional departments or private firms charged with doing urban planning or (2) they are members of a professional planning body that accredits planners. These people accept the role and therefore the responsibility for carrying out planning activities and contributing to the planning framework. They are the ones whose conduct professional planning institutes seek to hold accountable by various means, including registration, licensing, codes of ethics, refresher course requirements, and so on. My definition excludes people who simply comment on planning from the sidelines, even though their often-critical assessments are welcome and vital to the well-being of the field. Many people who speak from that position have catalyzed changes to theory and practice (cf. Myers and Banerjee 2005).

I also distinguish the planning framework from planners and planning activities. "The planning framework" is a collective term that refers to the plethora of legislation, tools, and policies that inform land use practices in a jurisdiction.[9] Built up in response to the problems presented by rapid urbanization and industrialization, the planning framework, with a century of usage under its belt, is deeply embedded in the administration of local and regional governments. Its elements have been altered over time; however, because the changes have been piecemeal, the framework that applies (at least in the case at hand) continues to reflect its origins in the industrializing period and planning styles developed since the late nineteenth century (Wolfe 1989; Healey 1983, 263). Changes around the framework's edges have included the formal planning framework's adaptation to legislated measures to promote sustainable environments, to restore brownfields, to protect heritage, and so on.

It is essential to separate the framework from specific planning activities because the framework forms the ground rules that everybody uses in a jurisdiction, whereas planning activities can vary, provided they satisfy the formal constraints of the framework. The planning framework can be and is used not only by people designated as planners but also by politicians and the whole development industry, including lawyers, architects, builders, and others. A distinguishing feature of this case study is its illustration of how the planning framework was used by the many people involved. This is rarely elucidated by researchers who investigate planning practice. In this case the planning framework's importance to the outcome is inescapable. A society is likely to be more invested in its planning framework than in its planners. Indeed, planners do not have roles mandated for them in the framework, although by convention their training and experience have come to accord them opportunities to work with it on behalf of their employers and clients. But if there were no planners at all, there would still be a land use planning framework. The framework incorporates the basic or default planning process and can serve as a stand-in when local processes are not in place. Appendix 1 offers a brief description of some features of the planning framework that were relevant in this case.

The framework includes a set of legally binding requirements that govern land development and to which all who participate in development must adhere. These are not ethical standards. Ethical standards are the responsibility of the professional organizations of the various users of the planning framework, whether they are planners, lawyers, or members of provincial oversight bodies. The ground for judging a person's legal right to act in a proposed manner is one's individual property rights interpreted in conjunction with land use legislation that may constrain them.[10] The arbiter in challenged disputes among private owners and government bodies is most often a court or tribunal with a mandate to serve the public interest. Tribunal decisions are thus presumed to reflect the public interest, despite how hard a concept that is to define or defend. The public interest is not a fixed concept. Because elected city councils and appointed tribunals are the primary custodians of the concept for municipal purposes, the public interest can shift as their memberships change. The planning framework can be used to support a wide range of projects because members of councils and tribunals can articulate their ideological proclivities through its generalities.

The public interest is also tied to the concept of good planning, and for the tribunal involved in this case, the two appear to be equivalent (Chipman 2002, 111). According to John Chipman's (2002, 106) analysis of the Ontario

Municipal Board, before which the Yonge-Dundas case was heard, good planning falls under three broad themes: "conformity with approved planning policies, impact and compatibility [of a development], and adequacy of process."

Planning and Urbanism

The relationship between planning and urbanism is hard to sort out for many reasons, and this is particularly the case in Canada. In Canada, in French, a planner is an *urbaniste* or, occasionally, a *planificateur,* and planning may be *urbanisme, planification urbaine, planification rurale,* or, in some circumstances, *aménagement*.[11] In this book "planning" and "urbanism" are not used synonymously. Using Giorgio Piccinato's analysis (1987), Michael Hebbert (2006) illustrates how planning in the British-American tradition differs from urbanism in the Latin tradition. Canadian practices have roots in both Anglo and Latin traditions, so both planning and urbanism are used. Despite the difficulties that are raised by distinguishing them, the choice respects, first, the origins of the term "urbanism" in the late nineteenth-century upheavals of rapid urbanization and, second, its interpretation in an important land use dictionary, *Dictionnaire de l'urbanisme et de l'aménagement* (Merlin and Choay 2000). Here, "urbanism" is used to refer to reflection on and practices directed to shaping and managing urban space using some combination of normative ideas, data, and practicable actions. Over the years, different types of practitioners – surveyors, engineers, architects, planners, and designers – have dominated urbanism, and some have tried to carve off a chunk and treat the part metonymically, as if it was the whole. To add to the confusion, the tasks of various professionals have been inconsistent over time and across jurisdictions.

Planners bring one bundle of knowledge and practices to urbanism. Their tasks, as conventionally understood, were outlined earlier and mainly deal with policy for overall urban development, research and evaluation, and regulation. One can use planning to contribute to reflections on "the urban" and to effect change, but one can also use urban design, engineering, and financial savvy for the same purposes. Urbanism is a crowded field, but planning activities are expected to result in policies on land and built form and in practices that lead to implementation. Once formal planning policies are approved through the political process and carry the weight of statutory law, other fields are expected to respect them. The scope of planning activities can differ substantially from one jurisdiction to another.

To further complicate matters, "urbanism" as a term is used much less among English speakers than among speakers of Latin-based languages, which is a development that may have discouraged the formation of a broadly shared understanding of the word.[12] Despite the terminological difficulties, what other word so aptly conjoins and contextualizes the work planners and others do in contemporary urban areas?

Questions to Answer
I use the case study details to address two questions about planning practice and one question about theories. My first concern was to learn how Toronto ended up with a core area redevelopment scheme that sought to emulate the new high-energy, razzle-dazzle "shoppertainment" venues that were being built as urban development projects in the United States and Europe. I wanted Torontonians to know how that had happened, especially given that one of the project's newer elements is the controversial, not-quite-public public square. Thus, the first question is: How was urban planning practised in this Toronto case? I wanted to see planning as it was, not as it should have been. I answer the question by taking the long way around, by going through as many byways as possible to show in detail what the planners actually did and what tools, ideas, images, and arguments they used to arrive at and present their views. I am referring here to planners who were either public-sector employees working for the city, development consultants working on behalf of the business lobby in the immediate area, or private-sector planners making arguments for or against options.

As for the second question about practice, the deeper I found myself in the project, the more it seemed to me that the project presented a complex and not uncommon planning problem – that is, what to do with several blocks of a declining street dominated by an enormous shopping centre in the middle of an urban area. The story shows how planners approached the problem and worked through it within a specific political context, with economic conditions constantly changing, and while retailing was in a period of massive reconfiguration. As mentioned, I discovered that there were two fully developed plans: a street regeneration plan and a more aggressive redevelopment project. I wanted people who are interested in urban planning and related fields to see how the plans to fix this piece of a city changed and how the arguments for the two different solutions were made so plausible that both could be adopted. Given that the formalities of the planning framework did not change in any way that affected this project between the regeneration and redevelopment plans, the second question is: How did planners and others reason their way to two different recommendations for the same geographic space? How were the justifications and rationalizations structured and conveyed, quite literally, at the level of language? It seems to me that answering this question would help make the planning function and what planners do more understandable.[13]

The chapters in which these two questions are answered are somewhat like a planning manual because so many facets of planning in contemporary space are touched upon: the use of various tools; the interconnections among planners, politicians, municipal lawyers, and developers; the problems of citizen participation in planning; and the eternal matter of poverty and how plans affect the life chances of the least capable. These chapters pose a number of questions: How long is an economic cycle? What is a planning department's role with regard to supporting economic activity? Are reinvestment incentives enough to kick-start regeneration? What is a planner to do with too little data and too little time? Under what circumstances would another city's answer to a problem be a good answer for a problem in your city? When does the law trump ethics? What is the range of options for a planner with a strong sense of public duty? The Yonge-Dundas case provides an example of planners trying to figure out which way to move.

The third question mainly concerns theories: How does a planned intervention such as the one examined here correspond to planners' theories about their work? How did this planned outcome come about? What theory – or combination of theories, procedural or substantive, explanatory or prescriptive – helps us interpret this outcome? The case does not fit so-called procedural theories or what by convention are called simply "planning theories." Those are normative theories of process that describe what planners ought to do to plan well. Indeed, the actions of the city's planners during the redevelopment phase would be found wanting against any normative theory. On the other hand, the plan was approved and even praised by the city council and the adjudicating tribunal, both of which formally represented the public interest. How are we to square that fact with the injunctions of normative planning theory? Were the planners' actions right or wrong? The case is no better explained by substantive theories about urban phenomena, the so-called urban theories.[14]

Planners and Their Theories

Planning involves not only practice but also theorizing. One stands back from practice and asks questions about it. Those who do this and write up their findings are mainly in academia or are independent writers interested in urban matters, although practising planners occasionally write from a theoretical perspective too. Matters that tend to be investigated include how planners practise today compared to the past; why they practise as they do; the relationship between practice and outcomes; and how practice connects to theories and evidence about urban phenomena such as demographic changes, economic growth and decline, and much more. The reasons for those kinds of research are to provide observations on the role that planning practice plays in the development of human settlements and to improve planning's rate of success, however success is defined (see, e.g., Campbell and Fainstein 2003, 2-4; Nigel Taylor 1998, 167-68). To do this kind of theorizing, researchers typically use a range of mainly social science methods such as interviews, surveys, on-site observation, extrapolation from practice, and document analysis. Two or more methods may be used jointly.

Research studies about how planners practise are different from those that seek to show how planners ought to practise. While the two research approaches are not cleanly separable – for both can invoke images of normatively desirable means and ends – the basic purposes behind them differ. The first type of study mainly tries to show or explain actions that evidence confirms were taken, while the second seeks to illustrate the ethical correctness, or lack thereof, of particular actions that may empirically have been taken or may in theory be taken in the future. The research for this book was of the first type and, broadly speaking, took the following route: examined practice as actually carried out; noted the praise for it; and wondered why it was praised, given that the practice departed from theories. The route for the second approach, the road not taken here, would be something like this: start with a normative theory of how practice should be done; check practice as actually carried out; define the gap between theory and practice; and suggest how to fix theory and practice so the two better coincide.

The Relationship between Planning and Urban Social Science: Has the Analogue between Them Been Overextended?

Cases like Yonge-Dundas have mainly been interpreted by using theories from outside the planning field itself. Most often this has been via theories of urban political economy. Urban development projects (UDPs), of which this was an example, and urban development corporations (UDCs) were strategies governments frequently used from the 1970s to reposition cities in the so-called new economy (see, e.g., Bartley and Treadwell Shine 2002; Courcier 2005; Deas, Robson, and Bradford 2000; Fainstein 2001a; Gordon 1997; Moulaert, Rodriguez, and Swyngedouw 2002; Reichl 1999; Sagalyn 2001). Common characteristics of UDPs include taking a parcel of land with investment potential out of the usual regulatory regime (which might mean reducing development controls and permitting actions to be taken without public consultation) and allowing a wide range of options to be used to generate action, often with the help of specific financial incentives to make it more interesting for land developers to take up the challenge (including temporarily reduced or waived property taxes). This is usually called property-led development (Healey et al. 1992).

Although examining projects using political economy theories and concepts can provide many insights, it would not show, at least in this case, the contributions made by planners, planning activities, or the planning framework. Political economy theories swamp the actual practices of planners. They are not substitutes for theories of planning. The cases cited above, for instance, describe how politics and economics are articulated through UDPs, not how the planning function is executed and what its effect is on the outcome. Even regime theory, one of the most commonly espoused theories, would not explain this case. An urban regime is defined by its originator as "the informal arrangements by which public bodies and private interests function together in order to be able to make and carry out governing decisions" (Stone 1989, 6). Stone (1993, 2) says regime theory "holds that public policies are shaped by three factors: (1) composition of a community's governing coalition, (2) the nature of the relationships among members of the governing coalition, and (3) the resources that the members bring to the governing coalition." A regime is place-specific, and uncovering the structure of a regime in a given place should explain what occurs better than other explanations. For instance, one might expect to find a significant amount of informal cooperation among coalition members. In the Yonge-Dundas case this type of cooperation did not materialize. Those who wanted to put up office buildings took up a position in opposition to important retail property owners. (It is not unusual for landowners with different capital investment interests to argue over development.) Not only that, the two groups argued formally (not informally) over the interpretation and use of the *formal* framework (e.g., the provisions of the official plan and the community improvement plan).

Thus, the first issue this case raises has to do with the relationship of planning to the social sciences. Have planners overextended the analogue between their field of practice and the social sciences? The most obvious reason why urban social science theories cannot account for the role that planning, as a field of practice, plays in urban development is that planning is not a social science. This is widely acknowledged. But while theorists can momentarily forget, practitioners caught in the fray never can. As a field of practice, planning deals with urbanism, the dynamics of urban life and space. Its job is to find options for development that are plausible enough to be implemented. Even the language used can be a problem: the social science theories that planners use are sometimes collected under the single rubric "urban theory," which effectively reduces "urban" to those things that are amenable to investigation using the social sciences.

The social science theories most often used in conjunction with planning describe space as being socially constructed through a variety of complex and reciprocal relations and exchanges that involve money, power, gender, ethnicity, and so on. That assumption has been very fruitful in social science theorizing since the 1960s. However, its power also inhibits the contemplation of space in any other manner, such as in terms of proportion, pattern, extension, or the spaces between things – in effect, principles that can be used to generate spatial arrangements. Social science approaches to planning subordinate principles of spatial organization rather than allowing that they could also generate good planned milieus.

Planning theories are at risk of being taken over – one might even say colonized – by social science perspectives in which the activity of planning is conceptualized predominantly in terms of social science knowledge. When the space that planners deal with is conceptualized as a matter of social production with pre-established ends (making money, increasing social justice, etc.), the concomitant metaphor or image at work is one of purposiveness, of a design in which all the elements are to be brought under control of a central body. The case described in this book illustrates how the overextension of the social science analogue inhibits the theorization of planners' practices in other ways. Françoise Choay's thesis on the enduring figures in urban discourses, which I describe later, helps explain the significance of this tendency to accept a kind of colonization of the field's theories.

Relationship of Process to Substance: Are They Divorced?

The second issue for theory that this case highlights is related to the point just made: the perennially unresolved matter of how the process of planning is linked to the substance of planning activities. The turn to urban social science theories to bolster planning theory coincided with a period in the 1960s when planning theorists decided to give precedence to the process of planning rather than its substance. This remains the principal orientation among theoreticians of the field today.[15] For many, planning theory has moved beyond divorcing process from content. However, I agree with Nigel Taylor (1998, 152) who says that the distinction between procedural and substantive planning knowledge, which was made by Andreas Faludi in 1973, lives on and indeed represents a kind of "continuity in the development of planning theory."

My interpretation of the status of the planning theory divide is that the two types of knowledge, procedural and substantive, that planners identified in their work evolved into a binary and hierarchical relationship between those two main terms. The dominant term is "procedure": it gathers under its umbrella knowledge about how planners should plan normatively, work with data and other concerned people, and find opportunities and identify constraints.[16] The subordinate term is "substance," the repository of substantive knowledge and theories about the things that planners plan – for example, cities, regions, neighbourhoods, waterfronts, housing complexes, streets, and so on. Today, "planning theory" refers by convention to procedural theory, to just one part of the binary, however weakly or strongly procedural theory is attached to substantive issues.

Procedural theories flow along two main channels, each of which has several streams that are epistemologically and procedurally distinctive.[17] Theories in the channel that was developed first rest on concepts of rationality and betterment. One expects the latter to be achieved by applying the former. For planners, as for others, the terms "rationality" and "rational" raise endless problems concerning what they mean in specific contexts and how they can be used. For example, does "rational" describe decision-making processes in which each step of the way is based on careful reflection rather than guesswork, and for which the reasoning is made explicit so that it can be questioned (Nigel Taylor 1998, 70) – in other words, instrumental rationality? Or should the term be used to describe both the process of arriving at a decision and the goal – so-called substantive rationality? Or is it something else altogether?[18]

Despite the fact that rational planning includes theoretical conundrums and practices that cannot meet ideals, it has lived on. While it can take many forms, it tends to refer to planning in which means and ends are logically and justifiably connected and processes are reasonably transparent and consultative. It is associated with a series of steps to work from goals to options for implementation. Rational planning, then, addresses some of the problems manifested in urban and regional space by using knowledge generated rigorously in fields such as economics, geography, demography, and sociology, which its practitioners often combine with their own expertise in assessing and solving urban problems. Rational planning is also known as rational comprehensive, synoptic, managerial, deliberative, regulatory, or synthesizing planning. Who carries out the steps may vary, but public planners are centrally involved, as are people who are concerned about a given problem – residents, corporations, social groups with minority interests to protect, associations of homebuilders or environmentalists, or government agencies. The planner's expertise lies in bringing together knowledge from a number of relevant areas and from people with interests in the matter at hand and using the planning framework and practices imaginatively and appropriately to arrive at recommendations.

A second major type of procedural planning theory emerged in the 1980s to oppose rational planning. It challenged the epistemology and efficacy of science- and expert-based approaches. Its various formulations incorporate ways to question how a recommendation is being developed, who is involved, whose interests are served and not served, and what knowledge is being used. The planner establishes a process for communicating with those concerned about a given issue. Within that process, a degree of mutual understanding is sought about the issues and relevant knowledge to be used to solve the problem. Johan Woltjer (2000, 25-26) identifies consensus-oriented planning processes as being of three main types, although they can and do overlap: collaboration and learning, bargaining and negotiation, and persuasion and will shaping. In consensual theory, the planner is a centre person, negotiator, or facilitator with the task of developing a consensual outcome. The planner's expertise in procedure is crucial. The outcome is intended to incorporate the local or specialist knowledge of participants affected by the plan and to generate their goodwill and cooperation in the final decision making and implementation. Like rational planning, this type of theory also has many names. This highly simplified synopsis of what I collectively call consensual planning disregards a host of epistemological differences among proponents of approaches such as communicative, collaborative, and consensus planning, as well as equity, advocacy, and institutionalist planning.[19] Theorists debate whether it is sensible to pit rational theories against consensual theories as if it was a matter of one or the other. Both rationality and consensus are (normatively) desirable in a planning exercise; one should not be excluded in favour of the other. Ernest Alexander (1998) makes this point in theory. Woltjer (2000) tested it against six Dutch cases of infrastructure planning and concluded that the combination is needed and, at least in his cases, was used in practice.

Having long ago focused on process, planning theorists have continued to debate how best to connect the substance of planning to the process of planning. The two lines of theorizing, rational and consensual, are basic replies to that question. The first one uses reason to bring knowledge developed by planners, who often lean on the work and experience of others, to bear on a problem to reach the best option under the circumstances; the second one uses theories and techniques of communication to work toward an option on which people can agree. However, complaints have been raised about both lines of theorizing; critics say that they have led to theory emptied of content, which is the substance of what planning is all about – that is, city-regions and the lives of people in them.

Three broad responses to the so-called emptiness of both lines of theorizing can be discerned. The first seeks to incorporate substantive matters by tying planning theory to urban social science theories. Robert Beauregard (1990, 211) is one for whom the "drift away from the physical city" is a deep concern. He wants to return to the kind of city-centred planning theory that "was about cities in a substantive sense ... inseparable from social reform" (ibid., 210). The city-building process is planning's theoretical object, he says, and planning theory needs to be attached to it because it must be able to show the benefits of a better city obtained through its practice. His city-building process is described in social science terms – that is, a city is a phenomenon amenable to analysis regarding progress using the social sciences. Within Beauregard's strategy, planning theory would be normative and planners would admit to a political function and forget any claims to objectivity. His brief article was part of a point-counterpoint symposium and his fellow planner-respondents did not agree with his strategy because they saw it as politically naive (Foglesong 1990, 215; Bassin 1990, 217; Brooks 1990, 219). Fifteen years later, Fainstein (2005) reasserted Beauregard's point that city planning does not make its objective clear. She goes further, however, because she wants the purpose of city planning to be singular: "to create the just city" (ibid., 121) that would recognize "the historical roots and justification for planning" (ibid., 122). She too worries about the procedural-substantive split in theories used by planners. She calls the first "planning theory" and the second "urban theory." She wants planning theory to be tied to urban theory; otherwise, the objective of consciously creating a just city is unattainable because effective planning depends on its context (ibid.). When she writes about theory, Fainstein derives context from urban social science.

Another effort to fix the problem of "substantively vacuous" planning theories seeks to embed procedural theory within urban social science theories. Lauria and Whelan (1995, 8) describe planning theorists as having made a full circle from the empty rational comprehensive theory of the 1950s to empty communicative-style theories of the 1990s. For them, content in the form of a theory about the socio-econo-political workings of cities is essential. In their view, this might be achieved by embedding procedural theory in regime theory. However, as I have already suggested above, the result smothers the actual practice of planning beneath the weight of abstract political economy concepts. Allmendinger discusses the approaches proposed by those who see the merit of a political economy orientation to address the "contentlessness" of procedural theory. He concludes (2002, 66) by raising serious doubt about "whether a more critically aware planning could do without a methodology for making and implementing decisions." Despite all the insight that political economy approaches can provide, we still would not understand planning if we had not studied actual planning practices. Actual planning actions must be seen to be theorized inductively, not only situated within political economy frameworks to be explained deductively.

Finally, others imply that the claim that procedure is divided from substance is itself empty because the problem has been resolved by the newer planning processes based on consensus, negotiation, and paying attention to institutional relations. These processes are designed to recognize divergent views about substantive issues and to propose a process that involves representatives of differing views. If the process is competently and fairly conducted, then the result will be a solution to disagreements on substance. Thus, it is claimed, a good process is the best route to a good outcome. Quality of process leads to quality of place (Healey 2007, 1, 2). However, the assumption that the problem has been resolved through a new type of process does not satisfy all those who are concerned with this substance-process matter. Woltjer's (2000, 214-15) analysis of several Dutch cases that used consensual planning shows that these processes did not necessarily produce "a society and environment with a 'better quality' than would be the case with a rational planning approach": the selective participation of participants may be less ethical, and these processes may yield "inadequate results in terms of sustainability, consistency and cohesion." Another example is Fainstein, who, as we have just seen, claims that only by joining procedure and substance within a normative position on social justice can one figure out the desired outcome of planning and whether one's efforts are bearing fruit. To Woltjer's and Fainstein's concerns I would add two more. First, a public planner has a professional view about substance, and that view needs to be expressed at least as strongly as any other view in a process. This cannot happen if the planner is a fair – that is, neutral – process facilitator. Second, public planners are institutionally situated in such a way that, if they manage a process in which development stakes are substantial, there is always the prospect that a political solution will be invoked by elected officials who come in over their heads. When that happens, a planner's credibility as a facilitator is put into question, while his or her knowledge about substance has not been a vital part of the process. That is a lose-lose result. There is no doubt that planners need to frequently participate in consensual processes; but the reason for being present should be to bring planning's contribution to urbanism to the table.

My view, which is corroborated by the case study, is that the problem of putting process and substance together has not been solved, nor has it disappeared. The substantive-procedural binary, with its hierarchical form in which process ranks higher than substance, still exists, and theories continue to be built on the binary, even though it is not acknowledged. In fact, I do not believe there is a solution to the problem of putting substance and process together. Rather, it is a tension that will always be present. The tension should be recognized explicitly in planning theories. On the other hand, the hierarchical placement of process over substance can be corrected, not by inversion but by formally recognizing the value of both process and substance and consciously deciding how to balance them on a case-by-case basis. In this book, inspection of the planning practice in the selected case confirms the potential for taking this approach. Going further still, the case supports a reconceptualization of what counts as substance within urban planning.

Planner- and Planning-Centred Theories

The brief comments that describe rational and consensus styles of planning theories indicate that, despite their different orientations, they share three defining features:

1. They are first and foremost about planning and its processes; that is, they are not about urbanism and regionalism, cities and regions, or environments and rural areas, which are secondary or implicit.
2. Planning is led and executed by public-sector planners. The public-sector planner is at the centre of the action, including consensus-based approaches, where planners take charge of setting up the process and often run or mediate it.
3. A planner is expected to be able to choose the planning process that will be used.

In the redevelopment phase of the Yonge-Dundas project none of these defining theoretical features were obtained, while in the regeneration phase only item 2 applied: planning was led and executed by public-sector planners. This leaves a large gap between theory and practice. In this case, actions were not as planning-centred or planner-centred as theory suggests.

The data of this case show that economic and political arguments were filtered through a discourse on urbanism, not planning. This applied to all arguments, not simply those made by planners. Arguments may have stemmed from economic, political, social, or planning interests, but their proponents framed them within theories about cities that were implied rather than named or defined. Thus, those with money or political power used urbanism as a framing device to argue in favour of doing things one way rather than another. Money and power holders did not successfully argue for an approach just because they had the wherewithal to do so. Potentially self-serving demands of the moneyed and the powerful were passed through a framework in which urbanistic decisions were made, imperfect as the framework and those decisions were. Even the Eaton Centre's problem of a down-at-the-heels street outside the door of its expensive property could not be addressed until the Centre's owners were prepared to enter into a discourse on urban space. However, my claim about the use of urbanistic discourse is not naive. I am not in any way discounting the fact that statements made in these circumstances can be posturing, or even untrue, and made to bluff or wheedle things out of others. I recognize that such statements by everyone concerned will most often be deeply informed by self-interest. People's motives are always complex. My claim is that political and economic influences do not transcend all others. The data illustrated to me that planning as a field of practice had a specific role in the Yonge-Dundas case, a role that was governed neither by capitalists' nor politicians' interests. The impact of planning came largely from the skilful use of the planning framework by everyone, including planners. In other words, with few exceptions, everyone had to don the discourse of urbanism to some extent to have their interests in built space served. In the Yonge-Dundas case, the planning framework, with all its accoutrements, including the Ontario Municipal Board, which hears disputes about municipal land, was used as the locus of debates about urbanism.

As a framing device, urbanism is represented in the policies and procedures of the planning framework and consequently influences how planning is actually done in practice. Urbanism has been and continues to have a disciplining influence on who does what and where they can do it. On the one hand, innovation, by definition, is tamped down by disciplinarity. On the other hand, if planners seek to innovate despite the disciplining frame, they will want to know where openings are possible and how innovation is blocked.

On the first point, the growth of an urbanistic discourse based on attitudes specific to the nineteenth century and later is widely recognized in a general way. It relates to more ordered, built environments and the realization that these bring advantages and drawbacks. Urbanistic discourse has become public rather than confined to elites, as it was in previous centuries. Consider the following contemporary statements on cities and urbanism.

> Capitalism these last 200 years has produced, through its dominant form of urbanization ... an urbanized human nature, endowed with a very specific sense of time, space and money as sources of social power and with sophisticated abilities and strategies to win back from one corner of urban life what may be lost in another. And while it may be true that some are losers everywhere, the vast majority find at least minor compensations somewhere while the rest find solace and hope in the intricacy of the game. Every political movement against the domination of capital must, at some point, confront such confusions. (Harvey 1989b, 199)

> Good environment, as the economists would say, is an income-elastic good: as people, and societies generally, get richer, they demand proportionately more of it. And, apart from building private estates with walls around them, the only way they are going to get it is through public action. (Hall 2002, 402)

Raphaël Fischler (1998, especially 395-403) describes the proliferation of new norms and ideas of normality that have emerged over the last century or so, especially the standards of need associated with the industrial and welfare state. These needs brought about the creation of norms that underlie the concept of "standard of living." Yes, Fischler argues, the apparatuses that were created and became part of the welfare state were flawed, but they carried with them "a hope, an illusion perhaps, of basic universality and of rudimentary equality" (ibid., 404). He asks: What exactly are we losing?

Paul Rabinow examined the role of norms and special terms in building an urbanistic idea of society. For him, the process involved a piecemeal stripping away by experts of "architectural, historical and social references in the name of efficiency, science, progress, and welfare" (1989, 322). He calls the gradual normalizing of activities in cities "middling modernism," which names practices that lie between high culture (philosophy, architecture, art, science, and politics) and the quotidian and engages people who might be called "technicians of general ideas," people like urban planners who invented and used "the practices, discourses, and symbols of 'social modernity'" (ibid., 9).

Those four statements capture the duality of urbanism, the tension within which planners and others engaged in urbanism work. One outcome of increased regulation has been the erection of a framework that is supported by laws passed by governments made up of elected representatives and appointed arbitrators. Egregious harm is mitigated; some discipline is demanded; but many choices can still be made. The recognition of openings is essential.

That leads to the second point, innovation, and its tie-in with planning. For help, I turn to Françoise Choay's ([1980] 1997) thesis on the origin of urbanism as a discourse and theory. In her detailed study, Choay traced the emergence of an autonomous discourse on the organization of city space back to the early Renaissance. Discourse about city space became autonomous in the sense that, for the first time, it was independent of religious, cosmological, military, or family structures. It was the beginning of a discourse on city space per se. (Choay is careful to note that her analysis is specifically Western in orientation.) She describes two fundamentally different ways to build cities that emerged in the late fifteenth and early sixteenth centuries. One was via rules used to generate solutions in space; the other was via models to be applied as solutions. She shows that the first arose in an architectural treatise, a study of urban spatial configurations that meet natural laws, human needs, and aesthetics.[20] The second emerged in the utopian form of writing, which presents criticism of an existing situation counterpoised by its solution in the form of a model of its opposite. Compared to the rules approach, the model approach entails mirroring and correction; the generation of something altogether new "is always secondary, [because] it always proceeds from preliminary work on and against a given reality whose values are to be inverted" (ibid., 150).[21] The rules and model approaches have both been in continuous use since their creation. Then, around the 1860s, those two approaches started to be combined with science, and this combination was put to use to defend urbanistic actions. This amalgam is a third approach, and Choay argues that it is in the theory of urbanism that the organization of space comes to be defined in terms of scientific discourse (ibid., 233-34). It was a distinctly new approach because instead of merely using technical and later scientific data to inform city making or urbanism, this approach took its form from scientific discourse. Choay details when each of the three approaches started, traces their continuation, and identifies their unique combination of characteristics.

Before the third approach took form, there was a period, which Choay calls pre-urbanism, during which disciplinarity began to be manifested in urbanistic practices, attitudes, norms, and terminology. The medicalization of society has been traced from the eighteenth century onward, and "the birth of the clinic" approach, so fully illustrated in the work of Michel Foucault, has contributed to an increasingly therapeutic attitude to urban matters. The effects of medicalization were epistemological in the sense that the social sciences began to "bear the imprint of the medical approach," to adopt concepts of normal and pathological, and to apply them to the social body, and they were spatial in the sense that urban space was "subjected to the clinician's eye" (Choay [1980] 1997, 224, 225). Urban space became an object to medicalize. Once design fell into the hands of scientists, buildings were cut off from the aesthetic dimension, "whether it be realized through the organic unity of parts, the axiom of concinnitas, or ornamentation" (ibid., 225).[22] Through this analysis, Choay shows that neither disciplinarity nor medicalization, both of which were shaping urbanism then and which continue to do so now, was the result of economic imperatives alone. Urbanism has its own distinct trajectory.

By the later nineteenth century, the theory of urbanism amalgam began to appear in urbanistic writings. It sometimes comprised a hyperspatialized, utopian critique and solution, together with pretensions to scientificity that were used to show that the critique leads to the solution or the reverse – that the solution will solve the problem identified in the critique.[23] The result was a scientific theory of urbanism. While both the critique and the solution may be well devised, one leads to the other only through political and ethical choice, not through science. Choay cites a series of texts in which this pattern is found and begins with the text that she analyzed in the most detail and considers the very first text that employed the theory of urbanism – Ildefons Cerdá's *Teoría general de la urbanización,* the title of which inspired Choay's name for this third figure.[24] Cerdá's text has qualities similar to other works, including Camillo Sitte's *Der Städtebau,* Arturo Soria y Mata's *La ciudad lineal,* Ebenezer Howard's *Tomorrow,* Tony Garnier's *Une cité industrielle,* Le Corbusier's *La ville radieuse,* Frank Lloyd Wright's *The living city,* Paolo Soleri's

Archology, and Christopher Alexander's *Notes on the synthesis of form.* To this list could be added Kevin Lynch's *Good city form,* one of the most appreciated books in planning schools. Its first two parts, "Values and cities" and "A theory of good city form," are important in their own right; however, one does not depend on the other for its logic. In these books we find elements of both the "rule" and "model" figures, combined with variably-sized dollops of science, social science, and scientism (excessive belief in or the misplaced application of the scientific method), which are introduced to try to solve urban problems. Because the built-form solutions are sometimes claimed to be normatively in the best interests of the society, as supported by scientific evidence, the choice is rendered normatively scientific, which is a contradiction in terms.

If Choay's argument that these figures have endured is correct, we could expect to find signs of them in the mundane outputs of practice, such as reports and presentations, bylaws, legislation, and so on. I explore this hypothesis further in the final chapter, where I discuss two completely different orientations to urban space in the case study. The first, which occurred in the regeneration phase and hinged on the question, What is this place? tends toward the use of some generative rules and principles. By contrast, the second, which occurred in the redevelopment phase, responded to the issue by providing a model, which, although developed elsewhere, was supposed to be capable of delivering in this new location the mirror opposite of existing conditions. This second orientation effectively closed down innovation in that space.

We usually read that contemporary urban planning was prompted into existence by a number of social and pathological conditions associated with nineteenth-century cities. The descriptions rarely connect that newly growing planning enterprise to earlier discourses on space. Consequently, the extent to which the nineteenth-century ideas from which planning emerged were a transgressive and disruptive force in an already existing discourse on building urban space is missed (Choay [1980] 1997, 3). The idea that planning was only or could only ever be therapeutic, utopian, or a force for doing good emerges from this truncated perspective on the history of urbanism. We disregard or have forgotten other ways. One significant aspect of Choay's contribution to understanding planning is its reminder of the dangers of carelessly reproducing utopian models, a specialty of industrialism, because they displace spatial principles that have potential for innovation.

We end up face to face again with the problem of how to glue process and substance together in planning, but we now have new insight into the origins of the problem and ways to address it. Françoise Choay shows modern urbanism (including planning) disrupting a discourse on space, not starting one. A framework for interpreting planning qua planning can be glimpsed, one that gives room to its spatial concerns, its utopian analyses, and its pretensions to social science validity – but with a reminder to be wary of how they are combined.

To What Does "Planning" Refer?

The term "planning" aggregates distinctive elements, including planning activities, planners who work in both the public and private sectors, and the planning framework. Leaving these elements aggregated muddles attempts to understand theories that have been developed about planning activity, planners, and urban development. Because the parts can function independently of one another, to some extent, it is important to pay attention to which part is in play. Analyses can be plain wrong if the distinctive elements subsumed under the term are treated together. For instance, in this case, planning is done without planners, although the term normally implies that planning is carried out by planners; planning's legal and administrative framework is used by everyone, not only planners, because it establishes the rules of engagement for all planning matters, not only for planners; and planning activities are carried out by planners and by others. Planners can influence the framework and actions but not control them.

A second problem is that when planning is treated as a bundle of undifferentiated elements, distinctions between public-sector and private-sector planners, as well as between planning for public-sector interests versus planning for private-sector interests, are obscured. The common element is the planning framework. Private- and public-sector planners with training and expertise have the right to present positions to councils and adjudicating bodies. However, the notion of public interest is usually more constrained for private-sector planners: their employers' actions concern a site, not the larger urban tissue, and a shorter rather than longer time frame. Consequently, their interpretations of the public interest will often diverge. The best reason to have a strong official plan (or comparable policy document) that clearly states the direction in which the municipality wishes to head is so that a defensible policy framework exists against which to assess individual options, applications, and recommendations. It probably would not hold up to every challenge, but without it the chance of planners being able to justify an opinion on a development is much reduced.

Finally, when planning is treated in the aggregate, planners can become scapegoats for what people do not like about land development. In the Yonge-Dundas case, planners and planning activities were the butts of hostility expressed by various people toward constraints on actions. If private-sector interests or the ward councillor wanted to do something that was out of bounds, planners were often said to be the ones laying on the restrictions or snuffing out initiative and innovation. In reality, restrictions are not applied by planners; they emerge from the application of the planning framework that, as discussed, is developed and maintained collectively and is not controlled exclusively by planners. We tend to forget that planning activities are governed largely by legislation, influenced by elected representatives, and tested at law, and that planners try to find plausible options within that scope, often amid a pandemonium of interests. Furthermore, planners recommend. Politicians decide. However, if planners' proposals lack imagination and innovation, it is a genuine problem for which they are responsible and that they need to tackle.

Each of these four issues – overextension of the social science analogue, the process-substance relationship, planner- and planning-centredness, and imprecision about planning referents – raises a different question about how adequately a case such as this can be described or explained using existing procedural and substantive theories.

Investigative Approach

There is considerable debate about how to connect procedural theory, which is conceptualized as planning theory, to substantive theory, which is presented as urban theory. My aim in this research was to describe planning, as practised in the vicinity of Yonge and Dundas, in a way that could shed light on this debate. I did not want to marshal facts and fit them into existing theories, because I was interested in both process and substance, which at this time are split into different theoretical realms. The best way to loosen the grip of conventional interpretations while maintaining the ability to ask new questions and find new insights is deep immersion in the details. That is the route I have taken here, and I expressly disregarded, as much as I could, all of the planning theories and structured social science–based urban theories about what was going on during the immersion. I do not say this naively, assuming I have no biases, but rather to emphasize that I did not start with any of the conventional structural theories to explain what I found. I readily declare my bias toward democratic, open, and fair processes, toward urban form that is carefully scaled and contextualized and aesthetically interesting, and toward urban form that facilitates the pursuit of people's hopes and dreams.

To describe this poststructural approach, it may be helpful to compare it to more readily recognized structural approaches. Structuralism takes as a given the "thereness" of structure. The structuralist's task is to identify structures and show how they are constructed, whether by type (e.g., economic, social, political, or philosophical), by characteristics (e.g., strength and how parts interconnect), or by effects (e.g., rules, decisions, influence, and the capacity to command). Structuralists posit the existence of a structure that in principle is knowable. A structure provides constraints and possibilities for thought and action. It provides the range of logic within which actors act. But a structure is created reciprocally so that it places ranges on people's actions, and those actions, in turn, affect the structure's features. Structural approaches include social constructionism, structure-agency, institutional analysis, contemporary capitalist economy structural theories, and earlier approaches such as structural functionalism, Marxist and neo-Marxist analyses, and classical and neoclassical economics. Regime theory, referred to above, is a structural theory.

Structuralism claims to provide ways to objectively analyze sociocultural phenomena, without recourse to transcendental elements – that is, phenomena beyond the material universe – to explain them. It has gradually supplanted conventional science as the principal approach to studying on-the-ground social practices. Its approaches are not objective in the way that the scientific method is said to deliver replicable findings relatively untainted by observational bias; rather, they are systematic in that a researcher can reliably identify phenomena and validly assess their meanings because, in principle, other students of a given structure could repeat a study and arrive at similar conclusions. Producing relatively objective analyses of structures in this way has become widely accepted in the academy.

It is precisely on the structuralist claim that a structure can provide relatively objective truth that poststructuralists bring their challenge. The latter contend that structuralists, by seeking meaning via the concept of structure, have exchanged the anchor of truth – called God in earlier times, and science more recently – for the anchor of structure. Poststructuralists say that anyone who tries to illustrate this objectivity will find himself or herself enmeshed in metaphors and contingent meanings, never arriving at objectivity but remaining situated in a cultural soup of meanings. Poststructuralists do not try to rise above structure (as the "post" might suggest) but to think through it, primarily by not giving it life as a centre, or as a presence, which proposes the existence of something else that is absent. "Post" in "poststructuralism" does not imply a subsequent time period, either. It signifies an approach that does not assume that structure is a thing with a form evidenced by the obvious pronouncements of central figures through their practices and texts. The poststructuralist seeks to critically reflect on the dynamics of structuring, such as by asking how this field of practice or argument is being structured. Like structuralism, poststructuralism is loosely associated with various ways of reading human activities to make them more open to reflection. Some examples are genealogy, as developed by Michel Foucault; deconstruction, as developed by Jacques Derrida; and mimesis, as developed by Luce Irigaray.

In contrast with structuralism, poststructuralism has not been well received in the academy except in very weak forms. The strong forms severely challenge the objectivity of structure building among structuralists. Certainly, planning has very few examples. In poststructural approaches the focus is as much on what is absent as on what is present, on "not" as much as "is." There is no fundamental order, logic, or truth; rather, the assumption is made that people organize knowledge into structures at various times and for various purposes, including to convey order, logic, and truth. Each structure has flaws, the main flaw in every case being that a feature essential to the coherence of the structure will, on examination of the structure, be found to have been ignored or treated as if it was inconsequential. Thus, the coherence of the structure is called into question. For example, public-sector planners build the structure of their field on the claim that it serves the public interest. However, at the heart of the practice of planning are private interests that need to be recognized, tamed, encouraged, and so on. After all, cities are built largely from private capital and interests. The task of planners is not only to make plans on paper but also to make plans that generate and guide implementation. A plan without reasonable potential for follow-through is not much of a plan. This was one of John Friedmann's (1969) early contributions: that planning is not simply about decisions but also about action. However we look at that task (aside from a Marxist perspective), planners are hooked in some fashion to the market and its private interests because that is where most development comes from. Based on the kind of actions it must engage in to do its work, the structure of planning cannot be as coherent as some claim it to be if private interests are not recognized as part of its structure (Milroy 1989).

Poststructuralists try to understand how and why a particular truth, logic, or order is promoted and to inquire into what it leaves out and why. A new, also flawed, logic ensues, but it is one that better accounts for how power works in a given circumstance. We do not solve the problem of power; we keep reworking it. It is a hard approach to sell because people generally do not like the feeling of eternal openness. However, insights gained from working with the approach can be profound and can be used in various ways. In this case the question that emerged from attempts to interpret the data is, why are principles of spatial organization left out of theorizing planning?

Complaints are repeatedly levelled against poststructural approaches to dismiss them as irrelevant. One concern is that economics and politics should be the important factors in the pursuit of justice and equitable cities. Economics and politics are "real" and, thus, where the focus for researchers should lie. They are serious, politically engaged, and where the work happens. By contrast, poststructural approaches are often inaccurately reduced to discourse analysis, which is represented as frivolous, peripheral, and unable to lead to action. Most damning of all, poststructural approaches are called apolitical.[25] On the contrary, poststructural analyses can be deeply political, for they can question even what passes for political.[26]

Another complaint is that poststructural approaches are nihilistic because there is no conclusion from the findings. It is true that there is no conclusion. But this does not lead to nihilism. The findings undoubtedly demonstrate that we are always in a soup of meanings, habits of thought, and regulatory devices – we do not escape them. But we can make them more obvious to ourselves so as not to be taken in by them. This is where poststructuralism excels. What is done to change habits, and so on, becomes everyone's responsibility.

Both structural and poststructural approaches are useful for those who want not only to understand but also to change the status quo. One might hazard to say that structuralists believe they can find the levers that, if adjusted, would increase social justice – for example, finding the right way to connect the planning process to substance. Poststructuralists believe that exposing how levers come into effect and are valued provides people with the kind of knowledge they need to expose injustice that parades as justice – for example, revealing the origin and evolution of the utopian model in planning that when reproduced obviates hard analysis and innovation. Those who work in a poststructuralist vein, more so than structuralists, leave no doubt that thinking subjects must do the hard work to change practices. The choice I made to use a poststructuralist approach in this instance does not deny the potential value of a structuralist one to investigate other facets of the same case.

Methods and Sources

My research began in 1999. The primary method used for the case study was document analysis. Because the development was challenged by owners of some of the properties to be expropriated, there was a lengthy quasi-judicial hearing at which evidence was presented and arguments were made. That public hearing left extensive records of the formal planning of and legal arguments for and against the Yonge-Dundas development. Technically, the hearing was before a Joint Board because both planning and expropriation matters were being contested. However, in this case, both of the hearing officers were from the Ontario Municipal Board roster. I read the hearing documents at the offices of the Ontario Municipal Board over two separate periods between June 1999 and August 2001. Nik Luka, in his capacity as a postgraduate research assistant, helped me with that task. I also read newspaper reports on the project. I examined planning legislation, official plans, and economic studies of Toronto; attended selected meetings of the downtown community council of the new post-amalgamation Toronto; and reviewed the literature on contemporary core-area redevelopment that emphasized the experiences of cities that used similar combinations of public space, shopping, and entertainment as were being proposed for Yonge-Dundas. In addition, I reread a great deal of the literature on planning theories and planning practice to ponder them in the specific context of this case. Nik Luka also searched local histories to determine where Toronto's "heart" was in different periods and by whose definition, and he found records of earlier attempts to fix up this section of Yonge Street. Using that information, he wrote the first version of Chapter 2, "History," which I have altered considerably.

After reading and analyzing the information and writing the first draft of the study, I tested, corrected, and extended my information by conducting interviews with twelve people who were centrally involved in the case. With the exception of the ward councillor, who holds public office, these interviews, which were conducted and tape-recorded between June 2003 and June 2005, were done on the basis of confidentiality and the nonattribution of quotes. I was greatly helped by the insights of these people, and I have tried to capture them in the text. However, their voices are buried so that statements cannot be identified with individuals. I am very grateful to the interviewees for the generous amount of time they gave me and for their spirit of candidness, especially given that they could not know how I would interpret their views and actions. My hope is that I have been both accurate and fair.

In my discussion of planning tasks and planners, I have often used a position title or general role instead of the person's name. The decision to use a name has been based on whether it was possible to adequately indicate the source of a point of view, data, analysis, proposal, and so on. However, the names of journalists, companies, and organizations are generally used if they are the authors of documents. The rationale for my overall approach is that the study is not about specific people but about planning as a function, with its tasks, tools, structures, and specialists, all of which are embedded in the larger context of urbanism.

I offer this case as an instance of planners tackling an urban problem in a specific historical and spatial context. Critical analyses of it will lead to different judgments about the quality of the planners' contributions. The case is offered for just that purpose, so we can learn and better bridge theory and history by knowing the actions of planners (Fischler 1995).

Chapter by Chapter

Chapter 2 concerns the history of the study area. It focuses on five events between 1950 and 1990, each of which altered how Yonge Street was able to function in the context of the city as a whole. It sets the stage for the next five chapters, which begin in 1994 with the regeneration ideas that would subsequently be transformed en route to implementation. We see the problems the city was up against, and there is little doubt that this was a difficult area to treat. Chapter 2 also illustrates how rhetoric was used in this case. Rhetoric is an important tool in the promotion of redevelopment projects. The geographical location in question was identified as the heart of Toronto. The heart was said to be in disgraceful condition. If the heart was failing, then the city was inevitably on its way downhill. Indeed the predicted fate would spread through the whole region because was not Toronto, in turn, the heart of the region? Surely such a dire analysis calls for immediate, decisive action. Whether Yonge-Dundas was ever really the heart of Toronto is disputable. However, it was on the edge of the heart in the city's early days, and it was one of several hearts more recently. Facts did stop heart imagery, which began to appear around 1996, from being used, nor have they since – which is the very point of rhetoric. That is, whether Yonge-Dundas was ever the heart of Toronto does not really matter. What matters is whether that rhetorical flourish could serve the purpose of persuasion.

Chapter 3, "Regenerating," describes the city's plan, which began in 1994, to regenerate the few blocks in question with a range of relatively modest initiatives. This multifaceted approach went through standard planning processes that began with involving affected businesses, citizens, and many others. Reports about the steps that were being taken went through the well-established committee and council approval stages. The chapter lays out the reasoning for this strategy and what it entailed, details the main points of the studies and reports, and identifies significant players who were involved in reaching decisions about actions for this area.

Chapter 4, "Redeveloping," discusses the parallel planning process that came from the private sector and was championed by the ward councillor. The city was persuaded to join its efforts to the private one in a loosely devised public-private partnership. Initiatives from this new planning arrangement overtook the regeneration project and converted it into a large-scale redevelopment. This project was developed in secret. It involved taking a dozen private properties, selling six of them at cost to a private developer to build a specific structure, and using four for a city-constructed public square (two properties were intended for other related purposes). The chapter describes the characteristics of the land parcels, how development options were generated and costed, the planning issues that were under review during the approval process, and other technical matters that related to requests for proposals, revisions to the official plan, the zoning bylaw, and the use of sections of the provincial *Planning Act*.

Because this redevelopment project was challenged, and because property expropriation was involved, a quasi-judicial hearing was required to settle the dispute as to whether the project should proceed. The hearing produced extensive written records that detailed how proponents conceptualized and defended the project and how opponents argued that it contravened good planning practice, if not the law. Thus, Chapter 5, "Defending," offers a detailed description of the planning and legal arguments that were put forward in support of or against the redevelopment. It provides an excellent occasion to see the connections among planning actions, planning legislation, and various actors.

Once the project received all formal clearances in the latter part of 1998, implementation began and has been underway since. Chapter 6, "Implementing," describes the development taking shape in ways that were not always expected, given the arguments made in the course of promoting it. The chapter discusses the new public square, the redevelopment around the square and in the improvement area as a whole, the institution of the new Business Improvement Area organization and how it expresses its interests in the square and surrounding area, and where the problems that were not solved went to.

The last chapter, "Closing," is situated within the crucible of evolving contemporary urban form (as described in the first chapter), in which a combination of technological, economic, and social changes are at work, and in which the issue of the relationship between expansive urban development and small spaces needs renewed attention from urbanists. I address questions about the correspondence, or lack of it, between the practice described in the case and current theorizing about planning practice by referring to four issues: (1) the overextension of the social science analogue, (2) the process-substance relationship, (3) planner- and planning-centredness, and (4) imprecision about planning referents. The conclusion put forward is that the decision made by planning theorists to accentuate process over substance has kept eyes focused on planning per se and away from the larger question of urbanism, and this choice has exacerbated the tendency to focus on space only as a product of social relations. In the face of major urban reconstruction challenges beginning in the 1980s, the connection of procedural theories to urbanism was fraught with difficulties. Those actors who were prepared to fix tattered urban spaces could step over planners and their traditional approaches to use the elaborate planning frameworks that had been put together over many decades of the twentieth century. Many planning practitioners have since been drawn into the new work of urbanism. Practices changed. Theory has not caught up.

CHAPTER 2
History
With Nik Luka

Predicting a city's imminent heart failure is a common strategy when a group wants support for an action. We saw it in Berlin during the rebuilding of Potsdamer Platz (Sewing 2000) and in New York during the Times Square redevelopment (Reichl 1999, especially chap. 3). Speaking generally, using the theme of rise and decline to appeal to emotions is prevalent in city development literature (Beauregard 1993; Ward 1997b). The emotional impact is achieved with considerable effect through the use of metaphor, a semantic structure that is used widely to interpret something unknown in terms of something known. The use of an image like impending heart failure – even though it is blatantly metaphorical and therefore readily seen as somewhat exaggerated and not quite correct – can nonetheless become compelling enough to spur action aimed at diverting that danger, even in what is technically not a heart at all.

Toronto's case falls into this type of experience. The intersection of Yonge and Dundas was described both as the heart of Toronto and as a rotting core. Even if both claims were exaggerated, the imagery had an effect on the redevelopment process. Yonge Street as a whole is central to life in Toronto, but this particular intersection with Dundas Street was not important until the Eaton Centre opened in the late 1970s. Even that event spread no prestige to Dundas, east or west of Yonge, or to Yonge Street itself. In this chapter we review the evolution of these streets in the context of the heart and rot metaphors since these are the images used by the project's proponents.[1]

The corner of Yonge and Dundas was described as the heart of the city in at least three respects. Each description is a little bit accurate, but only a little bit. First, the corner was said to have been the historical core of shopping and entertainment in Toronto. The members of the Ontario Municipal Board (OMB), hearing the case for expropriation, accepted the idea that Yonge-Dundas had once been a shopping and entertainment mecca for Torontonians.

In its decision to allow expropriation to proceed, it said: "During the 1950s and 1960s, Yonge and Dundas was 'the' retail shopping strip, the people place, where the sidewalks were full of people, the retail stores, restaurants and movie theatres vibrant and successful" (Joint Board 1998k, 3). A newspaper journalist who specializes in Toronto issues expressed the same view when writing about the Dundas Square project: "With luck, the project will turn back the clock to the days when people came to Yonge and Dundas to find the latest fashions or to catch a show" (Immen 1998a). It continues to form part of the story as it is described on the Square's website. This image was not quite accurate.

Second, Yonge and Dundas was described as a symbol of the well-being of the entire city and even the region. At the 1998 public hearing into expropriations for the redevelopment, a prominent private-sector planner in Toronto said that "the low-rise retail strip in the area of Yonge/Dundas is the most important in the region, and its location by the Eaton Centre makes the strip functionally and symbolically important in the region" (Joint Board 1998h, 14). The City of Toronto's planner for the area used more subtle phrasing without emphasizing the specific intersection, saying, "There is a fundamental incongruity between the street's overall diminished role and appearance and the notion that Yonge Street is viewed as Toronto's main street and the 'front door' to visitors to the City" (Joint Board 1998b, Exhibit 69, 7). Another frequently used idea or phrase, which was first expressed in 1996, was that Yonge Street's condition was central to the city's "health, image and sustainability" (see, e.g., ibid., 23). The well-being of the city, if not the region, was said to depend on the successful redevelopment of this small area.

Third, Yonge-Dundas was called a focal point for public life and major celebrations and was acclaimed as such by "the people." The area planner argued at the public hearing that this intersection was "the location of City celebrations, protests and gatherings and has national and historic importance as a visual symbol of downtown Toronto" (Joint Board 1998b, Exhibit 69, 9). But there was a bit of slippage regarding the location. Throughout the city's history, celebrations, parades, and events have indeed taken place on different parts of Yonge Street. As early as 1837, a stretch well north of the intersection was the scene of a brief but legendary armed rebellion led by William Lyon Mackenzie, a newspaper editor and Toronto's first mayor. But in the 1850s, '60s, and '70s, King Street, which runs perpendicular to Yonge and lies about one kilometre south of Dundas, usurped Yonge's place as the street for public demonstrations, including those that marked Queen Victoria's birthday in 1854 and Canadian Confederation in 1867, the funeral cortège for the Compact sympathizer Bishop John Strachan in 1867, and the mobbing of a Fenian by Orangemen in 1878 (Fleming 1996). The intersection of King and

Yonge streets then became the focal point for celebrations – Queen Victoria's Diamond Jubilee in 1897, British success in the Boer War in 1902, and the armistice of the First World War in 1918. At that time Dundas did not even intersect with Yonge.

Large stretches of Yonge Street served as parade routes throughout the twentieth century, for King George VI and Queen Elizabeth in 1939, for circuses, Santa Claus, anti–Vietnam War demonstrations, and so on. The massive Pride Parade annually takes over Yonge Street from Bloor Street south to Gerrard. Spontaneous celebrations are also associated with Yonge. A respected observer of the city and its places noted: "There is a venerable Toronto tradition of crowds taking over Yonge Street for a night of merry wildness on special occasions, usually victories in sport" (Mays 1994, 198). In the early 1990s, crowds marked the victory of the city's Major League Baseball team, the Toronto Blue Jays, in the World Series by filling large stretches of Yonge all the way north past Lawrence Avenue. James Lemon (1985, 151) noted that hundreds of central city residents came to Yonge Street in 1971 to celebrate the provincial government's decision to halt the construction of the Spadina Expressway, which would have required the demolition of hundreds of houses and the destruction of stable inner-city neighbourhoods. Finally, crowd hooliganism has also been associated with Yonge, notably against Greek restaurateurs in 1918 (Gallant 2004) and, reportedly, in response to the Rodney King incident in Los Angeles in 1992. In the latter case, a number of white police officers in Los Angeles had been videotaped apparently beating a black motorist. When charges against the officers were dismissed, there were riots in central Los Angeles and outbursts of anger elsewhere, including in Toronto.

These types of events took place, and continue to take place, over different stretches of Yonge Street. Yet the heart of the city was claimed by project proponents to be, quite precisely, at Yonge and Dundas. As a final point, it is worthwhile to note that celebration, organized or spontaneous, has been associated with movement through space, not with a fixed place. Peter Goheen has argued that for nineteenth-century Torontonians the street, not the square, was the focal point for demonstrations, regardless of whether they were formal, informal, or mob-like. However, other public spaces could be used as adjunct spaces. Adjunct spaces "served both for public assembly and speeches associated with parades and occasionally as turf for riots. All were centrally located public open spaces, and hence governed by many of the same protocols of access and control" (Goheen 1993, 142).

The observations that were made in association with the redevelopment plans established a picture of a rotting heart that could be, and indeed had to be, repaired to keep the city from collapse, from presenting a poor image to the world, and from unsustainability. The rotting heart became a metaphor for the perceived deterioration of Toronto, which had been walloped by the deep recession and economic restructuring that took place between 1989 and 1994. The redevelopment was held up as a harbinger of whether Toronto would be world-class or ordinary.

The following discussion explores the history of lower Yonge Street and the Yonge-Dundas intersection to give a sense of their importance, or lack thereof, over the years. The street-related enterprises in the area in question gradually changed from sober butchers, haberdashers, milliners, and house painters to clothing retailers, taverns, tea rooms, restaurants, and cinemas to fast-food outlets, game arcades, massage parlours, electronics retailers, and souvenir stores. Much of what was happening to the retail and commercial segment of the street was tied to the large-scale influences that came with post–Second World War growth: the city's form shifted from being monocentric (centralized transit and pedestrian shopping) to being polycentric (decentralized, car-oriented shopping). This change was happening all over Canada and the United States.

However, the case study was also distinguished by a specific condition. The T. Eaton Company, which had been a major employer in the city in the first half of the twentieth century, owned a large proportion of the land in the subject area on the west side of Yonge between Queen and Dundas and at Yonge and College. It was a family-owned business that originated in Toronto but eventually established itself Canada-wide. Its Toronto activities were primarily department store retail, catalogue sales, and product manufacturing (mainly clothes). Family members were wealthy and carried on in a semi-regal fashion. In its later years, Eaton's had weak leadership and shoddy vision, which hobbled the company and prevented others from being able to reorganize Yonge Street's activities in the face of large-scale changes to this industrial-era city.

Toronto's city government had a mixed relationship with this powerful company. On the one hand, it was well aware of Eaton's importance as an employer and taxpayer; on the other, city government had to struggle to deal with its power. It had a strong tendency to side with Eaton's, but, as we will see as the story progresses, citizen actions derailed some of Eaton's worst plans. In the end, the fifth generation of the family brought the company crashing into bankruptcy. This occurred in 1997-98, just when the redevelopment project was receiving final approval.

Yonge Street

Yonge Street as a whole is important because its history is closely linked to that of the city itself. Indeed, "anywhere in Canada, the name 'Yonge Street' is instantly recognized as a Toronto place name" (Kluckner 1988, 70). It may be the longest street anywhere. In 1793, when the governor of Upper Canada, John Graves Simcoe, selected the "Toronto carrying place" as the capital of the new province of Upper Canada, he laid out a military road to allow for, in times of war, the quick movement of troops from the original fort and harbour northward, from Lake Ontario to Lake Simcoe (ibid.). Simcoe named the road for Sir George Yonge, the British home secretary at the time. From then onward, the street served as a reference point in several ways. For example, it became the literal and figurative dividing line of the city as streets were laid out and numbered from zero, starting at Yonge. Many Torontonians think of themselves as coming from either the east or west end, because families traditionally settled in one or the other, and they rarely crossed Yonge when moving house. Consider the following excerpt from a feature article in Toronto's major newspaper on Yonge Street's "dividing line" effect: "It's an age-old bias in the former City of Toronto: you're a loyal east-ender or west-ender and never the twain shall meet. The other side is, well, foreign" (White 1999).

Early Growth

As the small town (originally called York) grew during the nineteenth century, the most important cross street (east-west) was King Street, seven blocks south of where Dundas is today. Dundas did not exist at that time in the area near Yonge. In 1873 the Yonge and King intersection was identified as the "heart of the town" by one of Toronto's first historians, Henry Scadding ([1873] 1966, 276). The city's most prestigious businesses established themselves on King, and toward the end of the century the first fashionable shops also opened up along it. Scadding wondered, however, whether "the needs of the population and the exigencies of business" would draw the heart northwest, following the direction it had taken over its 100-year history, to what is now Spadina and Queen (ibid.).

By the early twentieth century, this "heart" had shifted a short distance straight northward to the intersection of Yonge and Queen streets. Queen Street, like Yonge, was laid out by Simcoe as a key military road, and it was considered the principal east-west axis of the city until the 1960s. It was originally called Lot Street, because it was lined by "a range of 100-acre lots which were granted as *douceurs* to the officials as compensation for having to come to York" (Arthur 1978, 14). These estates ran north to Bloor Street. At the intersection of Yonge and Queen, Toronto's two major retailers, the Robert Simpson Company and the T. Eaton Company, faced each other across Queen Street. Each catered to a particular clientele: "Eaton's for the masses, Simpson's for the classes," a local saying went (McQueen 1999, 18). In an era when most

Torontonians travelled by streetcar, the meeting of the city's principal crosstown Queen route and the north-south Yonge route (the spine of the system) made this crossroads extremely important. The Yonge-Queen intersection had thus become the undisputed shopping hub of the city; in fact, there was a special car stop on Queen adjacent to the main entrances of the two department stores. South of Queen, Yonge Street was lined with shops and boutiques. The principal retail product in the area was clothing. Kluckner (1988, 22) notes that at the turn of the century the garment manufacturing industry employed more people than any other sector in the city. In fact, the ongoing importance of this junction was demonstrated by the City of Toronto's (1963) *Plan for downtown Toronto,* which suggested marking Yonge and Queen with a dramatic structure over the intersection.

One consequence of growth and change was a concerted effort, which began in the 1890s, to transform Yonge Street into a formal avenue with an almost European character. Its role as Toronto's main thoroughfare was to have been affirmed by an elegant and continuous street wall of "majesty and controlled uniformity" (Lyon 1978, n.p.). During this period a number of fine buildings were erected along Yonge Street, such as the Board of Trade building at the corner of Front and Yonge streets, the Fairweather and Robert Simpson stores farther north, and the Ryrie Building at Shuter Street (one block south of the Dundas Square site). Perhaps for economic reasons, or perhaps because the focus of the city's property market had already begun to shift, the street wall was never completed (ibid.). Nonetheless, at the turn of the century, Yonge Street, between King and Queen streets, was the main street of Toronto. Period images of this area depict a bustling street, packed with people going about their daily business.

The 1920s to the 1940s

The intersection at Yonge and Queen was an important node, but Toronto retailing continued to change and grow. By the 1920s luxury clothing shops had opened along Bloor Street (Lemon 1985, 41), and more followed. Bloor Street runs from east to west about eighteen blocks north of and parallel to Queen Street. City officials acknowledged in *Plan for downtown Toronto* (Toronto 1963) that Bloor-Yonge was the focus for high-end retail, although they still considered Yonge and Queen the main shopping district. The differences between the two districts continued. Specialty shopping leapfrogged northward toward the Yonge-Bloor area throughout the 1960s, eventually spilling westward into the village of Yorkville, which in the 1960s had become the focus of Toronto's hippie counterculture. In the 1970s substantial private-sector redevelopment occurred, resulting in tony shopping complexes being introduced, especially Hazelton Lanes and the Holt Renfrew Centre. Both

2.1 The Toronto Plant of the T. Eaton Co., c. 1919. *Foreground,* store building; *left centre,* home furnishings store and its annex; *right centre,* three mail-order buildings; *background,* two factory buildings; *rear left,* Old City Hall. | Illustration courtesy of Archives of Ontario; Ditchett (1923, 11).

2.2 Looking north on Yonge Street, c. 2008. The street has been widened and turned into a boulevard in front of what was Eaton's College Street store, seen on the left. | Courtesy of Sherrill Rand Harrison.

complexes reinforced the current role of the Yonge-Bloor area as the provider of high-end retail in Toronto.

The most notable event of the period was the effort on the part of Eaton's to try to impose its designs on others. It wanted to shift shopping north by abandoning Queen Street, leapfrogging over Dundas Street, and re-establishing the shopping district at College Street. From the time it was founded in 1869, Eaton's had grown enormously from a small shop on Yonge Street to a major department store located at Yonge and Queen. It occupied what had become a disjointed collection of buildings that covered much of the area from Queen north to Dundas. The Eaton's buildings that were located in the quadrant defined by Dundas, Yonge, Queen, and Bay streets are illustrated in Figure 2.1. However, Eaton's wanted to consolidate its retail in a massive purpose-built complex (Dendy 1986, 291). To this end, it began to secretly buy up College Street properties near Yonge Street in the 1910s. The family hoped to transform College Street into Toronto's fashionable shopping street (McQueen 1999, 65). It was a bold move because Yonge Street was not fashionable in this stretch. In fact, anywhere north of Queen seems to have been considered undesirable. And its desired location ignored the fact that Bloor was already becoming the city's fashionable street (George Hume 1999; Lemon 1985, 41). In the 1920s Eaton's tried to persuade the Robert Simpson Company, its across-the-street competitor at Queen, to go north too and even offered it some of Eaton's landholdings along College Street (McQueen 1999, 65). But Simpson's wisely declined. The whole concept was ill-devised.

Notwithstanding cautionary signs, in 1928 Eaton's began constructing a shopping and entertainment complex that became known as Eaton's College Street and is currently known as College Park. The new edifice was art deco styled, complete with an upscale restaurant and one of the finest auditoriums in the city. The T. Eaton Company also deeded a strip of its land along the Yonge Street facade to the City of Toronto so that its new store could be offset by an appropriately handsome boulevard. This accounts for the unexpected widening of Yonge Street from Gerrard Street north to College Street, which is shown in Figure 2.2.

As is noted by Rod McQueen (1999, 67), the move to College Street was unsuccessful for several reasons. The building, in fact, became known as a white elephant because of its white limestone cladding. The Great Depression had set in, shattering consumer confidence, not to mention disposable incomes. Eaton's had to delay indefinitely the construction of the other phases of the development, including an office tower. The Depression notwithstanding, Eaton's failure was also a case of poor decision making. McQueen (ibid., 68) argued that the Eaton's College Street store was too upscale for its customers, who were predominantly working- and middle-class, not the wealthy elite of Toronto. With Simpson's still located at the shopping hub of Yonge and Queen, there simply was not enough pedestrian movement up Yonge Street to the College Street location – which was in the middle of a very long stretch of Yonge – neither at Queen nor at Bloor. Shoppers were not lured north in large part because of the very subject of this discussion: the Yonge-Dundas area. The original plan to close the Queen Street store was never realized, and for forty years two Eaton stores, just six blocks apart, operated on Yonge.

Eaton's, a major employer and an important property tax contributor, was very successful in the early decades at building and running a vertically integrated corporation that covered manufacturing, retail sales, mail order sales, and shipping. It was much less successful at understanding how a city functions, which is to say that it had a poor grasp on how its business operations fit into a larger physical and social context. Ironically, the view of one of the developers involved in one of Eaton's many schemes, William Zeckendorf of Webb & Knapp, was that Eaton's itself was the "biggest stumbling block in this city." He argued that its extensive properties were the source of lower Yonge Street's misery because the greater part of the company's land "lies idle, either as parking lots or as dusty, truck-choked warehousing. Sprawled out like a great patch of crabgrass on a lawn, the Eaton holdings effectively choke any new growth trying to get underway alongside" (cited in McQueen 1999, 164).

First Intervention: The Yonge Street Subway

Until the middle of the twentieth century, Toronto was a relatively dense, compact city that had businesses and shops in the centre and residential areas that spanned outward. Most residents walked or used streetcars. The first streetcar line in Canada was installed in 1861 on Yonge Street between King Street and Yorkville's town hall. Initially horse drawn, the lines were later electrified. Speeds and service increased, but Yonge, being the central north-south artery, was often congested. A proposal to build an underground streetcar line had been put before Torontonians as early as 1910, but it was defeated in a referendum (Toronto 1987, 10). By the late 1940s, when packed streetcars were running in two-vehicle trains along Yonge Street at headways of less than one minute (Lowry 1996, 65), the pressure to build an underground line surged. However, Yonge Street merchants dreaded trading surface streetcars, from which passengers could easily see their shops, for underground rail, with its more widely spaced stops. A popular line was, "A carstop is never too far from any store" (Ted Wickson, cited in Filey 1986, n.p.).

Despite the merchants' concerns, construction of the subway line from Front Street northward to Eglinton Avenue began in 1949 (Toronto 1987, 11). Yonge

Street thus experienced its first major trauma, because access was severely limited over the next five years. For months at a time, entire blocks were closed to vehicular traffic and the streetcars were rerouted on parallel streets while the trenches that would form the train tunnels were dug and the streets were rebuilt over them (Greenberg 1991, 196). Although pedestrians always had access to the shops and restaurants along Yonge, the curtailment of vehicular access in a rapidly motorizing city was the first of several blows to street-oriented retail.

The first phase of the subway, from Union Station to Eglinton, opened in March 1954. It was immediately successful as a mode of transportation, carrying 2 million riders in the first week of operation. The subway affirmed Yonge Street's role as the spine of the city and served to reinforce the stability of the downtown core (Lowry 1996, 64-65). In fact, by 1962 property values had skyrocketed, by as much as four times the city average, along the subway corridor (Toronto 1987, 33).

At the same time, however, the subway line had a significant effect on street-oriented retail activities along Yonge. When the subway opened, the streetcars were removed from Yonge. In 1973 the trolley buses were removed. It did not take long before the traditional strip retail gave way to concentrated development around the subway stations (Greenberg 1991). In fact, as early as the 1960s, some stretches of lower Yonge Street showed signs of decline associated with the subway. The merchants' fears had been well founded. Herbert Lowe, who owned a shoe store on lower Yonge Street, commented in response to a 1963 draft version of the *Plan for downtown Toronto*: "For small independent retailers, the downtown area has become a 'decaying heart of the city' ... It is not a matter of earning a living or making a profit, but rather a question of who can afford to lose money and hang on the longest" (cited in City People Community Planning and Research 1974, 20). Lowe believed that this was due to the subway exits that carried people directly into the Eaton's or Simpson's department stores. But other factors were at work, too. Lowe identified inadequate car parking and the rise of suburban shopping centres as issues.

The 1960s and the Rise of the Yonge Street Strip

Yonge Street changed throughout the 1960s and 1970s. The section from College to Queen Street began to offer more contemporary leisure and entertainment services rather than live theatre and classical music, which had been offered until the late 1920s. Entertainment had by and large shifted to movie theatres; Maple Leaf Gardens, the hockey arena, at College Street (opened in 1931); and taverns, bars, and restaurants, including two especially well-known restaurants, the Silver Rail and the Brown Derby.

When it prepared its 1963 official plan, the City of Toronto acknowledged the existing entertainment focus of Yonge and wanted to see it, together with shopping, emphasized and encouraged: "The east side of the street, from Gerrard to Richmond, has already taken on the distinctive character of an entertainment strip and this should expand as the population grows ... Any rebuilding should concentrate on shopping on the west side and entertainment on the east side, especially north of Queen, since these are important functions of the street" (Toronto 1963, 29-30).

The rate at which replacement activities moved into the area may have helped mask the fact that Yonge Street was no longer the shopping destination of choice for Torontonians. For decades shops had been moving away from the hub of Yonge and Queen. As already mentioned, fashionable boutiques had shifted to Bloor Street West and farther north on the Yonge subway line at St. Clair Avenue, which was closer to the affluent neighbourhoods of Rosedale, Moore Park, and Forest Hill. In the 1960s the Canadian department store chain Hudson's Bay Company opened a large store at Yonge and Bloor, at the intersection of the newly opened Bloor subway line and the Yonge line. This created a secondary core in an interceptor location and strong competition for consumer traffic on Yonge Street (see Joint Board 1998b, Exhibit 207A, 5). Shopping centres were opening in the growing suburbs and offering a wide range of goods and services in climate-controlled environments, which was a significant consideration in a region with cold, windy winters and hot, humid summers. As well, stores in this section of Yonge had gathered in the underground pathways that linked subway stations and major buildings.

But other activities were moving elsewhere, too. The Yonge Street area may once have served as a crucible of sorts for Toronto's budding music and arts scene, but by the 1970s this scene was relocating southwest to Queen and King streets. For example, the restoration of the Royal Alexandra Theatre in 1963 and the opening of several restaurants along King Street West in the 1970s were followed by the Toronto Symphony Orchestra moving to Roy Thomson Hall in the King West area in 1982. The symphony's departure from its long-time home at Massey Hall left the 1894 concert hall at Shuter and Victoria without a resident ensemble. And then, too, Yonge-Dundas was left without one of its anchoring entertainment functions.

It was not long before retail businesses along Yonge Street came to be dominated by record stores, novelty shops, and discount outlets, and by the early 1970s the sex trade was well established. The blocks between Dundas Square and Gerrard Street were host to a particularly raunchy range of taverns, exotic dance halls, body-rub parlours, and bookstores that allegedly sold pornography and the like, and they soon came to be known as the "Yonge

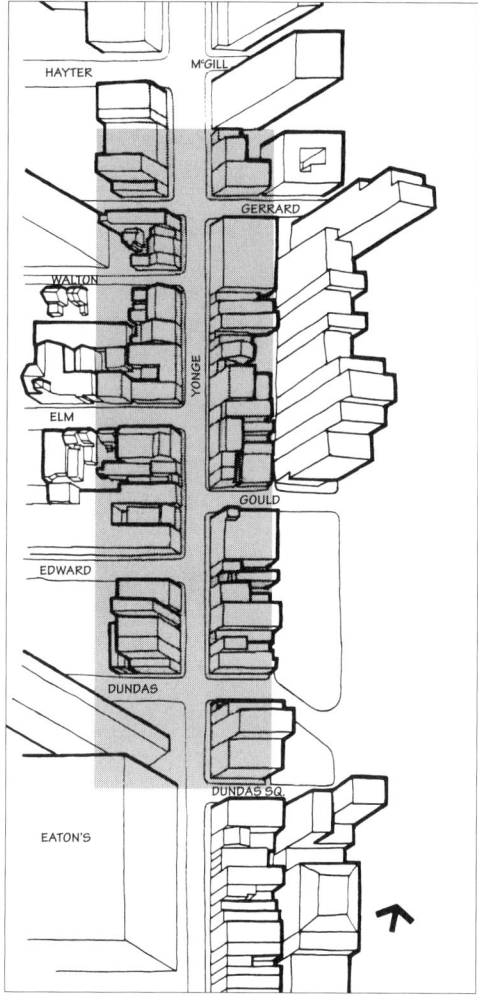

2.3 The built form of the Yonge Street Strip, as it was in 1975. | Adapted from Toronto (1975, 50).

Street Strip," the area shown in Figure 2.3. Myers (1977, 122) notes that there were about thirty body-rub parlours in the area in 1973 and about one hundred in 1975. Despite a clampdown on the sex trade, including the licensing of massage parlours, Yonge Street had clearly found a new niche in the retail market as the city's one and only strip. In fact, the redevelopment scheme tried to hold onto part of the strip's reputation – its flashing lights, noise, action, and intensity – but tried to attach it to uncontroversial retail aimed at higher-income users and families. The plan was to attract retailers who would not sell sex per se but who would doubtless use sexualized images to stimulate sales.

2.4 A section of Yonge Street temporarily converted into a pedestrian mall, c. 1974. | Courtesy of Archives of Ontario, RG 65-35-2-68.

Second Intervention: The Yonge Street Mall

In response to the shifts of activity that gave lower Yonge Street a somewhat tawdry image, beginning in the early 1970s a series of concerted efforts were made to reverse the decline. The central problem was defined as getting more shoppers into the area. An early effort focused on making the public space in the area more agreeable. A pedestrian mall was proposed. Pedestrian malls were popular in North American cities at the time. To test its feasibility in Toronto, Yonge Street was closed to traffic for six days in early June 1971. Benches, planters, fountains, and outdoor cafés were set up along the sidewalks and in the roadway. There were handicraft vendors, and the City of Toronto organized daily entertainments at noon and in the early evening. Torontonians seemed to find it "a smashing success that first year" (Myers 1977, 126). The following summer, the project was increased in size and duration. But the 1973 scheme was the most elaborate of all. Lasting for eleven weeks, it extended over two kilometres of Yonge Street, from Gerrard Street to King Street, with fountains, garden installations, information kiosks, and plenty of street furniture (ibid.; Kilbourn 1984, 22). Figure 2.4 shows the mall in operation. But the following year, the mall was closed down early, after being only six weeks in operation. Several reasons were given: the disruption in traffic was not justifiable, the mall became a gathering place for "degenerates," the experiment failed to increase sales for merchants, and there was an increase in nuisance crimes associated with crowd control (Myers 1977, 126-27). The reasons for closing it down were questioned by a local journalist who grew up on Yonge Street and who at the time was a newly graduated city planner. He and several planning school colleagues formed a cooperative that was hired in 1974 to study the mall. He said they surveyed every single merchant on the street where the pedestrian mall operated and "found that a majority of the merchants supported the mall. But the big department stores were against it. They didn't want people outside listening to speakers and street musicians. They wanted them inside shopping" (Stein 1996).

Another study of the mall was commissioned by Toronto City Council, which asked whether the mall should be made permanent. The study recommended that Yonge Street be closed to vehicular circulation from Queen Street south to Wellington Street and that the sidewalks from Dundas Street to College Street be widened. It is interesting to note that, according to this study, the portion of Yonge most suitable for a full-fledged mall was south of Queen Street, which suggests that the greatest concentration of activity was in that area and not near Dundas Street. Pedestrian counts taken in 1969-70 lend weight to this hypothesis. For example, over the course of the eight-hour day during which observations were made, the total number of pedestrians at the Yonge-Queen intersection was about 43,000, while the total number of pedestrians at Yonge-Dundas was about 30,900, or about 25 percent less. In addition, although the number of pedestrians at Yonge-Dundas was relatively steady throughout the day, foot traffic at Yonge-Queen more than doubled in the afternoon, suggesting that this area was a popular destination for leisure activities in the afternoon and evening. By contrast, the number of cars passing through the Yonge-Dundas intersection was considerably greater (Harrold et al. 1971).

That was not the end of the studies. A subsequent consultants' report recommended the opposite, that Yonge Street be kept open in its usual fashion because "the absence of vehicles and surface transit systems created a somewhat artificial atmosphere – an atmosphere which was sometimes exploited by hawkers and propagandists" (*Globe and Mail* 1974).

Ultimately, the pedestrian mall was rejected. It seemed to cause more problems than it solved. In Kenneth Greenberg's view, it "amplified the problems of prostitution, panhandling, and drugs, and created an atmosphere that was perceived to be unpleasant and out of control" (1991, 196). As constructed, the mall did not address the underlying socioeconomic or investment problems that, by that time, were clearly manifesting themselves along the street.

Third Intervention: The Construction of the Eaton Centre

The Yonge and Queen intersection was still the focal point of downtown shopping in 1963, when the City of Toronto was preparing its self-study prior to writing its official plan. However, there were early signs that the clientele of core-area retailers was changing. Their traditional clientele base had been shoppers from all over the city. Shoppers were now increasingly downtown workers. The general population was making more and more of its purchases outside of the core (Toronto 1963, 29). In response, the city looked to Eaton's to lead the way in reinforcing the vitality of the downtown shopping district. The official plan noted that "perhaps the best opportunity lies in any redevelopment of the extensive T. Eaton Co. Ltd. properties between Yonge and Bay, north of Queen. As a well-designed project this could have the great merit of building onto what is already the great downtown shopping centre" (ibid.).

By the late 1960s, Eaton's had acquired most of the land that extended from Yonge Street west to Bay Street and from Queen Street north to Dundas Street. Its retail operations were still spread throughout a disjointed collection of buildings that made up the flagship store at Yonge and Queen and the store at College Street, while manufacturing, catalogue sales, and warehousing were located in the area south of Dundas Street between Yonge and Bay. It was time to consolidate. Eaton's wanted to demolish the whole Queen-Dundas-Yonge-Bay area and build a new complex that would include office towers, a new flagship store, and an indoor shopping concourse. Discussions about a series of plans went on for more than fifteen years. Designs by I.M. Pei were supplanted by those of E.L. Hankinson; James A. Murray and Victor Gruen; and Haldenby and Mathers, in conjunction with Skidmore, Owings and Merrill, LLP, respectively (McQueen 1999, 163). By this time it was becoming clear that redevelopment plans included tearing down the Old City Hall, a classic late nineteenth-century sandstone building with a clock tower that stood at Queen and Bay, as well as the Church of the Holy Trinity near Dundas, which dated from 1847. In addition to the church's historical and architectural merits, it had social significance. It was the first Anglican church in Toronto in which "the working class residents of what was then the outskirts of Toronto could worship for free" (ibid., 164). In other churches, pews were rented.

Arguments over the sweeping plans to destroy these two landmarks continued in 1967, when a plan was rejected thanks to the work of an organization called Friends of Old City Hall, and in 1972, when another scheme bit the dust, rejected by Toronto City Council. That scheme was typical for the era: it called for a fortress-like megastructure that turned its back on the surrounding streets. The proposal was a dramatic change from the existing store, which was known for its elaborate window displays that drew enormous crowds at Christmas (Toronto 1990a). Under the new scheme, there would be no more traditional window displays because there would be no windows: "The basic principle behind the planning of the Centre was that all shoppers, and even casual pedestrians, would be drawn inside, leaving the city's streets and sidewalk-oriented businesses behind" (Dendy 1986, 291).

The plan also called for the demolition of the Church of the Holy Trinity and the Old City Hall. This sparked another uproar. Torontonians, having already lost many historic buildings, had become sensitized to their dwindling built heritage, and the proposal for an Eaton Centre was rejected by Toronto City Council in 1972. New discussions led Eaton's to hire the Toronto architect Eberhard Zeidler to develop a proposal that would better integrate the structure within the surrounding urban fabric. His design consisted of a huge galleria, which was modelled loosely on the Galleria Victor Emmanuel in Milan (which dated from 1867); office towers; and a new nine-storey flagship store for Eaton's, which was to be built with its main entrance at Yonge and Dundas (Toronto 1990a, 24; McQueen 1999). The galleria linked the new Eaton's with Simpson's department store, still at Queen Street. The two department stores were to be the anchors for smaller shops and restaurants located on several levels in the galleria. This scheme was thought to be much better: like Milan's Galleria, Zeidler's initial scheme called for a mixture of uses, including housing, a library, and genuine indoor public space (Dendy 1986, 291). But the developers were not keen on a mixed-use development, and the concept was dropped. Like earlier plans, Zeidler's also turned inward from Yonge Street.[2]

Construction of the Eaton Centre started in 1973 and took five years to complete. Once again, access to Yonge Street was made difficult in that area, just as it had been when the subway was being built (Lemon 1985, 160). However, although street-level merchants did suffer during the construction period, the popularity of the Eaton Centre, once completed, brought new life to a part of the city that had been stagnating, if not declining. When it opened in 1977, it was an instant success: the number of people entering the mall averaged 500,000 a week and increased to 750,000 a week during the Christmas season, and Eaton's total sales increased by 38 percent in the first eight months of operation (McQueen 1999, 207).[3] The number of people entering the Eaton Centre annually now runs to the tens of millions. Figure 2.5 shows

2.5 Toronto Eaton Centre interior, looking north, 2008. The photograph shows activity on several levels, the glass arcade effect, and the Canada geese sculptures. | Courtesy of Sherrill Rand Harrison.

the Eaton Centre's interior. According to one commentator, the redevelopment process gave Torontonians new confidence that city government could have a positive and formative role in guiding development (Dendy 1986, 293).

Fourth Intervention: Downzoning and the 1978 Yonge Street Revitalization Project

The Eaton Centre was an anomaly on the Yonge Street Strip: it could command much higher rents from retailers than other properties, and it attracted higher-income shoppers. A 1975 plan for the Central Area reduced the floor space index from 12 to 2 for the east side of the street (Toronto 1975).[4] This is how an economic researcher described that action: "The restrictive planning policies developed [after the Eaton Centre was underway] assured that the hugely successful experience could not be repeated on the east side of Yonge Street as the market would otherwise have encouraged" (Joint Board 1998b, Exhibit 207A, 17). The siting of the Eaton Centre right at the Yonge Street sidewalk, and its almost entirely closed facade, brought two-sided retail to a dead stop along the full length of Yonge Street, from Dundas to Queen.

Amid these circumstances, a consulting firm was hired in 1978 to develop a strategy to make the street healthy and vibrant (Lyon 1978). It recommended creating a European-style pedestrian shopping street.[5] The long-term vision for the Central Area included a pedestrianized downtown area (defined by Yonge, Bay, King, and Queen streets), a ring road system (consisting of University Avenue, College/Carlton streets, Jarvis Street, and Front Street), and extensive parking facilities at the periphery of the pedestrian precinct. Because traffic impact studies had not been done to establish the wisdom of making such dramatic changes, an interim plan proposed widening the sidewalks by reducing the number of vehicle lanes from four to two to discourage through traffic. A high-quality pedestrian realm would be created, with appropriate surface treatments; weather protection in the form of arcades, awnings, and glass canopies; plantings; seating; outdoor patios for restaurants and cafés; public toilets at street level; and enhanced entrances to the subway stations (Greenberg 1991, 196).

The 1978 revitalization proposal was nonetheless rejected. Yonge Street was not controlled by the city but by the Metropolitan Toronto government, which designated Yonge Street an important regional traffic artery. It refused to allow the number of lanes on lower Yonge Street to be reduced, in spite of the fact that it carried many more people on foot than by car.[6] Some attributed this refusal to the fact that the Metropolitan Toronto Council had more suburban than urban councillors – the former could not grasp the urbanity issue that was being presented to them.

Derailed but not defeated, the City of Toronto shifted its attention to enhancing the streets that intersected with Yonge and over which it had control. Changes by the city included widening the Gould Street sidewalk on the north side and installing permanent, canopied vendors' spaces and several chess tables and seats. These changes were very successful at the time.

In 1982 another move by city council was to designate the Theatre Block (bounded by Queen, Yonge, Shuter, and Victoria streets) as a redevelopment area. The block contains several listed or designated heritage structures, including the Elgin and Winter Garden theatres located at 189 Yonge Street, the concert facilities of Massey Hall at 15 Shuter Street, three historical bank buildings (at 173, 197, and 205 Yonge Street), and the former Heintzman building at 193 Yonge Street.[7] Between two of the banks was the Colonial Tavern, which was listed by the Toronto Historical Board solely to protect the facades of the banks it abutted. This is not to say that the Colonial Tavern had not had its own moments of significance. Members of Jazz Watch and the Jazz Action Society came to council to attest that "international musicians such as Duke Ellington, Count Basie, Oscar Peterson, Miles Davis, Dizzy Gillespie, Sarah Vaughan, and Buck Clayton found Toronto and the Colonial one of their favourite places to perform" (Joint Board 1998b, Exhibit 96). However, the Colonial Tavern had fallen on hard times and, by then, belonged to the city.

A revitalization concept for part of the block began to take shape when the provincial and federal governments announced they would contribute to restoring the Elgin and Winter Garden theatres, which were then owned by the province's Ministry of Citizenship and Culture and the Ontario Heritage Foundation. The councillor who headed the task force on the Theatre Block likened the initiative to "a cross between a miniature Lincoln Centre and Times Square, if all its theatres were to be cleaned up" (cited in Godfrey 1983). The idea was to demolish the Colonial Tavern, which was dilapidated, and create a landscaped passage between the two rather beautiful old banks from Yonge through to Victoria Street. The Colonial Tavern's golden age of jazz would be recalled through the design of the passage and by naming it "Jazz Place."

Meanwhile, the Pantages Theatre on Victoria Street was undergoing changes. The theatre has a fascinating history. With 3,373 seats, it was the largest and most elegant Canadian theatre that served both vaudeville and motion picture audiences (Mirvish Productions; for a different, colourful account, see Drabinsky 1995, chap. 14). It was designed by Thomas Lamb, built in 1920 by the Canadian motion picture distributor Nathan L. Nathanson, owned by Pericles Alexander Pantages until he was jailed in 1929, sold to RKO Pictures, which became Famous Players, and renamed the Imperial in 1930. The theatre was later divided into a six-plex cinema in 1973; half of it was seized by

Cineplex Odeon in 1986 through an administrative oversight by Famous Players. It was soon transferred to Garth Drabinsky's Livent, rebuilt for live theatre again under the name the Pantages, and reopened in 1989, only to be lost in bankruptcy proceedings to SFX/Clear Channel Entertainment. The theatre, having been renamed the Canon Theatre in 2001 in recognition of financial support from Canon Canada, is currently managed and programmed by Mirvish Productions. It is oddly configured in that it has a fancy, if small, entrance on Yonge Street, while the bulk of the building is on Victoria Street, where the box office is located.

The Elgin and Winter Garden theatres were built together as a unit in 1913. Like the Pantages, they were designed by Thomas Lamb and have spotty histories. The Winter Garden, fitted out like a botanical fantasy, was closed in 1928, while the Elgin continued as a movie theatre. The Ontario Heritage Foundation bought both buildings in 1981, renovated them at a cost of $30 million, and reopened them – the Elgin in 1985 and the Winter Garden in 1989 – as live performance theatres (see also Ontario Heritage Foundation).

The city was thus moving along with initiatives when it could see an opening. But private investment in the street's properties was not forthcoming, which meant public investments had modest effect. Within a couple of years, the city was gripped in a serious economic recession, as were other levels of government and the private sector. This would all but halt investments for about five years.

Fifth Intervention: Cityplan '91 and the Retailing Problem

The fifth intervention played out in 1994. Eaton's threatened to challenge the city's newly created official plan at the Ontario Municipal Board because, in the company's view, the plan did not adequately champion retailing in the core. The negotiations between the city and the company that ensued were directly connected to plans for redeveloping the Yonge-Dundas area, which is the subject of this book, so discussion of this intervention is postponed until the next chapter.

In concluding this look at the evolution of lower Yonge Street, it is obvious that its character, including the location and nature of shopping and entertainment over the stretch between King and College/Carlton streets, has been anything but constant. For a period in the first half of the twentieth century, portions of the street served as the city's shopping district of choice, but this changed after the Second World War. Major public-sector interventions have had mixed effects. To successfully change the pattern of use on Yonge Street is undoubtedly complicated. The city has been careful over the decades not to leap too quickly.

Before investigating the most recent proposals and actions, which are discussed in the next chapter, we turn our attention to the history of the Yonge-Dundas intersection. In arguments about fixing the area, the intersection was referred to as the "Main and Main" of the city and also as its heart (Joint Board 1998k, 3).

Yonge and Dundas

Although Yonge Street as a whole is clearly of great importance to Toronto, the idea that Yonge-Dundas has traditionally been a major urban hub is erroneous. Dundas has been relatively insignificant as an east-west axis. In the nineteenth century there was a Dundas Street that began far to the west of the city centre at what is now the intersection of Ossington Avenue and Queen Street. It meandered westward toward the town of Dundas, near the city of Hamilton (Careless 1984, 25; Armstrong 1988, 44), just as Kingston Road in the eastern suburbs led to the city of Kingston. The current incarnation of Dundas Street is the result of a civic improvement project of the early part of the twentieth century, the goal of which was to create a new east-west traffic link to improve the efficiency of the city's circulation networks (Careless 1984, 193). Starting in 1916, a series of east-west streets that ran a suitable distance north of Queen were joined together and renamed Dundas Street (Filey 1986).[8] The new crosstown route linked the west end road known originally as Dundas with neighbourhoods to the east, beyond the Don Valley.[9] This improvised street wanders across Toronto's orthogonal grid with a great many jogs and several unusual intersections.

At what is now Yonge and Dundas, creating the intersection involved forcing Wilton Street (on the east of Yonge) and Agnes Street (on the west of Yonge) to meet. At Yonge Street, these two streets were out of alignment by about seventy metres. Figure 2.6 shows the proposed route of the alignment. Several properties on Yonge Street and Victoria Street (to the east) had to be demolished so that the continuation of Dundas was straight enough to support a streetcar line.[10] This left a parcel of land that was called Old Wilton Square and later renamed Dundas Square (Joint Board 1998b, Exhibit 162, 7).

Throughout the nineteenth century, the streets around Dundas and Yonge were local in nature and largely residential in use. The housing was built and poorly serviced, and it was overcrowded. To the west of what is now Yonge and Dundas was one of Toronto's lowest-income neighbourhoods, a settlement area for successive waves of impoverished immigrants – Irish, eastern Europeans, Italians, and Chinese (Careless 1984, 157; Kluckner 1988, 135-42). The streets also housed Eaton's back offices, which supported the company's sprawling store to the south and its national retail activities. The company's

2.6 Plan to connect Dundas Street West and East. | *Daily Star* 1921.

central mail-order warehouse was located there, as was a multistorey manufacturing complex in which much of the clothing Eaton's distributed to its stores across Canada was made (Dendy 1986, 291; Lemon 1985, 39). Residents of the area provided cheap labour for these clothing manufacturers: "Sharing the blocks with the little houses and shops were factories of every size and description ... there was scarcely a block that did not have some sort of tailoring enterprise, ranging from well-organized factories in lofts to the meanest, most pitiful sweatshops in grubby lean-tos in the back alleyways" (Kluckner 1988, 135).

The 1934 Bruce Report on housing conditions in Toronto showed that dwellings with below-standard amenities began to be concentrated west of

Yonge, from about Dundas to near College, and increased in density as one moved farther west to Spadina and Bathurst (Toronto 1934, 16-17).

Still on the west side of Yonge, the city's poorhouse (known as the House of Industry) occupied almost an entire block on Elm Street, just a stone's throw from the Dundas Square site. Slightly west of that, on Centre Avenue, was the city's equivalent of a red-light district (Kluckner 1988, 135). Consequently, in the Toronto of old, steeped as it was in Victorian notions of morality, this area was often perceived as being marked by immorality and crime.

The character of the land use was no more polished on the east side of Yonge than on the west. There was likewise a mix of residential, commercial, and retail property or land, but there was only one major industrial use – brewing. According to an environmental assessment of the area prepared for the city by consultants, "the only industrial development in the area was the O'Keefe Brewing Co. Ltd. which was located on the east and west side of Victoria Street, between Gould Street and Dundas Street East. The O'Keefe Brewing Co. Ltd. discontinued operations at the site in the mid-1960s. The buildings were vacated and remained unused until demolition. The property was subsequently purchased by Ryerson Polytechnical Institute" (Joint Board 1998b, Exhibit 162, 6). Just to the northeast of the brewery was St. James Square, one of Toronto's few planned open spaces (Dendy 1993, 150). It was surrounded by three elegant buildings that housed the Normal School, the Model School, and the Department of Education. These buildings later became the home of what is now Ryerson University. When Ryerson was founded on the site in 1949, it was sitting in the midst of what Ron Stagg (1998) has described as "one of the less desirable areas of Toronto."

From 1899 the Society for Working Boys operated a home for disadvantaged youth on Gould Street, a block north of Dundas. In 1958 that building became the Ryerson Student Union building. Just a couple of blocks away, on the east side of Yonge between Gould and Gerrard (at no. 381), was the Yonge Street Mission. It has continuously operated at that location since 1904, serving various publics, most recently youth. It was named Evergreen in 1979 (Mathers and Mohamed 2004, 1-2).

The uses that have occupied the four corners of Yonge and Dundas over the years have not convinced us that the area has been the heart of the city, the main and main. The city's 1959 interim plan predicted that the area would consist of higher-density housing, with *local* shopping along Yonge Street north of Dundas (Toronto 1959). In the 1960s the City of Toronto (Toronto 1963, 40) noted that, aside from limited warehousing and manufacturing uses, and some wholesale or retail activity along Victoria Street, the area was primarily residential. The city's own interpretation of the area on the east side of Yonge at Dundas was as follows: "In all, this part of downtown is occupied by a number of distinct elements and several very mixed pockets. It is not a cohesive unit, but rather a backwater between more important, recognizable areas ... The area has no special advantage for office or retail business which would change its character" (ibid., 40-41).

A few years later, in 1971, the director of the City of Toronto Planning Board, on the subject of Dundas' role as an east-west axis, said that "any concept of Dundas Street as a cross-City connector seems questionable" (Toronto 1971, 2).

Although Dundas Street does have a role as a local shopping street in certain sections (e.g., in Kensington Market, west of Spadina), for the most part it is not distinctive. In fact, to the east of the Don Valley, Dundas is primarily a residential street. Clearly, Dundas, unlike Queen to the south or Bloor to the north, never did develop as an important east-west axis of any sort.

Taking the background of Yonge and Dundas into account, it is odd that this intersection should be described as the "main and main" of Toronto. If it *is* the heart, it has come by this distinction because of the Eaton Centre entrance, not because the intersection was especially distinctive otherwise. As we will see, that distinctive entrance was removed in the course of redevelopment because it was a magnet for people who liked to hang around, to proselytize, and to ply the informal economy.

Conclusion

The Yonge-Dundas area has been constantly busy over the years with retail or commercial and residential uses, as well as brewing, warehousing, and garment manufacturing. Whatever stylishness one could attribute to the area tended to be found closer to Queen than to Dundas. More raunchy activities had asserted their presence on Yonge north of Shuter and mainly north of Dundas by around the early 1970s.

The claim made by proponents of this project that Yonge-Dundas was once the flourishing and vibrant heart of the downtown is not corroborated by historical evidence. Nor is there substance to the claim that it was a fashionable part of the city that had fallen on hard times. In 1963 the City of Toronto described Yonge-Dundas as the "backwater between more important, recognizable areas." It has been given a nostalgic past that is more correctly attributed to other nodes on Yonge.

These facts did not stop the fall-and-redemption and rotting heart imagery from being used with considerable effect in efforts to generate support for redevelopment plans. The use of this type of blatant imagery is common in the business of selling cities and development. It is unlikely to work on its own, but as part of building up meaning through images, and as a form of rhetoric used in the course of trying to persuade, it is often part of a purposeful strategy for gaining attention. Indeed, speakers often use metaphors without being aware of doing so or of how inaccurate the imagery is, which is probably the case here.

On the one hand, we have no choice but to use metaphors. On the other, we should not be taken in by our own metaphors. Use of metaphor is built deep into Western ways of thinking, speaking, and writing. Consequently, we should be urged to ask in any given instance, what metaphor is at work? It should be opened up to critical analysis.

If the use of imagery in urban redevelopment is common, why do we need yet another story to illustrate it? The answer is because we still have not incorporated imagery and its effects into a theory of how planning works. Imagery is still treated as if it were an aberration rather than part of how planning functions. Certainly, metaphors should not stand unquestioned as the basis for a redevelopment project.[11] This is a central message of this book.

This chapter has also illustrated how the core of the city altered, over a century or so, in concert with changes occurring to its surrounding urban region. What was left was a small space that no longer provided the essential goods and services of daily life to the growing population on its ever expanding periphery.

CHAPTER 3

Regenerating

This chapter reviews the early stages of fixing Yonge Street in the area of the Eaton Centre in the 1990s. In this period the city decided the broad direction it wanted to take with built form and land uses. The pressures on the city to change what was happening on this stretch of Yonge are sketched out, and special attention is given to some key players. Near the end of the chapter, the emergence of a new initiative from a few of the private-sector owners in the area is discussed. The new initiative had become wrapped up with the city's plans by the time city council met in March 1996. This changed the way planning for this area was handled from then on.

Heavy Pressures from Capital Interests

The downtown section of Yonge Street underwent tremendous upheavals from the 1950s onward: the opening of the subway, the construction of the Eaton Centre, and the flight of retailing to the suburbs. Efforts to channel its vitality floundered. In the early 1990s, the city began preparing a new official plan to replace the 1976 plan. In the old plan, the part of Yonge Street around the Eaton Centre had been designated a prominent site and area and a priority retail street (Joint Board 1998k, 11-12). Its character was to be pedestrian-oriented retail or entertainment. In the course of preparing the new plan, colloquially called Cityplan '91, a draft proposal suggested that a "main streets" approach should be applied to the strip, an area that extended from Gerrard south to Dundas Square Street. This would require designating retail and commercial uses on the ground floor and dwellings above. At the time, the main streets concept was being promoted for many of the principal shopping streets in Toronto neighbourhoods.

The T. Eaton Company was dissatisfied with the official plan's treatment of the area around the Eaton Centre and its treatment of retail for the wider downtown. Therefore, it declared that it would appeal parts of the official plan at the Ontario Municipal Board on the grounds that the "objectives and policies ... as they relate to the City's downtown, and in particular to retail uses in the downtown, do not provide a sufficiently strong commitment to maintaining and enhancing the downtown as the economic and symbolic centre of the City and Region. In particular, the Plan fails to demonstrate an adequate understanding of the critical role that the retail sector plays in the vitality of the downtown and does not articulate specific policies that are required to ensure that this sector is able to continue to play this" (Joint Board 1998k, 12). Eaton's argued that its studies showed that the downtown area's share of the consumer goods market had dropped from 25 percent to just 6 percent in the twenty-one-year period from 1971 to 1992. Obviously, there had been an enormous shift to shopping in the suburbs; this had happened all over Canada and the United States. But Eaton's was implying that problems with the downtown market share stemmed from how the city was treating the retail sector in the core, not from deeper changes to the way the whole retail sector was conducting its business.

As a result of meetings between city staff and Eaton's representatives, the city said that there was no "substantive policy difference between Eaton's position and the Official Plan. The Plan implicitly assumes that the downtown will continue to be Toronto's pre-eminent centre. However, it previously was not considered necessary to explicitly state specific policies articulating the City's support for its downtown" (Joint Board 1998f, Tab 22). The negotiated settlement resulted in the city making some changes to clauses in its official plan. For example, it required the city to remove from the official plan statements such as "give greater recognition to the importance of the Central Area, particularly as a location for office employment" and replace them with statements like "support and promote the Central Area as an international centre for business, culture, entertainment, shopping, research and design, and institutions" (ibid., 2). It also required the city to add phrasing about supporting "the Central Core's role as the major focus for shopping activity in the Greater Toronto Area" (ibid., 3), and to commit the commissioner of planning and development to review limits on new retail floor space found in another section of the plan. These clauses were approved by city council and the Ontario Municipal Board (OMB) in September 1994 (Toronto 1994a).

Even if there was "no substantive policy difference," there remained a distinct difference of view as to the precise nature of Yonge Street's problem. The city planning department took the view that the problem was more social than economic and that the social problem stemmed from Eaton's having turned its retail centre inward toward an internal street system, thereby abandoning the public street. If Eaton's had had to admit that the problem was social, it would have had to also admit that there was a problem with the

Eaton Centre itself. The changes to the official plan were like a negotiated settlement on the street's problems. The lead up to it had given the commissioner of planning and development the opportunity to have focused discussions with Eaton's about the nature of the problem at Yonge and Dundas. Eaton's gradually began to change its perception of the problem after that point, but it did so slowly.

In his witness statement four years later, at the Yonge-Dundas hearing before the OMB, the staff planner referred to the changes to the official plan that had been required to satisfy Eaton's. He said that, among other matters, the modifications approved by the board had contributed to this broad policy. The board ramped up that observation by the planner considerably, writing in its decision that it found "that this effort by Eaton's was the catalyst that led to the ultimate founding of the Yonge Street Business and Residents Association" (Joint Board 1998k, 12-13), an organization, it implied, that was laudable because of the dedication it brought to the public interest in the Yonge-Dundas area. By 1997, the year the OMB was speaking so approvingly about Eaton's, the giant department store had already filed for bankruptcy protection. It was out of business one year later.

Social problems also existed in the Yonge-Dundas area. According to observations made by planners and others active in the area, as opposed to systematic research, it seems that users were flattening out or becoming less varied. The fieldwork of Jan Gehl (1996) and William Whyte (1980, 1988) supports the thesis that the biggest attraction of a public area is crowd mix. Too many of any one group can experientially flatten out a public space and make it less attractive. One can argue that in a place like Yonge-Dundas it is in the public interest to have a crowd mix that is socioeconomically and experientially varied. There was, then, a research basis for encouraging a different mix of people in the area, but no systematic research was done on who was using the area. No references to research on users were found in the Yonge-Dundas reports. References were either in general or made by innuendo.

The city's planning department did not have many tools for dealing with social issues, but it was called upon to "do something" and was involved with physical conditions in the area. So its approach in the first two years was to use its physical planning mandate to encourage other city and metropolitan government departments to focus their resources on this piece of geography in the core of the city – for example, to find more shelters for homeless people, to increase the resources for psychiatrically challenged people in the area, to find interesting after-school activities for youth that might reduce the numbers hanging around the intersection, and to do more effective policing. The planning department tried to validate other departments thinking geographically and working together to solve the problems of Yonge Street because its view was that if the street was cleaned up a bit – if crime and the perception of it was reduced, if litter and gum stuck on the sidewalks (a pet peeve of one of the active local business owners) were removed, and if blatant prostitution and sexual activities in streets, lanes, and doorways were reduced or eradicated – then economic improvement would follow. In theory, if challenged and challenging people seemed to be less dominant in the overall population of users, then others would be more likely to frequent the area. Proposed changes at that time were not focused on consumerism, strictly speaking, nor were they necessarily socially discriminatory. City staff hesitated to engage in any social engineering on Yonge Street and, as is evident in their planning reports throughout the years, had largely accepted the grittiness as part of the street's character in that stretch. However, this modest social strategy was reversed later on.

Another source of pressure on the city resulted from an application from a developer concerning a corner site at 350 Yonge Street, two blocks north of Dundas. The request, made in March 1992, sought permission to build a mixed commercial and residential building at a height of sixteen storeys. Neither the use nor the height fit either the old or the emerging new official plan. In technical terms the proposed building would have achieved 9.24 times coverage, whereas zoning allowed for 2.0 times coverage; it would have been over forty-seven metres high in an area zoned for eighteen metres; and it would have been more residential than commercial, whereas the reverse was specified in the official plan. Even though the development's features were out of step with the city's expectations for the area, the city's Land Use Committee seemed to want to use this application to force a decision that would end wrestling over just what to do with this stretch of Yonge Street. Therefore, it exempted the site from the new zoning bylaw and, in effect, put the site on hold, returning to it only after the city adopted the new official plan and zoning bylaw. Then, in September 1993, after the official plan and zoning bylaw had been adopted by city council, the committee asked the commissioner of planning and development to study the planning controls that were affecting the Yonge Street Strip between Gerrard and Dundas. Its answer to this redevelopment request, while long in coming, was the culmination of its effort to reach conclusions about which way to push Yonge. The committee had to wait until late 1995 for a reply from the planning department, but when it did come it was indeed fully contextualized within a study of planning controls, design, and current and proposed land uses.

These two private-sector initiatives – from Eaton's and from the 350 Yonge Street site – inevitably refocused the city's attention on the Yonge-Dundas area. Further incentive came from the effects of the deep recession the city was experiencing, the end of which only began to appear in 1994.

The arguments behind the initiatives and the city's emerging position are important to note. They involved the economic efficiency argument of highest and best use and the public interest argument, two debates that are rarely separable. Both the city and the capital interests associated with the Eaton Centre wanted to keep low-rise retail in the area, but for very different reasons. The city, via its planners, wanted to see the existing land parcels used in the interests of preserving the distinct place that the Yonge-Dundas intersection had become in the city of Toronto as a whole. It produced a design study that gave substantial evidence as to why this was a sensible approach. The city's interests also included maintaining the value of the Eaton Centre, which was paying approximately $50 million annually in property and business taxes. On the other hand, the Eaton Centre wanted to improve the street around it simply to keep up its attractiveness and the value of its property, but it did not want competition either from upscale retailers who might choose to locate outside the Centre rather than within it or, possibly, from new office space with underground retail. The Eaton Centre had two office towers to keep filled, and new interior shopping would compete directly with the Centre.

Two different ideas in good currency emerged to help resolve the differences between the city and Eaton's. One was the so-called urban-box format (as compared to the big-box suburban format). Urban boxes fit the scale of the streetscape the planners wanted to promote yet would not compete forcefully with the retailers Eaton's wanted to attract into the Centre. (See Figure 3.1 for an example of the urban-box format.) The other idea was to reiterate the inappropriateness of office uses in the area. Both ideas suited Eaton's and the city. The city consistently maintained that the strip was a unique area that should be preserved and that there was still plenty of space south of Queen and elsewhere for office development.

Meanwhile, commercial property developers represented another fraction of capital, and they argued in favour of the highest and best use. They had long wanted access to this section of Yonge and had blamed the condition of Yonge Street on the city's policies, which kept the height limit at eighteen metres. They wanted sixteen to thirty storeys with ground-level retail or services, surface setbacks to provide plazas, underground retail, and connections to the subway and the underground pedestrian system. This was precisely what could be found south of Queen and east and west of Yonge. The developers wanted to lay out the same pattern at Yonge and Dundas. All they needed was zoning permission, which could perhaps be obtained through a precedent-setting case, such as the 350 Yonge application might become. If this occurred, the current pattern of ownership, distinguished by small properties held in dozens of hands, would rapidly convert to a few large assemblies,

3.1 HMV's "urban box" form on the east side of Yonge Street, north of Dundas, 2005. South of HMV, on the right, is a small section of the hoarding with advertising that wrapped around Parcel A, the cinema-anchored site where redevelopment was stalled for several years. | Author's collection.

as had already happened at the Eaton Centre, the Atrium, and west toward Bay Street. Small landholders could make windfalls from selling; large developers could make high profits from building. The fate of the Eaton Centre would be highly uncertain.

For the city there was no obvious common ground for negotiations with commercial building developers. The developers were single-minded; they wanted to put up tall buildings to maximize their return on investment. Evidently, the stakes were very high – none more so than those that concerned the city's planning department and how it would define the public interest.

Getting Started: Early Steps

In the course of trying to sort through this tangle between Eaton's and the city, efforts were made through the city's Economic Development Committee to establish a formal Downtown Task Force composed mainly of private companies, each of which would pay for the privilege of sitting on the committee and helping shape policies and development in Toronto's downtown (Toronto 1994a, 93-97). Formal private-sector involvement in downtown planning is uncommon in a Canadian city but often associated with US planning. The city demurred and approved an arrangement of two committees – one broadly focused, the other narrowly focused. The former, a downtown retail revitalization committee, would "develop a strategy for increasing the general public's use of downtown Toronto for purposes such as shopping and entertainment" (ibid., 88). The latter, a Yonge Street improvement committee, would focus on that street alone. The revitalization committee did not get off the ground, but a version of the Yonge Street–focused initiative did. What Eaton's lost – potential control over planning in the entire city core – when the private-task-force idea proved to be a nonstarter was partly recaptured just months later when it helped launch an association of businesses on Yonge Street in its own bailiwick. The commissioner of planning and development – who spent the summer of 1994 stick-handling the Eaton's situation, including trying to convince Eaton's that its Centre was a major factor in the erosion of Yonge Street's vitality – made his own wry observation in his recommendation to city council on how to structure these committees: "In addition to amending the Official Plan, Eaton's also has recommended that the City establish a task force 'to monitor the economic and social vitality of the City's downtown and to develop and initiate a strategy to deal with real and perceived problems in the downtown'" (ibid., 97). (For help with dates and actions, please see the chronology in Appendix 2.)

In keeping with the spirit of the council's wish to move regeneration of Yonge Street forward, planning staff began meeting with interested parties in the Yonge-Dundas area in the fall of 1994. They gradually assembled a list of issues, approaches that could be used to address them, and, in particular, ways to better accommodate street activity (Toronto 1995b, 8). By April 1995 a community committee was established at a public meeting; it met three times that spring before it brought out a report. The committee was composed of representatives from the local business association, which was just forming, other nonaligned local retail property owners, the Eaton Centre, street vendors, street portrait artists, street musicians and buskers, students, the ward councillor, Ryerson University, and staff from both the metropolitan-level transportation department and several city-level departments. Their meetings were open to the public (ibid.). In general, the committee wanted to see the appearance and management of the area improved, and it developed proposals to those ends.

Given subsequent developments, it is worth noting that this committee also paid attention to social issues: it "discussed the interrelatedness of social issues to the physical planning solutions and the need to address social problems in the area on an immediate and ongoing basis" (Toronto 1995b, 8). It recognized that it did not have, but should have, social-service providers represented on the committee. Some initiatives such as community policing and greater security measures were under way. In December 1993 the police service had opened a substation inside the north entrance of the Eaton Centre. But it was recognized that much more was needed to meet the circumstances, because Yonge Street "is an attraction for the homeless and those persons who have turned to panhandling. In a city of Toronto's size, the poverty and unemployment throughout the region is very visible in such public places as downtown Yonge Street. The host community becomes the community [that] must address the problems which extend beyond the jurisdictional role of the City of Toronto" (ibid., 16). At that time, social welfare costs were shouldered by the provincial government; funds were passed to municipalities through the regional level of government.

The first report said that the initiatives it was proposing should be seen as a continuum of activities "with the objective of improving the physical appearance of public and private land and buildings on and near Yonge Street between Gerrard and Queen Streets and adjusting the regulatory system to accommodate a variety of street activity in a managed fashion ... Implementation will be incremental over several years, but should continue as an ongoing investment in the downtown, to support the area as one of Toronto's most public and pedestrian places" (Toronto 1995b, 17).

The report concluded by identifying some future tasks, one of which was for staff to look into whether the area should be designated a community improvement area under the *Planning Act,* because this status would allow the city to acquire land, offer municipal grants and loans, and be involved in other improvement initiatives. In mid-1995, then, the possibility of the city acquiring land was at least being allowed for in the planning for the area. (For a description of the basic characteristics of the area, such as land uses and built form, see Appendix 3.)

The planning department recommended that the meetings of this community committee continue and that its membership be broadened to include social-services representatives and local residents.

In-House Preparatory Studies Used in Decision Making
The relative clarity of direction for revamping Yonge Street would not have been possible without the findings from an important urban design study. That study was informal, internal to the Planning and Development Department, and not intended for the public. Nonetheless, once a committee was about to start work on planning the regeneration of Yonge Street more inclusively, the observations in that study provided a significant point of departure and framework for that task as orchestrated by the Planning and Development Department. Perhaps not coincidentally, the study was finished just four days before the first public meeting in April 1995, at which a community committee was formed to start work on what to do with the area. The study later

became part of the public record in the documents of the OMB hearing (Joint Board 1998b, Exhibit 126).

The urban design study provided details for nine block frontages between Gerrard Street and Dundas Square Street. The built form of the area included densities, heights, pattern of building, construction dates, usages, floor-plate sizes, historic building designations, and street and sidewalk features. Its main points were as follows:

- The land parcels are both narrow and shallow and not suitable for high-density development.
- The street is both narrow and north-south oriented so that high-density development would easily shadow it, reducing pedestrian comfort and, consequently, pedestrian usage.
- A general increase in density at one site would likely trigger a switch of primary uses so that street-related retail would become secondary to high-density residential or office commercial uses.
- Coverage could be changed from 2.0 times commercial coverage to 3.0 times commercial coverage and was recommended because it fit the existing buildings and retail culture of the street and would allow for the new form of urban-box retailing.
- The area should not have the current residential zoning because it did not fit into the city's main-streets concept, which encouraged a mix of shops and dwellings on main neighbourhood streets. This was not a neighbourhood street. The report said the main-streets designation may even contradict section 9.9 of the official plan, which seeks to heighten the significance of retail in this area.
- There is no logic to giving Ryerson University a presence on Yonge Street, although this is often proposed, because gregarious retail and sober university activities are not complementary.
- Current physical, commercial, and social characteristics are "fundamentally inter-related and are not only consistent with the planning policies that currently apply to the street, but with minor modification could be the basis of continued positive, incremental and compatible development" (Joint Board 1998b, Exhibit 126, 9).

The final point became central to the city's position on how it would push the street in the first regeneration phase. For example, the overall regeneration plan adopted by city council a year later, in March 1996, was nearly identical to what was proposed in the urban design report; however, site coverage had been raised to 4.0 and the height had been raised from eighteen to twenty metres. But in general this was the base analysis developed from data about the area. It was intended to generate "positive, *incremental* and compatible development" (Joint Board 1998b, Exhibit 126, 9, my emphasis). This study sharply focused the city planners' position. The head of urban design, who wrote the report, was unequivocal that the type of high-rise development envisaged for the 350 Yonge Street site did not suit that part of the street at all. The way forward was low-rise mixed retail and commercial uses. He was also clear that the existing residential designation should be removed to discourage gentrification. That planning actions should lead to taking a dozen properties and developing a public square is neither expressed nor implied in the report's conclusion. Research interviews confirm that the planning concept for fixing the street at that time was indeed "incremental," focused on slightly altering the regulatory controls to make the area more attractive for private development.

The report's position on avoiding gentrification was bolstered by a 1994 visit to New York by the commissioner of planning and development (who had previously worked for the New York City Department of Planning) and his chief planner to look at the Times Square redevelopment plans. On seeing the garishness of Times Square, they saw a potential parallel with Yonge-Dundas. The garishness itself had a value they believed should be retained. But that was where the comparison with Times Square seemed to end. Their observations evolved into a three-pronged strategy: eliminate residential uses, substantially revise the sign bylaw, and plan for incremental change. With respect to the first prong, they reasoned that residential uses were incompatible with the type of area they were trying to sustain, if in a somewhat reinvigorated form. One planner described the "fault line" that starts to emerge when uses are fundamentally incompatible. As he described it, someone may find it amusing to live above a Zanzibar Dance Club, but not for long. Those who do end up living there, either as tenants or owners, will eventually put pressure on the city to sanitize the club or close it. The situation is similar to that of suburbanites who fight to move farms farther from their properties because of the smell. So the city planners recommended removing the allowed residential uses so that the raucousness of the area could be left in peace, so to speak.

The focus of the second prong – signage – resulted from what the commissioner and chief planner observed in Times Square. They learned that New York had imposed a minimum, not a maximum, sign size for the Square to reinforce the dynamic, youth-focused, "bright lights" feel of the area. Toronto had previously allowed large signs in the area but had not enforced large signs. Signs are usually considered from the position of the maximum allowed. The third prong was to plan for incremental change, which is illustrated in much of the remainder of this chapter.

The only other study that backed up the regeneration plans was prepared a few months later, in October 1995.[1] It was described by the area's planner as "a street survey" (Joint Board 1998b, Exhibit 69, 10), and it reported the activities of businesses in the strip on Yonge Street, from Gerrard to Dundas Square, as well as provided numbers and percentages in each category (Toronto 1996e, 2):

1 two-thirds of the retail stores fell into three categories: electronic and music stores; discount or speciality clothing stores; restaurants;
2 eight stores or bars provided adult-oriented products or services;
3 upper floor uses varied from retail to office to vacant, with "less than five residential units above stores";
4 six stores were vacant.

The first conclusion the report drew was that the Eaton Centre provided more diversity of merchandise than the street; therefore, the street was doing poorly. However, parallel occupancy information for the Eaton Centre was not presented, so the possibility remains that two-thirds of its retailers also delivered in the three categories of electronics and music, discount or specialty clothing, and restaurants. Why was such a simple comparison not done? The second conclusion was that the HMV chain store on Yonge was the only example of a property expanding retailing onto the upper floors and, thus, developing the urban-box format (Joint Board 1998b, Exhibit 69, 10). While this near absence of vertical retailing was a fact, it did not lead to the conclusion that owners could not be encouraged to expand into the upper floors the way HMV had done, especially if the building envelopes were expanded by changing the zoning and if the city's intentions for the street were made clear. The HMV urban box had approximately 40,000 square feet (about 3,700 square metres) of gross sales area, a size not unlike what might be built in the suburbs (see Figure 3.2).

Seen in the strongest light, this street survey backed up the need to allow modest changes to built form on the properties. With slightly more height allowance, retailers could fit the urban box onto Yonge Street sites. With the urban design study and the street survey in hand, the city had the evidence it needed to put a regeneration plan that emphasized low-rise retail space in place. In this case, considerations of highest and best use were combined with considerations of the public interest to encourage a nonresidential, antigentrification policy that would retain the unusual strip character of this section of the street. Apparently, this solution suited local property owners and others who participated in the community committee. However, the solution did not suit others. Regeneration would probably reap steady property

3.2 Looking south on Yonge Street, 1999. Note the bulk of the Eaton Centre on the west side compared to the small-parcel built form on the east side and the contrast in animation and shadow on each side of the street. | Author's collection.

increases for current owners but not the windfall that would accompany high-rise redevelopment led by the private sector. It certainly was not the solution office-building developers wanted. It was also a highly contextualized response, one that was specific to Toronto and even a particular part of Toronto: the solution was not à la mode, it was not at all like some of the celebrated core redevelopments in the cities of Britain, Europe, Australia, and the United States. Not yet.

It is significant that the solution mixed paying attention to the long-term public interest (as the planners understood it) with financial gain, but not windfalls, for property owners. It was not an "economy first and foremost" solution. At this point it was a managed solution in the conventional sense of planning as managing built space and negotiating the shoals of Scylla and Charybdis – highest and best use to encourage the market in conjunction with keeping an eye on public interests.

Public Planning Reports

Once the basic groundwork was laid, the project continued to evolve in a dynamic, focused way. The city's planning department was clearly in charge, community representatives were involved, and social issues, which were so central to the problems of the area, were at least nominally part of the agenda.

Staff members then asked council to pass a bylaw that would designate a portion of Toronto's downtown as a community improvement project (CIP) area. Council, using section 28 of the provincial *Planning Act,* did this in October 1995. The designated area extended from Gerrard Street south to Queen, and was later extended north to College. Figure 3.3 shows the re-investment area and the community improvement area. The CIP designation gives a city powers it would not normally have "to acquire land, construct, repair or rehabilitate buildings, to lease or dispose of land acquired or held by it, to make grants or loans to land owners as an exception to the *Municipal Act* provisions respecting bonussing, [to] enter into agreements with other levels of government and the private sector or issue debentures for the purpose of the Community Improvement Plan" (Toronto 1995a, 8). Almost all of the report on the community improvement plan was devoted to describing the planning and economic development rationale for a grant and loan program for facade improvements in the project area and to explaining the details of how that would work. There was brief mention of streetscape improvements underway, and notice was given that a "broader conceptual plan for revitalization of Yonge Street and the downtown [was] emerging" (ibid., 15), which could require amendment of the plan. By November 1995 planning policy for the area was "to maintain Yonge Street as a pedestrian retail street where intense and specialized retail activity can function and support other downtown activities" (ibid., 135, para. 1.4).

The designation of a CIP was discussed at a public meeting held by the Neighbourhoods Committee on 6 December 1995. The notice in the newspaper advertising the meeting said that its purpose was to discuss the community improvement plan for the Downtown Yonge Street Community Improvement Area. It said that the plan made recommendations on community improvement projects, including a facade improvement program and streetscape improvements. This was the scale of activities the public was being asked to consider and comment on. After successfully passing through the committee and budget approval system, the community improvement plan was approved by city council on 22 January 1996. At council the plan was linked to the earlier June report that had had the community committee's involvement, but it was presented as going beyond it.

To follow the progress of this project, it is necessary to note that involvement by citizens seemed to fall off after the spring 1995 meetings, while involvement by members of the business and institutional sectors – those whose workday obligations logically included keeping abreast of this project because of direct, clearly definable interests – was maintained or increased. For example, among those who addressed the council committee in December 1995 were

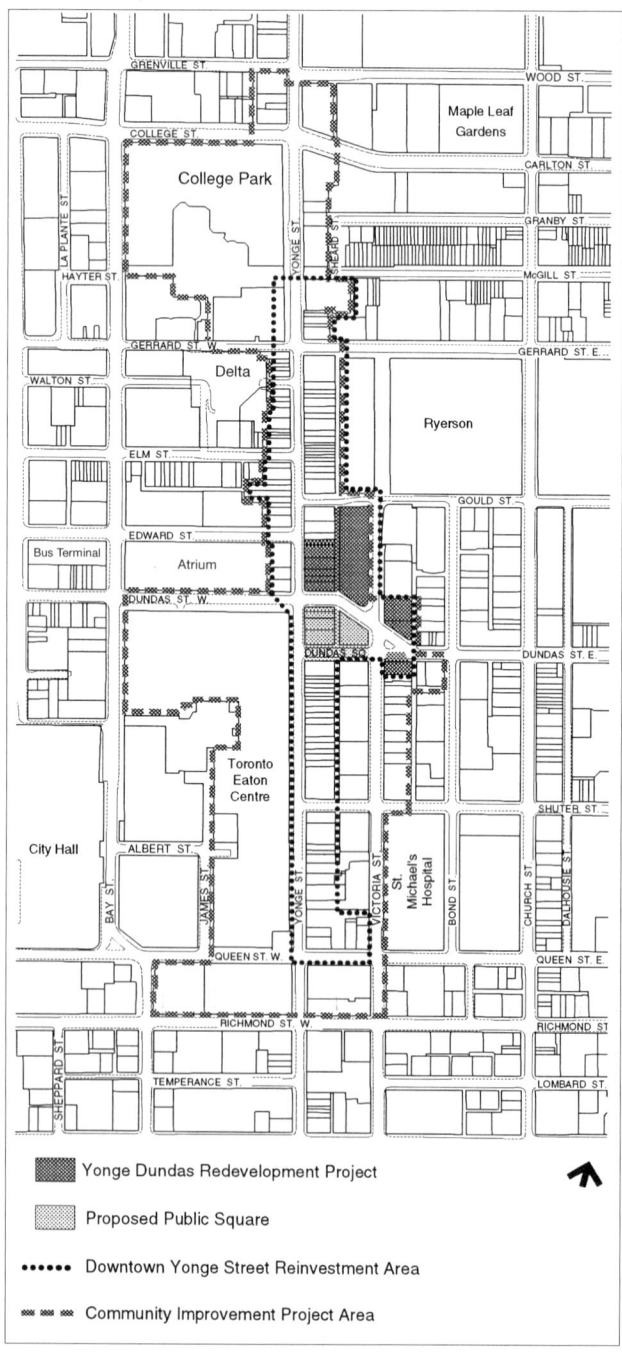

3.3 Reinvestment area and larger community improvement area. |
Adapted from Toronto (1996f, Map 6) and Toronto (1997a).

three of the small businesses in the immediate area and a professor and student from Ryerson University's School of Architecture. In addition, money was beginning to flow toward the project for the facade program, and reminders were appearing in reports that land acquisition could be in the offing.

However, no record has been found in the media to suggest that anything more dramatic than a gradual regeneration program was underway. One assumes, therefore, that Torontonians who followed municipal affairs believed that a slow-drip regeneration process was being planned, one that would attract investment because, at long last, the city could now give clear directions on its intentions for the future of the area.

Regeneration Plan at City Council, March 1996

Momentum was strong. By March 1996 a substantial report had been prepared that laid out the rationale for the actions on Yonge Street. It was approved by city council, along with two other related items.

The report began by referring councillors to the new "three lenses approach" to planning that had been adopted by city council four months earlier (see Appendix 1 for a description). The three lenses approach is a way to recognize "that different areas of the city should be treated differently in the planning approaches used to achieve local and City-wide goals. Downtown Yonge Street generally fits into the Reinvestment Area category as a mixed use area in need of revitalizing. For Reinvestment Areas, the focus would be on greater flexibility and diversity of uses with certainty of built form. With certain limitations, this approach is appropriate for downtown Yonge Street" (Toronto 1996e, 1).

Recall the discussion of theories about planners' work in Chapter 1. The planning commissioner then presented an argument for why a different set of tools would be required at this location than would be the case, for instance, in a stable area. In this example of planning practice, activities were formally selected according to what the problem was broadly specified to be. In this instance, the planner worked within a managerial style of planning and introduced a range of planning solutions suited to areas that confronted different development issues.

The planning commissioner was clear, too, about his report's connection to the development application for 350 Yonge Street. He said he had not reported earlier in order "to allow for a general direction on Yonge Street revitalization initiatives to emerge" (Toronto 1996e, 1). There was a purposeful chain of events, each of which involved a thoughtful engagement with a new facet of the problem. By the time of this report, most of the elements were falling into place, at least in the eyes of members of the planning department. The street was much better understood physically, as well as in terms of the role that specific sections played. This allowed the planners to be more certain about where the revitalization action should be concentrated, and it emboldened them to argue that this was a distinct part of the city that could be retained as such – and that to do so was in the public interest. For instance, the planners identified five sections of Yonge Street to which they needed to be attentive: the downtown section, which included the strip from Gerrard south to Dundas Square; two related sections, one of which went north to College, while the other went south to Queen; a section north of College, where the uses on Yonge Street were oriented toward the residential areas east and west of Yonge; and a section south of Queen, which was viewed as part of the financial district.

Thus, the College to Queen portion (the first three sections) was identified as an area that either did not belong to anything else or was not otherwise claimed. It was residual. This reverses the usual attribution that makes it the heart, the very centre of the city. The planners asked: Where does this place begin and end? Is there something unique about this place? If yes, should the uniqueness be retained? Even if, at this time, some of the media and politicians called the area the heart, it would be at least a couple of years before a planner did so in print. Planners saw the area as being open to circumscribed reconceptualization. Severe constraints existed if (1) sun was to be retained on the street; (2) one recognized the long-standing official plan policies that designated the area for entertainment and shopping, not residential or high-rise commercial use; (3) one acknowledged that surface transportation arrangements could not be changed much, given that both Yonge and Dundas streets were governed by the metropolitan level of government, not by the city; and (4) the city's priority of protecting the value of the Eaton Centre was respected. Besides being a major taxpayer, the Eaton Centre was also a key tourist attraction for the city. So both tax revenue and tourist dollars were implicated in its fate. (See, among other sources that indicate the city's interest in retaining its value, Toronto 1994b). Taken together, the possibilities for the small area began to coalesce around a rather short list of options. Figure 3.4, a schematic, shows the built-form context of the new planning amendments presented to city council.

The plan was called a "comprehensive planning approach," and the report writer said that this meant the plan would be inclusive and seek "solutions for the social and economic needs of the variety and diversity of people who either live, work or visit on Yonge Street" (Toronto 1996e, 11). Some planning theorists at that time severely criticized the comprehensive planning approach and, indeed, declared that it was already dead. Regardless, this report retained a clear reference to a traditional planning concept that the public interest is served by paying attention to a wide range of interests, not simply economic

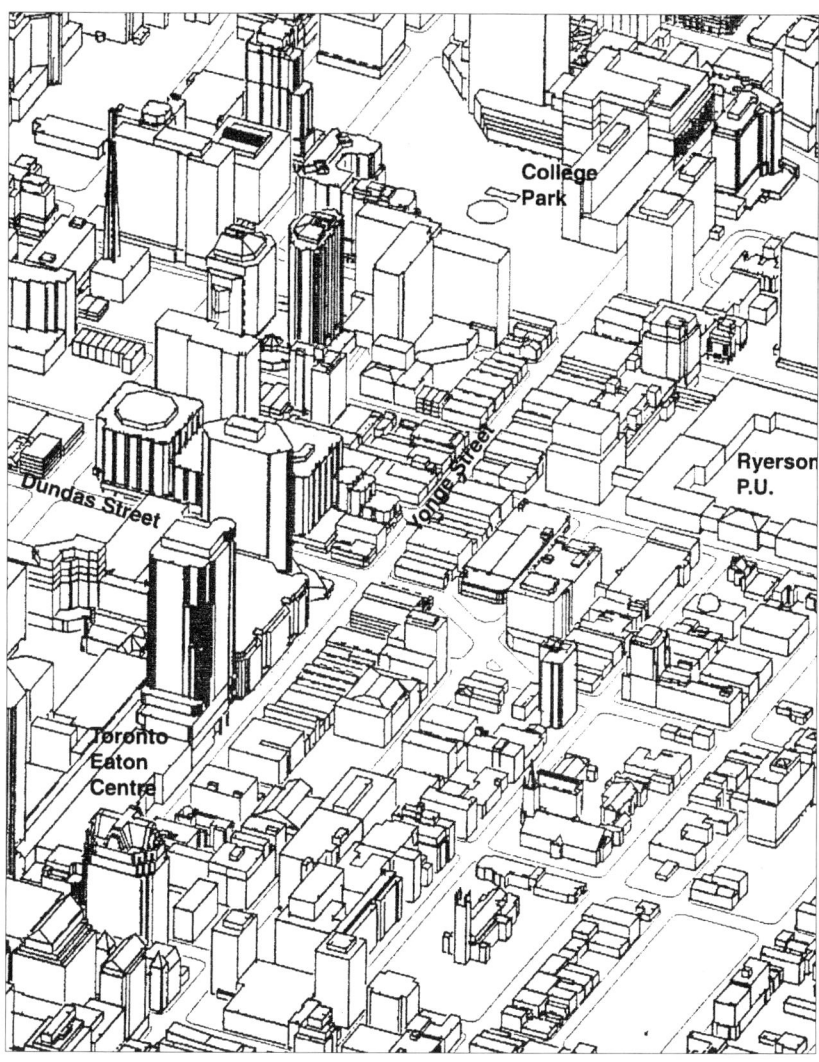

3.4 Yonge Street's built-form context, 1996. | Adapted from Toronto (1996f).

ones. That idea was captured by the following proposals put forward in the report: increase coverage from 2.0 to 4.0 times the lot area as of right for retail and entertainment uses (no increase from 1.5 for residential uses); designate the area a reinvestment area; relax parking requirements associated with new development; improve streetscape (sidewalks, lighting, and trees); protect heritage buildings; improve facades; review signage policy; institute permissions for sidewalk vendors, portrait artists, and musicians; and so on. The city planners did not see themselves as planning a new direction for

Yonge Street. They expressed their view of the constrained reconceptualization by saying, "To try to 'plan' a new direction for Yonge Street would seem antithetical to its very nature as Yonge Street will continue to gradually change on its own as it has over the past decades" (Toronto 1996e, 19). Rather, it saw the task as facilitating change, in part, by being "responsive to the market by deregulating planning controls" (ibid.). The report writer advised the council that there was still concern about social issues: "The community and the City have agreed to not separate [these issues] from the physical planning initiatives. A Community Services Strategic Plan is under preparation for the north portion of [the ward] which will in part place an emphasis on identifying the particular needs of the various service agencies which work on Yonge Street and the potential solutions available" (ibid., 25).

With one substantial study (the urban design study), one very light study (the "street survey"), and a tremendous amount of planning experience and direct knowledge of the area and the broader city context, the planning department produced a way forward for downtown Yonge. It is perhaps surprising that little hard information – for example, the range of people who used this part of downtown or the state of investment in the area – came into play. Given the emphasis on people's use of the area, on shopping and entertainment, and on the specificity of this area in the context of Toronto as a whole, it is notable that those topics were apparently not the subject of even modest surveys or inquiries. Knowledge about the state of the retail sector in the study area was expressed solely in generalities, and there were no details about the people who actually used the retail and entertainment venues in the area or about the people who used the street.

On the other hand, many isolated facts, or presumed facts, were bandied about, and their effect was to magnify the scope, validity, and persuasive force of the small amount of hard information that was presented. Lists of information used in the course of shaping the March 1996 plan are found in Appendix 4. These fact-like statements are taken from reports to city council, reports for the Yonge Street Business and Residents Association, and correspondence between that association and the city. I culled all statements that were directed toward building up the rationale for the recommendations for fixing the area. The statements are often generalizations and platitudes. I present them in their best light. That is, if any verification for an observation could be found, regardless of whether it was precise or general, it is attached to the statement. Most statements are uncorroborated. I have separated the statements of what was said to need fixing into two main categories – people's use of the area and economic activity. The reason the two categories of information are listed at all is to illustrate the tenuous nature of the data underpinning the recommendations.

Uncorroborated claims from a series of reports and correspondence coalesced to form the rhetoric of persuasion. These claims led to a modestly substantiated justification for a proposed action. Perhaps, for this scale of regeneration, there were enough verifiable claims, citizen involvement, and applied expert reasoning to justify the proposed incremental program.

Why was this program approved by city council? Some potential explanations follow. First, the knowledge and experience of the most senior planners seem to have translated into a high level of trust in their judgment from the majority of city councillors, and this trust offset the relative lack of hard information about how the goal of encouraging renewal would be achieved. Second, city council did not demand hard evidence to support the initiative. Recall that no studies were done on area users and the competing entertainment areas that were emerging to the southwest of Yonge-Dundas. Third, councillors did not wish to inquire deeply into the matter of whether they were authorizing changes to the physical environment for the purpose of changing the type of people in it. This raw form of environmental determinism had been widely denounced in Canada and the United States at least since the days of urban renewal struggles in the 1960s, including those in Toronto. Environmental determinism is the view that changes to physical form will result in changes to the behaviour of individuals. Perhaps a fourth explanation is that councillors were unsure about whether this was a modest, incremental program of only localized consequence or the first volley in a much larger game. This view was promoted by the ward councillor in city committees, where he said that the planning department's agenda was not nearly powerful enough to effect the total image change the street needed (see Toronto 1996b, 88-90).

A system based on "you keep out of my ward and I'll keep out of yours" operated in Toronto's local government. In such a system, the ward councillor is very powerful in his or her own ward, where he or she pays close attention to initiatives and shepherds development changes. Other councillors are expected to keep their noses out of that ward's business unless extraordinary circumstances warrant otherwise. The fact that Yonge-Dundas was the downtown core did not alter the expectation that other councillors keep their hands off the ward's business. Only on a few matters in which much larger city interests were concerned were other councillors drawn into the ward's issues. Finally, the particular councillor serving this ward was known as personally very active in his jurisdiction and ready to resist challenges to his decisions about what was right or wrong for his ward.

Central and Not-So-Central Players

Up to March 1996, the planning department was the central player. The evidence suggests that the Yonge Street Business and Residents Association and the ward councillor then eclipsed the planning department. As we move further into the case, there is significant change in the way planning in the reinvestment area proceeded, which lends credence to the idea that entrepreneurial planning arrived in Toronto with this project. In this sense, Yonge-Dundas is a pivotal project because it started out with a managerial, comprehensive style of planning and converted to an entrepreneurial project style of planning over the course of two years.

The Yonge Street Business and Residents Association

The Yonge Street Business and Residents Association (YSBRA, pronounced "wise-bra") was started in March 1995. Thirteen founding members chipped in $5,000 each to start the ball rolling. Founding members included not only Eaton's but also some of the companies intimately connected to it: the development company, Cadillac-Fairview, which owned a major share of the Eaton Centre; TD Bank, which was also a part-owner of the Centre; the Eaton Centre, the corporation that managed the Centre; and Cineplex Odeon, which had an eighteen-cinema enterprise at the north end of the Centre at Dundas. There were no small businesses or residents on the list of founding members (Joint Board 1998b, Exhibit 216). Some sources suggested that two small-business owners, Arron Barberian and Robert Sniderman, not Eaton's (as others claim), actually started the movement in the area. Apparently, there were two sets of interests that worked simultaneously: the well-financed large businesses organized in YSBRA and the two small businesses. The small businesses resented the Eaton Centre for its effect on the street. Nonetheless, they came together under the banner of the big business group, having been persuaded to do so by the ward councillor. By November 1995 YSBRA's executive committee listed on its roster members from smaller businesses, notably, Mr. Sniderman's Senator Restaurant on Victoria, Mr. Barberian's Steak House on Elm, and the Pantages Theatre on Yonge. All of the small businesses had substantial histories in their existing locations. A year later new YSBRA members were asked to pay only $500 to join, and YSBRA was trying to raise $200,000 for its Yonge Street improvement work.

There are few signs that the owners or tenants of properties that catered to poorer people on the street were active in YSBRA in its first three years of operation, and there are no signs of participation among those who owned properties that would eventually be expropriated. For example, Vahe Kerim, whose property was expropriated, partly owned 289 Yonge, managed the building, and ran the Jewellery Exchange on the ground floor. He was invited to be a founding member of YSBRA but declined, and in the spring of 1996 his views about the Yonge Street area and its future were sought out by members of the Yonge Street Regeneration Program Steering Committee (Joint

Board 1998g, 7). Another example of one whose property was expropriated and who did not participate in YSBRA was the owner of 323/325 Yonge. His tenant was KFC (formerly Kentucky Fried Chicken, the fast-food chain), and he spoke as a witness at the OMB hearing. He said he was not a member of YSBRA, had never been approached by YSBRA, and had not known YSBRA existed until he attended the hearing. He also owned a property, no. 322, across Yonge Street (ibid., 1).

In contrast to the image of YSBRA's membership conveyed above, a list of members prepared for the OMB hearing shows that, at least in 1998, the general membership ranged widely. This list was appended to the witness statement of Mr. Barberian and was dated 14 January 1998. However, the names on it do not match another list of financial contributors that Barberian appended. With the exception of Barberian himself and Mr. Sniderman, the ten executive members listed in a third appendix are all representatives of major corporations with real estate interests in the area (Joint Board 1998b, Exhibit 34, 223-30).

YSBRA was incorporated as a nonprofit organization in July 1995 (Joint Board 1998b, Exhibit 216). By November 1995 the association had taken the mayor and ward councillor on an evening walk around their properties; met with the police to encourage "a more visible police presence"; met with the editorial board of the city newspaper with the highest circulation, the *Toronto Star*, "with the aim of securing a more positive coverage of events on the street"; and had run a competition to get a new trash can designed. YSBRA described itself as working "as a partner [with the city] rather than as a protagonist in addressing key issues: safety for tourists, employees, residents and shoppers; clean and litter free streets; an attractive streetscape" (Joint Board 1998b, Exhibit 216). YSBRA's self-declared focus on safety, cleanliness, and aesthetics is standard for street-based retailing associations. On 12 December 1995, YSBRA asked a consultant to prepare a report on how to improve Yonge Street. The hiring of this particular consultant was said to have come out of a meeting YSBRA had with former Toronto mayor David Crombie (Joint Board 1998k, 19). YSBRA received the report, titled "Downtown Yonge: A program to promote the regeneration of Toronto's main street," on 24 January 1996. The contents covered an area from just south of Queen Street to just north of College/Carlton Street and presented a work program and budget for 1996. The goal of the program was "to substantially increase the proportion and range of the residents of Greater Toronto, and visitors, who use Downtown Yonge Street" (Soskolne 1996, 1). The program described was premised on a close collaboration between the City of Toronto and YSBRA (ibid.). For each quarter, objectives and tasks were laid out for "campaigns" on street appearance, promotion, marketing, and redevelopment. The report represented a qualitative change in tone, from planning to marketing, and it considerably ratcheted up intentions, from fixing existing spaces to redeveloping them. The consultant laid out the principal elements of the recommended program (he did not use the word "plan"), including "aggressive implementation of measures which will improve the appearance, safety, and cleanliness of the buildings and public space on the Street; a concerted promotion campaign aimed at attracting more customers to the Street; a carefully targeted marketing campaign aimed at increasing the number of quality retail and entertainment facilities on the Street; and a strategically focused re-development program aimed at improving the quality of possible retail premises and environments on the Street" (ibid.).

In the first quarter, the tasks included were "to initiate analysis of use and market potential of the Street, and initiate preparation of Street Promotion program [that is] public relations and media campaign; street-related programs and events; storefront exhibition space" (Soskolne 1996, 3). The redevelopment program had a third-quarter task to "begin land-assembly activities if appropriate" and "issue, if required, requests-for-proposals," while a fourth quarter task was to "co-ordinate implementation of Public-sector elements of projects" (ibid., 5). In YSBRA's hands the project of revitalizing Yonge Street was driven by public relations and promotion and marketing activities; if success in these activities demanded some expropriations and redevelopment, then so be it. A dominant attitude associated with this market-driven approach was that one needed to get a number of major international retailers to locate on Yonge Street. Some US companies in that category were phoned and invited to come up and take a walk on the street. YSBRA promoted a very aggressive commercial urban redevelopment model that had yet to be seen in Toronto.

It is not far-fetched to suggest that YSBRA, and possibly other people as of December 1995, envisaged redevelopment in a manner that went well beyond what had so far been described in the city's reports. That image entailed expropriations and the city building something. The possibility that properties could be redeveloped was noted in reports as early as July 1995, but the intention to do so was not expressed. Comments about opening up the potential for "larger format category retail and entertainment uses" had been made (Toronto 1996e, 9), and it was suggested that "certain prominent corners or sites may be appropriate for land assembly and comprehensive redevelopment" (ibid., 16). The phrasing is a matter of interest because, at various times, including at the OMB hearing in 1998, interested parties inferred or declared that the idea of expropriation and redevelopment was entirely the work of the public-private partnership between YSBRA and the city. However, as was noted earlier, the potential for land assembly was already there once the community improvement plan was passed. Still, it is my understanding, based on interviews and documents, that assembly may have been envisaged for the square but was not articulated, and that prior to the involvement of YSBRA there had been no intention whatsoever to create the major development, called Metropolis, that would be designated for the northeast corner of Yonge and Dundas. In the end, the extent, form, and quality of the expropriation and redevelopment were products of the YSBRA–City of Toronto collaboration and its marketing ambitions, not of a wider planning process.

The timing of the consulting report to YSBRA lends further evidence to the argument that the redevelopment scheme that was eventually adopted was based on one simple street survey and exactly one substantial, but informal, in-house design study that advocated incremental change.

Two weeks after YSBRA discussed their consultant's report at a meeting, the association asked to enter into a public-private partnership with the City of Toronto to promote its aims. Its request was formally approved by city council in early March 1996. I use the term "public-private partnership" (PPP) because this is the accepted term. This is also the term the ward councillor used when he first introduced the idea in writing to the Economic Development Committee; it expresses the way that the parties liked to think about their work on this project. City documents tended to call the partnership a "collaboration," and, in execution, the latter term is more appropriate. (Appendix 1 discusses public-private partnerships as part of the planning framework.)

To all appearances, the approval was a smooth, untroubled event. It was handled as follows. The commissioner of planning and development was obliged to give his opinion on the union. It was his responsibility to send his views in writing to the ward councillor. His letter managed to be both approving – saying the initiative met "planning rationale" – and circumspect. In fact, despite several readings of this letter, I am unable to deduce with any certainty the commissioner's position on the collaboration. His letter appears to have been carefully worded. On the other hand, he had been quoted in the press eighteen months earlier as having said that he hoped there would be a private-sector-driven solution to Yonge Street (Hurst 1994). The commissioner, Robert Millward, reviewed the initiatives taken in the Yonge Street area and wrote to Councillor Kyle Rae on 7 February 1996 that YSBRA's proposal was "a proactive initiative which would complement work already underway"; in his view, "the Association is acting in the public interest in pursuing this collaboration with the City for the revitalization of Yonge Street" (Toronto 1996b). A second letter was sent by the chair of YSBRA (who at the time was also the vice president and general manager of the Eaton Centre) to the mayor on 8 February 1996. It explained why the arrangement was a very good idea (ibid.). The style of language used in the letter and verb tense slippages suggest that the letter was written largely by the consultant for YSBRA's chair to adapt and sign.

Once the councillor, mayor, planning commissioner, and YSBRA chair were formally on board, the process to approve the PPP went into motion. At about this point, politics and marketing began to have the upper hand over the development process and forced planning to the margins. The ward councillor was the driving force, according to interviewees, and this view is supported by print media accounts, council minutes, the OMB's written decision, and other documents. The ward councillor was amply supported by council, including the mayor.

The Ward Councillor

There is no doubt that the ward councillor, Kyle Rae, was a strongly committed supporter of initiatives that would give Yonge Street a boost. The vice-president of YSBRA called him the organization's cheerleader (Joint Board 1998k, 18). For a politician, such an image can be a double-edged sword. If he was cheerleading for a group like YSBRA, which had clearly defined financial interests, he could not champion opposing interests. Nor would he be well placed to negotiate contesting points of view. But if the ward councillor was on one's team, he was a powerful ally.

Kyle Rae had launched his political career by supporting, with spectacular success, gay-community issues. His leadership in and dedication to that cause led to a relatively positive atmosphere for gays and lesbians in Toronto. He became a politician to be reckoned with, and his often left-leaning positions on issues were challenged gingerly by right-leaning politicians who sought to stay clear of accusations of gay bashing. He brought a lot of energy to his job. Thus, for a range of reasons, Rae had a strong grip on his ward (Ward 6 of the old City of Toronto, Ward 27 in the amalgamated city). By the time YSBRA formed and the PPP was launched, he was in his second three-year term of office, having been elected in 1991 after several years spent in community activism.

Rae frequently characterized city problems in terms of the behaviour of individuals: X would not do Y; therefore, policy Z is failing. In this case, policy Z was fixing Yonge Street. The people whom he identified as X and what they were failing to do, Y, changed again and again. For example, according to press reports in 1994, the ward councillor was highly critical of the Eaton Centre and its owners (X), even going so far as to say that if Yonge Street had deteriorated, the Eaton Centre was to blame (Hurst 1994). According to Councillor Rae, the Centre was built in such a way that it was sucking life off Yonge

Street, and Eaton's was not recognizing this (Y). As the months rolled by, the ward councillor stopped criticizing Eaton's and reportedly turned his attention to new Xs and Ys: small-business owners who were not maintaining their property (Wong 1997; Young 1999); Cineplex Odeon, which had not updated its movie facilities (Moloney 1997); the Yonge Street Mission's young adults centre, which was not keeping its "kids" indoors (Joint Board 1998b, Exhibit 75, probably 3 or 4 June 1997); elected officials who were not taking action against squeegee kids (ibid.; Toronto 1997g); Toronto taxpayers who lacked pride in their city because they did not support the Yonge-Dundas project (Moloney 1998a); the Toronto Transit Commission, which was engaging in "extortion" when it balked at some costs for a new subway access associated with building Dundas Square (Kuitenbrouwer 2001b); the private sector, which was slow to act in the Yonge-Dundas area (ibid.; Tompkins 2003); municipal staff who interfered with the private interests that ran Dundas Square (Hume 2002); and people who did not like Dundas Square because it did not have a couch and TV in it (Wanagas 2003). Despite Councillor Rae's penchant for assigning blame to so many, he continues to be re-elected with a very strong plurality.

For Councillor Rae, the solution was new entertainment-based, family-oriented development (Immen 1999). That was his ideal. Clearly, it did not match the planners' proposal, which was based on the decision not to try to redesign the street but rather to activate the market to do some moderate redevelopment. By contrast, the ward councillor believed that much more intervention was needed to revive retail activity and that planning's modest proposals would not get Toronto there. Rae had in his mind's eye an urban entertainment centre he had seen in Los Angeles – that is, Universal Studio's CityWalk. It had a major bookstore, about eight theme restaurants, and a cinema megaplex. He thought it was amazing retail space, and he wanted that for downtown Toronto – specifically for his stretch of Yonge Street. This put him well outside the bounds of where the planning department wanted to go. Inevitably, one or the other had to yield.

Residents' Associations and Local Institutions

In 1993 residents living on the east side of Yonge in the Dundas area incorporated their then informal association. The Toronto East Downtown Residents Association (TEDRA) was the last resident association to form in the eastern core of the city. It saw itself as representing a very troubled area, one that had long been trying informally to deal with a range of issues related to drugs, prostitution, and poverty. According to its founders, the event that finally made them decide to organize occurred in December 1991, when the police of 51 Division, who handled an area east of Jarvis Street, pushed drug dealers across the street into their area west of Jarvis and thus into a different policing precinct called 52 Division: "Overnight the plaza at the southwest corner of Jarvis and Dundas became a drive-in crack drugstore" (Joint Board 1998b, Exhibit 34, Tab 1A, 13-14).

The members of the association had other issues on their plate as well: three banks, two federal buildings, and a huge warehouse with 3,500 workers closed down, taking their employees and their business out of the area. There were many new developments seeking approval that required residents to deal with the planning department and appeals at the OMB (Joint Board 1998b, Exhibit 34, Tab 1A, 13-14). Merchants along Dundas saw themselves as being cut off from the Yonge Street clientele because, looking east from Yonge, the street jogged south and seemed to disappear. (Recall the seventy-metre disconnect when Dundas Street was formed in the 1920s.) Also, area residents felt that because too many social service agencies and subsidized dwellings had been established in their area, it was now hard to attract more self-sufficient residents. The balance was off.

At the beginning of the Yonge-Dundas planning work in 1994, when the city was first sorting out what needed to be attended to, TEDRA was fully involved in meetings, committees, and discussions. It wanted the city to see the Yonge Street problem as one that not only ran on a north-south axis but also involved knitting east to west across Yonge. Conceptualizing the issue as a solely north-south matter left TEDRA out of the discussion. However, to see it as a problem that cut off the area east of Yonge from that street's energy framed the problem – and, thus, potential solutions – in a different way. TEDRA's relationship to Yonge was complicated. On the one hand, members of the association wanted Yonge's homeless people and drug users off that street so it could draw itself closer to Yonge's vibrancy; on the other, they suspected that if Yonge Street were "cleaned up," those who were "cleaned out" would shift east to their area (Dennison 2003). This was a dilemma and only the beginning of TEDRA's woes.

At the suggestion of one of the metropolitan-level councillors, TEDRA secured over $45,000 in provincial funding that had been made available for community economic-development initiatives. Those 1995 funds were later bolstered by a further $55,000 from another source. The project members' terms of reference included the following: to develop a geographic information system (GIS) of land uses and demography; to conduct a household market survey to learn about residents' shopping patterns, education, leisure activities, travel patterns, and health; and to recommend community economic development opportunities. A great deal of energy went into producing a report of more than a hundred pages, which came out in October 1996 and described the state of the neighbourhood. It included an astounding eighty-one recommendations for action. Among the recommendations was one to take down buildings on Yonge Street south of Dundas to build a square, but it is questionable whether that recommendation could have emerged from the survey data. The report and its recommendations had little impact, and the GIS was not developed.

Around this time a member of TEDRA's board of directors was providing input to YSBRA's initiative on Yonge and sitting on YSBRA's board of directors (Joint Board 1998b, Exhibit 34, Tab 10, 218 and Exhibit 34, Tab 12, 231-34). However, as so often happens, at the same time that TEDRA was formally drawn into YSBRA's fold (as of 1996), its interests received less, not more, attention. Indeed, its voice became muted and then silent once the public-private partnership between YSBRA and the city was formed. The social problems that TEDRA wanted to tackle became invisible to the project's central proponents. Thereafter, "east-west" had meaning only insofar as making the square, and its immediate vicinity, was concerned. Eventually, TEDRA was accused of giving in to moneyed interests, and it became a target of one of the most radical activist organizations in the city. The Ontario Coalition Against Poverty helped organize a march, which made "stops at the homes of the leaders of the Toronto East Downtown Residents Association and Seaton Ontario Berkeley Residents Association, accusing them of colluding in a 'big-business plan' to 'cleanse' the neighbourhood in preparation for major Yonge-Dundas redevelopment" (Kastner 1997).

Another geographically defined association in the area was the McGill-Granby Village Residents' Association, which represents a tiny area just north of Dundas (from Gerrard) and east of Yonge. It represents ninety or so homeowners and some apartment residents, but not commercial or retail interests. Its representatives, like TEDRA's, worked with the city and YSBRA during the planning of the Yonge-Dundas changes.

The young adults centre, called Evergreen and run by the Yonge Street Mission (YSM), on Yonge just south of Gerrard was peripheral to the project in the sense of active engagement, but it was central in the sense that it was where youth congregated. An ongoing chicken-and-egg discussion revolves around whether the YSM acts as a magnet for youth or simply serves those who happen to be there already. The YSM's view is that it serves those who are there. In the past, when older people who were hard hit by war or the Depression were on the street, the YSM served adults. Today, the people on the street are young adults, so the mission serves them. In fact, Evergreen sends anyone over the age of twenty-five to other resource centres because its managers have found that younger people can be preyed upon by older people and that youths are more likely to find alternatives to street life if they are kept separate from adults. The youths who congregate in the area are male and female, poor, and ethno-racially mixed. A substantial proportion of the youth population is black. A pastoral worker at Evergreen warned the project's proponents of the tendency to identify youth with crime and thus stereotype and scapegoat youth, especially those who are black.

About three blocks from Evergreen, at Victoria and Dundas, there was a Salvation Army hostel for homeless men. This became another issue for the cleanup project. However, because the Salvation Army's operations at that location were funded largely by the city, control over whether it continued was very much in the hands of the city – more specifically, the ward councillor.

Approvals at City Council, March 1996

At the 4 March 1996 council meeting, three items that concerned the Yonge Street initiative were approved:

1 the Downtown Yonge Street Community Improvement Project Plan [bylaw 1996-0135] that had previously gone through consultation and committee processes
2 the designation of a "reinvestment area" (according to the new three lenses approach) for part of the area from Gerrard south to Queen
3 "Downtown Yonge: A program to promote the regeneration of Toronto's Main Street," the report of YSBRA by its private planning consultant, which had had no community consultation.

The proposed changes included the amendment of section 18 of the official plan to accommodate the reinvestment designation at this location. Existing density provisions were to be set aside and replaced by general-planning objectives and built-form principles with which successful development proposals would have to be consistent. The zoning bylaw increased the coverage potential from 2.0 times to 4.0 north of Dundas Square Street to Gerrard, and it increased the height limit from eighteen to twenty metres, with no change to the five-hour angular plane requirement for sun. Retail, service, and entertainment uses on the east side of Yonge were exempted from having to provide parking.

The YSBRA consultant's report and proposal were positively mentioned and described in the commissioner of planning's report: "I am of the view that the initiative is a valuable implementation vehicle which will encourage regeneration in a tangible and action-oriented manner" (Toronto 1996f, 26).

The commissioner asked that his report be circulated to all interested parties, specifically YSBRA, the McGill-Granby Residents' Association, TEDRA, and

Ryerson University. The reinvestment area designation still had to go to a public meeting of the Planning Advisory Committee scheduled for 17 April 1996. The commissioner was slated to make final recommendations to the Land Use Committee on 23 May 1996.

Although the city's reports continued to go through a full consultative vetting process, YSBRA's report did not. In February 1996 it went to the city's Economic Development Standing Committee, then to the Budget Review Group, then to the Executive Committee, and it was approved without discussion at city council on 4 March. That is, all the reviews were effectively internal to the city. Although meetings of the Economic Development Committee were open to the public, there had been no public announcement that the YSBRA report would be considered at its February meeting and that the report would be the basis for major redevelopment, which would operate in the coming year through a new PPP funded by the city to the tune of $250,000, not to mention staff time the city would provide. Likewise, the city council meeting was open to the public, but because no councillor had objections to the report (it was treated as "ward business" and not as a matter in which other councillors should involve themselves), the report was not discussed: it was adopted along with several other items in a single motion and vote.

From the point of view of a reasonably well-informed Toronto resident, it appeared that the city was still operating from a plan of incremental change. Only those deeply engaged in the project would have been able to see that what had gone through open, public consultation and what was coming into being were two very different things. Print media did not mention the Yonge-Dundas issue during this period.

Kyle Rae energetically realigned initiatives regarding the street. In his report (probably dated 8 February 1996), the councillor said he had had three meetings with YSBRA and other unnamed members of the public, during which they had "jointly identified what [was] wrong with the street" (Toronto 1996b, 88). The wording strongly suggests that the city's planning department was not centrally involved, if it was involved at all, in these discussions. The meetings were chaired by former mayor David Crombie at the request of the ward councillor. Rae went on to say: "I believe that a strong consensus has developed that the short term agenda for revitalization, which the City is aggressively moving forward with, needs to be buttressed by marketing, promotion, re-use and redevelopment. Long lasting revitalization of Yonge Street needs an expanded private sector involvement. It will not be achieved by the improvements the City can make on its own" (ibid.).

The period from December 1995 to February 1996 was nothing short of hectic regarding the Yonge-Dundas area:

- The consultant was asked on 12 December 1995 to prepare his proposal.
- He reported on 24 January 1996.
- Three meetings were held between YSBRA and the ward councillor.
- A letter from the planning commissioner to the ward councillor was sent, which said that the initiative would complement the city's efforts.
- Another letter, sent on 8 February from YSBRA's chair to the mayor, assured the city that private interests on the street were behind these new mid- and long-term initiatives (these were the letters discussed above).
- The ward councillor prepared the report of 8 February for the Economic Development Committee.

The rationale for action in the Yonge-Dundas area still rested on the two reports mentioned at the start of this chapter, and there is no evidence that further investigation of conditions or the role of this area vis-à-vis other parts of the downtown core had been done. These two reports were arguably sufficient for a modest incremental program in a case in which there had been considerable consultation, but it is hard to justify them as adequate when the costs and risks to the public escalated rapidly and when the style of management became less accountable to the public. The downstream effect was that when proponents were challenged about the logic of the project, they increasingly used weak arguments to try to explain it. Chapter 5 sets out how planners, lawyers, and various experts built post hoc cases for the major expropriation and redevelopment scheme that came to dwarf the incrementalist, regeneration-style original plan.

Conclusion

The Yonge-Dundas project began as an incremental, highly contextualized form of revitalization. Its underlying strategy, which has been uncovered during research, included avoiding gentrification, retaining the grittiness associated with the area, working with local interests, modifying the existing planning regulations, and dealing with social issues by trying to draw in people and organizations that had the tools to deal with those matters. The project's stated objective was to increase the general public's use of Toronto's downtown Yonge Street for shopping and entertainment. Its approach was comprehensive in the sense that it tried to pay attention to various interests and to balance them as it implemented change. The project also borrowed from elsewhere. Thanks to a visit to New York by the planning commissioner (who was a former planner in New York City's Department of Planning) and Toronto's chief planner, the plan was inspired by two specific features of the 42nd Street–Times Square redevelopment. One feature was finding new uses for old buildings, not by changing the built form of the street but rather by working with it, such as in the case of the urban-box form. The other feature was the sign bylaw, which set minimum, not maximum, requirements for size and wattage to encourage a bright lights, high-energy, slightly garish, ungentrified look. The tools used to implement the strategy included the reinvestment lens; the community improvement project, with its permissions for making grants and loans to businesses; discussions with affected businesses, residents, and street users; the official plan, with its zoning bylaw; and the tremendous planning experience, acumen, and knowledge of planners. This was what planners contributed to urban development.

This menu did not suit the ward councillor or, it appears, the mayor. Their vision was much closer to and eventually merged with a market-driven plan to sell Yonge Street to contemporary international retail and entertainment uses that could be brought in as tenants. In the redevelopment phase, planning will follow politics; comprehensive, managerial planning will evolve toward an entrepreneurial, market-based activity; and justification for proposed actions will change to rationalization and reliance on the adversarial argumentation skills of a top expropriation lawyer to win the day for the project.

The description of planning regeneration offered in this chapter illustrates how a plausible and ethically justifiable solution to the Yonge-Dundas problem was constructed. In my view, the solution was plausible and ethical because it would have led to adequate redevelopment on the street, retained the area's character and raised it a notch or two up the scale, and been fair to land owners. It would not have merely displaced problems. The planners did not have the tools to deal with the social problems directly but had enough skills to bring the various agencies together to focus on this sociogeographic space to get its microeconomy back on track, and planning contributed some regulatory modifications. That is, the planners practised a theory of planning that called for bringing professional tools to bear on a problem to create a plausible, ethical solution within specific city conditions.

CHAPTER FOUR
Redeveloping

Although there was no in-depth study of Yonge Street's problems, the small-scale initiatives the city worked on in 1994 and 1995 were unlikely to make matters worse. In fact, by early 1996 they seemed to be improving matters. The facade program was a huge success. Several owners had already renovated their facades or announced plans to do so. An informal survey of businesses in the area showed that many were pleased with improvements. In addition, the economy was picking up again after a brutal five-year recession.

But in March 1996 city council approved in principle a much more aggressive plan, which had been put forward by the Yonge Street Business and Residents Association (YSBRA). Under that scheme Yonge Street would be re-imaged, to use the terminology of the moment; it would be converted into an object to be marketed and sold to the new breed of retailers who understood shoppertainment. Toronto would "city-build" by using a US model to gain downtown pizzazz.

This chapter covers the period from March 1996 to summer 1997. During the remainder of 1996, the Yonge-Dundas project ran down two parallel tracks: the regeneration project went through the necessary public approval processes while the redevelopment project moved from the early conceptual phase to preliminary feasibility studies, which were conducted in secret over six months. Resources were organized by the city and YSBRA to redirect the outcome in the Yonge-Dundas area. By the end of 1996, a new proposal emerged that identified four land parcels that had been designated for redevelopment. Several properties would have to be expropriated to assemble two of the four parcels. This chapter explores how the proponents addressed the feasibility of the project and the rationale behind this particular type of redevelopment.

In 1997 the redevelopment project was fully defined and approved by the city. Was this planning, and, if so, in what sense? What did planners contribute in this phase? Are there theories of the work planners do that account for the actions described here?

A Public-Private Partnership as Steering Committee for the Project
On 4 March 1996, Toronto City Council approved several initiatives, including YSBRA's Downtown Yonge project, and a public-private partnership (PPP) between the city and YSBRA.

A week later some members of YSBRA and delegates from the city met to structure the new PPP. The terms "steering committee," "public-private partnership," and "collaboration" were applied interchangeably to the PPP. It is important to note two things. First, a steering committee in Toronto may advise the city on a specific topic, but it has no mandate to hire, make contracts or policy decisions, or spend funds. In this case, the PPP did all of those things. If the PPP was a steering committee, it was not, contrary to practice, registered on the city clerk's list of steering committees for 1996. Second, the collaboration between the city and YSBRA was passed by city council in March 1996 on the assumption that staff would give it formal structure and bring it back to council for approval. The agreement between the city and YSBRA would "serve as the 'rule book' for the partnership arrangement" (Toronto 1996b, 90). It was to have been presented to city council by the end of April 1996, but was not. The only formal trapping was a grant agreement that authorized funds to flow from the city to YSBRA and required quarterly reporting. The money flowed; the regular reporting did not. The first and possibly only quarterly report came up at city council's 16 September 1996 meeting, some six months after the PPP had been approved. Yet, in a report from the commissioner of urban development services to city council a year after the collaboration was initiated, it was called "a successful example of a public-private collaboration on an important initiative aimed at achieving the revitalization of the City's main street" (Toronto 1997e, 62).

Attendees who represented the city at the first meeting of the PPP steering committee were the ward councillor, four city employees from the legal and finance departments, and two city employees from the planning department. From the private sector, there were five business members, a private consultant, Ron Soskolne, who was identified as the program director, and a secretary employed by YSBRA. It is not clear how many of these people formally constituted the steering committee and, in particular, whether the program director was a member. The quorum was set at four members, with a minimum of two representatives from YSBRA and two from the city (Joint Board 1998b, Exhibit 75, minutes of 11 March 1996, 1).

The steering committee's job was to coordinate redevelopment. It was a working group of city officials and YSBRA members that was supposed to provide a degree of oversight. But since most of the work ended up being done on a confidential basis by a tiny subcommittee and a legion of experts, its oversight function lost all effect.

The program director's contract was with the private association YSBRA, not with the steering committee or the city. He and YSBRA held the right to select all consultants, although the city was to be consulted on an informal basis (Joint Board 1998b, Exhibit 75, minutes of 11 March 1996, 2). The program director had use of an in-trust account and was to prepare a monthly statement of expenses for perusal by the representative of the Department of Finance (ibid.). The estimated cost to implement YSBRA's first year of work was $400,000, of which at least $250,000 was provided by the city. At least $100,000 was raised by YSBRA. The program director was paid out of city funds. The public side of the collaboration was to provide office space and the equivalent of 2.5 full-time equivalent positions, mainly from the planning department but also from the City Solicitor's Office and the Department of Finance. YSBRA would provide secretarial services and cost estimating services (presumably to estimate redevelopment options because it had several real estate specialists among its executive members). In addition, it was the private side's task to conceptualize and drive the project, while the city's task was to smooth the project's political passage.

The program director was hired expressly by YSBRA to develop a vision for the area. According to the testimony of one of the initial members of YSBRA, who was its vice-president and a member of the steering committee when the program director was hired in March 1996, the director was given free rein "to come up with a scheme to 'instill life and vitality to Yonge/Dundas as was done in Times Square'" (Joint Board 1998k, 19). Based on this testimony, the Times Square image was in the minds of steering committee members in March 1996. But as we saw previously, it was probably adopted earlier in January (if not December 1995), when the planning consultant was first contracted to develop a scheme.

From the point of view of YSBRA and the program director, fixing up the area really began when the program director formally came on the scene in January 1996. Until then, the city had been putting on band-aids – the facade improvement program, legislation to regulate street vending, initiatives to get the city to do better maintenance, and so on. But more substantial actions had also been taken, including upzoning to 4.0 times coverage and introducing the community improvement project (CIP). Ron Soskolne's consultations in the first months with owners and investors about what the problem was led him to conclude that radical surgery was needed. Three points about the program director's conclusion should be kept in mind: (1) he arrived at it not through structured studies but rather through individual consultations, (2) it is already implied in his January 1996 report (that is, before he began the consultations), which puts in doubt the source of his solution to the problem, and (3) it seems to have been entirely different from that of the city's own planning department. The steering committee apparently viewed the new plan that would emerge from its work as totally different from the regeneration plan. In effect, the city was paying the program director out of a separate pocket to divert its own staff's planning and to bring about a marketing-based model of entertainment development with only the most superficial inquiry into what the model's effect had been elsewhere or how, or if, it suited Toronto.

Meetings of the steering committee were held on 3 April and 1 May. By the third meeting, held on 24 June 1996, a new approach was needed. The program director reported that he had had "meetings with stakeholders, about 35 to date," and his observations from these were recorded in the minutes. Curiously, two versions of these minutes were filed at the Ontario Municipal Board (OMB). The following are the program director's comments as they were recorded in Versions A and B (Joint Board 1998b, Exhibit 75, minutes of 24 June 1996). It is interesting to note how people are described in the different versions.

Version A
Ron Soskolne reported results of his meetings with stakeholders, about 35 to date: (1) Overall there is a negative perception of Yonge Street because (a) tourists are the primary customers and (b) the Torontonians who currently hang out on the street are undesirable. (2) Generally there is very positive interest in the Regeneration Program. His conclusion is that very little more can be accomplished in attracting quality retailers until there is something to show in the way of concrete positive changes.

Version B
Ron Soskolne reported results of his meetings with stakeholders, about 35 to date: (1) Overall there is a uniform negative perception of Yonge Street, with tourists being the only reliable customers, with Torontonians a negative force. (2) Generally there is very positive interest in the Facade Program. His conclusion is that very little more can be accomplished in attracting quality retailers until there is something to show in the way of concrete positive changes.

First, it is not clear who "the stakeholders" were: they could have been members of YSBRA or its steering committee for the regeneration project, city staff, residents, or others. "About 35" tells us that the program director was electing not to be precise about how many stakeholders had been consulted and how many had reported these views. The information is useless – or worse than useless, because it is dubitable and malleable – for recommending or making planning decisions. Second, according to the program director's comments, tourists are good; Torontonians are bad. Can this be true? If so, in what sense? Serious generalized allegations are made. Third, the facade and regeneration programs are referred to as if they are interchangeable. Fourth, "concrete positive changes" were occurring – they had been reported already. The person, or persons, who wrote the minutes means something much more precise than "concrete positive changes" but has chosen to be obtuse.

These "stakeholder views" were used as if they were reliable enough to carry the weight of the following recommendations:

1 Continue the important street clean up program.
2 Redevelopment planning. As there are very few appropriate premises in the area, there needs to be full commitment by the City to an aggressive redevelopment plan.
3 The hiring of two specialists, a legal advisor on land acquisition – Ron recommends Stephen Waqué of Borden & Elliott [sic] – and a consultant to prepare a detailed economic analysis – Ron recommends KPMG based primarily on credibility.[1] (Joint Board 1998b, Exhibit 75, minutes of 24 June 1996, 2)

There was unanimous approval to proceed with the hiring.

These two consultants would later be referred to by council as "the expropriation team" for the expropriated owners. Two weeks before this hiring decision was put before the steering committee, city council approved YSBRA's decision to retain Stephen Waqué – that is, YSBRA, rather than the steering committee, was the client of record. The city also instructed its in-house solicitor to place Waqué on a continuing retainer with the city as the client if the current planning strategy, which was leading to expropriation and owner compensation, proceeded (Toronto 1996a, para. 4b). Given this earlier hiring by YSBRA and approval by the city, the steering committee was asked merely to rubberstamp the hiring of Waqué at its 24 June meeting. The vote at the meeting was hollow and belied the idea of democratic oversight. The hiring process was undertaken by a privately constituted business association, not by the steering committee. With this gesture, the city and the private interests it collaborated with brought into their tent a highly successful expropriation lawyer who would then be seamlessly passed on to the city's expense account if the city decided to take and redevelop private properties. According to the available public records, Waqué was on the YSBRA account where private interests could work with him while expropriation was being explored, but he would be on the city's retainer once expropriation proceeded.

A close reading of either version of these minutes tells us that YSBRA was committed to aggressive redevelopment, and the construction of the wording suggests that because there were "few appropriate premises in the area" an aggressive type of urban renewal, with expropriation and bulldozing, was what YSBRA, with the help of its program director, envisaged. It also tells us that we cannot be sure that the city had made a clear commitment to aggressive redevelopment. The wording suggests the city was being challenged at this meeting by the program director to make a decision.[2]

If the city had not yet made up its mind to proceed down this new path, it did so around the time of this meeting. The meeting was attended by five representatives from the city (the ward councillor, the city solicitor, and one member each from the legal, finance, and planning departments), four representatives from private business, and the program director and the secretary. The planning department was represented by a person who was somewhat down the line of command in the department. This person had been designated the "program manager" at the initial meeting on 11 March. A little later he was named the program planner. When the planning department put two people on the project, they split the tasks. One wore the business hat and was named program manager; the other wore the planning hat and was called the program planner. This was an effort by the planning department to recognize that in becoming a project proponent, it needed to maintain some separation between the municipality's financial and business interests on the one hand, and the private interests of the YSBRA-led collaboration on the other. The line that separated the two was thin.

The ward councillor liked the new ideas that were brought by YSBRA's consultant precisely because they were not "planning" ideas but, rather, marketing ideas that he believed would generate the needed retail lift that planning alone could not achieve.

Was the redevelopment project going to proceed with or without the planning department's support because of the councillor's determination? While this question cannot be answered definitively, my understanding is that it would have proceeded because political momentum had driven much of the public planning influence to the margins. The planning department had to find its position in this set of real circumstances. It put aside any resistance it may have had and got behind the project. This was convenient for the YSBRA-city collaboration because the planning department had the tools needed to implement the project as it was envisaged – particularly the CIP. Unless the city set up an independent development agency of some kind, development had to occur within the legal authority allowed under a CIP, which was part of the provincial *Planning Act*. If the planners were not on board with the new scheme, then its proponents had to find a way to use the CIP without them. If they were on board, then the planners had to explain why regeneration, which they had supported as the solution, was no longer appropriate. One of their arguments was that redevelopment was an extension of regeneration. This post hoc rationalization would backfire if data and studies were looked at too closely. As Chapter 5 shows, however, the expropriation lawyer ensured that details and statistics were not central to the OMB hearing and, instead, played up the rhetoric of city building.

At the June 1996 meeting, the program director stated that extreme confidentiality was needed regarding the redevelopment program "and recommended that a narrow sub-group be formed to be responsible for the process" (Joint Board 1998b, Exhibit 75, minutes of 24 June 1996, 2). In a formal moved-and-seconded vote, the eleven people at the meeting elected a previously prepared list of four people to sit on this subgroup: the ward councillor, the program director, the program manager, and a representative from a local business. These four were to be formally sworn to secrecy, but, as it turned out, the city thought it was inappropriate for its staff to swear to secrecy, so only the two outside members were sworn. Attempts at secrecy were not entirely effective. If there was any oversight of this project, which was now run by senior staff, consultants, and one councillor, it fell to the city's Board of Management, which was made up of the four newly appointed "super" commissioners who replaced the previous, more numerous group of commissioners (see Appendix 2, Chronology, Spring 1996).

The person who moved the list of four to sit on the subcommittee that would work in secret on the redevelopment had been a member of YSBRA from the start, was a long-time property owner in the area, and was one of the true insiders. He would later bid for and win one of the parcels that became available because of the redevelopment project. His own property was not expropriated.

The steering committee served as a fig leaf. It gave the appearance of public oversight of a project that primarily used public funds, yet the project was driven overwhelmingly by private interests. The steering committee was not registered; it followed few if any agreed upon rules; and it worked mainly in secret. In effect, the city's existing plan was overridden, and the planning department's work was outsourced, not to develop a new plan but to get feasibility studies done for an idea that had been presented by the development consultant hired by YSBRA. The job of changing the area was given to an association of private interests that had clear and undisputed financial interests in the outcome of the redevelopment and no open accountability to public interests. Private interests were assumed to map perfectly onto public interests.

This is city development in action, with planning in tow. The main goal of this book is to identify and assess the contribution of planning to the overall development outcome. In this case, the planning framework tool, called the community improvement project, was key. And it was convenient, but not essential, for the planning department to wield it.

Regeneration-Related Activities

Approvals for New Planning Amendments
Meanwhile, the city carried on with its regeneration-related Yonge Street activities. Amendments to the Downtown Yonge Street plan were considered at a public meeting in April. City council had adopted these amendments in principle the month before at the meeting on 4 March. Prior to that meeting, the amendments had passed through the committee system (particularly the Land Use Committee) and had been circulated to relevant people and groups, including the two resident associations (McGill-Granby and Toronto East Downtown), YSBRA, and Ryerson University.

The amendments were then brought to a public meeting because under the *Planning Act* they could change the official plan if approved. The notice for the public meeting succinctly described the essence of the changes, as it was envisaged by the commissioner of planning and development and described in his reports to city council since the previous November. At the meeting the public heard a presentation and had the chance to ask questions and comment on the following proposals:

- increasing the nonresidential density permission from two to four times the lot area in the zoning bylaw for the general area between Gerrard Street and Dundas Square
- designating the area, generally between Gerrard and Queen streets, as a reinvestment area in the official plan and replacing density numbers with planning objectives and built-form principles
- increasing the height limit on Yonge Street, generally between Gerrard Street and Dundas Square, from eighteen to twenty metres
- removing the parking requirements for certain retail, service, and entertainment uses in the area between Gerrard and Queen streets.

The nature of what was discussed at the public meeting is noted in detail to show the type and scale of changes that were proposed through the open processes associated with regeneration.

At subsequent meetings in May and June, the report was finalized. However, consideration of the associated draft bylaws was put off because of the parallel initiative the PPP was working on.

The Facade Program and Other Renovations

The facade program was extremely successful according to all reports. Its success was immediate upon its announcement. That is, property owners were already stepping up to the plate once the new planning amendments went through council. All of this predated the announcement of the new square and other major redevelopments that would be made in December 1996.

In September 1996 the facade improvement progress report called the program "enormously successful" and provided data to back up the claim (Toronto 1996d, 38-39). Within the first few months, a city expenditure of just over $160,000 for ten grants had drawn out private investment of almost $1.4 million in work underway or already completed. Over and above this was the superb renovation of the Ryrie Building (finished in late 1996) and the announcement by the Eaton Centre of a facade improvement estimated at around $25 million. All this was kick-started by the regeneration plan, not the redevelopment program, but media reports later misrepresented the impetus for these improvements.

The commissioner of planning and development had expected that 15 percent of the ninety-three eligible owners would apply over the three-year life of the program. Instead, 15 percent applied within the first four months, and many more were in the pipe. The response was surely a strong indicator of pent-up demand for clarity about the street's direction and for more flexibility regarding property development. The new planning amendments, widely discussed and circulated in the course of being created, had stabilized the planning conditions for the area.

Actions of the Secret Subcommittee

Work moved into high gear as the steering committee's secret subcommittee prepared to present its redevelopment project to city council in December. Early in the summer of 1996, the ward councillor and the program director happened to be in the Los Angeles area, where, in the interest of figuring out how to redevelop Younge and Dundas, they met with Universal Studios. At about the same time, the program planner went on a professional development trip to New York, which had been organized by the planning department for about two dozen staff. The trip was not related specifically to the Yonge-Dundas redevelopment, but in the course of their time there the group visited Times Square and 42nd Street and met with Rebecca Robertson, president of the 42nd Street Development Project. On his return the program planner sent the chair of Toronto's Board of Management a memo, to which he attached a *Fortune Magazine* article (from 24 June 1996) on Disney and 42nd Street because, he wrote, "it reviews subjects we saw while in New York City and nicely summarizes where we would like to go on Yonge Street with the Regeneration Program. It is good background reading for your briefing ... set for ... July 31st" (Joint Board 1998b, Exhibit 192).

A memo sent in October to the Board of Management from the program manager on the subcommittee gives a sense of the feverish activity and the number of people to whom work had been farmed out in order to explore the feasibility of the secret plan. There were consultants doing appraisal work, making business valuations, and preparing the financial models. City legal staff was working on ways the development could be handled. Planning staff was putting together the overall project package. The budgets of the steering committee and the city had to be juggled so that the numbers worked. Soft costs associated with consultants' services were being paid for out of the steering committee's budget, but it was depleted rapidly. Either more money would have to go into that account or the services would have to be paid for directly by the city (Joint Board 1998b, Exhibit 83).

The first draft of the redevelopment plan was ready just in time for the city council meeting of 9 December 1996, where it was reviewed in camera. The following day, council publicly announced its approval in principle to proceed to the next phase on the redevelopment trajectory.

Key Physical Elements of the Redevelopment Plan, December 1996

With this report to city council, "redevelopment" was introduced, whereas the discussion before had been about "regeneration" (Joint Board 1998b, Exhibit 53). Four principal land parcels were involved (see Figure 4.1), and the site encompassed just over 1.2 hectares (three acres) of land. While some changes occurred over the next eighteen months, the essentials of the plan were laid out in the report. The report includes what was proposed and how its proponents intended to carry it out. Figure 4.2 shows a conceptualization of the finished redevelopment, while Chapter 6 describes how the project evolved. Figure 4.3 is an artist's conceptual drawing of the square and its surroundings following redevelopment.

Parcel A – Northeast corner of Yonge and Dundas: This parcel was to emerge from a land assembly undertaken by the city. The city would acquire six privately owned properties that faced onto Yonge, close the city-owned lane behind them (O'Keefe Lane), and obtain air rights over Ryerson University's parking garage, which backed onto the site from the Victoria Street side. The city would turn the assembled land and rights over to a developer at cost. The developer had to have a cinema client who wanted to establish itself as the anchor tenant. The total project would generate about 720,000 square feet (around 67,000 square metres) of new building that would front onto both Yonge and Dundas.

4.1 Development parcels in the Yonge Dundas Redevelopment Project. *Parcel A*, cinema-anchored building; *Parcel B*, eventual hotel and other uses (not redeveloped as of 2008); *Parcel C*, the Torch plus entertainment, commercial, and retail uses; *Parcel D*, public square and underground parking. | Adapted from Toronto 1998a.

Parcel B – 277 Victoria Street and two adjacent properties: The main building at 277 Victoria had been purchased by the city for $4 million two years earlier. It was proposed that it could remain in city use for the short term, but in the plan it was destined eventually to become a 400- to 600-suite hotel with 130 to 150 residential units above it and four levels of retail in a podium below.

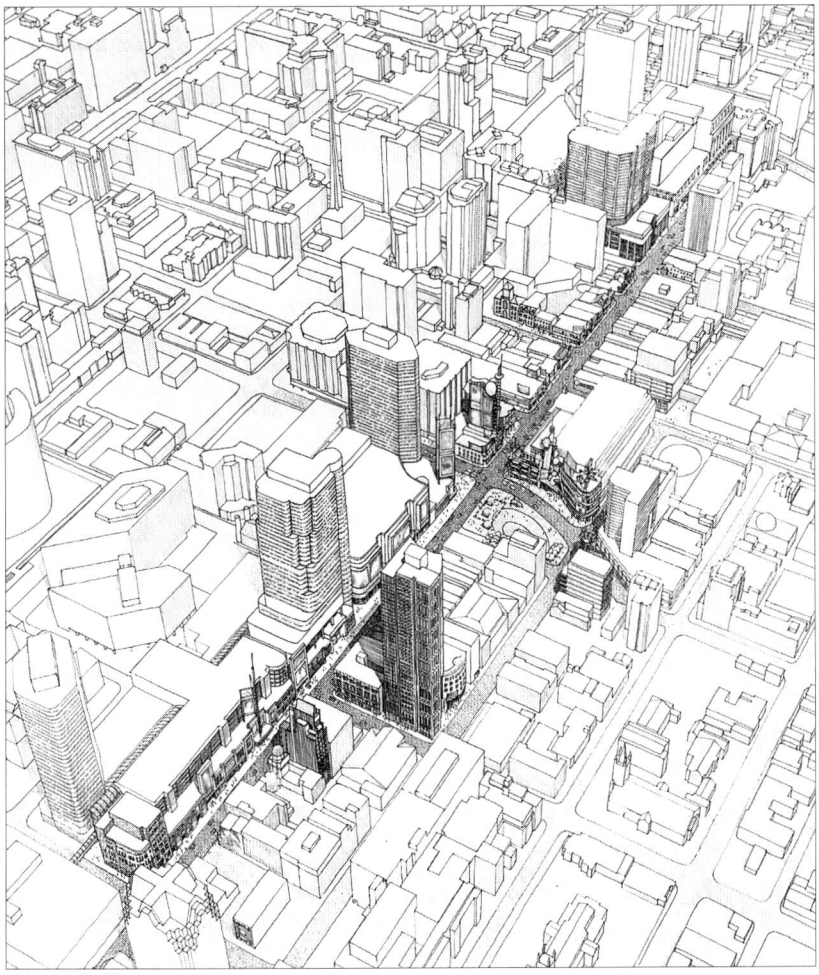

4.2 Original illustration for the redevelopment of the Yonge-Dundas area, 1998, by Gordon Grice & Associates and based on site models, photographs, and architectural drawings that were available at the time. | Courtesy of Gordon Grice & Associates.

Parcel C – The Salvation Army property and the Triangle: In the 1950s, the Salvation Army constructed a building at 37 Dundas East (also with the civic number 259 Victoria). At the time that these redevelopment plans were underway, the building was being used as a men's drop-in centre, and for a couple of winters it also served as a hostel with over sixty beds. The hostel was almost fully funded by the city as one of its emergency winter shelters. By withdrawing funding, the city would likely alter the building's use. Under the pressure of

4.3 Conceptual drawing of the future square and surroundings, 1997. | Toronto (1997h).

circumstances, the Salvation Army was prepared to sell its property and relocate its services elsewhere in the area.

Parcel D – Public square, with underground parking garage: Nearly 40 percent of this parcel belonged to the Parking Authority of Toronto (PAT). An arrangement was worked out between PAT and the city whereby PAT would build and operate a 250-car underground parking garage on the site, and certain revenues from the garage would flow to the city, where they would be used to offset the cost of developing the surface as a public square. Another small portion of the square would come from closing a further stretch of O'Keefe Lane that belonged to the city. Finally, four retail properties that faced onto Yonge Street were also to be acquired by the city.

At no place in the December 1996 redevelopment report is reference made either to knitting the east side of Yonge to the west side or to dealing with social concerns. These goals had been considered in the earlier regeneration plan discussions with stakeholders in the area and their associated reports.

Why This Precise Location Was Chosen

Since it had been decided that land assembly and redevelopment were necessary to revivify the street, the report to council explained why this particular location had been chosen. The choice was said to have resulted from analyzing various sites and locations within the community improvement project area that stretched along Yonge Street from south of Queen to north of College/Carlton. The report said that the following criteria were used:

1. access to existing infrastructure: subway and PATH[3] connections
2. presence of listed or designated historic buildings
3. recent retail investment and existing long term tenancies
4. prominence of location and potential for creating sense of place
5. proximity to the Toronto Eaton Centre and Ryerson University
6. opportunities for public benefits, amenities and parking facilities
7. retail market interest in key, high profile locations. (Joint Board 1998b, Exhibit 53, 9)

The report then commented on the criteria:

> The analysis demonstrated that the vicinity of the Yonge and Dundas intersection offered the most potential taking into consideration the factors listed above. The intersection is considered the "unofficial" heart of Toronto, has the highest pedestrian counts of any Yonge Street intersection including Bloor Street, has a subway station, is the gateway to both the Toronto Eaton Centre and Ryerson University, has sites that are not constrained by historic buildings and is recognized in the marketplace as a prime retail location and among the most high profile street retail addresses in the City. While the land ownership in the area is generally fractured, the area has the benefit of two large land holdings owned by the City of Toronto and Ryerson University ...
>
> The creation of public amenities and associated new buildings at this location would signal a significant departure from the past pace of incremental change on Yonge Street. Past attempts at renewal have not achieved change on the scale required to improve the nature of the street. This project would have the potential of becoming the commercial heart of the City and give a focus to the core. The square will create value for property in the vicinity and stimulate further reinvestment. (Ibid.)

A rationale such as this for the specific location was certainly necessary because it would be demanded in legal challenges to the expropriations.

Why an Urban Entertainment Centre with Cinemas?

Why did the anchor for Parcel A have to be an entertainment centre? And why cinemas in particular? Based on what he had seen elsewhere in North America, YSBRA's consultant believed that cinemas, and only cinemas, could create a critical mass of new activities. It was the new way cinemas were set up that gave them their appeal. The new form was the megaplex, which comprised about fifteen or more screens set in an urban entertainment centre (UEC). The UEC brought together an agglomeration of interrelated uses. In the consultant's view, "playdiums" were almost entirely electronic entertainment centres, whereas UECs combined electronic entertainment centres with book and specialty clothing stores, for example. However, there is quite a bit of similarity between the two in practice. Some say that UECs work in much the same way as cities: people patronize a UEC because it gives them what they need for a given aspect of their lives.[4] From another perspective, however, UECs are yet another example of businesses targeting people and parsing uses to maximize their return on investment. Those aged eighteen to thirty were targeted, and uses designed to entertain that age group specifically were identified for the UEC.

The UEC and the Eaton Centre were seen as complementary facilities. The UEC's cinemas were not intended as a tourist destination so much as a draw for residents of the region, although retail and eating establishments were directed toward both tourists and residents. The UEC would be for urban recreation – a paint-the-town-red type of entertainment; the Eaton Centre, which was already a major tourist attraction, would remain focused on merchandise. The synergy between the two facilities was intended to lengthen the stay of visitors in the Yonge-Dundas area.

The program director believed that he needed to attract a megaplex to the corner of Yonge and Dundas because that kind of facility was going to locate somewhere in downtown Toronto anyway. He had learned this from discussions with people active in the local development industry. His job, as he saw it, was to capture the megaplex for the corner of Yonge and Dundas. So the desire to snare the megaplex for this corner has to be seen as an attempt to keep the megaplex from setting up a competing entertainment area. This development would be of concern to the ward councillor. Recall that the centre of gravity of entertainment in Toronto had begun, following the decline of the Yonge Street area in the 1970s, to re-emerge to the south and west. Indeed, at the very time that the Yonge-Dundas plans were proceeding, city council declared that an area southwest of Yonge-Dundas was "the entertainment district," complete with street plaques and a business association that proposed to make good use of its new entertainment designation. The city's choice of location was based in part on its desire to create an area where large bars could locate without their noise disturbing neighbourhoods. The future of Yonge Street and this new entertainment area were decided without a study of how to accommodate entertainment in the city as a whole. Perhaps when planning was at the regeneration scale, this type of study was not necessary.

But conditions were different at the redevelopment scale, particularly with its unremitting focus on organized large-format entertainment.

A playdium called Festival Hall, which was anchored by Famous Players with fourteen cinemas, prepared to open in 1999 in the declared entertainment district. It ended up including a large bookstore, restaurants, bars, a giant four-floor video arcade, and a climbing wall – all of which were accoutrements of a "pop culture palace," as its architect described it (Michael Kirkland, cited in Dault 1999). In fact, it had all the signs of a UEC of the type being planned for Parcel A at Yonge and Dundas. The ward councillor for the Yonge-Dundas area said he was the only city councillor to vote against Festival Hall. He said he did so because the playdium was not on the subway lines. The entertainment complex failed within about three years, and since then the 40,000-square-foot building has changed hands a couple of times and been converted to nightclub use.

The Recommended Development Option

The strategy that looked most promising to the proponents at this stage and the one they recommended to council for further study involved a one-two punch approach designed to get the land to a developer quickly. (All seven options presented to city council are included in Appendix 5.) First, the city would hold exploratory talks with property owners to see if they would sell under option to the city. The idea was that the six properties north of Dundas Street East would be sold to a single developer, while the four properties to the south would be kept by the city for the public square. The kicker was that owners who refused this option would have their properties expropriated.

Once the six properties north of Dundas were acquired by the city, they would be sold as an assembled parcel to a developer who responded to an open request for qualifications. It was a risky strategy because the costs of acquiring the land were unknown – the program director had not investigated the willingness of property owners to sell or enter into agreements with the city – and the revenue from immediately reselling the land to a developer was "undetermined" (Joint Board 1998b, Exhibit 53, 13). The strategy also committed the city to a cash flow for a period of time. In the heady days of planning this redevelopment, "a period of time" was estimated to be at most two years, or to the end of 1998 (ibid., 19). As things turned out, it would be many years before the developer finished paying the city for this site.

The report said the reason for recommending the one-two punch strategy was in part because negotiations with various potential developers and end-users suggested it would work for them (Joint Board 1998b, Exhibit 53, 14[6.0]). Expropriation was shaped to suit developers, not those whose property was being expropriated, as if property owners did not merit equal consideration. The ward councillor and the program director reportedly spoke about owners negatively on several occasions in the media (Wong 1997). Property owners were treated as barriers to progress at Yonge and Dundas, and the rhetoric served to keep a solid consensus in place at city hall as a major shift in capital interests took place on the street.

Feasibility and Cost Estimates
Several studies were undertaken to arrive at a municipal cash flow analysis and development pro forma. The feasibility study showed that the city would have to pay for Dundas Square with parking garage revenues and for replacement office space with money it received from selling 277 Victoria Street. However, the feasibility study showed that these costs needed to be balanced "against the achievement of the overall objective of the Redevelopment Project to renew the Street and the tax revenue arising from increased assessment" (Joint Board 1998b, Exhibit 53, 12[4.1]).

Scholars at the Canadian Centre for the Study of Retail Activity at Ryerson University were asked for their view on whether the type of project envisaged would increase tax revenues for the city. The downtown core of Toronto was said to have a 7 percent share of the overall Metro retail market.[5] They replied that one clear measure of market share was the level of retail employment the project would help stimulate. The effect would at least help hold onto existing market share (Joint Board 1998b, Exhibit 53, 12). They estimated that the number of retail employees would increase from 700 to 1,100 (ibid., 3). Based on the assumption that the market share could be maintained, subsequent analysis showed that a combination of direct revenue would generate about $5.5 million, while indirect revenue would generate up to $25.4 million.

Net expenditures that needed to be financed by the city ranged from an optimistic estimate of $13.4 million to a pessimistic one of $17.1 million (Joint Board 1998b, Exhibit 53, Appendix 1, 19). In addition, if expropriation was undertaken, the city would need "maximum cash requirements at any one time, up until the project completion [of] up to $30 million. This [was] the cash flow requirement after all properties [had] been acquired, but not yet sold" (ibid., 19). The two scenarios are reproduced in Appendix 6.

Some of these estimates were vigorously challenged by the appellants at the expropriation hearing. Unfortunately, the final net costs can never be known: the city disclosed gross but not net costs because disclosing the latter would reveal what the city paid for the land, a secret that is retained under municipal privilege. The project gross costs circa 2004 were about $67 million for land, the square, and billed soft costs.

Planning Issues under Review

There were eight planning issues associated with the redevelopment that underwent ongoing review. Four are discussed here.[6]

Parking: An early estimate of the parking demand created by the redevelopment was 700 spaces, and it was thought that at least 350 of them could be located under the new square. Because the 277 Victoria site would be awkward for parking and loading, it was suggested that it might be necessary to consign most of the first floor to these uses.

Traffic and transportation: There were numerous traffic and transportation issues, including reconfiguring streets and changing traffic signals. Pedestrians are not mentioned in the section that discusses traffic issues or anywhere else in the report. Notably, the subject of traffic is introduced with this preamble: "Traffic impact will largely be a function of the number of parking spaces provided" (Joint Board 1998b, Exhibit 53, 17[d]). There is no hint of a connection to official plan policies on pedestrianization, the reduction of downtown traffic, and so on.

Ryerson University: Ryerson's parking garage, which would have been a logical piece of the redevelopment site, was not for sale. If it was sold or expropriated, the university said, it would lose a cash flow source that was vital to its well-being. The redevelopment options were designed to keep the garage in place and use air rights over it. The Joint Board report stated, "further discussions are planned to address Ryerson's issues and attempt to bring them into a constructive relationship with the City and potential developers on this project" (Joint Board 1998b, Exhibit 53, 18[f]). In due course, the idea emerged that Ryerson would use twelve of the proposed thirty cinemas as classrooms in the mornings and they would convert to cinemas in the afternoons and evenings.

Public square: The report does not tackle the planning issue of whether the site was appropriate for a public square, nor does it suggest that the issue had been previously examined in detail or that it will be in the future. It says that "creation of a public square at this location would address Official Plan policy which has identified this area of the core as a Parks Acquisition Priority Area" (Joint Board 1998b, Exhibit 53, 18[h]). (The official plan identifies the entire core area of the city, not this specific site, as an acquisition area.) The report goes on to say that the square is envisaged as an urban plaza (not a leafy park) because of the "commercial environment of Yonge Street" (ibid., 18[h]), and that it would be developed through a competitive design process.

Earlier in the report, the new "super commissioner" in charge of planning and development, the one under whose name the report was issued, said that the square should not be created alone: "The analysis has also demonstrated that the square must be created within an environment of new retail space in the vicinity. There is a strong linkage between creating the new environment and creating a successful public square. Creating the square in isolation does not address the broader need to change the environment of Yonge Street and is not recommended. Municipal benefits referred to would not be fully achieved. *Indeed, creating the square alone could exacerbate existing social and economic problems on the street*" (Joint Board 1998b, Exhibit 53, 10, my emphasis). It is not clear which analysis is being referred to in the first sentence. What is clear is that the square would be a public space created from the perspective of socioeconomic considerations, not spatial principles.

The lack of evidence to support the claim that the new square had to have new retail spaces is a concern given that the goal of the redevelopment project was "to substantially increase the proportion and range of residents and visitors who use Downtown Yonge Street" (Joint Board 1998b, Exhibit 53, 1).

The Rationale for Redevelopment over Regeneration

The report writers said that the following points summarized the rationale for redevelopment (Joint Board 1998b, Exhibit 53, 1-2):

City Building:

- the City is in the unique position to make decisions which strengthen the urban character of downtown Toronto and contribute to the quality of life and work environment for future generations
- the regeneration of Yonge Street as a main shopping street and the provision of improved public amenities is a key to maintaining the economic and social well-being of the downtown and the region

Planning and Design:

- a significant opportunity exists for a public square with underground parking, new retail and entertainment space and a landmark building for hotel and residential uses in the vicinity of the Yonge and Dundas intersection
- three development scenarios have been developed which are supportable from a planning and design point of view

Market:

- the Redevelopment Project is well-timed in terms of this investment cycle and interest in bringing new retail to urban street locations in major North American cities
- Yonge Street is experiencing some new investment as a result of market trends and the expectation of meaningful change to the character of the Street (e.g., The Gap, Urban Outfitters, Le Chateau)
- considerable development and tenant interest has been identified for new retail and entertainment space in the vicinity of Yonge and Dundas.

Based on this set of rationales, the city's argument is as follows:

Premise 1   city building is possible
Premise 2   as goes Yonge Street, so goes the city and region
Premise 3   a square is possible
Premise 4   scenarios are supportable from planning and design points of view
Premise 5   the timing is right for the market
Premise 6   change has begun
Premise 7   potential tenants are showing interest in new retail and entertainment space
Conclusion   redevelopment is necessary.

Logically, none of these premises leads to that conclusion. The proponents showed that redevelopment was possible; they did not show that it was necessary. Yet they acted as if the conclusion were the only logical option. They confused first-phase feasibility studies with planning studies. The plan's objective, to increase the proportion and range of residents and visitors using the area, is noticeably absent from the rationale.

The planners' logic underscores some of the project's fundamental problems and issues. First, the project was based solely on feasibility data that said that the project could be done but did not address whether it should be done. Second, the decision to move from modest to major redevelopment was based on poor reasoning. Third, the principal paradox of the area was not treated as a puzzle that had to be resolved before a treatment was designed; rather, the paradox, as stated in the report, was listed as a "barrier to renewal": "The vicinity of Yonge and Dundas is a prominent location yet it suffers from vacancy, poor property maintenance and violation of municipal by-laws, lack of reinvestment and underutilization and a lack of public amenities" (Joint Board 1998b, Exhibit 53, 7). The paradox was: Why did a central location such as Yonge-Dundas have meagre reinvestment in property? Casting the paradox as a barrier rather than as the central problem may have been inadvertent, a case of poor reasoning that was not caught, because there was so much momentum behind an already-chosen solution. But it helped to disguise that private interests were driving both the goal of the project and the means to achieve it. It is likely that no one at city hall had the time, interest, or inclination to critically examine the progression of this project, to challenge the data and logic on which it was based. The ward councillor seemed to have a lock on discussion. And no one who worked outside of city hall could challenge the project because it was being planned behind a veil.

Why did planners not point out the lack of data to justify scaling up from regeneration to redevelopment? This question is central to understanding the role of planning in urban development. Why not give private developers a chance to do the assembly and have a fully open competition? Why not invite the current landowners into a consortium to redevelop the area? Why not wait to see what effects the changes in the zoning would have? Or even, why not make a detailed assessment of the effects from changes already instituted and use that as the grounds for arguing that the next steps of expropriation and assembly were essential?

During the planning-as-regeneration phase of the project, it was possible to read into the reports that low investment in property was the key paradox to resolve. The planned response was to allow for larger building envelopes and more flexibility in how a property was configured. However, to scale up to the planning-as-redevelopment phase, more data was needed. The rationale provided by the public-private partnership should not have been taken at face value because the partners were already committed to redevelopment and eager to move to feasibility studies for what they already knew they wanted to build and from which the private proponents would benefit financially. Thus, from the moment the city agreed to join this public-private partnership, it was prepared to replace evidence-based planning with market feasibility. The steering committee, which was to provide oversight in the public interest, effectively stifled criticism.

Next Steps

The report writers had prepared a list of tasks that they recommended be undertaken next if the city was prepared to adopt the December 1996 report in principle and take the next steps: the city should issue a request for qualifications (RFQ) to the development industry to determine its interest in developing the parcels; negotiate conditional acquisition agreements with affected property owners; determine how many properties would have to be expropriated; and help those private developers who intended to build in ways consistent with the redevelopment project's objectives to get access to their sites. After reassessing the situation, city council would then need to decide whether to proceed with the project or terminate it based on an assessment of stage-two feasibility work.

Some of the features of the regeneration plan (approved in principle at the 4 March 1996 city council meeting, with final approval in June) were to be rolled over into the new redevelopment project: (1) the whole project area would be treated as a single, one-lot site even though it actually comprised separate sites, (2) the reinvestment area designation would be expanded to coincide with the lands proposed for the whole redevelopment site, and (3) the site would be prezoned as shown in the regeneration plan. One exception was proposed: in the regeneration plan the commercial density had been doubled from 2.0 to 4.0. This rezoning would not apply to the four properties to be taken for the square, presumably so the city would not have to pay the higher price for the newly upzoned properties when it took the lands either by purchase or expropriation. The facade program option was also removed.[7] These changes set a tone that was not conducive to productive negotiations.

A project that began as a proposal to YSBRA by a private consultant in January 1996 had become by March 1996 an initiative that paralleled the city planning department's regeneration plan. By December 1996, the project was the main planning scheme. By the fall of 1997, it subsumed most, but not all, of the regeneration plan within its structure.

Public Meetings
City council's approval in principle of the redevelopment project was considered at a series of three meetings.[8] Approval would necessitate changes to the official plan, zoning in the area, and the existing CIP.

The first meeting was mandated by the *Planning Act*: before city council acted, it was obliged to give those affected by changes to the official plan a chance to air their views in public. The planning department recommended an official plan amendment (OPA), with corresponding zoning bylaw amendments, and some changes to the community improvement plan. Changes to the latter were called for to clarify the strategies the city might employ to achieve its aims. For example, strategies might include "land acquisition and disposition, joint venture partnerships, redevelopment incentives and other strategies" (Toronto 1997a, s. 16.2, 9). The city also sought to improve the information provided within the CIP about the criteria it would use to "evaluate opportunities and land disposition," criteria that would continue to be tied to the overall objective of making tangible improvements to Yonge Street (ibid.).

Of the seventeen people who addressed this public meeting of the Land Use Committee, six represented properties that were to be taken under the redevelopment scheme. All the others were active proponents of the redevelopment. One of the central instigators of the redevelopment, who was himself a local business property owner, was quoted as saying, "We're all behind this with the exception of a few people who own buildings in the area" (Moloney 1997). The few unsupportive owners were those whose property was about to be expropriated.

After the representations and discussion, the Land Use Committee adopted the planning department's recommendations and approved the amendments. It also directed that a stage-two feasibility analysis be started that would include continuing negotiations with owners for taking their properties, negotiating with potential lead tenants for Parcel A, and launching an RFQ process with the development industry regarding the other parcels (Toronto 1997a, s. 16.2, 5-6). The Planning Advisory Committee gave its approval to the amendments on 17 March.

Although the city's reports stressed the strong support the project had received from organizations that ranged from the Toronto Board of Trade to local residents' associations, issues were raised at those two meetings and through correspondence. The issues can be grouped into six topics: design of the square, downzoning, land speculation, tax and employment benefits to the city, the continuity of retail on Yonge Street, and the size of electronic-games establishments (Toronto 1997a, s. 16.2, 13). Appendix 7 shows how these issues were summarized by the planning department for city councillors to read.

Modifications were made along the way to the basic redevelopment plan, but by 6 May 1997 council was ready to approve the project and ask that property acquisition negotiations continue. Changes were heard at a public meeting of the Land Use Committee held on 5 June.

A complicated piece of the approvals process then began at a city council meeting held on 23-24 June 1997. It was clear that some of the property owners would contest the planning amendments and the expropriations that would result from implementing them. The city's preferred choice was to avoid having the planning matters challenged at all by disgruntled property owners at the OMB. If that failed, it wanted the planning and expropriation appeals to go forward at the same time. In the terminology of Ontario planning law, the first appeal would be a "public hearing" on planning issues, while the second appeal would be a "hearing of necessity" on expropriation matters. The city wanted to run the planning and expropriation processes "in parallel instead of sequentially in order to avoid undue delay which would be deleterious to the advancement of the Redevelopment Project and the participation of the private sector" (Toronto 1997b, 92). The city presented a motion to the OMB that asked for approval "to dispense with the necessity of holding a public hearing relating to the planning approval process regarding certain OPAs, zoning by-law amendments and a Community Improvement Plan" (Joint Board 1998j, 3). The OMB heard the request on 14 August and refused it. In November 1998, when the OMB was assigning costs after the hearing ended, it scolded the city for this action. The OMB noted that if speed was the issue, the city had several other tools it could have used yet chose not to employ. The result was to put property owners in the difficult position of having almost no time to prepare their appeal of the planning issues. The city was required to pay all costs associated with that motion to the board.

The outcome was that expropriation notices were sent to affected owners and they launched appeals of the planning amendments as well as the expropriations. Those matters were heard jointly the following March at the OMB.

Seeking and Assessing Occupancy and Development Offers

Cinema Company Competition, Parcel A

Before the redevelopment plan went to city council on 9 December 1996, discussions had already taken place, probably beginning around July, with at least one developer and three cinema companies that could be potential tenant anchors in the Metropolis project. Until this point the Ontario cinema market had been shared primarily by two large firms, Cineplex Odeon and Famous Players. AMC, of Kansas City, Missouri, was trying to break into the Canadian market and had several projects underway in Alberta, Quebec, and Ontario. It also did a lot of work with Disney. Famous Players was not interested in the Yonge-Dundas project; this left two major players in the running. Cineplex Odeon had eighteen screens operating in a multiplex format in the Eaton Centre, kitty-corner from Parcel A. Offers came from Cineplex Odeon and AMC. At that time, Cineplex Odeon was a known quantity but was held in low esteem by the ward councillor, a point that came out in the OMB hearing. The ward councillor favoured AMC, which was also the program director's choice, and the latter had already convinced AMC to locate at Yonge and Dundas.

At the in camera council session of December 1996, the two cinema companies that showed interest in the project were discussed by name. Consequently, the developer, PenEquity, was also discussed because AMC considered PenEquity its developer of choice in the region, and the two firms were already working together on other proposals and projects. City council also had before it a letter dated 2 December 1996 from AMC that established the company's intent to be the anchor tenant in Parcel A (Joint Board 1998c, 1). Contrary evidence about what city councillors knew and discussed was offered by counsel for the appellants at the OMB hearing in March 1998. But the weight of evidence suggests that city council made its decision to proceed with this project when its members already knew the companies that would be involved, at least with Parcel A.[9] When the project, which had been approved in principle by council, was revealed to the public on 10 December, it appeared as if the developer would be selected by an open selection process. The winner would emerge from a fair competition adjudicated by the city. The selected developer, being the lead agent in his own project, would then decide on his anchor tenant. But the city had established the cinema anchor tenant in the fall of 1996, before the report was submitted to council; it needed a way to demonstrate that its process for finding a developer was fair.

The consultant from KPMG, who had been hired by the steering committee's program director back in March, was asked to make a financial analysis of the proposals from the two cinema companies, AMC and Cineplex Odeon. In his report, dated 22 January 1997, he said the AMC proposal was the better of the two. He addressed it to the city's planner for the downtown district and sent a copy to the program director.[10]

Comparing the two offers is impossible because in the publicly available version of the financial analysis, Cineplex Odeon's figures are included while those for AMC are expunged. For example, the paragraph on AMC's development costs looks like this:

> Hard development costs of   were estimated for AMC Entertainment (including tenant finishing estimated at   . Soft costs of   are assumed for consultant fees, contingency, and interest during development, and a cost of   is included for acquiring the Ryerson land, for a total estimated development cost of   . Based on the gross land area of 88,025 sq. ft., the total development cost is estimated at   million. (Joint Board 1998i, Tab 8, 3-4)

The comparable paragraph on Cineplex Odeon's development costs looks like this:

> The Cineplex Odeon hard development costs estimate was $133.15 (including tenant finishing estimated at $60.00). Soft costs of $30.00 are also assumed for consultant fees, contingency, and interest during development, and a cost of $20.00 is included for acquiring the Ryerson land, for a total estimated development cost of $243.15. Based on the gross land area of 84,000 sq. ft., the total development cost is estimated at $20.42 million. (ibid.)[11]

The city chose AMC as the anchor cinema tenant. It then had to get AMC a developer.

Developer Competition, Parcel A

At its meeting on 6 May 1997 city council acknowledged that it knew that by choosing AMC it was also implicitly choosing PenEquity Management Corporation. Nonetheless, the city had issued an RFQ for all four parcels on 20 February 1997. The RFQ had generated seven responses by the deadline on 24 March 1997, including one from PenEquity. Four of the respondents – Cadillac-Fairview, Henderson Development, Millennium Partners, and Swisscan Developments – were interested in developing all of the parcels, whereas PenEquity was interested only in Parcel A, Oceanic Adventures International Corporation was interested only in Parcel B, and Senator Developments was interested only in Parcel C. The selection team completed its evaluation on 2 May 1997, nearly six weeks after the deadline. Five members of the city's staff made up the selection team (Joint Board 1998b, Exhibit 157). The sixth member was the KPMG consultant hired by the project director a year earlier.

In the meantime, because PenEquity was AMC's developer of choice, the city's Board of Management had instructed that negotiations proceed with PenEquity even as the RFQ was underway (Toronto 1997a, 18). The deal with PenEquity was concluded before the RFQ deadline. The KPMG consultant assessed it as a good deal. However, the city financial officer's response to the KPMG report, which came less than a week later, was that KPMG's report "did not help in assessing the financial risk to the City because ... no verification has been made on ... the accuracy or appropriateness of the assumptions" (Joint Board 1998b, Exhibit 90, cited in Joint Board 1998b, Exhibit 259, 29). Indeed, the KPMG report concludes with disclaimers that cover its entire analysis.

A financial consultant to the appellants, who prepared an analysis of the same report for the OMB hearing, describes some of the risks to the city that the KPMG report did not address:

> Risk of incorrectly estimating expropriation land values
> Risk of City holding land for 12 months
> Risk of "Total Project Costs" overruns
> Risk that other unverified PenEquity assumptions are incorrect
> Risk that Excess Acquisition Price Notice causes PenEquity to walk.
> (Joint Board 1998b, Exhibit 259, 30)

The financial consultant's report elaborates on these points. It is instructive to note the degree to which the city may have put itself at risk because of its publicly declared wish to pursue a particular kind of redevelopment. As a public corporation, the city had to tip its hand, which made it next to impossible to negotiate in the best interests of the corporation.

Results of the Request for Qualifications

The RFQ submissions were assessed by the selection team, and its recommendation was sent to the commissioner of urban development services.[12] In a report to city council dated 6 May 1997, the commissioner noted the link between AMC – which offered "a significantly better business deal" – and PenEquity. He wrote that "pursuant to direction from the Board of Management, negotiations have been undertaken with [PenEquity]. These negotiations have resulted in a proposed agreement which is being recommended for approval" at the city council meeting (Toronto 1997a, 18). The recommendation to council was that Parcel A "be the subject of an agreement between the City and PenEquity on the basis of negotiations as discussed previously in this report. *The potential exclusion of this site from an RFP was anticipated as a possibility and noted in the Request for Qualifications document*" (Toronto 1997a, 19, my emphasis).

Why did the city bother with the RFQ for Parcel A? Once the city received the KPMG report that compared the financial offers of AMC and Cineplex Odeon and came down in favour of the former, its choices were limited. If it chose AMC, it chose PenEquity by default. AMC had made it clear that it was working with PenEquity on thirteen other projects and that the two companies had been looking at opportunities together for over three years. The project director had himself approached AMC and PenEquity to propose that they develop and anchor Parcel A:

> While still in the process of undertaking our search for sites in downtown Toronto, we were approached by Ron Soskolne to submit a contingent development proposal for the Yonge-Dundas site on the basis that the land would be assembled by the City. The fact that the City was also prepared to make a substantial infrastructure investment in terms of a public square indicated to us that it was prepared to invest in improving the social and economic conditions on the Yonge-Dundas corner and addressing the perceived and actual problems with respect to crime, including drug trafficking, panhandling and prostitution. Toronto is a safe and clean city, yet Yonge and Dundas is anything but clean and safe. (Joint Board 1998b, Exhibit 42, 3)

It seemed only a matter of time before AMC got the nod. A condition of AMC's interest in Yonge-Dundas was that land assembly had to happen by mid-1998 or it would look elsewhere, and PenEquity's condition was that, once offered, the public square had to be built. Rather than being hindrances, those conditions worked to advance the steering committee's ambitions: it could use them to put pressure on city council to act quickly and to head off questions about placing a public square in that particular location. With or without an RFQ, a surprise outcome was unlikely. PenEquity had effectively won the competition before the RFQ process that was held to give the appearance that the city was fairly sourcing developers.

This was all laid out in a much simpler form in the question and answer notes prepared for use by speakers at the press conference that announced the choice of developer for Parcel A:

> Why did PenEquity win the bid over many other experienced international companies?" (Let city answer first)

Following the RFP and RFQ process, the City of Toronto selected PenEquity out of seven initial candidates and four or five final candidates for the following three reasons: (1) PenEquity is working closely with AMC on developing other entertainment centres in Ontario, Alberta and British Columbia and brought AMC to the table. (Joint Board 1998b, Exhibit 15, Tab E)

Despite what was contained in the question and answer notes, an RFP had not been called, and it was not PenEquity who brought AMC to the deal but the other way around.

Once the PPP decided it had to have a cinema company, of which there were only three major ones in North America, and once the program director attracted the interest of one of them, AMC, the city became vulnerable, particularly in light of AMC's connection to PenEquity. The agreement between the city and PenEquity established the uppermost price that PenEquity would have to pay to get the six expropriated properties from the city. If the cost of expropriation was lower than this fixed amount, then PenEquity would pay less, but if expropriation exceeded that amount, the city would absorb the excess and be out of pocket. PenEquity's ceiling amount would not budge. The agreement would also allow the city to sell to PenEquity extra density rights, over and above those already acquired in the new height and density permissions, and it would allow the city "to participate in future revenue or alternatively to cash in the participation value at an agreed upon price" (Toronto 1997g, 66). Furthermore, as Torontonians later discovered, the terms of agreement were loose enough that PenEquity did not put a shovel in the ground until 2003, five years after the OMB decision cleared the way for the redevelopment to proceed, and construction stalled again the next year. By 2006, PenEquity had substantially but not fully paid the city for the land; final payments were due at project completion.

A Request for Proposals

Of the firms that responded to the RFQ and showed interest in developing all four parcels, two were interested in further discussions about Parcels B and C, but neither wanted to immediately prepare a proposal (Toronto 1997b). Nonetheless they and other developers with whom the staff had been in contact were interested in a formal RFP. Therefore, staff asked city council to approve an open proposal call to the general development industry.

An RFP for Parcels B and C was issued on 15 July 1997 for a 28 August close. In August the commissioner of development services reported that more than sixty documents had been mailed out or picked up by interested parties and that other inquiries had been made. The RFP described the area in upbeat terms and indicated the development activity that was already occurring. Some of the initiatives the RFQ described were the Parcel A and Parcel D developments, but it also listed signs of invigoration that were independent of them:

- New retail tenants such as upscale clothiers, restaurants and specialty shops.
- Municipal streetscape improvements and improved public amenities in 1996 and 1997.
- Twelve façade improvement grants for buildings between Gerrard and Queen Streets on Yonge.
- Development approvals granted for a unique, New York-style condominium building on Yonge Street south of Shuter Street and a 40,000 square-foot new retail premises on Yonge Street north of Queen Street.
- An approved project for a new 1,400-seat live theatre, including improvements to the Pantages Theatre backstage and a new residential hotel building.
- Planned improvements to the Toronto Eaton Centre and the Atrium-on-Bay, both in the immediate vicinity of Yonge and Dundas Streets.
- Several new high quality residential developments, the most recent one which is the Merchandise Building at Church and Dundas Streets. (Joint Board 1998f, Tab 16, 3-4)

Does this list suggest that the street was in the process of repairing itself with the help of the new height and density regulations – that is, thanks to the regeneration initiatives? An expert witness for the opponents of expropriation argued at the OMB hearing that the street was renewing itself, but the board dismissed his evidence (Joint Board 1998b, Exhibit 233, especially pages 4-5).

Only one proposal was received for Parcel B, the hotel and residential complex at Victoria and Dundas Street East. The city declined to consider the proposal "on the basis that there is an unresolvable existing or potential conflict of interest" (Toronto 1997f, 17). Given that there was no acceptable proposal for Parcel B, the commissioner recommended some changes. The city would remove some properties (54-74 Dundas Street East and 100 Bond Street) from the expropriation list. The property at 38 Dundas, right next to the city's own 277 Victoria Street, would remain on the expropriation list, but the city would try to negotiate options to keep open the possibility of a joint venture in the future for that consolidated site. Part of the city's interest in this site was based on the fact that it could, in exchange for a payment, use the *Planning Act*'s section 37 bonus zoning provision to grant height and density above the existing as of right zoning. The money could help finance the square (Toronto 1997f, 17). This approach fit logically with an analysis that was done in the stage-one feasibility period before the 9 December 1996 city council meeting in which it was shown that the market for a hotel building was not ripe, although it was improving. The city's consultant on hotel space suggested a delay of at least two years.

Two proposals generated by the RFP for Parcel C were evaluated. This was the site that the city had bought from the Salvation Army – a triangle of land in the odd-shaped intersection of Victoria and Dundas Street East. One submission came from Senator Restaurant Limited, the company of a founding member of YSBRA who, at the time of the RFP submission, was its chair and a member of the steering committee (although not the secret subcommittee). The other submission was from a long-established Toronto home furniture and decorator business. The commissioner recommended the Senator Restaurant Limited proposal and based his decision on the advice of a review committee made up of staff from Corporate Services and Urban Development Services and the KPMG consultant. The commissioner's report – which was discussed in camera – said it was the best overall proposal for the city. It offered to pay cash for the land and to renovate the existing building to accommodate a restaurant, retail uses, and offices. Senator Restaurant's developer would be PenEquity, the same developer who had won Parcel A. Senator's price was $1,025,000. The other proposal offered $1.8 million, although it carried a comparatively large mortgage. The city valued the land at $1.6 million. Several years earlier, in 1988, the Salvation Army property alone had been assessed at a market value of $1,760,000 (Joint Board 1998b, Exhibit 151, B-1). City council approved the Senator Restaurant proposal at its October meeting (Toronto 1997f, 18).

Ten days later, on 16 October 1997, the owner of Senator Restaurant Limited resigned as chair of YSBRA and from the steering committee of the Yonge Dundas Redevelopment Project (Joint Board 1998d, 20). Conflict of interest on the part of the owner of Senator Restaurant was not alleged during the OMB hearing, but the line of argument from the appellants' counsel implied that he had lurked near the outer edge of virtue. The latter wanted to know why it had taken so long for the owner to step down from the very body that was formally partnered with the city to make the redevelopment happen. Although in frequent interviews with the media he described his actions as being in the public interest, the owner of Senator Restaurant had also acted in his own interests as he tried to foster the redevelopment of the area in which he had business property. The OMB was disturbed by his actions (Joint Board 1998d, 21), but it declared that it was satisfied that there had been no wrongdoing. However, in the course of explaining its position, the board made some inaccurate statements about the owner's official positions with YSBRA.

Dealing with Property Owners

Were the small-business owners targeted for expropriation negligent because they did not appeal the original community improvement plan for this area? The board suggested that owners should not have been surprised at the intention to expropriate (Joint Board 1998j, 8). However, as the descriptions in this chapter and the previous one show, it was in no way obvious that expropriation was anticipated in the original community improvement project and official plan amendments, nor was it anticipated in the studies supporting them. Indeed, the central argument made here is that the original plans and accompanying consultations and reports to city created the conditions for an incremental regeneration plan; expropriation came to public view when the plans were secretly delivered to and approved by city council in December 1996. Property owners then began to see that their lands were to be taken. There was nothing in the print media before December 1996 that would have alerted landowners.

It can be argued that the city (1) intended, from about June 1996, to use expropriation to acquire properties on the east side of Yonge, (2) masked that intention until December 1996, and (3) did not encourage existing landowners to find redevelopment solutions that fit within the new official plan amendments and CIP.

First, the city's intention to go along with the private-capital interests in YSBRA and to expropriate property was likely fixed by June 1996. By that time the city planners were challenged by the steering committee to get fully behind redevelopment. This was also the period when the steering committee was pushed to one side and the oversight of redevelopment plans was put in the hands of a secret four-person subcommittee. The intent to expropriate property is evident in steering committee documents about a Times Square–like redevelopment that would demand some expropriation and in a briefing memo to the Board of Management about the planners' trip to New York. None of this was public information.

Second, the city, as part of the PPP, masked the intention to expropriate. The CIP legislation permits "redevelopment." And redevelopment could imply expropriation that would invoke other legislation. However, expropriation had not been discussed publicly, either as a general possibility or as something that could occur at the Yonge-Dundas intersection. Until June 1996 the emphasis was on setting conditions for existing landowners to redevelop their properties in larger building envelopes and to meet built-form performance objectives.

Several pieces of information illustrate the desire to mask intentions. (Note that masking expropriation intentions is logical when one is trying to pay the least possible amount for land. The argument here is whether that was the proper role of the city on prime core area land where other options were being promoted.) The ward councillor, the program director, and the city's contract expropriation lawyer met with the deputy minister of the province's Ministry of Municipal Affairs and Housing on 18 September 1996 to try to have the hearing into the expropriations waived (Rae, n.d.).[13] Lead counsel for the appellants at the OMB hearing drew this information from one of the city's planners on the stand. The deputy minister's reply was allegedly something to the effect that a request like this would have to be considered by the provincial cabinet, and its approval would require very good reasons (Joint Board 1998d, 18, item 5).[14] After that meeting the project's schedule, dated 24 September 1996, indicated that in April 1997 the properties would be acquired at values backdated to the day before city council announced the redevelopment plan.

Insider knowledge about the city's intention to expropriate was revealed at the OMB hearing. In one instance a restaurateur who had been one of the instigators of YSBRA said he was so worried about his property being expropriated that he could not sleep the night before the 9 December council meeting (Joint Board 1998d, 18). He was not a member of the secret subcommittee, but he acknowledged that he knew there would be expropriations. In another instance, the OMB (in its written decision) expressed concern about whether another restaurant owner who had been awarded the right to develop Parcel C had insider information about the project. In this case, the property owner was the chair of YSBRA and the steering committee when plans were laid in June to December 1996. There was also evidence about the ward councillor: under cross-examination at the hearing, the councillor said that "he had *never* been counselled that expropriation was necessary" (ibid., 19). But as the lawyer for the property owners pointed out, this declaration directly contradicted the councillor's rationale for seeing the deputy minister on 18 September 1996 – to have the hearing of necessity waived – and the evidence of the project director, who testified that he had kept the councillor fully informed.

Third, existing landowners were not encouraged to find redevelopment solutions that fit within the new official plan and zoning regulations. This claim is backed up by three incidents. The program director "*had been* instructed [by the city] to approach the landowners to determine their interest to sell or become part of a consortium" (Joint Board 1998d, 18, item 6). He did not act on the request of the city's Board of Management. The program director was a private-sector development consultant employed by YSBRA who served on the steering committee's secret subcommittee and directed the whole project. It is unclear whether his conditions of employment allowed him to be instructed by the city to do something specific. Agreements between YSBRA and the city did not cover such an eventuality; on the other hand, the municipality would be the body to seek expropriation because the law does not permit a private organization like YSBRA to do this. Therefore, it would be the city that would have to defend the need to expropriate if a hearing was demanded. Consequently, the municipality needed to have all the bases covered, so to speak, and one precaution was to find out if property owners in the area wanted to engage in any form of redevelopment of their properties. But the program director gave evidence that he did not, in fact, consult with the property owners who were facing expropriation. Thus, as the opponents' lawyer argued, they were never "given the opportunity of considering a joint venture" (ibid.). From the program director's point of view, that would have been inappropriate because it would have given away the plan and caused the prices demanded by existing owners to escalate. It was a matter of confidentiality.

Another instance occurred at a meeting of the city's Policies and Priorities Committee held after the OMB decision was released and in preparation for city council to take the final decision on redevelopment. One of the city councillors on that committee asked if the possibility of entering into joint ventures with the small businesses had been investigated. In response the program manager on the file said that it had been difficult to treat all of the small businesses in the area equally; so, no, the possibility of a joint venture had not been examined. Finally, the owner of the World's Biggest Jean Store said that he and others had been offered opportunities within the new regeneration plan, such as the facade improvement program; however, when they tried to take steps toward property improvements, the ward councillor told them to hold off for a bit, but he did not tell them that they were going to have their properties expropriated (Toronto 1998c).

After the council meeting on 9 December 1996, at which the city approved moving the project to the next phase, a company was hired to conduct negotiations with the ten affected property owners. It was to use figures that had been prepared during the June to December secret planning phase for the negotiations. This resulted in one signed offer to sell from the owner of 299 Yonge Street (Toronto 1997a, 18).

Other City Actions That Affect the Area

Signage

In the summer and fall of 1997, the city approved a media tower that would sit over a new extension to the Atrium on Bay Street. The tower would rise fifty-five metres above the street and have the capacity for signs up to thirty-nine square metres apiece. Soon after, other approvals for huge signage were then given for the Eaton Centre facade, Metropolis on the northeast corner of the intersection, the Torch on the eastern side of the square, the top of the building on the south side of the square, and for yet another media tower over a new extension to the Eaton Centre on the intersection's southwest corner.

The bylaw to permit the continuation of this already existing practice of large signs did not require the redevelopment program for its approval. First, huge signs had long been a feature of the area, the most dramatic being the two enormous flashing records on Sam the Record Man's store. One of the first facade program grants, approved by the city in late 1996, went to Sam's (347-349 Yonge Street) to renovate its signs. Several minor variances had been granted since 1993 for oversized signs, including those for Future Shop, HMV, and Pizza Pizza. Indeed, the vast majority of applications for oversize signs in Toronto were for buildings within a one-and-a-half-block radius of the Yonge-Dundas intersection (Joint Board 1998b, Exhibit 247, 5). Second, uses in the area would continue to be primarily retail and entertainment (this was made apparent in the response to Eaton's challenge to the official plan on the priority given to retail in that area). Third, according to the March 1995 design study, no new residential use would be added. Fourth, future measures taken in the area would support the demarcation of the area as an important commercial intersection (the design study recommended incremental changes to allow the area to be more of what it already was). Large signage was already justified by previous studies and decisions.

Policing Initiatives

In 1993 the Metropolitan Toronto Police opened a substation, a branch of the police district called 52 Division, in the north end of the Eaton Centre. The district is the most concentrated part of Metro Toronto in the largest city in the country, so it is to be expected that it would require substantial policing. Metro Toronto's population was 2.4 million, and it sat in a census metropolitan area with a population of about 4.7 million. The blocks around Yonge and Dundas streets had long been associated with the problem of drug dealing. Indeed, this seems to have been the case for at least thirty years.

In April 1997 a special anticrime initiative called Operation Broom, which focused especially on drug- and sex-related activities, was started within 52 Division. It operated throughout 52 Division, not just around Yonge and Dundas. It had the support of the Eaton Centre, the Atrium on Bay, Ryerson University, and local residents (Moloney 1998b). Operation Broom was supposed to last for five weeks but was extended to at least the spring of 1998. The figures for the first six months of operation (131 days from April to mid-

Table 4.1 Number of police "contact events," 1995-97

Events – 1995, 1996, and 1997	Number
At the properties on Yonge Street to be demolished for the redevelopment project	499
At the first property north of those to be demolished (HMV)	580
At the first property south of those to be demolished (Hard Rock Cafe)	43
At the Eaton Centre	7,098

Sources: Adapted from Joint Board (1998b, Exhibit 37) and *Might's City Directories* for 1995, 1996, and 1997.

October 1997) were 404 arrests and 818 charges, for an average of about 3 arrests and 6 charges a day (Joint Board 1998b, Exhibit 34, Tab 6, 1). The great majority of these charges concerned illegal drugs – selling, possessing, or stealing to purchase drugs.

The proponents of redevelopment brought the police on board to bolster their arguments. The main line of reasoning the police used had two prongs: first, Yonge-Dundas was attractive for those in the drug trade because of the physical configuration of the small buildings on the east side of Yonge, with their hidden corners; and second, small-business owners do not use sophisticated equipment for security, so they do not adequately discourage crime in and around their buildings. This analysis led the police to claim that larger, more modern buildings with owners who knew about security would make the crime problem go down. Supporting this line of thinking with data became a problem for the proponents because the data showed the reverse. Table 4.1 shows the number of police "contact events" that occurred in the three-year period from 1995 to 1997. The table shows where the majority of events were reported to have taken place.

According to figures for crime incidents by category and patrol area in 1996 and 1997, crime in all main categories (with the exception of drug offences) on the east side of Yonge Street, from Dundas south to Queen, went down before redevelopment had been approved.[15] One assumes the dramatic increase in drug offences was because Operation Broom was effective and criminals were being caught. However, on the west side (the Eaton Centre), several of the main categories of crime – robbery, shoplifting, break and entry, prostitution-related offences, and drug-related offences – went up. Operation Broom was tackling prostitution and drugs. Table 4.2 provides figures for the area by category and compares them to larger areas of the city. Total criminal offences on the west side of Yonge Street (including the Eaton

Table 4.2 Drug, prostitution, and total criminal offences for selected police reporting scales, 1996 and 1997

Category	Location	1996	1997	Variation (%)
Drugs	Metro Toronto	5,897	6,450	9.4
	Central Area	4,057	4,506	11.1
	52 Division	453	984	117.2
	Patrol Area 5211	88	194	120.5
	Patrol Area 5213	33	180	445.5
Prostitution offences	Metro Toronto	2,309	2,385	3.3
	Central Area	1,935	1,829	−5.5
	52 Division	342	293	−14.3
	Patrol Area 5211	68	57	−16.2
	Patrol Area 5213	2	4	100.0
Total criminal offences	Metro Toronto	261,816	229,096	−12.5
	Central Area	126,610	112,371	−11.2
	52 Division	33,964	31,964	−5.9
	Patrol Area 5211	2,026	1,843	9.0
	Patrol Area 5213	5,993	5,901	−1.5

Note: Patrol Area 5211 is located on the east side of Yonge Street from Queen to College; Patrol Area 5213 is located on the west side of Yonge Street from Queen to Dundas.
Source: Adapted from Joint Board (1998b, Exhibit 37).

Centre) were approximately triple those on the east side.

Squeegee Youth

By 1997 a small but increasing number of youths were engaged in squeegeeing – that is, washing car windows while drivers stopped at traffic lights. In mid-1998 police estimated that there were about 200 squeegee kids, some were full-time and some were part-time or seasonal, some were homeless and some were partially housed. City council struggled with two interpretations of the phenomenon. One was that these youths were a pest and a menace to ordinary people and should be forbidden to carry on their trade. The other was that the youths were displaying an entrepreneurial attitude that should be harnessed rather than crushed by regulation and that they should be urged to turn those talents to more mainstream pursuits.

Squeegee activity became an issue for several city bodies in 1997. The planning department was one of them, as were the city solicitor's office, community and neighbourhood services, and committees that dealt with emergency and protective services, finance, and policing. Since both the planning department and the Community and Neighbourhood Services Department had experience working with youth at risk, they were both drawn into the mayor's

Youth Employment Summit and the Youth Subcommittee of the Children's Action Committee (Toronto 1998d).

In June 1997 city council supported the second interpretation and its members believed that street kids could be dissuaded from squeegeeing by the offer of alternative employment. City council agreed to put money into a pilot project in which the city would be a partner with youth services agencies. However, by August 1997, the ward councillor for the Yonge-Dundas area tried to convince council to reverse that decision. Councillor Rae wanted tougher action. He said youths were "obstructing sidewalk and vehicular traffic, harassing and intimidating drivers and posing a threat to the safety of members of the public and their property" (Toronto 1997c). However, he said the police had advised him that they could not control the problem using existing provincial legislation. Instead, the councillor proposed that the city amend its own Municipal Code (chap. 313) concerning streets and sidewalks. He wanted the amendment to "prohibit any person from approaching an operator or other occupant of a motor vehicle while the vehicle is stopped at any intersection on any City street for the purpose of performing or offering to perform a service in connection with the vehicle, with the exception of emergency repairs requested by the operator or passenger of the vehicle, or otherwise soliciting the sale of goods and services to the operator or passenger of a vehicle" (ibid.). He wanted squeegee kids to be charged with illegal vending of a service. The prohibition discussion would later expand to include all panhandling (ibid.).

Regulating panhandling in public space is, appropriately, a complex matter. The city solicitor advised the municipal council that the province had not given the city authority to deal with panhandling as if it were a public nuisance under the *Municipal Act,* for example. Basing his advice on past court decisions, the city solicitor believed that the city would have to make a very strong case "that actual obstruction, inconvenience or a threat to public safety does occur as a result of the prohibited activity and great care must be taken in crafting the by-law so as to target activity which can be demonstrated to lead to these problems" (Toronto 1998b, 2). He noted that these prohibitions could contravene sections of the *Canadian Charter of Rights and Freedoms,* for instance, those that deal with the right to peaceful assembly, freedom of expression, equality rights, and the right to life, liberty, and security of the person. Furthermore, he advised that criminal law was a federal not a municipal matter and that offences that covered loitering, mischief, or intimidation already existed. If squeegeeing was a problem of that sort, the criminal law could be invoked.

The city solicitor proposed some complex options for council's consideration, but he essentially counselled against trying to use municipal powers to clear "the streets of persons on the basis of who they are (i.e., panhandlers or squeegee kids) as opposed to their participation in an activity which is within the jurisdiction of Council to regulate or prohibit" (Toronto 1998b, 3).[16] He preferred provincial legislative action. One route would be to ask the province to amend the *Provincial Offences Act*; another would be to require the province to bring in new legislation, and that is what happened. Mike Harris' Conservative government, then in power provincially, believed it was important for street people to be regulated and therefore made its proposed legislation, *The Safe Streets Act,* the centrepiece of the fall 1999 legislative session. When the legislation was passed, the attorney general solemnly announced: "Our government believes that all people in Ontario have the right to drive on the road, to walk down the street or to go to public places without being afraid or feeling intimidated" (Bourette 2000).

Meanwhile, the city considered a report to put another $500,000 into initiatives to assist street-involved youth to stabilize their lives through access to housing, medical attention, drug rehabilitation, education, and employment. The number of squeegee youth dropped to a very few.

Administrative Reorganization

The switch from the regeneration to the redevelopment plan occurred during a time of municipal reorganization. In the late spring of 1996, the mayor introduced a board of management regime that reduced the number of commissioners from ten to four; each super commissioner was responsible for several municipal functions. None of the existing commissioners (including the commissioner of planning) was allowed to compete for the new posts. The new administrative structure was strongly supported by the ward councillor for the Yonge-Dundas area. The planning commissioner who had developed the regeneration plan with his staff was consequently somewhat sidelined during the spring and summer that year (although he completed all the approvals for the regeneration plan) and he left the city's employ in September. Meanwhile, a lawyer who had previously served in various minor government agencies became the commissioner of services that included planning.

Conclusion

The proponents of the Yonge-Dundas project insisted that redevelopment was simply a continuation of the regeneration plan. But the data presented and the arguments made do not support this claim. Regeneration as it was publicly presented did not imply land flipping and land assembly via expropriation, despite being set within a community improvement project area that permits expropriation under certain conditions. Nor did the data and rationale underpinning the regeneration plan support the shift to redevelopment. The background planning rested on two modest studies, some loosely applicable information, and the savvy of city officials, the local ward councillor, and local property owners. The program director's view was that the city started to fix the area when it approved the development, and the ward councillor did not view the redevelopment as planning, because he believed planning was inadequate to the task of fixing the area.

Redevelopment took the form of a marketing plan devised for the purpose of importing a particular core area image that had been chosen because it was believed that it would work to clean up the Toronto intersection. But no study supported that belief. The proponents of redevelopment wanted a financially and politically feasible development strategy that would land a developer for Parcel A that would bring the right tenant in tow. This would bring the international core-redevelopment model to Toronto via Disney, Times Square, Leicester Square, and so on. All Toronto had to do was accept the merit of the model and provide the labour, enthusiasm, land, and capital. The project was standard international issue and bore many of the marks of the 42nd Street redevelopment in New York, but at a much smaller scale and faster pace. The Yonge-Dundas redevelopment was made possible in large part by the specific people involved: the program director, with his reputation and contacts both in Toronto and the development industry more widely; the ward councillor, who wanted nothing more than a snazzy cleanup of that part of his ward; and the mayor, who was a strong supporter of the ward councillor and led, with his help, an administrative reorganization that resulted in the planning department reporting to a lawyer. The redevelopment also rested on insider dealing, which was possible because the structures that governed development were murky at best and opaque at worst. The area was thus made ready for companies such as AMC and ClearChannel to fly in as tenants, occupy prime retail and commercial space, and profit with the help of some of Toronto's city-building establishment.

If that was the context for planning, what kind of planning was it? First, the substantive image of what a city core should look like and what it should contain led both the regeneration and redevelopment projects. This is contrary to the dominant model of planning theory that puts process before or above substantive matters. Second, planners' tools were needed by the proponents to legally carry out their project, so control over those tools was important; however, these tools could be wielded by others if the planners refused to use them. Third, municipal planners were placed in a box that constrained their actions to those that fit the new private-led redevelopment, which came to dominate thanks to a private-sector development consultant and politician who worked assiduously with certain capital interests on the street. Contemporary theories of planning, in which the planner is far more free to voluntarily select the style of planning that will ensue, have no answer for the question of what happens when a development goes ahead without the planner's support.

In the Yonge-Dundas case, the slide toward rationalization, or *Realrationalität,* was underway. Therefore, a lot of energy had to go into creating a justification for the scheme at the OMB hearing.

CHAPTER FIVE
Defending

The material in this chapter relies heavily on the documents that framed the hearing at the Ontario Municipal Board (OMB). These are the expert report of the program planner, who was the city's inside planner on the project for three and a half years; evidence submitted by the program director, who was a private consultant for the steering committee, or public-private partnership (PPP); the closing arguments of the counsels for the appellants (private-property owners) and respondent (the city); and the decision and report written by the members of the OMB who heard the case. Each document makes selective references to earlier reports, activities, and statements to build up the rationale for the position its writer is espousing. Key premises of the field of planning are that objectives and proposed solutions are well correlated, that they can be shown to be so using good reasons and reasoning, and that the objectives have been worked out in cooperation with the community that planners serve or, at least, in keeping with a defensible notion of the public interest. Consequently, the map of the city's reasoning in the Yonge-Dundas case is worth reconstructing.

Regardless of whether she or he appears before the public, council, committees, boards, or, as in this case, the OMB, a planner needs to be able to say why she or he holds a view. Indeed, one needs to be able to say why one's view is both right, in the sense of correct, and good, in the sense of ethical. Arguments can take many forms, but three types are commonly seen in planning cases. A justified argument is the form that planners should strive to provide because it pays attention to both evidence and ethics. On the one hand, justification is a process of rational argumentation by which support for claims is marshalled from data about relationships (fit, aesthetics, norms, causality, and associations) and from experience in related situations (e.g., if we do x, we know from past experience that y will likely result; or, if we are not legally permitted to do c, then the choices are a or b) to show why a proposed action is right, appropriate, proper, logical, and legal. On the other hand, a justified defence of a planning proposal also demands an argument based on ethical judgments – the claims that one's society assume have merit for resolving ethical conflicts (see Curtler 2004, especially chap. 4). Therefore, an argument may be justified if it meets two conditions: (1) evidence supports the claim and (2) the claim can be shown to be ethical. Ideally, this would characterize a right (correct) and good (ethical) argument.

The public interest usually stands in for the ethical portion of the justification for a public planning action and is a generalized notion that is rarely explicated in clear, straightforward detail. The public interest is what a city council wants to see achieved and believes it can argue successfully is in the best interests of its residents. In this case, redevelopment, which involved expropriation, was represented by the private-sector planner as being in the public interest. He promoted the idea to large and small businesses in the area; in turn, they promoted the idea to the ward councillor, who promoted the idea at city council, in the planning department, and in the rest of the city, especially through the media.

The second type of argument is explanation. Explanations should satisfy the first part of a justification by providing evidence to support a claim, but they have no claim on goodness in an ethical sense. For example, an argument could be made that car use in a city's core has gone down because parking rates have gone up by 35 percent. In principle, one could amass the data necessary to support the claim that one action satisfactorily explains the other. (Whether this is a good thing is not part of the issue in this case, although it could be if a planner wanted to make an argument for higher parking charges to improve core-area air quality, for instance.) The basic criterion underlying this kind of argument is that the data and the claim are related.

The third type of argument is rationalization. Rationalization does not provide verifiable evidence for claims or rest on a sound ethical basis. Curtler says that rationalization "is a weak form of argument in which a conclusion is held *despite the fact* that reasons do not support that conclusion" (2004, 131). The facts may support some other conclusion but not the one the proponent is making. For example, in this case, the argument for redevelopment was a rationalization. The reasons given did not support that conclusion. This is not to say that redevelopment was necessarily wrong but that proceeding with it was not supported by the reasons given.

In planning contexts, proposals and actions should be justified – that is, they should meet empirical, experiential, and ethical standards. The empirical basis can be derived from fields, such as economics, demography, or geography, that specialize in explanation or from experiences in fields such as urban design or architecture. The ethical basis requires the backing of the public interest, however it is deduced. Feeding data and ethics through a planning framework with its substantive tools can result in a justification for a planned intervention.

This chapter shows the city hovering between justification, explanation, and rationalization regarding this project. The project could be justified at the beginning, and up to about May 1996, when claims about what should be done were supported by experientially based evidence that was specific to the area, when the public interest informed the plans. The nature of that justification was conveyed in Chapter 3. The case presented at the OMB was primarily concerned with the later redevelopment project, and Appendix 8 describes the bylaws that were considered by the board. Proponents of redevelopment called upon the regeneration project and the support it had as a foil for their own initiative. This sleight-of-hand masked the need to justify the more elaborate redevelopment scheme. Once the new solution appeared, attention turned to figuring out the feasibility of implementing it and away from figuring out if this was the correct, justifiable solution to the problem. Although the new scheme was more interventionist and shared little with the initial plan, and although there had been no systematic analysis to measure the success of the regeneration plan, which was already underway, the new scheme was promoted simply as an extension of the plan for which public approval had been built. A double-fisted argument was made. As was shown in Chapter 4, the city argued that redevelopment was merely an extension of regeneration – all it needed was feasibility studies. In this chapter, I show the city defending a new vision, one that replaced regeneration with redevelopment. The evidence gathered for this research shows that the impetus for and organization of the redevelopment project was separate from the regeneration plan, although it took place in the same geographic space. It shows, too, that the objective of the redevelopment project was to create something that members of the Yonge Street Business and Residents Association (YSBRA) wanted.

The City's Planning Argument: Evidence

The city's Planning and Development Department naturally focused its expert testimony on the planning tools it had used, including the official plan, the *Planning, Municipal,* and *Expropriation Acts,* and more general knowledge about cities, land development, community organizations, and the Yonge-Dundas area. The public-private partnership between the city and YSBRA was not the respondent in the case. It fell to the city to take that role because the steering committee had no fiduciary status.

The planner's argument took this basic form:

- Yonge Street is in decline.
- Yonge Street is a top priority for the city.
- Something needs to be done before the situation worsens; the time is right; the city must seize the moment.
- Reinvestment incentives are not enough.
- A double-barrelled solution is needed: reinvestment plus redevelopment.
- Redevelopment would permit a new vision for the street.
- The new vision could be the one used in many other North American and European cities.
- The city has the tools to implement redevelopment and a new vision.

Yonge Street Is in Decline

At the hearing, the planner's evidence for decline was the same as he had previously used. One piece of evidence used throughout suggested that the stores were not properly maintained and were doing less well than stores in other parts of the city. This was weak evidence for several reasons:

- Experts did not agree on how well these businesses were doing.
- Rather than physical blight, social blight, which had not been used as a redevelopment justification under section 28 of the *Planning Act* in the past, was put forward as a justification.[1]
- The city already had the tools to charge businesses that were not acting legally under existing offences.
- The variety of stores on the street was not shown to differ from those in the Eaton Centre, even though the latter were directed to more affluent consumers.
- The decline of this part of the street had already been associated with the Eaton Centre drawing higher-end retail into the mall and with the deep recession of 1989-1994, not with the level of acumen or civic-mindedness of local retailers.

The fact that the people who used the street were poor, homeless, or criminally active was repeatedly introduced as evidence of the street's decline. While there was some truth to these statements, they were no more than "eyeball" estimates that did not take into account others who used the street and in what proportion.

Yonge Street Is a Top Priority for the City

According to the planner, "Yonge Street's condition is seen as a top priority for the entire City because of its economic and social importance to the health, image and sustainability of the City ... as the City's historic[al] main shopping street, [it] serves as a visual symbol of success or decline in the downtown"

(Joint Board 1998b, Exhibit 69, 4.2, 23). He then said that Yonge-Dundas was a project for the whole downtown core, that "it represent[ed] an 'act of faith' in the traditional commercial centre which [was] intended to provide economic and social stability," and that the project would compensate "for the southwestern shift in the centre of gravity which ha[d] been occurring downtown" (ibid., 8.0[a], 57).

The planner tried to appeal to emotions about a past era when the general area, but not the precise intersection, was a retail and entertainment hub of the city. No evidence was brought forward to show how the project would ease the shift in the centre of gravity. Indeed, there was no sign that the competition with the area southwest of Yonge-Dundas, the formally designated entertainment district, was taken into account.

Something Needs to Be Done before the Situation Worsens

Something needed to be done right away, the planner argued, "in advance of the full consequences of decline" (Joint Board 1998b, Exhibit 69, [1.4a], 7). The reinvestment strategy had not proved adequate to the task, in his view. Allusions to urgency were made frequently: certain decline was ahead, time was running out, the time was ripe for immediate action, it was important to catch this economic cycle, the city was losing ground compared to US cities, and so forth. Reinvestment-fed regeneration did not constitute the "something" that was needed because it would not jump-start a new image for the street. The time was right, but the time would not be right for long (ibid., 5.8, 40). The planning recommendation was to redevelop now.

Reinvestment Incentives Are Not Enough

In his expert report, the planner repeatedly stressed the need for "'significant strategic change' to break the pattern of dysfunction" (Joint Board 1998b, Exhibit 69, 7[f]; cf. ibid., Exhibit 53, 7[2.0], para. 1). He called for a strategy of "reinvestment incentives *and* substantial change through municipal intervention" (ibid., Exhibit 69, 7[f], 26), which would achieve the new vision. A strategy of reinvestment incentives would be inadequate on its own, he argued. He said that as planning proceeded through 1996, "the reliance on private investment through the proposed 'reinvestment incentives' was increasingly considered a limited, 'single track' solution especially given the constraints on the street and lack of privately initiated redevelopment in the past" (ibid., 28). His report goes on to describe the stage that thinking had reached by February 1997 when

> the Regeneration Program showed that the magnitude of renewal that is required for real improvement to the street and the barriers to renewal which exist,

necessitate a redevelopment project as a "significant strategic change," essentially as an implementation vehicle which will better ensure that the reinvestment incentives will be taken advantage of by others on the street. This finding demonstrated a linkage between the reinvestment incentive approach and the redevelopment project. This linkage is that without the redevelopment project as a catalyst, the incentives would not achieve any substantial change and, indeed, may exacerbate speculation. Thus, it has been argued that should the Redevelopment Project not proceed, the reinvestment incentives approach should be rethought as a means to achieving renewal on their own. (ibid., 4.5, 28, my emphasis)

To announce in February 1997 that redevelopment was needed because regeneration was not working was premature. It had been less than a year since increased floor coverage and height had been approved as of right; the city was only about a year out of recession and was still busy finalizing its plans for the area. Why would reinvestment have begun by landowners who knew they were on the outside of the game? There is no evidence to suggest that the strategies already employed were not working and would not work.

The planner also argued that reinvestment alone would not bring about substantial change and might make speculation worse. Although speculation was offered as a reason why redevelopment with expropriation should proceed, information to substantiate the potential for speculation was not expanded upon in the hearing documents. In the view of the program director, the speculators were the small-property owners who, instead of participating in redevelopment on their own, were waiting for windfall profits.

A Double-Barrelled Solution Is Needed

The planner listed elements of the problem and showed why mere reinvestment would not solve it. It was a long list of nine items (and speculation was not among them). Every item did not entail redevelopment: some could have been fixed under the reinvestment incentives program (e.g., lack of community leadership and participation or lack of investment in appearance). Four are examined here.

Concentration of Social Blight

This is the terminology used in the report. This language comes closer than any other used thus far by the planners to say in print what the project's long-stated redevelopment goal had only implied: that redevelopment was intended to discourage the presence of unwanted people in the area. The elected ward councillor used similar language.

To make this point, the planner and the city's legal counsel divided the labour. The planner dealt primarily with the poor and homeless; the lawyer dealt with criminals. Nonetheless, both skated around the issue of who, exactly, they were describing and which of their activities constituted barriers to fixing the street. The number of homeless people, panhandlers, drug users, and pushers in the area was not provided; a picture of who used the area for what purposes was not drawn.

The issue of social blight was presented as follows:

> While it is perhaps unavoidable that Yonge Street as the City's main street attracts some of the marginalized and socially and economically disadvantaged individuals in society, especially given the street's current condition, the degree of vagrancy, loitering, panhandling and homelessness is quite pronounced on Yonge Street and particularly in the vicinity of Yonge and Dundas. From a planning point of view, this concentration at the City's main intersection is not mitigated by countervailing forces. One of the objectives of renewing any street is to achieve a better balance of activity, both within the public realm and within private development. A concentration of persons with similar economic or social problems in one area (ghettoization) is not helpful to the individuals affected nor is it supportive of other efforts to attract reinvestment to the area and is especially damaging given the prominence and visibility of the location – downtown Toronto's main shopping street and prime tourist destination. (Joint Board 1998b, Exhibit 69, 5.6, 37-38)

This statement is an elaborate explanation of the long-held goal of increasing the range and number of residents and visitors who use the area. The next paragraph referred to how this view of the city was to be interpreted through the community improvement program in the *Planning Act*. People in poverty were the topic of the first paragraph, while criminality was the topic of the one that followed. Panhandling was placed in a list of criminal activities, even though it is not a criminal activity: "In terms of the relative importance of social problems such as the concentration of criminal activity that persists at Yonge and Dundas, they cannot be rated lower than the problems identified such as unsuitable building forms. Accordingly, the reference in Section 28(1) describing the Community Improvement Project Area as areas in need of improvement for '*any other reason*' is read to include vandalism, theft and drug dealing and panhandling as well as matters of building form, strategic location and other matters set out in this Report" (ibid., 5.6, 38, my emphasis). The OMB's interpretation of the phrase "any other reason" would be central to the city succeeding in its case.

The planner then put forward the well-known trickle-down economic theory as a way for the board to contextualize the city's use of redevelopment to solve social blight: "Planning reports recommending the Yonge Dundas Redevelopment Project have never maintained that the project is a panacea for all the social ills which confront this street. However, a strong downtown is a critical component of continued growth and social stability. While the project itself is not held out as a direct solution, it is expected to make a substantial contribution to assessment growth which is a key ingredient in enabling the city to provide solutions for those in need" (Joint Board 1998b, Exhibit 69, 5.6, 38).[2]

The next paragraph presents arguments about security and the potential to enhance it via public-private initiatives, including the Yonge-Dundas redevelopment:

> The Redevelopment Project is likely to reduce opportunities for crime because the concentration of people who take advantage of poor situations will be diminished. Casual participation in crime which is concentrated at Yonge and Dundas will be less likely and not as easy to commit given the physical design improvements which are included in the project. The project, given its support by the Yonge Street Business and Residents Association, should increase opportunities for partnerships in security and safety. The establishment of a Business Improvement Area, which the YSBRA is now organizing, will confirm and entrench local management of the street. Based on initiatives undertaken by other BIAs in the City, such as the Bloor Yorkville and Bloor West Village BIAs, the marketing, promotion and enhancement programs will be of assistance. The YSBRA has already begun outreach to social service providers on Yonge Street and it is expected that this will continue to the benefit of all concerned. The YSBRA has also strengthened communications with the Toronto Police Service and coordinated efforts to address problems needing police support. (Joint Board 1998b, Exhibit 69, 5.6, 38)

Later in the hearing, OMB members applauded YSBRA's involvement in security and went so far as to recommend that YSBRA participate in managing the security of the public square in the manner of Bryant Park in New York.[3]

The report then discussed homelessness, which is considered a different sort of problem confronting the street, one that is only partly a planning responsibility:

> Homelessness is a more problematic issue which has both macro and micro level symptoms and consequences. At a micro level, improvements to the

arrangement of buildings at Yonge and Dundas and better management of the street will reduce opportunities for sleeping in the street. At a more macro level, the community through both YSBRA and TEDRA have been working with social agencies to establish relationships and networks for solving community issues. Co-ordinated effort and community participation provide better results in getting the homeless into shelters and advocating for more long term housing solutions which meet people's needs. (Joint Board 1998b, Exhibit 69, 5.6, 38-39)

The report then described the solution colloquially and, perhaps inadvertently, in ways that seem to match a regeneration strategy more than a redevelopment one: "The application of the 'broken window' theory is a way of viewing community improvement on Yonge Street. People tend to feel safer, stay later or longer and shops tend to reinvest more when perception of safety increases. So-called 'quality of life' crimes which generate negative perceptions and fear and an increased perception of crime have not assisted Yonge Street in attracting new tenants and broadening the merchandise and customer mix" (Joint Board 1998b, Exhibit 69, 5.6, 39). Nothing in the paragraph suggests redevelopment as a solution.

In the final paragraph of the section, redevelopment was invoked as a step toward improving Toronto's East Downtown. Redevelopment might have been a solution, but the information provided at the hearing and throughout the report and other documents does not support the planner's argument. Indeed, one could argue that "cleaning up Yonge" would chase these problems into that area and concentrate them even more: "The East Downtown's recent experience with the drug trade and increase in violence, noise, littering, weapons problems and vandalism has begun to characterize the neighbourhood. Both the police and the community believe that improving the East Downtown is in part dependent on improvements to Yonge Street, its western edge" (Joint Board 1998b, Exhibit 69, 5.6, 39).

Whether the true intention after March 1996 was to seriously engage with the problems of East Downtown is difficult to say. Throughout 1994 and 1995, the intention seemed to be there; afterward, it was less likely, which raises the question: Was fixing the western edge a way to ensure that urban decay east of Yonge stopped migrating west, as the program director said (Joint Board 1998e, 25), or was it a way to bolster Yonge Street so it could then turn eastward to help its neighbour, as the program planner suggested? With regard to the latter half of the question, nowhere does there seem to be any analysis of what that help might look like; therefore, there is no hint as to whether it is realistic to assume that that is what the planners would deliver. As is mentioned earlier and shown in an aerial photo (see Figure 5.1), the built form

5.1 Looking south down Yonge Street to Lake Ontario, c. 1997. The photo illustrates the contrasting built form on either side of Yonge. Structures on the east side tend to be low-rise and relatively few properties have been assembled into single development parcels. On the west side, there has been considerable land assembly and large footprint, high-rise construction in recent decades. The location of the proposed public square is highlighted. | Joint Board 1998b, Exhibit 42, 16.

and land uses on the east and west side of Yonge Street are nothing if not dramatically different.

Unsuitability of Buildings and Faulty Arrangement
The planner argued that the proposed redevelopment was needed to obtain suitable spaces for new entertainment-plus-retail types of businesses. In fact, the redevelopment, as proposed, would provide only one such structure and it would require land assembly, either private or municipal. The city wished to undertake the land assembly itself to ensure that it would be done immediately to meet market and social blight pressures. This argument had potential only from the point of view of timing. Correcting social blight through urban renewal could not be defended honestly if proper evidence was brought forward. Furthermore, the city's planner acknowledged under crossexamination that the new 4.0 times coverage was adequate to encourage private land

assembly. Nonetheless, the appellants could not overturn this argument during the hearing, although they did try to propose alternative development schemes and show why putting thirty cinemas at the location was unrealistic. But these arguments did not defeat the basic point that, without land assembly, there was no potential to build *this* type of structure in *this* area.

The desire to have an urban entertainment centre (UEC) like everyone else was, however, a case of the tail wagging the dog. The UEC was expected to revitalize the street. The evidence did not actually show that a UEC would lead to wondrous economy boosting results. Horton Plaza in San Diego was referred to as an example at one point, but it is more like an open-air Eaton Centre than a UEC. The New York 42nd Street project was not a UEC, and Chicago's redevelopment was not centred on a UEC. Both redevelopments were cited as similar in spirit to what was being proposed in Toronto. New York and Chicago had once had scary downtown areas; they now had shoppertainment, and their cores were healed.

On the other hand, the city had just increased development envelopes to 4.0 times coverage with increased commercial capacity as of right and the option to ask for more density if the developer was willing to make a deal with the city by compensating it with the provision of some public good. The hearing spent considerable time deciding whether this new built-form allocation was adequate for the new kind of retailing and eatertainment, and it concluded that it was. Through expert witnesses, both the appellants and the respondent agreed that this was adequate. There was still no convincing evidence in support of the proposed redevelopment. It is well within the realm of possibility that a private land assembly could have been encouraged with the new planning amendments in place.

A Discouraging Response from Property Owners
The planner argued that the city had to act because landowners were not acting. He noted, "Through several business cycles, no private redevelopment applications have been filed with the city, no effective land assembly has taken place, no substantial improvements in the merchandise and tenant mix of existing stores has taken place and no existing land owners, affected by the project, appear to have provided significant tenant inducements to upgrade buildings" (Joint Board 1998b, Exhibit 69, 4.7, 30).

The planner left out a few details when he argued in this manner for city-led redevelopment at Yonge-Dundas. He did not mention that there had been a private redevelopment application in the works since 1992 (350 Yonge Street, which was resolved in 1998). Indeed, analysis of the details concerning this case suggests that the city itself was trying to figure out which way to push Yonge Street and had reached a conclusion only after it completed the urban design study in March 1994 and digested it in 1995.[4] The first sign of a strong position from the city on what it would or would not accede to came toward the end of 1995. The city's stance followed decades of annoyance expressed by the development industry. The development industry had been prepared to put up high-rises anywhere and everywhere, including at the corner of Yonge and Dundas, but the city's 1976 Central Area Plan had dropped the height limit from 12.0 to 2.0 times coverage. The industry did not think it would be worth its while to build at such a low height in that location. The industry was still trying to break the city's determination on this issue. As it happened, Eaton's intervened. This was a clear case in which the interests of capital were fragmented. The city had to deal with fights among private interests as it tried to keep an eye on the public interest. The city's response was reasonable but slow.

But the city could not have it both ways. This point was made by the counsel for the appellants. If the city thought it was appropriate to take its time to figure out what it believed would be good strategy for Yonge Street, it could not then turn around and complain that development applications had not been filling planners' in-boxes while the city deliberated.

The planner also compared the lack of investment in the Yonge-Dundas area with the enthusiastic response by developers in the Kings, two large parcels of land in south central Toronto that were undergoing redevelopment. However, the Kings and Yonge Street were hardly comparable. The former was largely abandoned employment space, while the latter was built and functioning space. The former attracted international capital for large, mixed developments, while the latter was almost entirely in the hands of domestic development capital and geared toward retail, at the city's insistence.

Finally, although the program planner's expert report was undated, it was written, at the latest, in early February 1998. The new zoning regulations had been adopted by city council in mid-1996. The deep five-year recession, during which Toronto's development industry had been decimated, had just ended. The reinvestment incentives program had been underway for no more than two years, and the facade program was demonstrably successful. Special policing had had a four-month run, and the city and the police claimed it was successful. Merchants were said to be happy with the direction in which things were moving, in part because the energy of the street had not diminished (so the program director argued, although he did not provide evidence), and a bonusing scheme for redevelopment had been introduced. It was therefore too early to argue from evidence that property owners could not meet the challenge of renewing the street.

The problem with the timing was that the city was involved in a partnership with the private sector, money had been spent, the flames of anticipation had been fanned, and only one city councillor was paying close attention, one whose agenda was clear. There seemed to be no way to stand still or turn back.

Overcrowding and a Lack of Public Amenities

The city always maintained that the square and UEC formed a redevelopment package. Its position was that the square was an inalienable part of the project: the project had to have the square, and the square should not be built without the rest of the project. Indeed, the link between the two helped fuel speculation that Metropolis' developer had demanded the square, even though it had not.

Why were the square and the project linked? The idea of a square with a parking lot beneath it was a brilliant move on the part of the planners in several ways. Nobody argues against new public squares, and everybody knows that parking is a headache that demands constant attention. City councillors know this better than anyone. Because parking space would be provided beneath the square, the city could say to future redevelopers of surrounding sites that they would not have to contribute a percentage of their property toward public space and that they could offset parking demands by contributing to the city in some other way. This was a major incentive for owners to redevelop existing properties, an incentive that had not, at the time of the hearing, had the opportunity to work its way into the real estate plans of area property owners.

However, the advantage to private developers was not a basis for the city's stated support of the square. This benefit was noted in one paragraph of the report that was buried under other details (Joint Board 1998b, Exhibit 69, 4.6[a], 28-29). It was a fine investment incentive. Is that the reason it was buried? The incentive encouraged regeneration-scale investment; it did not particularly support redevelopment. In fact, it made it all the more necessary for the city to show why it would not build the square unless the rest of the redevelopment went ahead. The planner presented the city's build-as-a-package position this way: "Creating a square only and, in isolation of other improvements, doesn't address the need for new retail space. New retail space without the square does little to significantly change the environment of the street and the sense of place nor does it address the broader array of concerns" (ibid., 7.2, 48). One item in that array was social blight, specifically the potential to exacerbate it if only the square was built. Legal counsel for the city dealt with that issue.

Instead of making this rich incentive package a highlight of the rationale, the planner's arguments in favour of the square were as follows: the official plan allowed for it, the population of the area was increasing, the sidewalks were crowded, and it would help the Dundas Street East problem (see Joint Board 1998b, Exhibit 69, 58-59 for eight reasons the square was said to be a good idea).

The square was indeed allowed for in the official plan, in the sense that the whole central core of Toronto (not this intersection specifically) was said to be deficient in park space. Furthermore, "portions of the East Downtown bordering Yonge and Dundas have areas which are farther than 200 metres from a local or district park" (Joint Board 1998b, Exhibit 69, 5.3, 36). Elsewhere, the planner introduced population figures for Ward 24 of the new City of Toronto and figures for expected population increases based on building applications filed between 1990 and 1997. The conservative growth estimate was 16,000 people (ibid., 3.2.2, 15). At least two things were odd. First, the square was not conceptualized as a park or, even, a local space. Yet the planner said that, for the East Downtown, "the open space serves a dual purpose as a local amenity for residents and workers" (ibid., 7.2, 48). Second, population figures for one scale were being used to support a claim made about a situation at a different scale. This is called an ecological fallacy.

The planner also argued that the sidewalks were crowded. This was a new argument. It is interesting that it was used after the amalgamation, when the city had at last gained control over sidewalks and streets from the defunct metropolitan government. It could now widen the sidewalks, if it wished, to narrow Yonge Street, a strategy it had used to much acclaim on St. George Street, just a kilometre west of Yonge. How crowded the sidewalks were is not revealed. In the planner's expert witness statement, new information showed that a "pedestrian demand study" was completed before the city changed its regulations regarding the use of A-frame signs on the street. This is how the study described pedestrian congestion: "Yonge Street itself has narrow sidewalks and offers little relief from pedestrian congestion. The City has taken initial steps to maximize sidewalk availability by prohibiting marketing areas in front of retail premises on Yonge Street in order to preserve the 3.66 metre (12 foot) width of the sidewalk for pedestrians. A review of pedestrian demand was undertaken prior to this prohibition in 1996 and there was found to be consistently heavy pedestrian use and occasional surges in demand" (Joint Board 1998b, Exhibit 69, 5.3, 36).

A pedestrian count was done for the city by a consulting firm in October 1997 – that is, after the redevelopment plan, with all its elements, had been presented to and adopted by city council. This study was not mentioned in the expert report, though it was part of the evidence adduced. The street was said to lack "pedestrian amenity which would complement and stimulate private retail reinvestment" (Joint Board 1998b, Exhibit 69, 5.3, 36), whereas the square would increase "the amount of retail frontage now visually exposed to Yonge Street from 50 metres to 225 metres, considerably improving the opportunity to create new retail and entertainment premises which are street-related; this would in turn, strengthen retail continuity and the presence of the Street" (ibid., 8.0[c], 59).

Finally, the planner argued that the square would offer "a tangible step in bringing some additional investment along the Street to the east of Yonge" (Joint Board 1998b, Exhibit 69, 5.9, 41). Dundas, he said, was blocked from the view of shoppers on Yonge by the Yonge Street stores and, he continued, "there are no inviting and animating uses immediately east of Yonge which would begin to draw pedestrians eastward" (ibid., 41). As the history of Dundas Street in Chapter 2 showed, his statement was quite accurate, and, indeed, there never had been an eastward draw at this junction. He argued that the square would open up Dundas Street East by "establishing visual and physical linkage from Yonge Street and vice-versa," making a change for the East Downtown from isolation to connection (ibid., 8.0[c], 59).

Redevelopment Would Permit a New Vision for the Street

Having presented the benefits of a double-barrelled strategy of reinvestment incentives and redevelopment, the planner argued that the strategy could lead to a new vision for the area. In particular, the square and new retail would create a critical mass that would give a concrete form to this new vision. Indeed, in his view, the new public space was not merely a response "to the planning objective of fundamentally altering the context of Yonge Street," it also added "definition to the intersection to create a 'sense of place'" and "permitted the reimagining of the Yonge and Dundas intersection which now resemble[d] no particular place and could be any intersection in the city." But, he continued, it would not be just any space: "The City and community see it as a special place and special location." The square would be an appropriate way to symbolize this status. Yonge and Dundas would "become a 'big city' central place" (Joint Board 1998b, Exhibit 69, 8.0[c], 59).

From this justification one can sense the excitement, perhaps even passion, of this planner who wanted the area to become special in an international style. On the other hand, from the way he describes the area, one is left wondering what the sense of place would be. He refers to "the planning objective of fundamentally altering the context of Yonge Street." "Context" means surroundings, not the place itself but the milieu within which something sits. Fundamentally altering context is not what this report was about. Also, it had been asserted in the earlier regeneration report that fundamentally altering the street was *not* the objective: cleaning it up while maintaining its basic characteristics was. Previous reports had also asserted that this stretch of Yonge was unique; in contrast, the planner argued that it resembled "no particular place and could be any intersection in the city." The city was contradicting its earlier arguments in favour of regeneration and claiming that redevelopment was simply a continuation of the regeneration plan. The appellants' counsel tried to highlight these contradictions but was unable to do so in a manner sufficient to slow down the energy that the respondents had built for an international-style solution for an ailing city core.

The New Vision Could Be the One Used in Many North American and European Cities

According to the planner, there was a ready solution that had been tried and had succeeded elsewhere: a UEC and public square managed by a public-private organization in the interests of facilitating shopping and entertainment experiences. With this argument, the intersection, as a symbolic place, was transformed from the tacky but unique heart of the city to the generic heart of the city – a copycat heart.

The City Has the Tools to Implement Redevelopment and a New Vision

The planner argued that the city had all the tools needed to fix the street. And just as importantly it had a vision as a guide. The tools, the grounds for their use, the objectives to be achieved, and the failure of attempts to acquire properties through purchase as allowed for in section 30 of the *Expropriation Act* – all these favoured the city's position.

Argument Made by the Steering Committee's Program Director

For the program director, the expert consultant who developed the vision, the Yonge-Dundas redevelopment was a "unique" opportunity. The following quotation provides a taste of his use of language and imagery and conveys what he, as a consulting planner, wanted to do to reinvigorate this part of Yonge:

> The project presents a unique opportunity to attract to this publicly-important location a critical mass of highly desirable retail and entertainment operations which will effectively re-establish the street as a major destination for a broader range of citizens and visitors. The uniqueness of the opportunity stems from a variety of interrelated factors: "The on-going evolution of the retail and entertainment business in major cities has produced a new format and scale of product – the flagship or super-store/category-killer/megaplex (e.g. Chapters, Indigo, HMV, Niketown, Sporting Life, Crate and Barrel, Virgin Megastore, All-Star Cafe, Dave and Busters) which offer the consumer the 'biggest and best'

of the category in a single location and in a spectacular environment. These products tend to function as destination uses and do not need the critical mass of a shopping mall to successfully operate their businesses. Therefore they tend to be developed as free-standing structures and thereby are capable of being street-related although this opportunity is often lost particularly in suburban settings." A parallel trend is the evolution of the Urban Entertainment Centre. Existing entertainment districts such as Times Square are being dramatically revitalised, while in other places new entertainment districts, such as the Irvine Spectrum or Toronto's Entertainment District, are coming into being. These districts are growing to accommodate the increasing tendency of people to seek opportunities for an out-of-home multi-faceted recreational experience which includes entertainment such as movies, theatre, dining in an interesting restaurant, and browsing for small-scale, "impulse" purchases such as books, CD's, sports equipment, apparel, or gifts. Moreover, the essential characteristic of this experience is that it happens in a pedestrian mode – it is an urban phenomenon whether located in a suburban or downtown centre. (Joint Board 1998k, 7; for quotes, see Joint Board 1998b, Exhibit 55A)

In the course of his statement, the program director named three criteria for a successful UEC; in the process, he reduced urban redevelopment to a UEC. It is worth emphasizing that a UEC is a business venture that seeks to achieve some range of marketing and urban revitalization goals. A successful business venture is not the same as successful urban redevelopment, although there will be some overlap. Urban redevelopment was the presumed subject of the OMB hearing, but upon reading the proponent's documents and the OMB's decision, it is evident that it was repeatedly reduced to UECs and their attendant needs. For example, the program director said that the criteria for a successful UEC are as follows, as reported with approval by the OMB:

> The first is the need of a major cineplex or grouping of cinemas to act as an anchor. Another alternative is a very large concentration of live theatre, as, in his New York experience, the combination of a megaplex cinema and live theatre increases the anchor effect.[5] The second is the choice of good quality theme restaurants that act as entertainment in themselves, labelled "eatertainment" in the new industry jargon. Examples are Planet Hollywood, Celebrity Sports restaurants and bars, and the Hard Rock Cafe. The third is the creation of a unique "sense of place" through public space and memorable architecture. The "place" must be pedestrian friendly but active. The public square must act as a draw and not break the rhythm of the retail environment.[6] (Joint Board 1998k, 28-29)

The program director said that the potential to provide this kick-start at Yonge and Dundas already existed, but timing was everything. The OMB stated:

> While the market is ripe for such a facility in Downtown Toronto, such market [sic] is not infinite. It is critical that the UEC be located at Yonge/Dundas which will serve to regenerate the area and if not captured here, now, it will go somewhere else and take the associated retail opportunities with it. Flowing from that will be the further arrest of the recovery of Yonge Street. It was his view that as long as the project can be brought into being as soon as possible, and at a price that is viable, it will be an assured success. It was also his opinion that it was critical that it be developed in this business cycle. [The program director's] opinion was that "this is Yonge Street's opportunity to seize the moment." (Joint Board 1998k, 28)

Comments about the City's Planning Argument

This was a complex case for the city's planner to defend. From the point of view of a planning department that wanted its project to proceed, the approach taken was good and ultimately successful. What it says about planning – both in practice and in theory – is another matter.

As has been discussed, the written evidence in support of the argument was broad and multifaceted, but wafer-thin throughout. Sorting out whether evidence actually existed for claims and whether this evidence was solid was a huge task. The appellants had an uphill battle. One unsubstantiated or irrelevant or semirelated bit of information was piled on another, creating the impression that if all of that information and all of that effort had been put into the case, there must be some truth to it, even if it seemed a bit fuzzy.

Was the argument a justification in the sense that it met both empirical and ethical demands? The city did present solid pieces of evidence, and it had the capacity to exert its will. This is not in doubt. But did it have the evidence to support redevelopment as a solution? And was it ethical to expropriate one owner's lands to turn them over to another private owner in this circumstance? Not without much better evidence than was presented to this point in the hearing. The city's task was to demonstrate that the public interest overwhelms these shortcomings.

The Appellants' Legal Arguments That the Project Was Not Justified

Owners of nine of the ten Yonge Street properties that were singled out for expropriation challenged the city's intention. Several legal firms were involved. One firm, however, represented the interests of several owners. The arguments presented for that group form the basis of this discussion. The firm is called here "the counsel for the appellants," even if it did not represent all appellants or all of their complaints.

The appellants claimed that expropriation was unsound and unfair for the following reasons:

- The city hindered the development of the strip in the past.
- The city was now rewriting history to make its case for taking these beleaguered properties just as conditions were improving.
- The city's plans would likely fail.
- The street was beginning to cure itself.

The appellants said their own redevelopment plans would have begun with private assembly by the majority of current landowners (Joint Board 1998b, Exhibit 206). While the schemes they presented at the OMB hearing were of some interest to the members who heard the case, they were problematic as replacements for the city's scheme because they did not respect the city's official plan in several ways. For example, they did not meet the land use or height requirements. If the city chose to change the zoning bylaw to accommodate the appellants' proposed buildings, redevelopment was thought to be unlikely within the economic cycle because real estate values were expected to level off or fall. The appellants primarily proposed office buildings. These would empty at night, detracting from life on the street. The vice-president of the Eaton Centre said he wanted buildings that did not empty out at night, and that it was "of 'absolute importance' to have an open area at Yonge and Dundas" to draw the action now centred around his main entrance eastward across the street (Joint Board 1998h, 1-2; also see Joint Board 1998g, Tab 5, 4). In addition, these alternatives to the city's plans did not create "a sense of place" or "arrival" that were as commanding as the city's vision. The appellants' expert planning witness conceded this point under crossexamination (ibid., 3).

The City Hindered the Development of the Strip in the Past

The appellants' counsel, citing the program director, argued that the city had not helped the strip even though the city was now prepared to argue it was "'in decline,' 'dilapidated,' 'seedy' retail activity which perpetuated the 'poisoned atmosphere' since 1975" (Joint Board 1998d, 4[3]).

The appellants' lawyer argued that the conditions at Yonge and Dundas were of the city's own making. The evidence he presented to support this claim was that the city, beginning with the 1976 official plan, had imposed restrictive planning policies on the strip. He cited a 1986 consultant's report prepared for the city that said that the city had "avoided the forces of change primarily by prohibiting them" (Joint Board 1998d, 3[2][a], citing Joint Board 1998b, Exhibit 106, 30) and that Yonge Street needed the city to give it development potential so that rehabilitation of the current structures would be encouraged.

One of the appellants' witnesses, an expert in economic research, testified that policies and programs imposed by the city precluded any major redevelopment or intensification on lower Yonge Street:

> Given that the Eaton Centre, on the west side of Yonge Street was achieving the highest rates of sales and rents of any retail facility in Canada, it follows that the east side of Yonge Street with its depreciated building structures would come under strong redevelopment pressure ... In our opinion, the east side of Yonge Street below Dundas Street, and the sector of Yonge Street north of Dundas Street, would also have been redeveloped for intensive retail and office use during the 1980's, but was prevented from doing so by deliberate policies implemented by the City of Toronto. (Joint Board 1998b, Exhibit 207A, 7)

The witness provided this explanation for the decline. First, development density had been severely reduced – from a floor space index of 12.0 to 2.0 – in the Central Area Plan of 1976. Second, the zoning created an illogical geography of building rights that was inimical to economically practical development. Third, buildings deemed to be of historic value on the east side of the street were taken directly into public ownership and subjected to municipally led redevelopment that has been unsatisfactory (Joint Board 1998b, Exhibit 207A, 16-17).

The witness continued to develop his explanation for why redevelopment on the east side had been such a problem and returned to the issue of the influence of Eaton's:

> The second of these policies [zoning] requires some further explanation ... The planning policies in place for the Eaton Centre at the outset of that development, permitting the functioning of the economic investment flows, thus permitted the extremely economically successful investment experience of the Eaton Centre project ... The restrictive planning policies developed subsequently assured that the hugely successful experience could not be repeated on the east side of ... Yonge Street as the market would otherwise have encouraged. (Joint Board 1998b, Exhibit 207A, 17)

Elsewhere, he made the point that it was not so much the Eaton Centre but rather subsequent policies that had prohibited "two-sided" retail – that is, retail on two sides of the street. Most of the shopping centre on the west side of Yonge Street was equivalent to a four-block solid wall. The facade renovation the Eaton Centre was planning would go some way to rectifying that problem.

An important planning lesson was being learned in this case. The economic research witness concluded his written evidence this way: "It is our opinion that the planning restrictions which have been in place for the past two decades, combined with the City's direct actions in the lower part of the block have been responsible for putting the potential of the lands 'in limbo' so to speak, and preventing rational feasible development from taking place" (Joint Board 1998b, Exhibit 207A, 18). The appellants' counsel said the city had even recognized in its early 1996 planning report that its policies had been a hindrance: the report showed that 50 percent of the buildings were over allowable density (Joint Board 1998b, Exhibit 49A, Tab C). As well, both the program planner and the program director said that the low-density, mixed-use zoning designation was inappropriate (Joint Board 1998d, 3[2][f][g]).

The City Was Now Rewriting History to Make Its Case

According to the appellants' counsel, the city was claiming a decade-long decline of the properties on the strip to justify their expropriation. The city was attempting to show that there was "blight" so that it could trigger public-sector involvement in redevelopment. In the counsel's view there was no evidence that would warrant public-sector involvement via section 28 of the *Planning Act* (Joint Board 1998d, 5[5]). Indeed, he held that, until June 1996, there had been no mention of blight, dilapidation, or serious decline; no alarm bells had been sounded; and no call had been made for a huge redevelopment or public square (ibid., 11[d]). He supported his position with reference to planning reports from 1993 to 1996. Indeed, research for this book substantiates the key point made by the appellants' counsel. He argued that in the February 1996 report the planners had opined that "to try to plan a new direction for Yonge Street would seem antithetical to its very nature as Yonge Street will continue to gradually change on its own as it has over the past decades. The City can, however, facilitate change and be responsive to the market by deregulating planning controls" (ibid.).

Counsel said that as soon as YSBRA's project came along, an expropriation team was put together (Joint Board 1998d, 11[2]). His view was that the expropriation team knew it could not use the *Municipal Act* (section 191), because its stipulations prohibited selling the lands to a private developer (ibid., 12[e]). On the other hand, redevelopment under section 28 of the *Planning Act* would allow the city to sell or lease the acquired land to other users. However, there was one condition: the city would have to show that the area was blighted. Consequently, the city and others had to construct a history for the area to justify urban renewal. Counsel called this "backfilling the case" (ibid., 12[2][e] and 12[3]). After citing some evidence for this "rewriting of history," counsel for the appellants acknowledged this much: "There is no question that this section of Yonge Street looks tired today, having weathered a bruising retail depression over the past 9 years. There is no question, however, that there are absolutely no signs of dilapidation, blight or serious deterioration in this section of the Street" (ibid., 13[4]).

The next part of counsel's argument came from his verbal questioning of the program planner. On the matter of blight, the latter said that his written report referred to "social blight" and made reference to social and criminal problems in the area. Counsel for the appellants apparently questioned the program planner extensively on this issue to illustrate that the city had not identified physical blight anywhere and to lead to the conclusion that expropriation under section 28 of the *Planning Act* would be unfounded.

The appellants' lawyer fixed on blight as a "physical manifestation," as it was interpreted under the earlier urban renewal legislation. But this line of argument took him straight into the proponent's trap. The lawyer for the city would show that *social blight* could be used as a reason to invoke expropriation.

The City's Plans Would Likely Fail

The appellants raised several challenges to the city's redevelopment plans. Three are considered here. The first drew attention to the disjunction between the goal and the tool to be used to achieve it. The goal to "substantially increase the proportion and range of the residents of Greater Toronto and visitors who use downtown Yonge Street" could not be achieved using cinemas, said the appellants. They presented the following pieces of evidence (Joint Board 1998d, 23[B][3]) to support their argument:

- Almost half of movie goers are between the ages of 12 and 29, and in urban areas only 14 percent are in family groups, which raises the question of whether cinemas respond to the objective in any real way.
- The demographics will be influenced by the retail mix, which is still unknown.
- Movie distributors will largely determine which films AMC can show.[7]
- The market draw will be ten miles at best, that is, from within the new city of Toronto.

These empirically verifiable statements seem logical at first glance. In combination they at least raise doubts about the link between the long-stated goal of the project and the likelihood of achieving it. However, the OMB rejected these points in favour of others put forward by witnesses for the proponents.

The second aspect of the plans that appellants challenged was expropriation. They argued that it would distort the operations of the market by bringing thirty new screens onto the market at once. The appellants' lawyer tried to build a picture of a misguided city using public monies to help overbuild cinemas that in turn would lead to market distortion (Joint Board 1998d, 29[3]). His efforts were to no avail in this circumstance because the city's lawyer argued that, when it comes to OMB decisions and market effects, the "case law states that the Board will not interfere with the marketplace" (Joint Board 1998e, 36); that is, its decisions should deal with the development issues. By contrast, the appellants' lawyer did not cite any case law on his point.

The third rationale that counsel for the appellants presented for why the city's plans would not work was that the square was not needed:

- The developer, PenEquity, had not demanded it (Joint Board 1998d, 27[E][2]).
- If the development on the northeast corner did not proceed but the square did, the city would have a problem that it itself had identified (ibid., 27[E][4]).
- The retail linearity of the east side of Yonge would be interrupted (Joint Board 1998d, 28[E][7]).[8]
- Putting a square or park on this site was not in the city's official plan.

Counsel for the appellants disputed the respondent's technically correct but highly generalized point that there were provisions in the official plan for the development of more open spaces in the core of the city *as a whole*. In his view there might be a higher concentration of open spaces in this area than anywhere else in the city (Joint Board 1998d, 28[E][6][b]).

The arguments for why the city's plans would likely fail concluded with a rationale for why the appellants' alternative development scheme was a better option for the city.

The Street Was Beginning to Cure Itself

The appellants' counsel cited evidence that the street was curing itself: the real estate market for office and retail was rising; there was considerable investment in area properties; and the facade improvement program was successful (Joint Board 1998d, 9[E], [F]). Under crossexamination, the program planner had to acknowledge that a floor space index of 4.0 would lead to the assembly of land parcels (ibid., 10[G]).

In the opinion of the appellants' lawyer, the solution to social problems in the area was *to deal* with the social problems. However, the police testified that they did not have the tools needed to deal with the social problems. In that case, said counsel, either the city or the province should give the police the tools they needed (Joint Board 1998d, 10[H]). Indeed, he went on to say that the way the Yonge-Dundas issue was handled prior to the redevelopment scheme was to make social problems a special consideration. For instance, the June 1995 Yonge Street Improvement Plan deals "in length with social issues while discussing the physical building façade and street activities proposals and rather than attempting to engineer social change through the City's proposed project and the C.I.P. amendment before you, it stresses the development of a Community Services Strategic Plan as a coordinating tool for community service providers" (ibid.).

Meanwhile, the appellants said that the recession had also influenced real estate investment decisions by property owners. The recession had just lifted and the city was just beginning to help the area, as was witnessed by the adoption in March 1996 of proposals for 4.0 times coverage, the facade program, and other changes. The city had also finally resolved the 350 Yonge Street redevelopment application. The direction for the street was becoming clearer.

After all of these developments, it was unfair, counsel for the appellants argued, for the city to seek to expropriate these properties.

Comments about the Appellants' Legal Case

Appellants are poorly situated in contexts such as an OMB hearing. They are not likely to be planning experts and therefore must rely on experts their lawyer brings in from outside the situation. They may turn to their regular lawyer whose specialty may be corporate, small-business, contract, or tax law. If their lawyer is not practised in municipal and especially expropriation law, they can be placed at a further disadvantage. (In this case the appellants hired a lawyer who was an expert in municipal law.) The quality of the questions the appellants' lawyer puts to the expert witnesses to answer in their sworn testimonies will reflect his or her prior knowledge of planning and the relevant law. Those questions also depend on the lawyer's ability to rapidly identify the key issues of a case. In this instance the city, realizing that expropriation and redevelopment would probably be involved, hired a top expropriation lawyer in the very early stages of establishing the PPP and kept him informed throughout the process. The tactic paid off in terms of the quality and coherence of legal reasoning that underlay the city's witness statements and expert documents. The relationship between the appellants' lawyer and expert witnesses was not as symbiotic; perhaps it rarely is, unless appellants can see a legal battle looming early on and are financially able to bring legal counsel on board and keep it in place. A close relationship is crucial for keeping the lawyer up to speed on all of the planning points being made in what is essentially a land use planning court. Continuously briefing the lawyer from a position of knowledge helps the lawyer build the best case, be effective in examination and crossexamination, and argue clearly and on point in the final summation. The case at hand bears out those problems.

Finally, the appellants had a problem of strategy when it came to whether to propose an alternative redevelopment scheme. As it happens, they chose to present an alternative. On the one hand, it showed there was private-sector initiative with respect to these parcels and that assembly was possible. But on the other, as one clearly sees in the board's decision (see Appendix 9), the very existence of a counterproposal, which involved assembly, showed the hearing board that assembly was desirable to the private sector. The owners had not taken any concrete steps toward assembly. Their high-rise commercial proposal was completely out of line with the city's wishes for regeneration, meeting neither its built-form nor use intentions.

The appellants' arguments against the redevelopment are both weak and strong, but they are verifiable. Their counsel built his argument on public policy and ethics, focusing on fairness as a matter that should enter into the deliberations. For him, the city's expropriation plan was unfair because new policies that were beneficial to his clients had just been approved for the street. But he could not find a way to make fairness count.

The City's Legal Argument That the Project was Permissible

The approach taken by the city's lawyer in his concluding argument was entirely different from what had been heard from the consulting and staff planners because his role was different. He had to marshal all of his expert witnesses' evidence, debunk the alternatives proposed by the other side, argue legal points, and, finally, present the case for the city's project in a way that would make its strong points seem invincible and the weak ones defensible.

His summary argument took this form:

- There is a way to change the cycle that is underway at Yonge and Dundas, and it is called city building.
- City building can bring an exciting, contemporary image to the area, whereas the appellants propose only dusty, old 1970s-style solutions.
- Neither reinvestment incentives nor the appellants' proposed alternatives will generate a nice new public square, but the city's scheme will.
- The square is essential to resolving the clash between economic interests and crime.

- Expropriation can be used against "social blight" with a CIP.
- The appellants' experts never established that thirty cinemas would be impossible as a business venture.
- The timing is propitious.

There Is a Way to Change the Cycle That Is Underway at Yonge and Dundas

By using the leitmotif of city building, counsel tried to raise the discussion at the hearing above mere detail and carry it into the realm of the passionate activity of creating cities. He wanted to emphasize the city's commitment and vision while he downplayed detail and avoided questions about whether the city had perfectly executed every step along the way. He was making room for the possibility that he would have to ask for forgiveness for the city if it was shown that, in its spirited enthusiasm, the city had acted too quickly or left a *t* uncrossed.

The city, counsel said, was profoundly committed to the project: "That commitment is grounded in a firm belief that we are engaged in the task of City Building and that the decisions which are made by this Board in this case will be directive of the future growth and prosperity of this priority area of the City; which area is acknowledged as the visible symbol of the City's economic well-being" (Joint Board 1998e, 1-2). He went on to say that the city's main concern was always to do what was best for Yonge Street and the downtown core.

City Building Can Bring an Exciting, Contemporary Image to the Area

The new image, as the lawyer described it, would be similar to the one for the recently redeveloped Times Square in New York – not literally a copy, but like it in "the sense of place, excitement and energy represented by that world class icon" (Joint Board 1998e, 44). A Toronto version would work, he proposed, if it was "smaller in scale and finer in grain, and [paid] more attention to built form, micro-climatic conditions and environmental concerns" (ibid.).[9] A UEC and public square could, in combination with the other elements of the city's proposed project, provide the dynamism to ensure the corner had new pizzazz.

He wished to show that his opponents' plans were old-fashioned and had been long out of favour: "Perhaps the appellants could claim City Building too, although in the sense of returning to the twelve times coverage policies that were in place in this area before the 1976-78 Central Area Plan. That approach invites the rejection of 20 years of Official Plan policy and practice and has no demonstrated support beyond those among the appellants who support it" (Joint Board 1998e, 3).

But what did "city building" actually mean in this context? Among some planners it is a rhetorical flourish. Ordinarily, those who use it want to capture in a single expression the business of taking the city in hand, fixing it up, and marketing it. The term "city building" belongs to the new language developed for the entrepreneurial approach to cities – let's not wait for things to happen, let's make them happen! The city's counsel was correct to apply it to the project he was defending, and he was being ironic (and particularly cutting) when he used it in conjunction with the appellants' alternative schemes.[10]

Neither Reinvestment Incentives Nor the Appellants' Proposed Alternatives Will Generate a Nice New Public Square, But the City's Scheme Will

With respect to the ongoing reinvestment incentives, the public authority's counsel needed to respond to the appellants' counsel, who claimed that Yonge Street was curing itself. Steering clear of any evidence, he noted that the street had improved, but he argued that it may be said to have cured itself only if one's ambition for the street was to reach no higher than its condition before the last recession. Legal wrangling is not for the faint of heart.

The real drive behind his argument was to suggest that part of the cure had come as a result of announcing the redevelopment; therefore, to stop the redevelopment now would stop the cure. A brilliant argument. Why? Because no hard evidence was presented about the matter of whether the cure was well underway before the redevelopment plan was announced in December 1996. Therefore, no one could bring a strong case against his assertion that it was *not* happening. He stated, "To give in to the argument that the announcement itself has been a sufficient catalyst and there is no need to carry through will only create greater uncertainty in the marketplace respecting such proposals" (Joint Board 1998e, 60). Counsel for the city made OMB members hearing the case realize that it was impossible to put the project back in the box. Once city council had announced its support for the project – possibly in December 1996, but certainly in May 1997 – the city could not back away. Had it been forced by the OMB to do so, it would have been shorn of credibility in the development industry, and its extensive work on tackling this part of Yonge would have been thrown back in its face. Assuming that the board could see the consequences, there was only one decision it could make.

Counsel for the city spent much time demolishing alternative schemes and showing why expropriation was fully justifiable because he wanted to show that the city had become a developer out of necessity, not choice. The private sector had failed in the past and was continuing to fail with plans that did not respect the official plan. What was more, the city had all the tools it needed to take action.

The Square Is Essential to Resolving the Clash between Economic Interests and Crime

Part of the city's case was that it had a right to defend its economic interests against criminals. It had a substantial economic interest in the well-being of the Eaton Centre, "a retail centre of super regional significance" (Joint Board 1998e, 22). The area's significance had been reconfirmed in a recent OMB decision in which it was described as being of provincial significance (ibid.). Its well-being was threatened by criminal activity occurring "somewhere" in the vicinity, so the argument went.

There certainly was criminal activity. One expects it in the centre of a large city, even if one regrets it. However, the evidence for where the incidents occurred or what types of crime they were was not compelling. Many black youths frequented the area. A member of the clergy who ran a youth drop-in centre noted in his public statement that the fact that youth are attracted to Yonge Street does not necessarily translate into increasing levels of undesirable activity (Joint Board 1998g, Tab 5, 8). He warned listeners about the tendency to attribute crime to youths just because they are youths, and he warned that this error was even more likely if the youths were black (ibid.).

To avoid this error, it is essential to know crime figures and where crime is occurring. Ordinary people without any political motive or special training would ask to see the crime figures and locations of incidents to help assess the situation. But the legal counsel's strategy was to stay away from details regarding who was using the area, where they were congregating, and what they were doing. He stated, "Yonge and Dundas has become a focus of adverse criminal and social activities, the most severe example of which is the problem with crack cocaine dealing and usage addressed by Project Broom" (Joint Board 1998e, 23[5]). Counsel used the term "adverse" in association with both criminal and social activities and then proceeded to focus exclusively on criminal activities in the form of drugs. He continued, "It does not matter, in this context, whether or not murders occur at Yonge and Dundas as a result of altercations which start in the Eaton Centre. The fact is that both the Eaton Centre and the strip are threatened by this adverse social condition" (ibid.). Here, counsel shifted from drug activities to murder, of which there had been one in recent years. Through the rhetorical use of the association of ideas, he managed to focus the attention of his audience – most importantly, that of the OMB members hearing the case – on high danger. At the same time, he wiped out the picture (which anyone who knows the area well would have from simple observation) of a place where thousands of people pass through each day and replaced it with an image of a place where youth congregate. Thus, the city's lawyer created through rhetoric the very conflation that the reverend running the youth centre had warned against: youth (mainly black) equals crime.

Despite the best efforts of counsel for one of the appellants to deduce what was happening from the crime figures, the picture remained incomplete (see Chapter 4). But the figures do show incidents taking place at a much higher rate within the Eaton Centre than outside it. Counsel for the city more than once dismissed as irrelevant the desire to know more about crime:

> In my respectful submission, it is not relevant to know how many drug arrests were made on each premises [sic] or on which quadrant a recent stabbing murder took place. The important thing to understand is that the intersection is a problem area which, notwithstanding the application of the highest concentration of police resources in the City, demonstrates a problem which has not been arrested ... As [the detective] indicated, statistics are not kept with a view toward answering inquiries such as those that might be put at this hearing. They tell part of the story, but to examine them in detail would overemphasize them in a way I think inappropriate. We have the pictures of the condition of the roof at KFC before this hearing started. The Board has viewed the premises where [the detective] indicated there was drug dealing, whether arrests had been repeatedly made on those sites on repeated occasions or not. In fact, [the detective's] evidence was that typically arrests are made elsewhere. I will not review the statistics and any detailed information in my argument-in-chief, but I am prepared to respond in reply if it is raised in detail by the appellants. (Joint Board 1998e, 42)

Consider another example of counsel for the city shielding data from inspection. When one of the lawyers for the appellants attempted to obtain information about arrests, detentions, and expulsions from the Toronto Eaton Centre by private security personnel, retail store personnel, or the Metropolitan Toronto Police Force, the city's lawyer said that asking the vice-president and general manager of the Eaton Centre to provide this information went beyond the call of duty. After all, he continued, the executive was not a party to the case, he was electing to give evidence, he was not being compensated for giving his time, and, therefore, he "should not be oppressed with disclosure requirements that have marginal if any relevance to the matter about which they are to give evidence" (Waqué to Heisey, Joint Board 1998b, Exhibit 39, 1). Furthermore, counsel for the city argued that he had "no way to control [the executive's] conduct with respect to producing documents" (ibid.). He wrote to the counsel for the appellants:

Is there no other way we can address some of your concerns? Can we not agree that there is a significant problem with criminal activity at Yonge and Dundas, that this is a vitally important location for the City of Toronto, locally, regionally, and on a world scale, at least with respect to the business of tourism? Or that the land use planning process has a role in addressing this problem? Perhaps we will also have to agree that there are different visions before the Board as to the correct approach to addressing this issue. However, is it really necessary to deal with everything in a "tooth and nail" basis? (Ibid., 1-2)

Given that the redevelopment was about conserving the economic value of the Eaton Centre for both the city and the Centre's owners, it was brazen to say that asking the vice-president to produce data already in his possession would oppress him. Perhaps because it was so astonishing, it was a perfect reply.

Counsel for the city used rhetorical skills to defend his client's position in a forum where rhetoric, persuasion, and "facing down" one's opponent were more important than the fair presentation of facts. Indeed, from counsel's perspective, it was the role of his antagonist, the lawyer for the appellants, to force the board to pay attention to the facts. If he did not do so, then rhetoric would win.

The city's counsel also claimed that the square would be easier to police than the front door of the Eaton Centre (Joint Board 1998e, 32). One may wonder what evidence there was for this claim, because the argument is usually made in reverse: it is easier to police private spaces than public spaces because a private owner can use more security devices, strategies, and facets of the law of trespass. The space was ambiguous. The triangular sidewalk enlargement at the Eaton Centre entrance was technically owned by the Centre, but it seemed to be public space because it was a seamless extension of the sidewalk. This generous apron of space had been a design concession to the city when the original site development approvals for the Eaton Centre were reached. It was used as if it was public; you might say that it was used exactly as the city intended.[11]

The proponents may have viewed people's propensity to hang around the general area of the triangle as a signal that a public space would work, yet at the same time they did not want certain types of people to fill up the new square. The vice-president of the Eaton Centre testified that "it was of absolute importance to have an open area at Yonge and Dundas and that an urban entertainment centre was preferable to [the appellants' office-building design] because that would empty out at night and it was important to attract a broader mix of persons throughout the day and evening" (Joint Board 1998e,

60-61). The executive of the Eaton Centre wanted to push the loitering away from his building. The Eaton Centre provided what was, in effect, a private, internal street that paralleled Yonge. The Centre had to handle security within its own building. This must have been a financial burden. If cost was really the problem, however, it did not require redevelopment to solve it but, rather, a way to manage the costs.

The city's counsel said that although there was much work to do with regard to the square's design and how the activities on the square would be regulated, there was no reason these issues could not be handled the way they were for Nathan Phillips Square in Toronto and Bryant Park in New York, both of which served as examples of what could be achieved (Joint Board 1998e, 32).[12] In fact, these two squares are handled entirely differently. Nathan Phillips Square is fully public, open to all, and programmed. Bryant Park is privately patrolled, open only for approved behaviour, and, instead of being programmed, is a space for contemplation. The difficulty the city's lawyer was trying to skate around was that the arguments in favour of and the promises made regarding Dundas Square demanded a fully public square – in line with the very popular Nathan Phillips Square; however, the private interests in the area wanted more control over the square to keep the number of vagrants and youth in check. To reach that goal, they would need more private control, which explains the reference to Bryant Park.

Expropriation Can Be Used against Social Blight within a CIP

The strategy the city's counsel used to argue for expropriation included making the case that this was not a hard-luck story whereby the city was taking property from small businesses and residents. The city's counsel said the appellants were, "for the most part, investors in real estate for whom real estate is a commodity. The issue is money" (Joint Board 1998e, 6). He contrasted this to his client's position: the city was not doing this project for the money, but for a higher purpose, namely, for the good of Yonge Street, the city, and even the region, for which the few blocks of Yonge Street were vital as an indicator of economic well-being. He added that the city was not interested in exactly which developer or which tenant obtained the northeast corner of Yonge and Dundas; it only wanted the redevelopment project accomplished with the least risk and exposure for taxpayers. The latter point was presumably made to declare that the city was neither attached to the selected developer and anchor tenant nor against others, including the appellants. The appellants, the city's counsel argued, had simply not come up with an adequate plan, and the city was therefore taking the matter into its own hands. It was thus asking the provincial authorities to let it do what needed to be done with the tools the province had given municipalities to use when such problems arose. The city had a clear, straightforward vision for the street that it sought to implement within the scope of the tools at its disposal. It is within this argument in particular that the reach toward "justification," especially the moral position of furthering the public interest and the neutrality claim that it was treating all parties with the same dispassion, is attempted.

In sum, the city's counsel argued that the city's motives were in the public interest, and he suggested that the motives of the appellants were the obverse – for private gain.

The city's counsel then turned to the legal tests that needed to be met for the board to be convinced of the validity of using expropriation to implement the project. Requirements under both the *Expropriations Act* and the *Planning Act* had to be addressed. However, he said that expropriation was always a political action in the end, and even if the board approved it, everyone knew that the approval would be but a granting to the city of permission. If the city decided to proceed with expropriation, it would have to answer for it politically, before electors.

Under section 6 of the *Expropriations Act,* certain past decisions apply when interpreting the legislation. Relevant interpretations used by the city's counsel are briefly noted here.

- The objectives of the city are not open for inquiry on the part of the inquiry officers of the OMB because they are assumed to have been adequately determined by elected officials.
- The words "fair, sound and reasonably necessary" characterize a legitimate expropriation and are to be treated as a single set of tests, not three independent ones, and "reasonably necessary" does not mean without a shadow of a doubt, as in criminal law, but rather "reasonably defensible."
- Because the objectives are beyond review, the focus falls on whether the location chosen for expropriation is the best one.
- Rights of landowners are to be compensated fully and fairly. (Here, the lawyer emphasized that losing title to land is different from losing property value via downsizing or the siting of obnoxious facilities. In the former, compensation is paid; in the latter, compensation is not ordinarily forthcoming, given past cases.) (Joint Board 1998e, 10-11)

With his last point, the lawyer seemed to be strategically positioning himself to counter the appellants' argument that they had been downzoned when the city removed the new 4.0 times coverage from their properties, and the possiblity that this argument would find favour with the board. This position and the point that appellants saw real estate as a commodity, not as a matter of public interest, were intended to raise the city's moral stature by lowering that of their opponents.

The city's lawyer then sought to show that, when examined closely, this was a conventional expropriation case. His points were as follows (Joint Board 1998e, 12-16; see also Appendix 9):

1. four of the ten properties are for a public park or square and underground parking;
2. taking the six properties from one set of commercial owners to turn them over to another set of commercial owners had been done previously for the purpose of enhancing the creation of a public square (the example was lands taken on the south side of Queen Street opposite Nathan Phillips Square for the construction of the Sheraton Centre);[13]
3. the basic reason for expropriation is to enhance economic development:
   a. tourism is vital to the local economy;
   b. this is a tourist area because of the Eaton Centre;
   c. evidence given by a planning expert witness illustrates why cities today need to expropriate for tertiary sector activities, not just for hard services;
4. no precedent is being set:
   a. the city has done land assemblies several times before; and in this instance the appellants have shown that they couldn't or wouldn't do it;
   b. a previous court decision in a comparable case showed that land could be taken for ultimately private commercial purposes;
   c. there is case law that is relevant although not on point, together with the standard planning and law reference text, that says it is normal for private developers to be involved in redevelopment plans;
   d. this is simply a case of a municipal council deciding what it sees as best for its jurisdiction.

Those are the principal points with respect to the *Expropriations Act*.

With respect to section 28 of the *Planning Act*, the city's lawyer elected to frame his argument in these terms: just because expropriation can be used as a tool does not mean its use should contradict good planning sense. He said, "The decision to initiate an expropriation is a serious step, but it is a political one and the use of the implementation tool should not overwhelm, from a policy perspective, all the other factors and considerations that go into establishing good planning and good city building" (Joint Board 1998e, 17).

One of the points the city's lawyer sought to drive home was that "community improvement" in section 28 refers to an area. Nothing in it says that a specific project must take place in the worst part of an area. It is possible, he argued, to use the approach of looking for a trigger that will spark further development. It would then be a red herring to argue that if this redevelopment is to go ahead it has to be in the most debilitated section. A viable strategy would be to choose a strong point and use it as a catalyst from which to build outward (Joint Board 1998e, 20). The lawyer was referring to recent planning wisdom that, not surprisingly, was both advocated and practised by one of the city's main witnesses. However, this reason had not been used in earlier reports. Like several other key arguments, it was developed after decision making took place, not before it, as the word "planning" in common-sense usage suggests.

The lawyer's next point built toward a key claim. He noted that there was substantial agreement among the parties to the hearing about the unsuitability of buildings: many structures had "small frontages, dysfunctional ratios of width to depth and low ceiling heights, outdated mechanical and electrical systems"; "in this sense, they are faultily arranged or unsuitable" (Joint Board 1998e, 21[d]). This had been fully demonstrated through testimony. However, he argued, this is not all there is to community improvement. Community improvement "does not have to meet a specific objective standard of condition, but simply that it is an area 'the community improvement of which *in the opinion of the Council is desirable*' (Section 28[1] of *The Planning Act*). Council's opinion on this point has been unanimous on three occasions and the Minister of Municipal Affairs and Housing and his Staff have come to the same view. Certainly, it cannot be said that their opinion is unreasonable" (ibid., 28[4]).

Counsel then argued that the legislation allowed for redevelopment because of various cited physical conditions or "for any other reason." He argued that, in this case, the words "or for any other reason" could apply to social blight: "For example, if the general words after the phrase 'dilapidation, overcrowding, faulty arrangement, unsuitability of buildings,' were: 'or for any like physical condition,' then it would be clear that the *ejusdem generis* rule applies. However, the use of the adjectives 'other' and 'any' indicates that a broad interpretation was to be maintained to permit exercise of discretion of Council referred to above" (Joint Board 1998e, 28-29).[14] And this argument survived. After the hearing the board asked the city's counsel to reply to several questions, one of which was whether there were any cases "directly on point and argument on the meaning of the words 'for any other purpose' in s. 28 of the *Planning Act*." He said there were not (Joint Board 1998a, 2). Thus, given the decision of the OMB in favour of the city's plans, a precedent-setting interpretation emerged from the case.

Counsel for the city then discussed the public square and why it was needed. His subtle juxtaposition of subjects suggested that the square was connected to his just completed argument that interpration of the statute for expropriating land should include taking land to deal with social blight. The square would thereby be a tool in the city's effort to combat blight and, consequently, an essential element in the redevelopment.

The Appellants' Experts Never Established That Thirty Cinemas Would Be Impossible as a Business Venture

A contentious section of the hearing had to do with whether the city was at risk if it settled on an anchor tenant in the PenEquity development that promised a thirty-cinema megaplex. How could there possibly be a market for thirty new cinemas? What would be the effect on existing cinemas? Did building this one take into account the other megaplexes going up around the region? What would the effect be on Festival Hall, which was located a few blocks to the southwest and nearly ready to open? What about the eighteen-cinema facility across the street in the Eaton Centre? Who would AMC's market be in terms of age, income, and domicile in the region? In reply to these questions, counsel for the city replied that, despite all the evidence, it was never conclusively shown that thirty cinemas would be unfeasible. A weak defence, indeed, but he argued that no other evidence was technically required by the OMB.

In retrospect the debate seems surreal. Immediately after the hearing, cinemas began closing all over town. Cineplex Odeon went bankrupt. All cinemas in the Eaton Centre closed. AMC lost 80 percent of its value.

The Timing Is Propitious

A central point in the city counsel's argument was timing. He argued that the city could deliver its proposed redevelopment within the same economic cycle while the appellants could not (they had admitted this). During cross-examination he managed to elicit from one of the appellants' expert witnesses that he, the witness, would be deeply concerned if changes to Yonge and Dundas did not occur in this cycle.

Another route the city's counsel took was to appeal to emotion and to belief in serendipity, if not to the possibility that the stars themselves were aligned. This was a special moment. He said, "City Building is, by its nature, a passionate exercise. Part of the reason for this is that the opportunities for significantly redirecting the course of growth of the City are limited. They result from a rare confluence of circumstances and events ... There are moments of rare alignment when public consensus, political will, and the market are all aligned to be harnessed to a common purpose and may achieve a significant result, if permitted" (Joint Board 1998e, 3). In other words, the project is bigger than all of us; there can be no going back.

Comments about the City's Legal Case

The city's lawyer snookered his opposition on virtually every point. While the appellants focused on physical blight, the respondent's counsel pulled the rug out from under them by successfully arguing that section 28 could be used to counteract social blight. The alternatives proposed by the appellants were presented as being uninspired and old-fashioned; worse yet, they demonstrated a need for large land assembly that could not be accomplished in the economic cycle. They also failed to show the potential for lots of "flowers to bloom" along the street within the new 4.0 times coverage. Appellants were unable to make headway with their claim that the process was "reprehensible and shocking" (Joint Board 1998d, 17[6][1]) or with their argument (called "ideological" by the city's counsel) about the proper role of the public sector in redevelopment.[15]

Despite much evidence and testimony in their favour, the appellants did not even win one of their most interesting points: that to build thirty cinemas in this location for the purpose of changing the predominant demographic profile of people using the Yonge-Dundas area to families was surely unrealistic. But the problem for the appellants was not poor evidence on the viability of thirty cinemas: it was that it was not the board's business to worry about the viability of replacement facilities; rather, their concern was the appropriateness of taking the land and whether the basic planning was in compliance with regulations. As the respondent's counsel argued, the city's proposal for the redevelopment of the northeastern corner had only to be "reasonably defensible," not defensible beyond a shadow of a doubt. His clincher was that no one had shown that the plan was impossible when a big US cinema company came to town and said thirty cinemas was the magic number for Yonge and Dundas.

The OMB's Reasons for Ruling That the Project Was Permissible

The OMB said its decision was based on whether the project and request for permission to expropriate met the tests in the *Planning Act* and the *Expropriations Act,* which had been outlined by the respondent's counsel. The board agreed with the city on everything:

- that it had the correct provisions in place in its official plan to use the CIP section of the *Planning Act*
- that there was no objection to the phrase "for any other reason" being used to treat social blight or, as the board chose to express it, being used "to attain the economic and social benefits that will come with the creation of the catalyst which is intended to lead to the 'improvement' of the community

so delineated in the CIP and the community improvement project area" (Joint Board 1998k, 40)
- that the expropriation was reasonably defensible
- that properties could be resold or leased to private interests under both the *Expropriations Act* and the *Planning Act,* section 28.

Four sections of the board's decision are reproduced verbatim in Appendix 9. One reason for including them is so that readers interested in municipal and planning law can easily refer to them in conjunction with the analysis presented here. Another is to show how heavily the board leaned on the closing argument of the city's counsel for its case law, definitions of terms, selection of items to highlight, and organization of the grounds for decision. Like Tweedledee and Tweedledum, either could have spoken for the other. Recall that board members, the respondent, and the appellants made a joint trip to New York to review the 42nd Street Development Project. One wonders if there would not have been excellent opportunities – while strolling, waiting to board the aircraft, and so on – to chat about the underlying principles of such redevelopments. The board identified with the city's position and went even further by recommending that the city adopt a privatized, New York-style of management for Dundas Square.

In the end, expropriation is a political decision: the board approved expropriation, but it was up to the city to execute it and take the heat for it, if there was any. In early July 1998, the councillors of the new City of Toronto voted 38 to 7 to proceed with the land acquisition. Expropriation notices were to go out in August, the site was to be turned over to PenEquity by mid-January 1999, and the cinemas were to be completed by fall 2000 (Moloney 1998a). That was the prognosis from the city's ward councillor in those heady days when it was still possible to ignore the gloom descending over the cinema industry, when it was a good bet (but still not a certainty) that shakeups in the cinema industry would drive some companies to bankruptcy and require the rest to drastically revise their expansion plans.

The Program Director Had the Vision

In coming to its decision, the Joint Board said in its report that it had reviewed the vast amount of information that had come forward. It recited the project's ambitions and noted that the trip to New York had helped the members to grasp what the city was proposing. It found that the vision for this project was that of the program director (Joint Board 1998k, 20), who had been hired by and was at first responsible to YSBRA, then to the steering committee, then to the secret subcommittee, and, finally, to the city. The board referred to the long passage from the director's witness statement, which illustrated "this unique window of opportunity," and it concluded by saying, "the Board accepts his opinions as its own" (ibid., 28).

The board also chose to agree with the program director's assertion that this vision had been successful in the United States (Joint Board 1998k, 28). We do not know what criteria were used to measure this success, or whether the director was asked to provide any evidence. Success seems to have been taken as self-evident: if development energy had been unleashed in Times Square, and if the panhandlers and sex shops had been made to disappear, then this was success.

The following question does not appear to have been asked: Would a development that seemed so propitious – and unlikely to be a success if delayed – have a certain ephemeral character that might not provide a long-serving, solid catalyst for something so important as the so-called heart of Toronto? Urban entertainment centres of this type were expected even then to have a relatively short shelf life. The proposal could be likened to a fireworks-like burst-and-die strategy. For core redevelopment, this was out of character for Toronto.

And the following question was likewise avoided: What actually happened to the homeless and panhandlers of Times Square in the New York of Rudolph Giuliani? A well-respected city columnist for the *Toronto Star* (and former city councillor) wrote that, in every important respect, the process and intentions in Toronto were like those in New York. But, he admonished, if the city bought the glitz, it also bought displacement, because that was the Giuliani solution. From his viewpoint, the political position of Toronto city councillors had shifted. While the right was more troubled by the project, the left (in particular the ward councillor) had bought into the "new economic and social order of free enterprisers and crime-fighters" who were prepared to buy the strategy of "moving the riff-raff from one corner to another," which is "hardly a way to deal with poverty and crime" (Vaughan 1998).

The Metropolis UEC Is Reasonably Defensible

In response to the question of whether the megaplex was reasonably defensible, the board said it preferred the evidence of the city's witnesses over those of the appellants. In its view, the former were more experienced in cinema marketing, while the latter had broader market and economic analysis expertise (Joint Board 1998k, 31). The city's witnesses thought that the new project would force some cinemas to close, but this would happen anyway, with or without the new megaplex. The board was impressed by evidence that one could "grow" the cinema-going market, a feat that would be helped by the patented LoveSeats that the prime tenant, AMC, would put into its new cinemas (even in the twelve to be used by Ryerson University for morning classes?).

The board also believed the Metropolis developer's estimates of potential tenants. It went even further and inflated them: the developer said that "as a result of enquiries, he was confident that the demand exceeded the amount of project space" (Joint Board 1998k, 29). But the board concluded not only that the UEC would rent up but also that there would be "spill over into nearby properties promoting the catalytic effect envisaged" (ibid.).

The Joint Board Elaborates on Its Support for the Redevelopment

To end this section on the board's decision, we turn to the conclusion and *obiter dicta*.[16] In the conclusion, sandwiched between a recommendation that the new Toronto city council show its commitment to the project and a recommendation that the subway entrance in the square be moved, the board said, "It is essential that YSBRA continue its efforts to ensure that the principles expressed in the CIP are fully realized. In this regard, the Board encourages its active participation in the maintaining of the area as a safe and clean environment which attracts the tourists and visitors and citizens of Toronto to Yonge and Dundas as has been accomplished by the BID [business improvement district] ... in Times Square" (Joint Board 1998k, 44).[17]

The board offered its opinion, without being asked to do so, on the proper way for the city to organize its planning and policing: the city should take a BID/Times Square approach. The board's stated opinion raises questions. First, did the board have a mandate to advise the city on the conduct of its future planning and policing? With respect to the board's decisions on planning matters, its task was to base them on the evidence presented at the hearing. That evidence can be wide-ranging, and it can be weighted by those hearing a case according to its perceived strength (see, e.g., Krushelnicki 2007, 91-93). The city said it would manage the new square the way it managed its existing ones; the board said it should manage it the way New York manages Times Square. This would later become an issue. Second, did the board understand what it was recommending? One of the city's witnesses was Rebecca Robertson of the New York state-governed redevelopment agency. She gave evidence about the redevelopment process. However, the BID, not the redevelopment agency, runs the day-to-day operations of Times Square. There is no sign that anyone from the BID – for instance, Gretchen Dykstra, its executive director – gave evidence.

In its obiter dicta, the board also offered views on panhandling that were based on comments made by the general public and city witnesses at a "public night" sponsored by the board and about how the owners whose property was soon to be expropriated might be feeling.[18] The board's comments are cited here in full:

> The Board was impressed with the comprehensive approach taken in Times Square with the co-ordinated efforts of the City, the police, the BID and the social agencies, to reclaim the streets so that they can be enjoyed by the general public in a safe, clean and unobstructed manner. The Board heard a great deal of evidence and complaints by the general public about panhandling, vagrancy and drug dealing and the need for the City of Toronto to take corrective action. The evidence of [the police detective] and a representative of one of the social agencies actively involved in this area was very persuasive and convincing. Both support the project but advised that many of the street people have adopted panhandling as an occupation to gain easy money to support their habits and [it] is not essential to survival. Both recommended to the Board that the City should undertake an active program to educate the general public to say "no" to these people and, in the alternative, to buy them a coffee or a hot meal. In addition, the City should pass legislation modelled on the Winnipeg By-law and the City of Kingston By-law and the experience in New York, to take action to prevent undesirable uses of City streets that act as a deterrent to economic vitality. Having said this, the Board is cognizant of the fact that the Winnipeg By-law has yet to face a court challenge, expected in the fall.[19]
>
> [...] The Board well appreciates the sentiment of the landowners whose properties are to be expropriated. Part of that reticence is the underlying fear and suspicion of not receiving compensation that reflects their perception of the market rise or increase in value as a result of the project which requires their land but will benefit adjacent lands not taken. These perceptions may have hindered a negotiated acquisition. The Board, as part of the services it provides, can offer mediation on request, either by this panel or other Board members, to assist in trying to achieve a negotiated settlement, obviating the need for a protracted and expensive arbitration to determine the compensation payable to the owners. (Joint Board 1998k, 46-47)

The tone of these observations by the board are surprising. They come from an institution whose job it was to impartially and intelligently review solid evidence before reaching conclusions based on the public interest and legislation. It refers to itself as "the Board," a manner of expression employed to indicate its neutrality and that its comments are not from people but an impartial institution. That the same format should be used when the hearing members express their views on matters outside the purview of the case or on matters that they cannot know about – such as how Torontonians should respond to panhandlers or the sentiments of the landowners – must surely be questioned.

A Short Delay

The appellants were entitled to appeal the expropriation in a court of law, and three of them did so. The decision was not in their favour, and a higher court refused to hear an appeal. The appellants were required to accept compensation for their properties. A synopsis of the divisional court's decision was prepared by another practising Toronto lawyer with expertise in municipal law and is cited here in full:

> The Court ruled that the Joint Board was correct in its interpretation of Section 28 of the Planning Act in its finding that the definition in that section of the community improvement area did not require that the lands be in a state of dilapidation, deterioration or blight before Section 28 could apply. The Court held that Section 28 was not confiscatory legislation that is to be construed strictly according to the Supreme Court of Canada in the Dell Holdings Limited v. Toronto Area Transit Operating Authority, [1997] 1 S.C.R. 32 at 44. The Court held that the Joint Board was not interpreting the Expropriations Act itself nor an expropriation matter as such in exercising its jurisdiction as a Joint Board under Section 28 and therefore the Joint Board was right to give Section 28 a broad and purposive interpretation. The Court affirmed that in reviewing decisions of the Joint Board under the Consolidated Hearings Act where the issues in question arise under the Planning Act, the standard of review is that of patent unreasonableness. Costs were awarded in favour of the City against the expropriated land owners. (Lord 1998, 2)

Conclusion

Whether the Yonge-Dundas redevelopment would proceed was contingent on the reception of legal sanction, after which the city could elect to put it to a vote in council. Receiving approval required presenting arguments to a quasi-judicial tribunal concerned with Ontario land matters. Appearing there required hiring lawyers to defend the various positions. The defence of each side of the case required constructing arguments. Therefore, an array of powerful elements were drawn into the decision-making process.

The city as proponent argued its case primarily on points of law, with substantial dollops of rhetoric. The appellants focused on policy – was the planning approach correct given the evidence? – and on ethics: was it fair to expropriate these properties at the tail end of a brutal recession, at a time when the city had nailed down new development possibilities for the street but before owners had had a chance to act on them?

Carefully argued, the law won. Through law we decide what it is possible to do, which may not be the same as the ethical thing to do. The power of the law, supported by the tribunal's hearing officers, won the day. While the improvements were being handled locally and nonconfrontationally in the regeneration scheme, it was still possible to marry evidence to ethics within the legal planning structure.

The role of the OMB was central. It decided to select as the winning argument the one that would yield a considerably more entrepreneurial approach to development than Toronto had previously seen, an approach used to develop Times Square, manage Bryant Park, and build London's Canary Wharf. The board's decision did not rest on having heard rigorous analyses of planning data but rather on its ability to envisage what the city was proposing as plausible. In addition, the law (as described by the respondent's lawyer) did not prohibit it. In its decision the board heaped praise on the private-sector planner, all but parroted the contract lawyer's arguments, and lauded YSBRA's energy and foresight; it wrote in far more restrained tones about the city's work. Was the board biased? Would it be in the interests of property owners whose property was about to be expropriated to ask this panel to provide mediation as the board proposed? Could any *subset* of the board mediate the dispute appropriately, given that this panel had been at pains to demonstrate that it spoke for the whole board?

The struggle between different types of capital interests could possibly have been resolved without invoking expropriation had the city not handed planning over to a private-sector business association. It resulted in a rearguard battle between, on the one hand, older-style developers and some small-property owners who supported older ideas about city development and, on the other, a coalition – led by the ward councillor and a private-sector consultant and his client, YSBRA – that promoted using the city as a tool to generate hyperentertainment consumption. Giving public planning decisions to private businesses has a multitude of effects, not the least of which is that one should not expect the public interest to be enhanced. Had the city kept a strong hand in shaping the planning and development decisions (even in a properly created PPP), it very likely could have maintained a stable environment in which to work out ethical solutions and the rational means to achieve them. As the concluding chapter will show, this lesson had already been learned in England.

Instead, a legal wrangle ensued that was very expensive for all concerned, and problems were displaced rather than solved. Whether Yonge-Dundas is a heart for Torontonians to be proud of is still open to debate.

CHAPTER SIX
Implementing

As soon as the Joint Board announced its decision to allow the city to proceed with its redevelopment, a press release was issued reminding Torontonians about the nature of the project and its history to date. Under the subtitle "Project receives broad public and private sector support, represents innovative public-private co-operation and captures market trends," the city described the project this way: "The development of an urban entertainment district along Downtown Yonge Street with a focus at Yonge and Dundas seeks to capture retail and entertainment opportunities, new trends in signage and vertical and street-related retailing to build a critical mass with a strong sense of place and arrival in an atmosphere of tremendous vibrancy and excitement" (Toronto 1998a, 3).

City council voted in favour of proceeding with land acquisition, by expropriation if necessary, for the Yonge-Dundas redevelopment. The overall net cost to the city was estimated at a mere $14.4 million. Property expropriation was completed by the end of July 1998, and arrangements were made for possession by 15 January 1999. Demolition occurred immediately afterward.

What is on the ground several years after the plan was adopted? The old adage "There's many a slip twixt cup and lip" neatly fits what can happen between the planning and implementation stages of a project. The description that follows shows what was implemented and how it differed from what was claimed would emerge in the heat of arguments for or against the project.

The Metropolis Urban Entertainment Centre: Parcel A

The planners envisaged Metropolis as an urban entertainment centre (UEC) that would sit on Parcel A. Urban entertainment centres were said to represent a new urban form because they attracted the public through some combination of entertainment, dining, retail, and education under one roof. Together, these were said to create synergy. Ideally, UECs were to be more like shopping malls than theme parks, because their market was primarily residents in a region, people who potentially make repeat visits. Tourists were secondary. Even though "urban" was part of their name, urban entertainment centres, its proponents said, could actually be located anywhere a crowd could be mustered, anywhere the "density, vitality, and eclecticism of amenities" could be generated (Beyard et al. 1998, 24; see also Pine and Gilmore 1999 on marketing synergy).

The Yonge-Dundas version diverged somewhat from the UEC model because it was supposed to be more of an entertainment centre and theme park than a mall. Access to the UEC's tenants was to be from the street, with no interior corridor. It also diverged from the model in that it was intended to attract tourists. Had the project veered toward a mall, it would have been in direct competition with the Eaton Centre. Instead, the two centres were expected to provide complementary functions – merchandise in one, entertainment in the other.

Initially, Metropolis was to generate 340,000 square feet (roughly 32,000 square metres), which was later reduced to about 283,000 square feet (about 26,000 square metres) – 117,000 square feet for twenty-four cinemas, down from the original thirty, and 166,000 square feet for ancillary retail). The Centre would have four storeys above ground along Yonge Street (higher on the Victoria Street side), two floors below ground, an underground connection to the subway, and entrances to restaurants, bars, and other services off the street. Inside, it would be anchored by AMC's megaplex and have franchises of several US chains that specialize in selling food, drink, and entertainment to the age and income group to which the Yonge-Dundas area was being marketed. Outside, the architecture of the building would be masked by kinetic advertising. With each new retail campaign, the wall's advertising would change (Hume 1998b; 1999b), just as would happen on the hoardings during the long wait for the building to materialize: L'Oreal cosmetics one week, Jockey shorts the next, and so on. By 2006 the space that could be leased had increased to 360,000 square feet (over 33,000 square metres), with three levels below ground and ten or seven storeys above ground, depending on the part of the structure.

The OMB had been convinced of the viability of this project in part because it deduced from the proponents' evidence that there was a surfeit of tenants anxiously waiting to be approved as occupants. By March 1999 the six buildings on the site had been expropriated, the laneway behind them was closed, buildings had been torn down, air rights had been negotiated with Ryerson University to build over its four-storey parking garage, and the anchor tenant had been secured – almost. Completion was set for fall 2000.

And then the unravelling began. The cinema business began to collapse. AMC closed its Toronto corporate office. It reduced the number of cinemas in Metropolis from thirty to twenty-four but did not pull out completely, even though it had cancelled participation in some megaplexes in the United States and was closing many of its multiplex facilities (Powell 2001b). It reportedly lost as much as US$29.1 million in the fourth quarter of 1999 (up from $19.1 million a year earlier), but things were a bit brighter in 2000, when its losses decreased. In 2005 AMC merged with Loews Cineplex in the United States. Meanwhile, Statistics Canada reported that movie attendance had declined (Dixon 2005).

The developer, PenEquity, would not reveal the names of tenants with whom it was negotiating, but now and then hints emerged. The first hard information about tenants set the tone for what was ahead. There would be twenty billiard tables and thirty-two bowling lanes, some of them in VIP rooms. The developer's media people said that bowling was shedding its accustomed association with suburban malls and being marketed in new and exciting forms. For example, there would be cosmic bowling for those who like loud music and strobe lights to ratchet up the challenge of hitting the pins. Family lanes would be built so that balls would not go off the track and fail to knock down any pins at all, which might discourage children. With an eye on the twenty-five-plus age group market with disposable income, there were plans for a cigar lounge, sushi bar, and two US chain knock-offs. One of the latter would be a bar that overlooked the square, could seat 500, and would be in the style of the VooDoo Lounge in Las Vegas' Rio Hotel. The other would be a 200-seat tapas restaurant like Florida's Café Tu Tu Tango (Theobald 2000).

The cause for further delays was laid at the feet of the Toronto Transit Commission (TTC), which, the ward councillor said, did not want to help the city and had "reneged on an agreement to cost-share the underground connection from the subway into the building" (Powell 2000). Whether such an agreement existed is unclear; certainly the TTC did not think so. The opening date was pushed forward again. By the end of 2000, PenEquity said there would be further delays because after talking for eighteen months with the Disney Corporation, negotiations had fallen through. Disney was to have financed another knock-off called Disney Quest, an interactive theme park similar to ones in Chicago and Orlando (Florida). The Metropolis version would have been much more impressive than the interactive development located several blocks to the southwest in Festival Hall at King and John streets. The long negotiations cost PenEquity $700,000 (Hume 2000b).

By 2001 there were rumours that negotiations had begun with Virgin Entertainment Group Inc. to install a Virgin Music megastore (25,000 square feet, about 2,300 square metres), and this time the model for the Toronto variant would be the one in Times Square. In addition, Future Shop was to put in a flagship store that would take up 26,500 square feet (about 2,500 square metres) on the second floor, but it would have its own entrance at street level. A Wolfgang Puck café (modelled after the one in Hollywood) was expected. Metropolis – with its smorgasbord of models from Hollywood, New York, Florida, and Las Vegas – had still not confirmed that it was fully leased at the end of 2001 (Immen 2001b; Lester 2001).

By March 2002 it was revealed that the city had not been paid for the land it had expropriated and flipped to PenEquity (Moloney 2002). The city eventually issued the developer a notice to pay $10 million toward the amount owed by the beginning of April 2002. The program manager for the city was reported to have blamed delays in payment on PenEquity's inability to secure tenants. But why was that the city's problem? Did it not have a development deal that was based on flipping the land to PenEquity? In response to further questions regarding why the city had apparently lost control over the timing of the development, the program manager was reported to have said that "such a high degree of optimism surrounded the project, it was felt that deadlines wouldn't be necessary" (Tompkins 2003). The project team assumed that because PenEquity was going to put up between twenty and thirty million dollars, it would be motivated to start quickly. The misjudgment was especially egregious given that one of the pillars of the city's argument against allowing the slow-drip regeneration plan to play out in the market was the need to catch the existing economic cycle.

By this time trees were growing on the vacant lot. Only in mid-2003 did crews begin uprooting the trees, clearing away the debris, and digging, but construction stopped again in 2004. By late 2006 the prospective tenants were mainly fast-food franchises and four regular mall retailers – HMV, Future Shop, Adidas, and Shoppers Drug Mart. A new Canadian Music Hall of Fame, which would cover 60,000 square feet (about 5,500 square metres) on three levels, was announced in 2005 and cancelled in 2006. By 2006 the building had topped out at ten storeys in one part and seven storeys in others, both of which were well over the height estimated during the OMB hearing. In early 2007 naming rights for Metropolis were sold, and it was reported that the Centre's new name would be Toronto Life Square. The Centre was now said to have 500,000 square feet (about 46,500 square metres) of indoor space and about 20,000 square feet (nearly 1,900 square metres) of outdoor signage capacity. Toronto Life Square would have "Canada's largest high-definition video display, measuring 30-by-52 feet, and the world's largest contoured trivision. The video display [would] be enhanced with 34-surrounding video panels that [could] be used individually to create marquis effects or as a display area of approximately 2,400 square feet" (*Novae Res Urbis* 13 April 2007, 9). Phased openings for tenants, scheduled for late 2007, occurred in 2008.

The Torch/Olympic Spirit and Redevelopment of the Senator: Parcel C

Two developments by Bob Sniderman, owner of the Senator restaurants and the Top O' the Senator jazz club, were approved by the city between 1999 and 2001: one was a new building providing approximately 33,000 square feet (about 3,000 square metres), and the other was a tower-like structure called the Torch. Both were eventually built, but the designs and uses changed during the process. The Torch was to occupy the former Salvation Army site, which had most recently served as a winter hostel for men. Figure 6.1 shows the Salvation Army building next to the Senator. The proposed new use was to be a fifty-metre-high media tower built in the shape of an inverted ice cream cone. The Torch and the Senator restaurants were to be connected by a bridge-like structure that would contain several cafés and entertainment facilities.

Both the Torch and the new Senator building were beyond the allowable zoning, so debate arose and a public meeting was required.[1] The city's head of urban design said the tower was an essential element of the Dundas Square project because without it the square would just bleed away on the eastern edge (Hume 1999a). The contrary position was presented at a community council meeting a year later when the re-zonings for the site were discussed.[2] The lawyer representing one of the business owners just east of the square argued that the Torch would block the view down Dundas Street East, a vista that people who were located east of the square had wanted as a principal outcome of the whole planning initiative from the very beginning. The complainant's lawyer said that the Torch and its "spectacular signage" created a barrier that obliterated, not just obstructed, visual access to her client's premises. The ward councillor opined that if the complainant had stayed in the redevelopment process, then it might have turned out more to his liking.

In response to the concerns raised, the developer's project manager said that the building was "transparent" to both pedestrian and vehicular traffic because it was raised five and a half metres (eighteen feet) above grade. This measurement did not match the mock-ups of the building, and with this the project manager was wading onto rocky shoals. Things became even more precarious when he said that the Torch had "always been thought of as a hinge point," a transparent connection between the realm of the square and the realm beyond it. At this point the ward councillor jumped in and moved the discussion to a line less likely to be challenged by the lawyer or other councillors. He asked the developer's project manager about the reaction to the Torch from those living on the east side in the new condominiums (few

6.1 Southeast corner of Dundas and Victoria streets, 1998. The Salvation Army building at that time served as a men's hostel. The three-storey building with the arched window on its right was the Senator, which included a restaurant and snack bar on the ground floor and a jazz club upstairs. | Author's collection.

were actually occupied at the time). Judging by the ease with which the manager shifted gears to speak about how excited the neighbours were – "at least the ones they heard from" (no numbers were offered) – it looked as if this question-answer sequence had been rehearsed prior to the meeting. The project manager added that the neighbours were extremely supportive of "the new, unique icon" that would "reinforce this special moment in the city's fabric."

After rescuing the project manager from the perils of a debate about design, and after the interlude on neighbours' feelings had brought back a feel-good tone, the ward councillor expertly addressed staff. Was the Torch a barrier or a hinge? The planner whose task it was to reply struggled somewhat but essentially made the following points:

- The Torch forms an edge to Dundas Square, not a boundary between east and west.
- The "spectacular signage" is of the sort already secured for Metropolis and is meant to revive the area like Times Square – to make it something new, something "quite beautiful."
- Staff had worked hard with the developer to make sure the sight lines offer as much transparency as possible.
- The building has an open arch structure.

- Staff brought the neighbours back a second time to review it.
- Staff are sure that it is not a barrier building but an edge to the square and that it manages to achieve the objectives of the official plan.

The planner's main point seemed to be that regardless of what The Torch was, it was what could be achieved given the conditions at hand. There was no further discussion. The process was managed straight into a vote. Motions to approve the zoning changes and the "spectacular signage" were carried without opposition. Much congratulatory talk – about how the project, begun in 1994, had progressed and about how the ripples of positive change could perhaps proceed farther east to the next ward – ensued on the floor of city council among politicians and proponents of the redevelopment. The sponsor of the Torch, his developer, and the ward councillor all received applause. Moments later, while waiting for the elevator to leave the council chamber, the Torch's sponsor, who stood next to me, said to the other proponents that the complainant's points were old-fashioned, that they were in the language of twenty years ago. How reminiscent his comments were of those used by the city at the OMB against the expropriated property owners. The restaurant and jazz bar owner had learned well the language of contemporary urban renewal.

The Torch was meant to be garish and over the top (Hume 1999a). The designer selected to create the cladding was Scéno Plus, a Montreal firm whose corporate motto is Technology, Art, Passion. Its goal is to "introduce powerful jolts of techno-architecture into often colourless urban landscapes" (Phillips 2000). The firm's most important client was Cirque du Soleil, for which it designed permanent venues at Disney World, the Bellagio Hotel in Las Vegas, and London's Battersea Power Station. Other clients included Paris' Paramount Opéra, which is a cinema multiplex, and Montreal's own classy Ex-Centris cinema complex on boulevard Saint-Laurent (ibid.). Patrick Bergé, founder of Scéno Plus, envisaged the inverted cone of the Torch as a "modern totem pole, its moving quilt of digital screens communicating news, sports and business updates, while flashing advertisements colour the night with the messages that will pay the bills" (ibid.). According to the *Toronto Star*'s architectural critic, the Torch advanced on the Atrium Tower's technology because it added movement (Hume 1999b); for Bergé, it went a giant step further, because there was nothing similar at Times Square. In the end, neither man accomplished a "mine is better than yours" coup because features of the Torch had to be scaled back due to cost. Figure 6.2 shows the original design for the Torch on the square. The advertising for the Torch would later be handled along with that for Metropolis. The Torch, as realized, is rather less than the original design of 1999 suggested it could be (see Figure 6.3).

6.2 Original design of the Torch by Scéno Plus Inc., 1999. | Courtesy of Scéno Plus Inc.

6.3 The Torch, 2008. The building stands on the southeast corner of Dundas and Victoria streets where the Salvation Army building once stood. | Courtesy of Sherrill Rand Harrison.

As for the new Senator building, its uses changed. It was to have been primarily retail. By 2002 its new use was a commercial spin-off of the International Olympic Committee. Called Olympic Spirit Toronto, this 52,000 square foot (about 4,800 square metres) complex on five levels combined entertainment, education, and retail facilities (the "trinity of synergy" model). It included an Olympics museum, an Olympic-themed retail shop, a full-service sports café, a 360-degree cinema, and a theme park in which visitors were to be "able to feel the spray of the bobsleigh, experience the sensation of actually leaping a distance of 29 feet in the long jump and be emotionally inspired with the sights and sounds of the Olympic Games" (Canadian Olympic Committee 2003).[3] Toronto's Olympic Spirit facility was the first of a series envisaged for a worldwide franchise. It officially opened at the end of September 2004 and closed less than two years later. In 2004 Bob Sniderman sold his holdings at the site (except for a small restaurant) and turned his energy to other projects.

The Square: Parcel D

The square was born into problems. Public consternation flows along two channels: how short on appeal it is and how far its current role is from what was announced for it. The result of the latter has been cynicism because it is unclear whether the square belongs to the public or to private businesses. A third matter, its physical siting within the fabric of that part of the city – the square is an island surrounded by traffic that is not a crossroads and does not knit east and west – has had no discussion.

The Winning Design

The winning design by Brown + Storey Architects was selected through a juried, international competition.[4] The competition brief described the square mainly by its physical characteristics, such as dimensions, and less so by its placement or function within a larger circulation and built-form context. At 3,250 square metres (0.4 hectares, or just under an acre), the park's design had to accommodate a focal feature, an entrance to the subway, and an entrance to the underground parking garage. It also had to accommodate the hectic signage that would nearly surround the square. According to the firm that organized the competition, there were few demands put on the designers. Indeed, the square "could have been just a concrete slab with a piano in the middle to meet the design requirements" (Immen 1998b).

The winners said their intention was to make the square simple, with clean lines, because there would be plenty of liveliness coming from the surrounding buildings. For them, a minimalist design could preserve the sense of space that would be created once the buildings on the site were taken down, and it would reflect the fact that the square came into being as a subtraction from the city fabric. They also wanted a space of calmness in the centre of the vibrancy created by the building facades and media towers around it. According to newspaper reports, the winner's design stood apart from the others because of that characteristic: others "were extremely busy, featuring elaborate fountains, multiple steps, reflecting pools, buildings and artworks ... even ... a stairway reminiscent of fire escapes that would give viewers an overhead view of a constantly changing light show" (Immen 1998b). Besides the kinetic lights and signs around the square, dense traffic contributed to its context. To some, the square is a traffic island, marooned; but for the designers the traffic was simply a condition they had to deal with. Their approach was to maximize the space and try to disengage it – make it more like an oasis. Whether island or oasis, the square is not anchored on any side.

The main features of the winning design were as follows: a floor of green granite that would rise about a metre from west to east; twenty-two recessed fountains in two lines and a lattice pattern of underground lighting toward the south side that would add contrast to the line of the floor; a line of trees and ornamental grasses along the south edge; a canopy along the northern Dundas Street edge where it curves east-southeast that would define that edge but also protect users from rain and sun; pedestrian access to the parking garage and to the subway near the northwest corner, which would take the form of a brightly lit opening looking down into the subway; and a combination raised performance stage and vehicle entrance to the underground garage that would occupy the southeast section. The total cost would be $2.5 million (Hume 1998a; Immen 1998b; Young 1999). The designers were given several more months to finalize the design. The winning design by Brown + Storey Architects is shown in Figure 6.4.

As the detailed work proceeded, Brown + Storey elaborated further on their concept. Known for their environmentally sensitive work in Toronto, they noted, for example, "that storm water running off the square would be collected in troughs at the edges of the square and recycled into the fountains" (Steed 2002). Brown talked about the square being "porous": "We're moving water through it, people through it, growing trees out of it – it's the new landscape, artificial, man-made, though the granite is real, natural. But we're making it porous, connecting the underground systems, pedestrian linkages, lighting, electricity, water, subway, everything that serves the upper surface. We're applying the same principles in any ecological system to the surface. That's what's interesting about the square. It's also about cultural infrastructure" (ibid.). Some critics made sense of the architects' intentions and liked them: their model won an Award of Excellence (*Canadian Architect* 1999) and a citation (*Architecture* 2000).

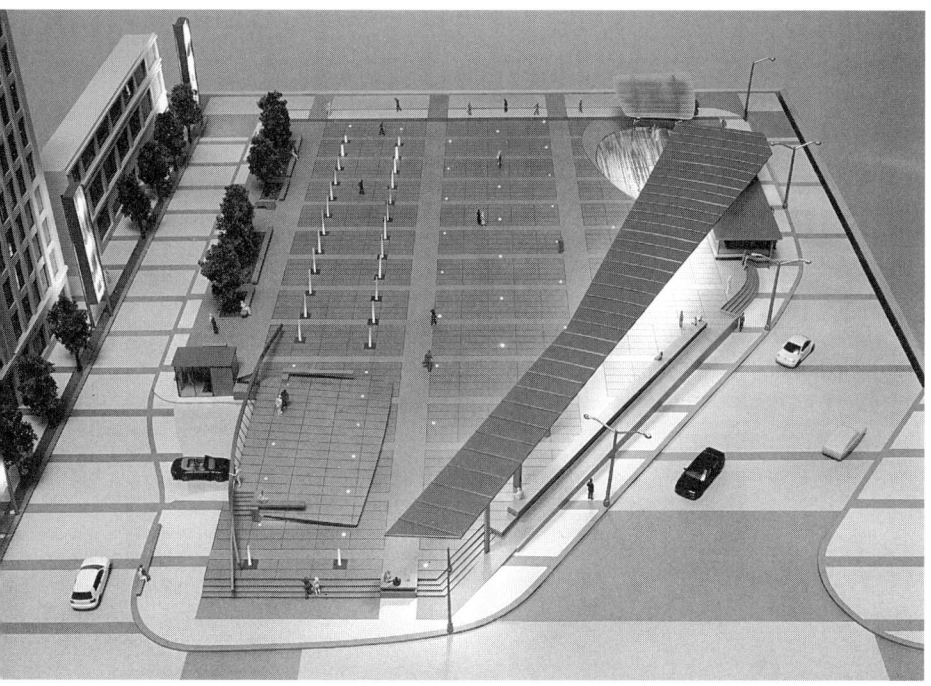

6.4 The winning design for Dundas Square, 1998, by Brown + Storey Architects. | Model by Richard Sinclair; photograph by Peter McCallum. Courtesy of Brown + Storey Architects.

The square was to be finished by the end of 2000 but was two years late. The bill for the square alone at that point was around $7 million, and much more was spent completing the light standards, washrooms below the surface, and the stage canopy. The square received bonus zoning contributions of over $500,000 from at least two new buildings. The contributions were the equivalent of subsidies by the city to the square, and they were negotiated by the city's planning department under section 37 of the *Planning Act*. One contribution ($300,000) was from the Trump International Hotel and Tower, and the other ($250,000) was from the Met, a residential condominium. Both buildings were nowhere near the square. Had the subsidies not gone to Dundas Square they might have gone, as such funds often do, to community centres, public parks, libraries, or assisted housing. They are intended to beef up community facilities the city cannot otherwise afford. The cost of completing the square kept rising.

Construction and Launch

The first task was to excavate for the 250-vehicle underground parking garage and then build it, which took longer than expected. One design challenge was ensuring that the slope of the square and the plinth on its southeast corner had sufficient height to allow vehicles to enter the parking garage. A series of delays was more troublesome. The first, in the summer of 2000, was a strike by the workers who supplied concrete. Then a flooding problem meant hydro transformers had to be relocated. Following that incident, tunnelling to connect the garage to the subway was done inappropriately, and, in the course of correcting this, the waterproofing membrane in the garage was damaged. Then the four-storey high piston designed to operate the parking garage elevator turned out to be two metres too short (Kuitenbrouwer 2001b). The final glitch – tiny but ironic – was that signage was missing when the garage opened in September 2001, so drivers circled in the bowels of the earth, searching for an exit (Kuitenbrouwer 2001a). That problem was quickly rectified, and the garage began functioning very well.

The hoardings around the square came down, unannounced, in November 2002. The green Brazilian granite flooring had been passed over for cheaper Quebec granite, which is technically dark green but looks dark grey. It has a special water-jet finish that, when wet, is supposed to have a shine to it. The quartz in the granite gives it highlights. The two rows of water jets and associated fibre optic lighting were tested and found to work well. An aperture planned for the north side of the square had to be delayed, but once completed it would consist of the actual stairway into the subway and a grid formation in an oval frame through which light from below would shine. As for the canopy on the north side, the architects were quoted as saying that it was not so much an edge as a way to mediate "between traffic-laden Dundas Street and the inside of the square. [They] wanted to create an inner space between those two worlds" (Hume 2002). The architects did not want a sense of front or back to the square. However, the fairly steep rise on the Victoria Street side and the placement and orientation of the stage created a distinct front and back.

The formal opening took place on 30 May 2003. Singers, bands, and buskers were hired. A crowd assembled. People waited to be entertained. Police were present in large numbers. Mike Gauvreau, the local drummer who had been entertaining spontaneous crowds for free outside the Eaton Centre's main door for over fifteen summers (*Globe and Mail* 1999), was not invited to perform. He was moved several metres west on Dundas so that his busking would not interfere with the high-priced entertainers hired for the occasion. Later that summer he moved his drums and base of operations a few metres down Yonge, still on the Eaton Centre side of the street slightly south of the square, then disappeared from the area for a few years, and returned in 2008.

In its first year, there was little acclaim for the square from the local media or the general public. Responses ranged mainly along the lower end of the spectrum from tentativeness ("let's wait and see how it gets used") to observations about perceived shortcomings (a highway aesthetic; poor seating; general emptiness; or to puzzlement and dislike: in Gertrude Stein parlance, "there's no there there" [Rochon 2003]). The canopy was described as "Gardineresque," a reference to the useful but detested elevated highway that separates downtown Toronto from Lake Ontario and is named after a former mayor. The descriptor captures the feeling of dismay that a piece of one ugly structure had been given lodging in another. There has been little applause for the square since. However, the square does match the designers' image of a space that holds itself back and allows things to happen in it (Steed 2002), like a stage setting (Hume 2000a).

The square is barely out of the box, so perhaps, with the designers, one has to allow that the square is getting used to the city and the city is getting used to the square as a space. It may gain a place in the urban imagery of Toronto. Certainly, it is important to separate observations about the design from its management.

Regulations for the Square: First Iteration

How Dundas Square would be managed has had four iterations so far. A quick summary is shown in Table 6.1. The first iteration, expressed repeatedly through the city approvals and OMB processes, was that the new square would be run like Nathan Phillips Square. The argument in favour of the square – as it was made by the planning department and accepted by the OMB – was composed of several reasons. One reason was that the area was deficient in open public space. Another was that the city intended to regulate activities in the square the way it did in Nathan Phillips Square, which was the successful apron of city hall (see, e.g., Joint Board 1998b, Exhibit 69, 53; Joint Board 1998j, 6). The OMB wrote that its understanding of the square was that it was to be "public," like Nathan Phillips Square. The evidence put

Table 6.1 Changing management of Dundas Square

Iteration	Timing	City department
1	Pre-OMB decision	Urban Development Services
2	Post-OMB decision	Urban Development Services
3	Post-2000	Economic Development, Culture and Tourism (from ch. 270 to 636, new *Municipal Code*)
4	c. 2005	Economic Development, Culture and Tourism

Source: Compiled by author from City of Toronto documents.

to the board by the programmer of Nathan Phillips Square was "that the city intends to control it through regulating the activities of the square and to program and promote activities in the square" (Joint Board 1998k, 6). The board further described the square as providing a sense of place and a feature that would encourage an increase in pedestrian-orientated activities. All of this illustrates that the picture conveyed to the public was of a new public square coming into being, one that would be owned by the city in the same way that Nathan Phillips Square was owned by the city and which the city would operationally manage along the same lines as the existing model for public squares described in chapter 270 of the pre-amalgamation *Municipal Code*.

Programming in Nathan Phillips Square is geared to community events. There is no charge to use the space, which is available for booking every day of the year. Only not-for-profit and charitable organizations can make bookings. See Appendix 10 for a sample of the events booked for Nathan Phillips Square over a period of several months.

The applicable *Municipal Code* chapters also stipulate compliance with human rights conventions. There are two basic conditions: any person or organization seeking a permit must comply "in all respects with the Ontario Human Rights Code" and must make its event open to anyone who wants to attend. Given the additional "right of entry" section (270-11), any person has the right to be in the public square as long as he or she does not engage in prohibited actions such as lighting fires and so on.

These, then, were the conceptions of "public" and "openness" that prevailed for Dundas Square, if only because no others were suggested at any time and because those were the principles and regulations that governed the template square. So that was the image the public would have had as it heard the arguments in favour of the development of Dundas Square. There was no obvious reason to think the city intended to do something different.

Regulations for the Square: Second Iteration

The redefinition of the square was pushed along by the OMB. When the OMB approved the overall development in June 1998, it attached conditions of approval to its decision, one of which said that a Nathan Phillips Square–type of municipal code amendment was to be prepared by 30 August 1998 (Joint Board 1998k, 45). The planning department provided a new draft bylaw on public squares (Toronto 1998e) that seemed generic because it was titled "Public squares" but was actually specific to Dundas Square. Dundas Square was the only diagrammed square attached as a schedule to the new chapter 270. The explanation given was that the chapter was called "Public squares" because Dundas Square did not yet have an official name.

Chapter 270 had three main features: (1) it was created so as to be open to a future consolidated bylaw governing use of the city's public squares; (2) it proposed that permissions for use and prohibitions for Dundas Square be the same as for other public squares; and (3) it added one exception to the second feature, which was to leave open whether commercial use of the square would be allowed. In effect, the planning department said that in order to meet the board's approval conditions, Dundas Square "should initially be regulated in a manner similar to Nathan Phillips Square" (Toronto 1998e, 5). It looked like the planning department was not recommending public-private management for the square, because that was not the form used for Nathan Phillips Square. On the other hand, the writers of the OMB/Joint Board decision lauded the kind of management of public spaces they had observed on their one-day visit to New York City's Times Square. That was the model the OMB had advised the city to use through its tone and words in its decision, including in its obiter dicta (Joint Board 1998k, 33-34, 44, 46).

City council decided that the planning department would hand responsibility for Dundas Square over to the Corporate Services Department and its facilities management group after the design competition was finished. The transfer occurred before formal approval for commercial activities and gated events was completed. With the reorganization of departments, which followed shortly after Toronto's amalgamation with six other governments, responsibility for Dundas Square shifted again, this time to the Economic Development, Culture and Tourism Department.

Regulations for the Square: Third Iteration

In December 2001 city council approved a new section on public squares for the *Municipal Code*.[5] Like chapter 270, chapter 636 deals exclusively with Dundas Square, with detailed elaboration of the Yonge-Dundas Square Board of Management (Article 2) and the use of the square (Article 3). With respect to how individuals can use the square when it is not rented, the stipulations for Dundas Square are virtually identical to those for Nathan Phillips Square.[6] Beyond that, Dundas Square differs from the template square in several respects. In essence, chapter 636 gives express permission for commercial uses and deletes the need to make all events open to anyone who wishes to attend (see section 636-18, Compliance with Human Rights Code).

Soon after the transfer from the planning department to the Economic Development, Culture and Tourism Department, the square's principal use was declared as serving economic development interests. Indeed, the department said that this had been the intended purpose of the square: "The Yonge-Dundas Square was intended to be used largely for commercial events for which a fee would be charged" (Toronto 2001a, 2-3). This completely contradicts the arguments made at the OMB hearing by the city. According to the new commissioner, Dundas Square was to be distinguished from other civic squares: the square would be a tool of economic development, and this mandate would be carried out in conjunction with the Business Improvement Area (ibid., 6, 7).

A wholly new "governance model" to manage the square, a Board of Management, was developed and approved by city council (Toronto 2001a, 7). Within the classification system of the city's agencies, boards, and commissions, it fell into the category of program operating board, "which means that it delivers a service which is closely aligned with a service provided by a City department and therefore should be included in the planning and budgeting process for the overall program delivered through the department" (ibid., 11), in this case Economic Development, Culture and Tourism. As a program operating board, the Board of Management is required to establish and maintain close functional alignment with that department.

The Board of Management's task is to act on behalf of city council, taking charge of the maintenance, operation, and control of the square. It holds financial responsibility for the square's operations, which initially included making the square financially self-sufficient by 2005 (Toronto 2001b). It is charged with operating the square on behalf of the City in accordance with prudent business practices (ibid.), and can establish booking policies for the square, hire staff and consultants, and enter into contracts for services. It has to prepare a three-year business plan each year with the assistance of Toronto's Economic Development, Culture and Tourism Department, through which it reports to council, and in consultation with the city's chief financial officer and treasurer. The Board is required to meet at least seven times a year and to deposit its minutes with the city clerk. Its volunteer board members receive no remuneration, but they are assisted by staff.

City council establishes the board's membership – that is, the number of members who will represent a given interest or constituency and its voting status. Of the nine voting members of the Board of Management, four are selected by the BIA. Another is the ward councillor. The other voting members include one member each from Toronto Theatre Alliance, Ryerson University, "a residents' association" (not specified, not even geographically), and the Yonge Street Mission. The last three are hard-pressed to meet the rule that says nominating organizations should propose members who "have a strong interest in economic development activities and the development of large-scale entertainment events" (*Globe and Mail* 2001). The BIA is expected to give the board "in-kind contributions such as administrative support, office space and marketing expertise" (ibid.). Thus the BIA and the

Board of Management of Dundas Square are intimately tied to one another, with other members having smaller stakes or being nonvoting technical or staff representatives of the Toronto Parking Authority, the Police Services Board, or the Economic Development, Culture and Tourism Department. The BIA plus one (such as the ward councillor) can always control the board.

The advent of Dundas Square introduced five new conditions for public squares in Toronto: (1) a commercial function within the city's structure, (2) a management board dominated by commercial rather than civic interests, (3) exclusionary uses expressly permitted instead of expressly forbidden on the square, (4) use of a square divided into primary (commercial) and residual (public) – that is, public leisure in the square is a residual use that is permitted if the square is not being used for a fee-for-permit event, and (5) no days are set aside for free civic events.

None of these changes was implemented by the planning department, but they all emerged as a result of how planners and everyone else used the institutional planning framework to redevelop the area. This included contradictory imperatives by the OMB that the city develop a Nathan Phillips Square–type municipal code amendment and that it take New York as its image for how to do this.

What the square was to be – and where it had come from – were laid out in the press release announcing its official opening on 30 May, 2003:

> Located at the intersection of Yonge and Dundas Streets, Toronto's most visible event venue can accommodate special events, promotions, commercial film shoots and receptions of various sizes and configurations. Available for permit 24 hours a day, seven days a week, the Square can draw audiences into diverse and creative environments ... When not booked by corporations and not-for-profit organizations for events, the Square becomes an urban plaza to be enjoyed by residents and tourists alike ... It is the centerpiece of the Yonge Dundas Redevelopment Project that began in 1996. Yonge-Dundas Square is part of the vision of the City of Toronto and its partners to redefine urban space and transform the heart of the city into a vibrant, safe and livable downtown. (Toronto 2003)

According to the press release, the square will be residually public at most, which contradicts arguments about its status that were made at the OMB. The press release also states that the square emerged from a project that began in 1996, which puts into question the city's claim at the OMB that redevelopment was a continuation of the regeneration plan that began in 1994. Finally, the press release suggests that to redefine urban space for commercial spectacles is to make it not only vibrant but also safe and livable. Does this suggestion also imply that public space, in the ordinary sense of belonging to the public, is less than or the reverse of vibrant, safe, and livable?

The Board of Management was given the task of achieving financial self-sufficiency within the first three years of operation and, to that end, was given the right to set fees. Rates were therefore driven purely by profit, not civic-mindedness. Indeed, on the most civic days of the year – the statutory holidays, Victoria Day, Canada Day, Labour Day, and New Year's Eve – the board charges premium rates. The fee schedule resembles a typical commercial holiday rates model: dead of winter rates are half those of the shoulder season; shoulder season rates are two-thirds those in high season; and high season rates are half the premium rate. Discounts on those fees can be obtained by registered charities and nonprofit organizations (but there is still a minimum $500 fee) or for multidate bookings. There are also rates for those who want a permit for a commercial photo or film shoot or to use the space for promotional sampling. Added to the fees are taxes and a range of services such as contract security services ("A preferred list of suppliers may exist" [section 3.29]; the security contract at the outset was with a US firm, Intelligarde), cleaners, on-site coordinators, electricians, and audiovisual technicians. According to the website of the Downtown Yonge Business Improvement Area, the square's management takes 10 percent of liquor sales and charges for kiosks set up to sell things, and takes 1 percent of admissions on gated events.

The square became a commercial venture on property owned by the city. If it is public, it is residually so – in its failed moments. The square was set up so that its space would be for sale 24 hours a day, 365 days a year. When the space is sold, the public can be kept out altogether. When it is not sold, the public can sit in it or walk across it under the watchful gaze of private security. If cynicism has been expressed about the square, it may be because its shift from public to private commercial space followed a partly secret set of processes under the aegis of the planning framework, which included an OMB hearing that further confused the square's status, and an unveiling that revealed that the square's mandate was to make money.

Regulations for the Square: Fourth Iteration

In mid-2005 the city lifted the requirement that the square become completely self-financing. It became evident to the Board of Management, probably as early as October 2003, when the square had been open only a few months, that it could not be both financially self-sustaining and a community resource. By late 2004 the board was petitioning the city for financial relief. However, none of the five conditions that make Yonge-Dundas Square a new kind of Toronto square were changed. Yonge-Dundas Square's website indicates that it still operates differently from others in the city; it is a square run by a Board of Management "as a business venture."

The Eaton Centre

The Eaton Centre had been planning or executing changes since it "saw the light" regarding the destructive effects of its opaque, fortress-like structure on the surrounding area. Well before the overall Yonge-Dundas redevelopment plans were completed and approved, the owners of the Eaton Centre planned to open up the long facade on the west side of Yonge by pushing out three metres onto sidewalk it already owned and making several new doors and shop windows. These plans were repeatedly claimed by the proponents of redevelopment to be among its successes, which was inaccurate.[7] To the revised facade Eaton's added huge backlit ads (6 × 18 metres) down the length of the street – a kind of horizontal media tower or media wall (Hume 1999b).

The T. Eaton Company went bankrupt in 1999 and moved out of the Centre. The store's 900,000 square feet (more than 83,000 square metres) of the Centre's total 1.6 million square feet (more than 148,000 square metres) remained eerily empty for several months. Then Sears moved in and tried to fill the gigantic retail space. Shortly afterward, in February 2001, Cineplex-Odeon went into bankruptcy protection, and a month later the eighteen-cinema cluster in the north end of the Eaton Centre suddenly closed. When it opened in 1979, this multiplex had been "the world's largest cluster of theatres under one roof," a fact that was noted in the Guinness Book of World Records (Powell 2001a; Drabinsky 1995, chap. 7). Whatever could be done with eighteen rooms that seated from 57 to 137 people on sloping concrete floors? Apparently nothing.

In 2003 major renovations began at the Centre's north end. The police substation located near the north entrance was taken apart during the summer because of the renovations. Whether this offshoot of 52 Division will be reinstalled after the renovations are complete will be a decision for the police to make because it will be at their expense. The Centre would be happy to have it reopened.[8] A clothing retailer new to Canada, the Swedish firm Hennes & Mauritz (H&M), opened at the north end of the Eaton Centre on three floors of newly constructed space (30,000 square feet, about 3,800 square metres). A new entrance to the mall was built, this time squarely on Yonge Street south of Dundas, with a narrower sidewalk in front of it to discourage loitering. Above H&M, another media tower – sixty metres high with five screens, all of them facing the square – was completed in late 2004.

6.5 The generously large triangular sidewalk at the Eaton Centre's main door at Yonge and Dundas, 1999. Normally filled with street vendors, proselytizers, shoppers, buskers, students, and people transferring between the subway and streetcar, the space was a design requirement associated with the development of the Eaton Centre in the 1970s. | Author's collection.

6.6 Reduced sidewalk at Yonge and Dundas outside the Eaton Centre, 2008. The main door of the centre was moved south (out of view to the left). | Courtesy of Sherrill Rand Harrison.

The redesigned features have not fully achieved what the Eaton Centre's owners had desired since at least 1997, which was to move all crowds away from its front door by appropriating Dundas Square as its "front yard," as one journalist called it (Hume 2003). Figure 6.5 shows the triangular apron in front of the Eaton Centre's main door in 1999, while Figure 6.6 shows the apron's reduced ampleness after reconstruction. Loitering has been reduced but not eliminated.

New Street Management: The Downtown Yonge BIA

The Yonge Street Business and Resident Association (YSBRA), which had come into being in 1995, evolved into a full-fledged Business Improvement Area (BIA) by July 2001. It joined the forty-six other BIAs in Toronto at that time, all of which were gathered under an umbrella organization, the Toronto Association of Business Improvement Areas. Business improvement areas are governed by the city via its *Municipal Code*, chapter 19, which is in line with a mandate delivered to the city by the provincial *Municipal Act*.[9]

Membership in the Downtown Yonge BIA (DYBIA) includes approximately 1,800 business tenants and 200 property owners whose boundaries are shown in Figure 6.7. Its budget is around $1.5 million for safety and maintenance, marketing, administration, and cost-shared capital expenditures.

The DYBIA is implementing the vision of the street in the interests of business tenants and owners. First and foremost is its focus on keeping the area safe and clean. From the outset the BIA assumed that it could not move forward much on other initiatives until this was accomplished, so more of its budget was dedicated to security and maintenance than to marketing. By contrast, other BIAs in Toronto tend to put marketing first.

Implementing a safe-and-clean policy has taken several forms. The BIA has extra police patrols on its streets. While the DYBIA believes it is well served by the city police for emergency calls, it wants more proactive policing than the Toronto Police Service can offer. In the BIA's view, private security services would not be sufficient for their types of problems – drug dealing, aggressive panhandling, and public urination. Therefore, they hire "pay duty" police officers to establish the presence they desire. These officers work in uniform but are not on regular duties assigned by their division. They are paid from the private funds of whoever hires them, yet they report to the police service, not to those who pay them. Whatever policing went on from the substation in the north end of the Eaton Centre at Dundas did not seem to serve the area beyond the Centre to the desired standard.

Ironically, one reason the BIA believes it cannot get enough policing is that the police division within which it sits also has to manage policing of the formally designated entertainment district southwest of Yonge-Dundas. That

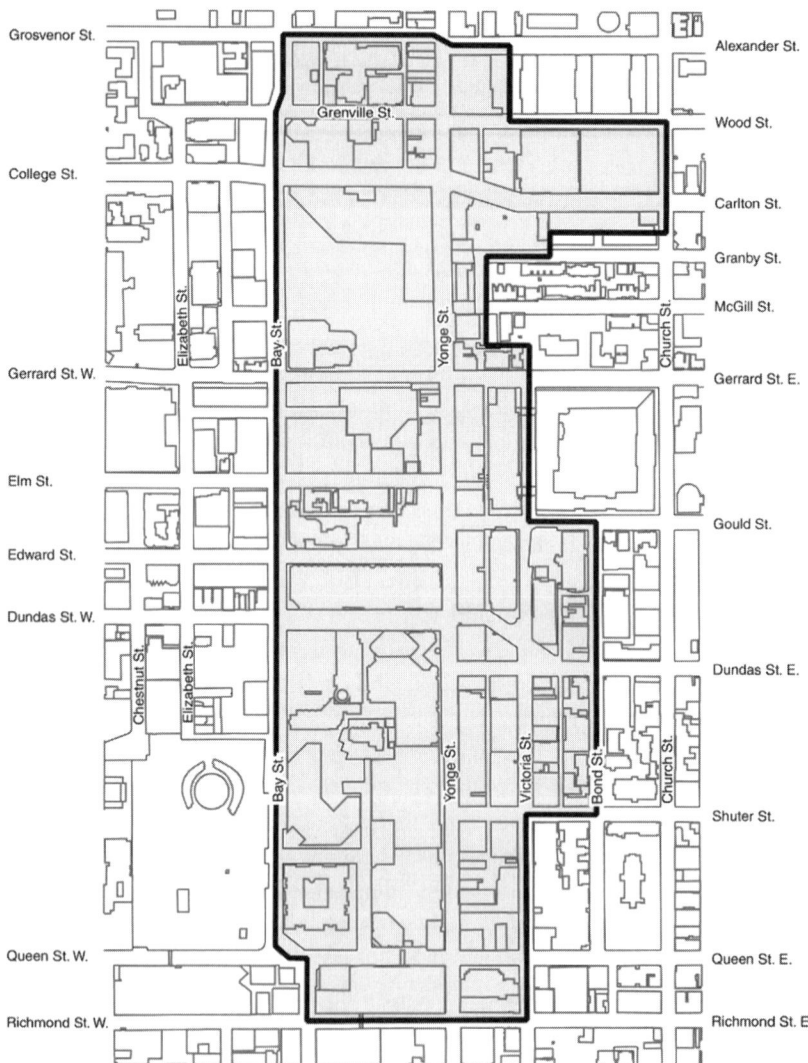

6.7 Downtown Yonge Business Improvement Area boundaries, 2001. | Courtesy of James Robinson, Downtown Yonge Business Improvement Area.

area takes a lot of evening and weekend resources. Queen's Park (the seat of the provincial legislature) and the consulate of the United States also place heavy demands on the same police division. They are sites of periodic protests. The DYBIA lobbied the city for more police resources but was unsuccessful. It was especially displeased to see extra policing being drawn to Toronto's entertainment district, which is a rational response. However, this problem developed because of city council's earlier inaction regarding, on the one hand, the emergence of the designated entertainment area at the same time that redevelopment at Yonge and Dundas was being pursued and, on the other, the power individual councillors can exert over city-wide decisions.

In addition, the DYBIA was not able to get crime data from the police service to help it better understand what was going on on its streets. To complicate the situation further, in 2004 the police service changed its precinct boundaries so that the DYBIA's territory fell into two of them. The dividing line is now down the middle of Yonge Street: 51 Division patrols the east side but, for some reason, not Dundas Square, which lies off the east side; 52 Division looks after the west side but makes a jog eastward to include Dundas Square. Metropolis and the Hard Rock Cafe, which lie north and south of the square, respectively, are part of 51 Division's duties. By 2004, the DYBIA suspected that crime was going down, or at least not increasing. (This was also the view of one of the nearby residents' associations; however, the other nearby association disagreed.)

According to the DYBIA, closed circuit television (CCTV) surveillance of the streets would be an asset. Two matters delayed immediate widespread installation. Legal issues were surmounted by putting up signs to say that people would be monitored by CCTV. The overriding hindrance was cost. The police wanted video surveillance in the entertainment district and at Dundas Square, but once they figured out the cost of monitoring the cameras, they decided it was impractical for them to shoulder the task. The BIA did not have enough funds for full camera monitoring, although it did put five cameras on the square from the outset. The cameras captured images of a fatal shooting, including the alleged gunman, in the square in July 2005. But two other shooting sprees (with one fatality) near but off the square in the same year generated calls for more cameras along the streets themselves. By 2006 police and the DYBIA were pilot testing and preparing for more CCTV installations. According to a press report, the manager of an electronics store at Yonge and Elm said the situation was worse than it had been ten years ago, "when the only thing he had to worry about were thugs breaking into his business overnight. Now he said he sees drug deals and gang activity going on at all times of the day just outside his shop's window" (Gandhi 2005). This was what the redevelopment approach was supposed to fix. At the same time, the executive director of the DYBIA was quoted as saying that he would have expected that "the millions of dollars that have been poured into revitalizing the area since the 1990s could have prevented these incidents from happening" (ibid.).

Another element of the program to keep the area safe and clean is the work of the three-person "clean team," which does tasks such as removing graffiti, posters, litter, and gum from the walls and sidewalks. Business improvement areas that do extra cleaning do so reluctantly: they believe this is the city's job, pure and simple. For its part, the city is also reluctant to see this basic city task being done privately, if only because it raises union issues with its own staff. Finally, the DYBIA had a consultant look at best practices in North American cities regarding how to handle social issues that are part of the BIA's strategic planning, and it joined a partnership that researches urban health issues in the downtown area (Educon Marketing and Research Systems 2003).

On the marketing side, the DYBIA hired urban designers to develop a streetscape master plan. Although the plan will not have the legal status of a secondary plan, it will nonetheless carry considerable weight. The DYBIA and the city split the cost of the plan's preparation under a special program available to BIAs. All capital improvements (e.g., specially designed traffic signal poles) will also be paid for through this cost-sharing arrangement.

Together with these initiatives, which were launched to ensure that the DYBIA's vision would be implemented across its territory, the association has an all but decisive voice on the Dundas Square Board of Management. It has, in effect, secured as its own project the spectacularization of this piece of Toronto. The private organization has used the tools offered to it through public legislation to turn public space and services to its advantage. That power was as much given to it as it was taken.

Local Organizations

The Toronto East Downtown Residents Association (TEDRA) has had a few tough years. It had been involved in the regeneration plan, had fully supported the redevelopment plan, and even had a seat on YSBRA's board of directors (Joint Board 1998b, Exhibit 34, Tab 10, 220). In 2000, TEDRA changed its name to Toronto East Downtown Neighbourhood Association (TEDNA) to reflect that its executive members were frequently people whose jobs, rather than residences, were in the area. Members were often employed in the area's many poverty-related organizations and agencies. As a residents' association, TEDRA had to restrict votes to residents, regardless of whether they were owners or tenants. The renamed organization was supposed to get around that restriction. Soon after TEDNA came into being, however, some residents who had been active in the local association for several years objected to a transformation that gave as much weight to the interests of social agencies as those of residents. Although the residents recognized that social agencies had interests in the area, they still wanted a residents' association that was capable of expressing their interests. These residents acknowledged that there were some places where the interests of both groups overlapped, but there were certainly others where they were opposed.

It was over these diverging interests that the residents had their greatest difficulty with the ward councillor. Consequently, having a combined organization with an agency-heavy executive that, in their view, shared more interests with the councillor than with residents was a problem. Using a modest version of the pack-the-hall tactic, a group of residents got itself elected to the board at a TEDNA general meeting and declared itself the legal successor to TEDRA and TEDNA, to their names and to their intellectual and material assets (see the Garden District Residents Association website). The group demanded that the papers and financial records be turned over to the new board and that three of the previous members of the executive explain certain accounting irregularities.

The ward councillor asked the new board to resign to invalidate the election. It refused – to no one's surprise. The board's central concern was that the residents' association had become a "cheering group" for the ward councillor and no longer operated independently from his influence. The new board has since carried on as a residents' association in the councillor's ward, the boundaries of which include Dundas Square (Sherbourne to Yonge and Queen to Gerrard). The replacement calls itself the Garden District Residents Association (GDRA) to reflect the area's historical association with Allan Gardens. The councillor has gradually had to acknowledge that the GDRA exists but does not accept that it really represents the community. Meanwhile, a new organization has formed that brings together those who run the social service agencies in the area and some residents. Probably by design and perhaps as a way to thumb their noses at the GDRA, members of the new organization chose to recycle the TEDNA acronym, but this time it stood for Toronto East Downtown Neighbourhood Alliance.

The number of shelter beds in the area is greater, by any measure, than anywhere else in the city – the area has far more than its share. The GDRA has argued that the homeless are transient and therefore identify with the services rather than the community. This situation raises conflicts because residents and small businesses believe that the homeless frequently misuse community spaces, making it difficult for others to enjoy them too. The GDRA says the representatives of the social service sector have a bona fide interest in the area, which is largely to maintain the status quo in terms of services provided, while the interests of homeowners, regular tenants, and small businesses, which is to see changes to the balance of uses in the area, are also legitimate. The GDRA wants the social service sector to participate but not take over the residents' association. Nor does it want the ward councillor to control the association. The degree to which this association challenges the councillor makes it distinctive in this ward. An open letter on the GDRA website, dated 21 January 2002, explained the new board's perspective: "If a neighbourhood association is to reflect the needs and aspirations of the whole community, it must be free of political influence. Having municipal staff on its board of directors or providing overt support to political candidates does not bode well for the integrity of such an association. If a councillor feels free to call for mass resignations to invalidate the duly elected board of an independent organization, such [an] organization is but an extension of a political office." The GDRA expressed contempt for the uncritical policies of the previous board, which supported the city at every turn and, in particular, did not force the city to deal with the rising number of social service agencies, facilities, and criminal activities. The current board is very clear that it will not be managed by the ward councillor.

Has the Yonge-Dundas redevelopment provided the benefits the association sought when it participated as TEDRA? It said it wanted the square because it would provide more open space. The current view is that the square is not an amenity for its residents and that there are already several excellent, or potentially excellent, spaces, including Allan Gardens and Moss Park, in the area. First, more attention to the existing spaces would have been preferable. Second, the idea of opening a vista has been completely defeated by the media towers and reconfiguration of the north end of the Eaton Centre. The effect has been to close down rather than open up the view lines. Third, no positive effect on crime has been achieved east of the square, and the GDRA believes it has the data to show this.

This almost bare-knuckle struggle over urban space has taken the classic form of the dispossessed versus ordinary home and business owners and tenants. The tension is not helped by the fact that the city has been unsuccessful in sharing socially assisted housing across all the wards, despite its considerable efforts over the years. At the same time, it would be naive to not realize that redevelopment in the area is in its early stages. Redevelopment will financially benefit those who hold out and, at the same time, will displace many of the very services the residents' association currently has trouble accommodating. We have seen this before.

By comparison, the McGill-Granby Residents' Association has remained in the ward councillor's good graces. It, too, was involved with the regeneration plans and redevelopment initiative. It likes the square, is relieved that crime and loitering has not gone up (as far as it can tell), and, overall, finds that nothing much has changed for its residents. Complaints about noise levels from concerts have been addressed by insisting that groups use the square's sound system, which curbs the decibels. Complaints about the flashing signs from people north of the square were expected to be resolved once Metropolis was finished because its height will block them out.

Why does the tiny McGill-Granby group sit on the Dundas Square board while the larger GDRA does not – even though the square falls within GDRA boundaries? The predecessor of the GDRA, TEDNA, was originally identified by name as the residents' association that should be appointed as a voting member of the Dundas Square Board of Management. The name of the McGill-Granby group, which represents a miniscule residential area by comparison, was nowhere to be found (Toronto 2001a, 3, 9, 18). At city council in December 2001, the wording was changed from naming TEDNA specifically to identifying a generic space for a member of a resident's association (ibid., 1). The ward councillor wanted the change. The tiny organization can see that its interests lie close enough to those of the ward councillor that it is willing to risk being managed by him to some extent. By contrast, the GDRA's interests are much further from the ward councillor's, and it is adamant about remaining free of political influence.

The reverend who ran the Yonge Street Mission and spoke against the redevelopment on behalf of the appellants at the hearing, warning about the dangers of associating black youth with criminal activity, no longer works at the mission. The Yonge Street Mission now supports the project wholeheartedly, and its executive director was appointed by the ward councillor to sit on the board of Dundas Square. The Yonge Street Mission celebrated its 100th anniversary party in the square in September 2004, at which time the ward councillor called the mission the one constant on Yonge Street. The mission even got into the spirit of spectacular consumption when it bought one of the media signs on the square as an investment. It rents the sign to ClearChannel.

Replacement and Renovation

Beyond those property changes already described, others were taking place in the vicinity. The Atrium Tower was erected by ClearChannel on top of a building near the northwest corner of Yonge and Dundas. It stands 67 metres high and has 1,860 square metres of advertising space that can accommodate fifteen to twenty advertisers (Theobald 1999). These billboards in the sky are "giant, sculpted signs, big and deep enough to accommodate objects as large as a car" (Hume 1999b). Hume observes that the media tower concept explodes the usual billboard into three dimensions. Where ordinarily there would be a building wall, now there is just pure structure with the paradoxical function of being both invisible and unavoidable (Hume 1999b).

Along the top of the building, on the south side of the square, SkyeMedia erected seven large signs, which were described in the application and public meeting announcement as seven spectacular backlit and front-lit vinyl roof signs that faced onto Dundas Square and Yonge Street. The signs range in size from twenty-eight to eighty-nine square meters, and one includes an electronic video screen (*Globe and Mail* 2001).

The Hard Rock Cafe, located on the south side of the square, underwent a $6.5 million renovation in 2001 and 2002. It also has an outdoor café that runs the length of the restaurant and faces the square. The twelve-metre high, terracotta-clad building carries a listed historical designation. It stands next to the forty-five-metre Hermant Building, which underwent renovation and improvement to its terracotta facade under the grant and loan program before 1997. It houses a number of jewellers and diamond cutters. Farther south on the east side of Yonge (no. 193) the Montreal distillery, Corby's, moved its head office into Heintzman Hall across from the Eaton Centre in 1998. The building facade was cleaned and repaired.

A number of new businesses and retailers have opened. Prior to redevelopment approval in September 1997, a new Gap store opened on the northwest corner of Yonge and Dundas. This was a relatively small store, located in a former bank, compared to its Toronto flagship store at Bloor and Bay streets. It was reported that Gap had a careful real estate strategy to pick sites in older urban areas that are on the upswing. The president of International Gap Inc. said he had had his eye on this location for a long time (Israelson 1997). By 2001 Gap's international strategy seemed to be to close smaller stores and increase the average size of remaining stores because a few large ones are more cost-efficient than several small ones (Bone 2001). Given that strategy, and with the large new H&M with its similar retail objectives of stylish clothing at moderate prices located directly across the street, it was only a short while before Gap closed its Yonge and Dundas store. Next door to the former Gap, a 10,000 square foot (about 930 square metres) sporting goods flagship store was opened by Bata in 2000 (Theobald 1999) but closed down soon after. Guess Jeans opened in 2001 (Immen 2001a). The Outfitters, an upscale retailer of outdoor clothing and equipment, opened where the Silver Rail restaurant had been (at no. 235) with much fanfare in late 1998, but it was closed down within less than a year by its owner, the Hudson's Bay Company. The closure coincided with the removal of the company official responsible for its opening in the first place (Slinger 1998; Strauss 1999). A David Bitton Buffalo store moved in.

Sam the Record Man shut down business in June 2007 after forty-six years on the east side of Yonge Street and a block north of Dundas at Gould (the store spent a total of seventy years in the vicinity of that location). The company had declared bankruptcy in 2001 and was rescued temporarily through reorganization. Father Sam stepped aside and left his sons Bob (owner of the Senator restaurants and the jazz club above them, and a major player in the area's redevelopment) and Jason (a musician) in charge. They kept only two of the company's stores, including the original one on Yonge, open. However, it too closed in 2007, and the building was bought by Ryerson University. The closure indicates how changes in communication technology have long affected retailing in this part of downtown Toronto. The owners tried to save that store, as well as their two restaurants and jazz club, by saving the Yonge-Dundas area from itself, but to no avail.

The area's precariousness and the closures of several stores have been attributed to the long delay in building Metropolis. One interviewee said that some firms came in too soon (e.g., Bata) and could not or would not hold on until Metropolis opened. Given that it took nearly ten years from project approval until most of the Metropolis tenants opened, this is hardly surprising. In the meantime the site was a hole in the ground surrounded by hoardings that ruptured the street's retailing rhythm, and around the site there was a covered sidewalk between the hoarding and street that was narrow, dark, and usually unkempt.

Changes were also taking place on the block east of Yonge, on Victoria Street. A new hotel and condominium complex opened in spring 2004. Called the Pantages Tower, it has 341 condominium units and 242 hotel rooms, and, at 45 storeys, it is well over the as of right zoning height. The project, first announced in the mid-1990s, had several setbacks on the way to completion. A 1,400-seat theatre was to have been built next to the then-existing Pantages theatre. Garth Drabinsky's Livent, which owned Pantages, was involved with this small theatre. However, when financial and legal woes beset Livent and its owners, the theatre part of the project was cancelled (Pendakur 1998; Bill Taylor 1998; MacDonald and Waldie 1998). The developer, Dundee Realty, sought and received permission to reconfigure the structure without the theatre.

Displacement

Hostel Beds

The Salvation Army's property at 259 Victoria/37 Dundas East had been used as a winter men's hostel since 1997-98. But it was wanted for the redevelopment plan by two parties: the ward councillor wanted to see hostel use erased from the area, and the city wanted the land so it could sell it to the developer of the Sniderman property next door. This would allow the Torch to be built and the Senator Restaurants property to be extended. Because the Salvation Army agreed to sell its property to the city, it did not become part of the contentious expropriation hearings.

The Salvation Army constructed the building in the 1950s.[10] Initially, it had been used as a supply space for books, uniforms, music, and the like. Later, the Salvation Army's Corrections Department and the national office's social services function moved into the space. The building's uses evolved: at one point it was used as a church and drop-in centre. The Salvation Army converted the property to a men's hostel in the winter of 1997-98. Its sixty beds for overnight drop-in constituted an official city winter shelter (that is, for use six months a year), and the shelter was funded almost entirely by the city.[11]

The ward councillor was quoted as saying that "operating the hostel in the middle of a tourist area is incompatible" and "people are intimidated and terrified by [the homeless]" (James 1998). The announcement that the hostel would be closed apparently caught the city's commissioner of social services off guard because "she too expected the program to continue" (ibid.) The councillor defended the decision to refuse to continue funding the shelter, reportedly saying, "There must be thousands of hostel beds in my ward. I invite other constituencies in the area to do their fair share" (ibid.).

Negotiations allowed the hostel a reprieve for one more winter before the city stopped funding that location. When the Salvation Army moved the shelter, it took it just slightly out of that ward. The Salvation Army bought another building at 107 Jarvis Street and opened another hostel called the Gateway to assist homeless men. The displacement of the shelter a couple of doors beyond the ward and into another area that carries more than its share of shelter accommodation reinforces evidence that there was no strategy in the redevelopment plan to deal with the then-growing problem of homelessness and social destitution. If the city's own commissioner of social services is caught off guard, it is difficult to claim that there was a plan. Certainly, the residents' association, TEDRA, had begun its cooperation with the city in 1994 on the assumption that its area would be helped by redevelopment. Moving the shelter elsewhere in the area did not meet that expectation. It generated some cynicism about the city's intentions and heightened struggles among residents and agencies in the area.

Chess Players

New management for Sam the Record Man in 2001 coincided with the relocation of the public chess tables on the Gould Street sidewalk. The tables, having been one of the city's initiatives to improve the street life of the area, had been located next to the store since the early 1980s. Figure 6.8 shows players using the tables in 1999. The tables were moved to the grounds of city hall.

6.8 Chess players on Gould Street, 1999, looking west to Yonge Street, where Gould terminates. Used year round, the chess tables animated that stretch of street. | Author's collection.

However, according to one press report, many of the players moved to a small park near the corner of Queen and Church streets, just east of the Yonge-Dundas redevelopment area, but in the same ward.

In the privatizing and sanitizing spirit of the times, the sidewalk beside Sam's where the chess tables used to be was at first fenced off. The area was reconfigured so that a high railing demarcated a space reserved for buyers of food sold from a kitchen on wheels in the fenced-off space. A few uncomfortable-looking bar stools and a ledge atop the railing were put in for patrons. The stools were lined up so that customers who sat and ate looked out at Gould Street, a vista that does not merit full-face attention even for the brief time it takes to eat a hotdog. How different the stools were from the generously wide, standard-height seats that allowed chess players to focus on the game between them or simply on conversation across the table and left the uninspiring streetscape to be seen out of the corner of one's eye. The story of the chess tables seems to capture distinctly different ideas about public space – use it the best one can under the circumstances versus use it in a utilitarian fashion for control and consumption.

Other Street Users

From the point of view of YSBRA, the main reason for undertaking the Yonge-Dundas redevelopment was to get rid of shopping hindrances. One can also say this was the city's (as well as the planners') ambition after it shifted to the redevelopment initiative. The goal was to be achieved by changing the building forms and by specific policing measures. As was noted in the previous chapter, the distinction between actual criminals or threatening behaviour and people who are associated with crime because of skin colour or poverty was glossed over so that criminality was attributed by implication to people who had every right to be in the area. The line between criminality and behaviour that fails to fuel retail and commercial interests was repeatedly smudged.

There was almost no protest against the displacement of poor people from Yonge Street. An exception was an event in August 1999 organized by the Ontario Coalition Against Poverty to protest the use of city money for this project instead of for homes for the homeless. About sixty homeless people marched silently around the expropriated properties, and some appeared quite disoriented. A sadder march would be hard to imagine. The marchers were outnumbered by police on foot, bicycles, and horses. Watching this from the sidewalk next to the Eaton Centre, a small boy beside us who was hoisted on his father's shoulders and intently watching the activity said, "Look, Daddy, a police parade!"

The police's approach to criminal activity was essentially displacement. The detective who testified at the OMB hearing that changing the physical space and its owners would reduce the crime rate because the crime was opportunistic was reported to have said just a year later that the troublemakers had been dispersed, although "they haven't always gone very far. The idea is now to keep them moving" (Immen 1999). But surely this strategy is ineffective for both the police and the city: as long as criminals are moving, it is harder for police to arrest them. Whose interests are served by displacing criminals to another part of the city?

In the spring of 2002, using extra funding from the BIA, the police launched another crackdown on drug dealers at the north end of the Eaton Centre. (An earlier crackdown, Operation Broom, was described in Chapter 4.) That action coincided with street youths moving their hangouts to the gay neighbourhood centred on Church Street. Cawthra Park and the steps of a well-known coffee shop were two favoured destinations. The youths' behaviour was reported to range from "unpleasant to homophobic to violent," and the coffee shop eventually had to close in 2004 because its clientele from the gay community found it too unpleasant or intimidating to frequent it. The displacement strategy was illogical to the chair of the Church-Wellesley BIA. His opinion was that these people need to be helped out; otherwise, he asked, will the police "keep them moving until we've pushed them all the way to North York?" (Dennison 2003).

At least four troubling displacements occurred because of the redevelopment: hostel services, anti-social activity, criminal activity, and people in poverty. Almost all of the displacements and their effects have made matters more difficult in the affected areas of the ward, while some problems have migrated farther afield. Had more negative externalities been exported out of his ward, the councillor would probably have had difficulty keeping his elected colleagues on side. If municipal memory was long enough, displacement would cease to be the successful strategy it so often is.

Conclusion

Facets of both the earlier regeneration plan and the redevelopment project were implemented. Regarding the former, buildings have been fixed up and made to address the street better. Large signage has been installed in several locations. None of the owners has redeveloped a property to the new, larger 4.0 times coverage. However, this is not surprising. The 4.0 times coverage was part of the regeneration approach to the street. Once the redevelopment plan was approved, it broke open the regeneration vision that had the power of the planning framework behind it. Landowners could interpret approval of the redevelopment plan, led by the ward councillor, as a Trojan Horse being manoeuvred into place. It would be only a matter of time before the Elm Street proposal of 1992 for 9.0 times coverage would look puny beside the buildings being approved for neighbouring sites. Indeed, a seventy-storey building was approved in 2007 for a block north of where the Elm Street project would have been.

Regarding the redevelopment project, the square opened to considerable controversy because of its appearance and how it could be used. It is too early to say how the square will fare in both respects, although it will be well used commercially. Yonge-Dundas Square added a new definition of "square" to Toronto's portfolio because it can be used commercially and house gated events. The Olympic Spirit rose and then collapsed as an enterprise on Parcel C. It provided some definition on the eastern side of the square, but the pedestrian's view eastward past the square is blocked almost as much as it was before redevelopment. The ward councillor later said it was not the view so much as the financial investment that those on the east side wanted and that it was beginning to happen because of the Yonge-Dundas redevelopment. Dubious claims of causality notwithstanding, the greatest impetuses for development east of Yonge were the favourable financing opportunities that derived from national macroeconomic policies and international investment choices fuelling the Toronto real estate market from the late 1990s, as well as city-wide planning and development policies.

One of the most striking outcomes of the redevelopment is the degree to which the City of Toronto gave the ward councillor the full opportunity to define and implement this project. Even though Yonge-Dundas was said to be the heart of the city and, thus, presumably of interest to everyone, the ward councillor controlled the area's reshaping as if it were any corner in the city. He played not only his role as elected official to the full but also the roles of proponent (by shaping the city's role as developer), planner (by shaping the planning department's response, pulling it and its tools into the service of his and YSBRA's vision), and browbeater (by attempting to shame others to act and respond to his project the way he wanted them to). Whether this is ward bossism in the sense in which the term is used in the United States or a case of "if you scratch my back, I'll scratch yours," other councillors supported virtually all the decisions concerning Yonge-Dundas.

An effect of ward-focused politics was the simultaneous emergence of two entertainment areas within a few blocks of each other. They were planned as neither competing nor complementary city spaces and are separated by unrelated uses, such as the provincial parliament buildings, a ceremonial route, office towers, and major hospitals. The area around King and John streets was officially designated the city's entertainment district, complete with street signs. Both areas have competed for similar facilities, especially a UEC-cum-playdium type of structure, as well as for city resources, notably, heightened policing. It was one thing to focus only on this short stretch of Yonge Street when incremental regeneration was the aim but quite another when major entertainment redevelopment was sought because other parts of the city were involved and, therefore, coordination was needed. The ward councillor had political interests at heart first and foremost. The political structure encouraged him to see his ward as the most important of his responsibilities, with city-wide interests coming second. He thus competed with any other councillor who wanted to attract entertainment uses. One outcome of the split districts has been weakened attention to problems in both of them. Another effect was that city staff were left to be the spokespersons for the city-wide perspective and for the long term. They can serve that role but not effectively if councillors do not play their part in council debates and not if elected officials take staff functions into their own hands. Staff members are, after all, advisors not decision makers.[12]

What problem was solved by the redevelopment? There has been more investment in local properties, but it cannot be said with any certainty that the regeneration plan would not also have attracted investment after the direction for the street had been determined in March 1996. In addition, a great deal of money has been lost by companies going into and then out of business in the area, and the city faced unexpected costs when it turned out that the square was not self-supporting. Whether the public using the area has changed is unknown because a study of users prior to the change was not done. People still hang out around the Eaton Centre north entrance. And it is not clear if crime has been reduced. Rather, the local neighbourhood group that has a seat on the Board of Management of the square says it thinks the crime rate is about the same; the DYBIA devotes most of its attention and much of its resources to criminal behaviour; extra policing is done; CCTV cameras are increasing; and drug trafficking and gang violence continue. Other problems have been displaced. The new square is being used by people for leisure and recreation, for entertainment purposes, and for some community events. The Eaton Centre is thriving. Ryerson has access to new lecture halls for selected hours. These are the principal effects after thirteen years of attention to Yonge and Dundas.

The entrepreneurial attitude in which the redevelopment plan was crafted brought a new kind of public space – in the form of a square designated as a public space for the use of a Business Improvement Area – into existence in Toronto. The leaders in this innovation were the ward councillor and the consulting planner hired by the local businesses. In effect, the city, a public body, led the commercialization and privatization of its own public space and insisted that it was really offering the public another Nathan Phillips Square. Yonge-Dundas was in the vanguard of Toronto's movement toward a more entrepreneurial approach to governance. To the limited extent that urban design informed the redevelopment plan, it did so only in the service of economic, social, and political aims – that is, it was in thrall to the idea of space as curative. The technical-aesthetic facets of space were given no role as a counterforce against the unrelenting therapeutic model that was promoted and implemented. In Françoise Choay's (1997) terms, "the rule" was entirely at the service of "the model."

With commercial signs covering almost every surface around Dundas Square (and often in it, too), the space exemplifies spectacularization. It is a civic space designed to promote not inclusivity but, rather, exclusivity as city policy. The city's rationale for the redevelopment was that the area had become dominated by threatening individuals who scared away other users, which resulted in a form of social exclusion in the area. No data supports this claim, which means that it may or may not have been true. If exclusion indeed existed, no single policy of the city promoted it. It happened as part of a conglomeration of events associated with urbanization, urban policies, and practices. With the redevelopment, the city traded that claimed exclusion for another, which it defined explicitly when it decided to market the area to consumers in specific age and income brackets. The area's complexity was reduced. But there were other options.

CHAPTER SEVEN
Closing

This book follows a planned intervention through two formulations – a regeneration plan superseded by a redevelopment plan. Both occurred in the same geographic space, in overlapping time periods, and many of the same people were involved. A wide range of issues was dealt with and many facets of the planning framework were used to work out each intervention. The description throughout is in response to the first question posed in Chapter 1: How was urban planning practised in this Toronto case?

The second question of how planners and others reasoned their way to two different recommendations for the same geographic space is addressed in Chapters 3, 4, and 5 in particular. In the regeneration plan, the space was conceptualized by using a combination of socioeconomic and technical-aesthetic factors that are associated with the question, What is this place? By comparison, the recommendations in the redevelopment plan were in response to the question of how these economic and social conditions could be changed. Consequently, they led to a plan that focused on political action that used the planning framework to reform the area. The Yonge-Dundas case provides an exceptional opportunity to not only see how a substantial change came about in a planning approach as players revised the conceptualization of the space but also delve into the formal defence of the change. Finally, because the planning work led to implementation, those actions could be followed to see what became of the planned solution. This broadens the picture of the effects that planners and others working within the planning framework achieved through this intervention.

This chapter addresses the third question: How does a planned intervention such as Yonge-Dundas correspond to planners' theories about their work? I consider why the regeneration phase looks like planning activity whereas the redevelopment does not. What distinguishing characteristics do regeneration and redevelopment have in this instance, and, specifically, which features of the regeneration and redevelopment cases fit or do not fit contemporary theories of planning? What insights, if any, come from examining these features alongside the four issues discussed in Chapter 1: (1) overextension of the social science analogue, (2) the process/substance relationship, (3) planner- and planning-centredness, and (4) imprecision about planning referents? A look at other property-led development cases shows that the approach can take several forms aside from the resolutely entrepreneurial one used for Yonge-Dundas. Other cases demonstrate the importance of technical-aesthetic factors for using a site well. Finally, I recapitulate the principal observations about planning activity, planners, and planning frameworks that, in my view, need representation in theories that planners construct about the work they do.

The Regeneration Phase Looks More or Less Like Conventional Planning Activity

The regeneration phase was managed by the City of Toronto's Planning and Development Department, with hands-on attention from the head of the department, the commissioner of planning. He worked with city council and its committees to reach a settlement with the largest property interest in the area, the owners of the Eaton Centre, regarding wording in the official plan, thereby heading off a legal challenge to the city's brand new official plan. He also came up with the proposal that won council support for a working task force to look into the Yonge Street area, and succeeded in directing energy toward it while staving off the formation of a committee of business leaders that would have been entrusted with generating planning policies for the entire downtown area. He used early and open consultation with a wide variety of interests to learn their assessments of the area's problems. He brought realism to the endeavour because he made it clear that planning could alter the investment climate in the area but could not solve its troubling social problems. However, the commissioner said he could encourage other departments and agencies to focus attention on the area at the same time that his department was trying to generate and implement solutions to the physical space and investment options – in effect, he used the planning activity as a catalyst to rally attention to a small but significant section of the city.

The planners were cognizant of and took into account the demands of various interests: the commercial developers' desire to put up office buildings; the city's implicit ambition to at least preserve, if not increase, the municipal tax base; the Eaton Centre's wish to secure its property value while holding off strongly competitive or antithetical uses on the opposite side of Yonge Street; the hope of Ryerson University and various business interests that the area be tidied up and made safer; and neighbours who wanted the area cleaned up but also wanted some of Yonge Street's liveliness pulled east in their direction. The planners recommended retaining the long-held sense of the place by finding a way to keep the basic configuration of land parcels and built form while attending to the expressed demands for some change.

Some research was done, but the planning staff relied primarily on its existing knowledge and experience of the area. The main exception was an in-house design study that clarified not only land-parcel widths, depths, and ownership but also the existing built form and the potential for changing it while keeping land use goals in mind.

The concept plan was built primarily on previous decisions about the area. However, the newly conceived reinvestment area designation was applied to part of the area, and ideas brought from elsewhere were used within the context of an overall, homegrown plan.[1] One of those ideas was to disallow any new dwelling units in the immediate area in order to discourage gentrification. Another was to institute a minimum sign size. Each step of the way conformed to the informal conventions of Toronto planning and the statutory requirements of provincial planning legislation and made use of many tools offered by the *Planning Act* and city policies.

A clear strategy emerged out of the assessment that the sky was not falling in the Yonge-Dundas area of Toronto: a measured response was designed with the expectation that it would gradually reignite investment. The street would be cleaned up a bit, but the steps taken were specifically intended to obviate gentrification. The plan was rational in that reason had been used to sort through the options, it was transparent and relatively consultative, and it balanced short- and long-term public interests.

If these characteristics convey "planning," why do they do so, and what sort of planning do they convey? At least six distinct features can be found in that brief recounting of the regeneration plan: statutory requirements, customary practices, a planning process, a discourse on urbanism, a public planning department, and various publics. Let me say a bit about the first four.

Statutory requirements are, in effect, the rules for engaging in planning. In Canada they are established by provincial legislation. A municipality is obliged to observe them, as is discussed in Appendix 1. As Hodge and Gordon point out, statutory requirements establish *who* may plan and *how* they may do it (2008, 217). A few examples from the case study are illustrative: the official plan, the community-improvement-plan section of the *Planning Act*, and obligatory public meetings to introduce amendments to the zoning bylaw.

The second feature is customary practices that planners acting in their professional capacity will ordinarily try to execute. These are mainly of two kinds and are sometimes referred to as planning methods: participatory practices and technical studies. The first are used to find out from interested parties information about key problems and potential solutions, and the second are used to investigate problems in detail and find solutions that can be supported by evidence or argumentation. For instance, one technical study of the Yonge-Dundas area showed some concentration in the type of retail goods offered in street-level stores; another looked into the urban-box format as a potential new retail space for the area.

The third feature is a planning process that, by its very use, acknowledges that customary practices are purposively selected. Choices are based on theories that depict the relationship between knowledge and action and between the state and citizens. This is where planning's procedural theories come into play. Chapter 3, on the regeneration phase, offers a sketch of a typical rational planning process in which the planner is a manager who works with the city's policies and the planning framework to arrive at recommendations for the elected councillors. Planners use a variety of data sources – writings, statistical projections, observations, and discussions – to create a picture of the area and its problems and then use that knowledge to shape recommendations for action. This planning activity is set within the context of the official plan. Once the official plan is drawn up and approved, the planning department's tasks include helping to generate development and recommending approval or refusal of applications for developments according to their fit with the policies and principles of that plan. Applications have to make an arguable fit because at any time a development decision can be appealed. This work is done by producing the best information possible within the constraints of time, money, staff, and imagination and by putting it forward persuasively.[2] The Yonge-Dundas regeneration phase looked somewhat like the typical model of the planning process (see, e.g., Hodge and Gordon 2008, 176). The main difference was that the feedback loops were not explicit, although the uptake of the facade grants and loans program was monitored, and the intention to monitor the effects of changing the building envelope seemed implied.

The fourth feature, which is hinted at in the preceding paragraphs, is a discourse on urbanism. A brief reminder of Françoise Choay's time-resistant figures is in order. The first figure, the rule, with its origin in the architectural treatise, refers to principles of building urban areas such as proportionality, scale, pattern, fit, light, and connection that can be combined to generate spaces for uses and things, all the while with an eye on natural laws; technical skills concerning building, communication, and transport; people's needs and desires; and aesthetics that engender appreciation. By contrast, the second figure, the model, refers to a way of achieving improvement in urban areas by assessing what exists, determining what is wrong with it, and modelling a solution that reverses what exists to correct it. The third figure, the theory of urbanism, is an amalgam that binds either the rule or the model or both to the idea that a science of urbanism is possible and desirable, a proposition that differs from simply using science and technology as sources of pertinent information that can inform urbanism. All of these elements can be engaged in discourses on urbanism.

The planners asked: What is this place in the overall context of the city? The urban design study, in particular, considered that question in light of the area's land parcels and building dimensions, which had generated a succession of uses over the decades; the current desire to keep retail in the area; the main street's width and north-south orientation and the effect sunlight has on shopping street users; and the potential physical forms that new retail spaces could take. The planning department also clarified that social issues could be helped but not solved by encouraging more investment in the buildings and infrastructure, because repairing this location needed contributions from others, too. The discourse on urbanism evoked a complex place and space that was amenable to alteration through the use of a combination of spatial and socioeconomic tools, including the innovation of promoting a new building form by offering extra investment potential, but no promise of utopian results. Urbanism in this planning exercise was expressed through the use of both technical-aesthetic and socioeconomic conceptualizations of space.

In summary, the regeneration plan looked like planning in terms of customary practices and the type of process used, which resembled the rational (or managerial) planning theory in which the planner is in charge of finding ways to advance a reasonable solution to a built-form problem. But the regeneration plan was not identical to any particular planning theory. Compared to the idealized rational model, the actual case was more consultative or, if it is compared to a consensual style, the planner took a more explicitly directive role by building his solution on notions of urbanism that revealed his experiences and understanding of spatial relationships, economy, social dysfunction, land-ownership patterns, private and public power relations, and the like. The regeneration plan was also less research-based compared to a rational model. But there had been years of studies, pilots, and consternation about the area, and it was, after all, in the centre of the city, only a few blocks from where the planners worked every day. They certainly knew how the area "felt" as a place. Also, the planners had just completed a new official plan along with all the city self-studies such a process entails. Significantly, the principal research was the urban design study, which was central to deciding the direction in which to push the street. It had so strong an influence on how the regeneration plan proceeded that conventional rational planning theories, tied as they are to urban theories that explain urban space as socially constructed, do not account for the case.

The regeneration does not look exactly like any theory of planning in another respect. The planning framework put some boundaries on what the municipality and its planners could propose and do. Frameworks are not accounted for in theories, yet they have substantial effects. They establish acceptable planning activity for a given jurisdiction, which may be quite different in Ontario compared to Illinois, Manitoba, New South Wales, and England; indeed, cities in the same provincial or state jurisdiction may differ due to local bylaws, practices, policies, and strategies. Frameworks also push practice toward plausible rather than ideal solutions because proposals must meet many challenges from citizens, developers, elected officials, and the law.

The Redevelopment Phase Does Not Look Like Planning Activity
The redevelopment phase was an initiative led by the private sector, with the public planning department playing a secondary role. Public funds in the form of investments, carrying costs, foregone taxes, and soft costs (especially consulting and retainer fees and staff costs) were used to increase the value of properties owned by the proponents. Even though public money was used for private purposes, oversight by those on the outside was virtually impossible. Using city funds to draw out private investment is common. Leveraging increases the effect of a strategic public investment by encouraging correlative private investment. For example, the facade program was a small-scale form of leveraging. But the redevelopment phase was not ordinary leveraging because public funds went to a program managed by a private consultant hired by private-property interests.

The city used a private development consultant as a development promoter in a poorly articulated public-private partnership even though alternatives to that approach existed. That alternatives existed was never denied by the city. Rather, during the quasi-judicial hearing, the city argued that it had the right under the powers given to it to choose this particular route to fix the street. Municipal politicians thus used their power to impose the model they wanted, including, in effect, having their own planning department work under the direction of the development consultant and one councillor.

The redevelopment phase was conceptualized from the start as street marketing, as a program to entice a better class of businesses to the area. The plan emphasized public relations, promotion, and gaining media attention. The manner in which the cinema company, AMC, was brought on board may have been unremarkable in private business but seemed devious in a public project, and it led to incommensurate versions of truth being voiced during the Ontario Municipal Board (OMB) hearing. The choice of developer and the transfer of six of the expropriated properties to it also clouded the redevelopment with suspicions about motives so that other dubious explanations for how this happened were bandied about for public consumption. The evaluation of bids was said by inside sources in the finance department to have been sloppy. The redevelopment program was said to be in response to what was wrong with the street as determined through one-on-one conversations with people whose identities and affiliations were not declared, but those people almost certainly included a number of the major property owners and other project insiders. The program also reflected the consultant's and the local councillor's opinion that the city could not fix the problems itself, least of all through planning. The project needed buy-in from private property owners and major corporate tenants. The process had no steps in it for finding ways to accommodate current users of the development area. It was directed toward removing the old and selling the new. No consultation that could be called impartial took place while ideas were being developed. Reminders that there was a public interest involved sometimes had to be foisted upon certain project participants. Efforts were made to avoid even the formal legal steps required by expropriation legislation. The owners were given no options regarding their properties: they either had to cede to expropriation by the city or fight a legal battle at their own expense. The approach to the public interest was idiosyncratic. The councillor said that he and a few others had figured out what needed to be done. The public interest appread to be defined in light of the wishes of a few private businesses of the area.

No research was done to find a solution to the problem. A solution was identified, and it was a model used elsewhere. It was claimed that once the model was applied, crime and loitering would fall, consumption would rise because of the bright lights and razzle-dazzle atmosphere, and because property values would rise, so too would property-tax revenue. All that remained was the preparation of feasibility studies to show whether the model could financially succeed and where, in the few blocks in question, the expropriations and demolitions should take place to maximize the model's success. The idea came first; the rationale for it came second. Even the way the square materialized was part of a socially utopian drive; it was not, as one would assume for such an important addition to public space, conceptualized and defined with respect to the principles of urban space. The extremely modest pedestrian study was done only after it was evident that the city would have to defend itself at the OMB. Chapter 5 shows that the reasoning used was largely rationalization, or *Realrationalität*, in Bent Flyvbjerg's terminology (1998). The premises presented by the proponent did not lead to the conclusion that was claimed. The solution did not grow out of knowledge of the Yonge-Dundas area but out of knowledge of a model that was used elsewhere to maximize the consumer appeal of city spaces. It was not mentioned that the effects of the model on other places had not been investigated by its

Toronto proponents, nor had the parallels between sites where it had been applied been compared to Toronto's site. Assumptions were completely untested.

The redevelopment bears little resemblance to the planning process described in the section above that discusses regeneration. To fit it into the conventional planning mould, one would have to accept that redevelopment was merely a continuation of the regeneration plan. In that scenario some of the prior steps could be said to underlie the redevelopment scheme. I have argued against accepting the claim of continuation for a number of reasons: (1) in the regeneration phase, the express intention was not to change the street in any fundamental way because it was unique, whereas that was exactly the intention of the redevelopment, which was to make the street different, not the "anywhere" it was denounced as being; (2) the regeneration plan called for incremental change to be determined by property owners, not expropriation and redevelopment by new capital interests; and (3) since the project was approved by the city in 1998, those concerned consistently asserted in written pronouncements that changes to Yonge-Dundas had started in 1996, when the Yonge Street Business and Residents Association formed a partnership with the city. Anything before that is ignored as if it had not occurred. The line of argument by the city at the OMB hearing had several strands, but the one that paid off was that those prior efforts at regeneration were too puny to have had an effect.

Therefore, in this study redevelopment fits no procedural planning theory and contravenes most customary practices. Yet, it shares with conventional planning an adherence to statutory planning requirements and a tendency to present arguments within a discourse on urbanism. In the case of the former, the city's intentions for redevelopment had to meet provincial requirements and be approved by the OMB at appeal. The fact that it met those requirements (as the regeneration plan would also have done) indicates the interpretive latitude of the planning framework. This seems logical given that planning's legal framework grew out of the desire to protect property values. The city argued that it was protecting the economic potential of this area by removing blight. A similarly surprising interpretative latitude was noted in British planning (Brindley, Rydin, and Stoker 1989, 1).

With regard to the discourse on urbanism, one finds a classic utopian model was applied with the assistance of scientism at its least subtle, and the combination looked very much like the third figure, the theory of urbanism. A model was found that could, it was claimed, convert bad into good, disorder into order, and an immoral place into a moral one fit for families. For an example of scientism in the service of spurious causality, recall the inscrutable crime data that was used to show the good that would come from getting rid of indentations in building faces, the small-business owners who did not understand security the way big corporations did, and the statements that lumped homeless people, panhandlers, and psychiatrically disturbed people together with drug dealers. It is the quintessential nineteenth-century theory of urbanism identified by Choay, a theory heavily skewed toward a social-therapeutic, hyperspatialized model that lacks reference to generative rules about building. Its proponents argue it will deliver the last word on contemporary city building. How did it happen that at the close of the twentieth century the City of Toronto took a nineteenth-century approach to planning an area it had come to fondly call its heart?

Comparing Theory and Practice
Although the redevelopment process does not fit contemporary planning theories, it is still necessary to deal with the fact that this was a planned intervention in a literal, descriptive sense and it was seen as good planning in a normative sense by both the city council that approved it and the OMB that tested it against statutory requirements. It is a problem for planning theorists – not municipal and provincial governments or even practising planners – to solve if their theories do not correspond to what is being done in their name.

Let us now return to the four issues concerning planning theories that were raised in Chapter 1 and reconsider them in light of the case data and the above comments.

Overextension of the social science analogue: The analogue is overextended to the degree that theorists equate the work planners do with social science or see planning as a kind of curative social science activity with origins only in the socioeconomic upheavals of industrial cities rather than as the continuation of a discourse on urban space. The recommendations of the regeneration plan were reached in part through a consideration of the technical-aesthetic features of the space. Only by ignoring these features, or reducing them to byproducts of social interaction, can the proposed plan be explained using social science theories. If this approach is followed, then something vital, a residual, within planning practice remains unexplained: the technical-aesthetic facets of space.

Indeterminacy regarding how to link the process of planning and the substantive facets of the thing planned: In the regeneration phase, process and substance were linked with no implied hierarchy between them, and substance included both socioeconomic and technical-aesthetic features of planning and urbanism. In the redevelopment phase the planning process resembled no extant procedural theory, if only because all procedural theories are normative and, in this case, the approach was chosen intentionally to break away from norms. As for substance, those in charge of the process seized on socioeconomic facets to get a model implemented.

The planner- and planning-centredness of theories: The argument regarding what to do at Yonge and Dundas had to do with conceptualizing space. Spatial conceptualization for such an area invokes urbanity, the reciprocity between urban tissue and conviviality. Urbanity, in turn, invokes urbanism, the reflection on, shaping, and management of urban areas using some combination of normative ideas, data, and practicable actions. Planners are one of many groups that contribute to urbanism.[3] Others are involved – developers, designers, architects, financiers, engineers, landowners, and so on – and all participate via the planning framework. A theory that is intended to get at what happened in the Yonge-Dundas case but centres on planners' actions alone, such as the procedural theories discussed in Chapter 1, will not be adequate because the planner's actions would be unconnected to the larger question of what the activity was about – urbanity.

Lack of clarity about planners, activities labelled as planning, and frameworks that govern planning in jurisdictions: Theories make reference to planners and their actions. However, these constructs are often vague about who counts as a planner and whether planned actions were the result of planners' recommendations. Who is being blamed for what? Could theories be clearer about those distinctions? Could analyses using such theories specify the effects of the framework, not to let planners off the hook but to keep from scapegoating them? Should the distinction between planners acting for the public sector and planners acting for a private development be made clear?

The assumption that space is socially constructed is a cornerstone of investigations into and theorizations about planning as an activity. The assumption has been borrowed from geographers and others since the 1960s and it is pervasive: it shapes substantive and procedural matters. Contemporary planning theorists have almost unanimously cloaked themselves with the assumption. The hegemony of constructionism hides the fact that planners' explanatory, descriptive, and normative models do not take into account the technical-aesthetic factors that are so essential to urbanism.

Using a Site Well

Chapter 1 briefly explored how changes to technical, social, and economic conditions have led to different patterns of urbanization and urban form since the 1960s. A number of writers have shown how those new conditions have altered planning practices (e.g., Albrechts 2001; Brindley, Rydin, and Stoker 1989; Courcier 2005; Imrie and Thomas 1999; McGuirk and MacLaran 2001). Notably, the iconic regulatory style has been displaced by a cluster of styles in which new approaches engage a range of strategies and actors in the tasks of reviving small core areas or filling gaps left in the urban tissue where rail, harbour, and industrial activities had formerly thrived. The Yonge-Dundas redevelopment was an example of planners breaking away from the regulatory or trend style, and an examination of the case reveals several actions that should not be repeated. A brief examination of a few other redevelopment cases will bring out further lessons regarding how conceptualizations of space, planning, and urbanism are connected.

The London Docklands urban development project was among the first of the property-led entrepreneurial type, and when it was first launched, the Thatcher administration in Britain sought to have as little public-sector involvement as possible. In fact it was so unplanned that one of the sites being redeveloped, Canary Wharf, failed in its first go around, and this failure, in turn, contributed to the spectacular downfall of its prime developer, Olympia & York (O&Y). Several analysts concur that lack of infrastructure planning led to inadequate transportation to this huge development site. Poor transportation combined with a failure to control new development on adjacent City of London sites as Canary Wharf worked its way to completion and occupancy, a combination that resulted in the latter being less accessible and, thus, less attractive to tenants.[4]

For researchers Brindley, Rydin, and Stoker, the London Docklands Development Corporation (LDDC) project was indeed planning, which they define very broadly as "all activities of the state which are aimed at influencing and directing the development of land and buildings" (1989, 2). The LDDC was one of several urban development corporations that resulted from a national-level policy of the Thatcher government. However, its work did not look like planning, they add, because actions came out of right-wing instead of left-wing ideology. For Brindley, Rydin, and Stoker, the new right was not against planning – after all, it used highly interventionist tools like urban development corporations and projects led by public-private partnerships. The new right was against planning approaches that were collectivist, welfarist, or critical of the market. The demands of the new right were for planning to be done more in line with developers' interests. The result was that a range of planning styles was spawned. The LDDC used leverage planning, one of the six potentially overlapping styles that Brindley, Rydin, and Stoker observed being practised in the 1980s throughout the United Kingdom.[5] Sue Brownill (1990, 32) also agreed that the Docklands project was a case of planning. She interprets the LDDC project as being "not anti-planning *per se*, but anti those aspects of planning that have attempted to restrict the market and to use planning to achieve social and community objectives." Property redevelopment used as the route to recovery from recession and economic restructuring is distinct from using a social welfare approach. The former has at its core the assumption that the benefits from development will automatically filter down to those who have been harmed by economic changes. However, there is no evidence that this happens. On the contrary, it appears that the gap widens between the poor and those associated with the new economic activities (Healey et al. 1992, 7; Fainstein 2001b; Moulaert, Rodriguez, and Swyngedouw 2002). Social problems must still be attended to. Consequently, a rapprochement became essential: free-wheeling opportunism had to circle back and hook up with planning activity to protect huge public and private investments in part by attending to local concerns.[6]

According to Susan Fainstein, if the LDDC was engaged in planning, "its style was entrepreneurial, and its staff ... [was] focused on implementation rather than planning" (2001a, 177). One of her interviewees told her there had never been a grand master plan and that the project executive officer simply wanted to make things happen. In her assessment, it was correct to develop the Docklands area as an office centre because it benefited the wider city, not just the people in the vicinity. The problem was the absence of planning to make adequate infrastructure available, to create conditions that would permit the new office space to effectively compete for tenants, and to ensure that social and educational programs for the area's residents would prepare them for new jobs in the area. With the passage of time, the area eventually became a financial success, and even local residents approved of it. But success came only after considerable changes were made to how the Docklands were being developed. Again, it was confirmed that some planning is required in order to attend to public interests, including protecting public and private-sector investments in a site, dealing with social issues, and ensuring that a new development fits properly into the broader jurisdiction. Regardless of a government's political stripe, planning is needed to deal with the broader context of urbanism – the dynamics of urban decline and redevelopment over large city-regions.

Times Square, as shorthand for the whole 42nd Street redevelopment, was the model most cited for the Toronto project. It too was driven by a utopian discourse on urbanism. Before all else, it is important to note that the scale and symbolism of Times Square far outstrips the Yonge-Dundas project, just as the LDDC and Canary Wharf projects do. If the first run at the LDDC was on the outer edge of what could be termed "planning," and if its second try embraced some aspects of planning of necessity, analysts say that Times Square was off the planning map altogether. Lynne Sagalyn studied the project intensively over several years and said the city's planning department had almost ceased functioning and could only react to this project, which was led by successive mayors (2001, 71). It was not planning but, mainly, deal making, in which the city was seeking short-term gain at the expense of the long-term public interest (ibid., xii, 70). Thinly disguised risk taking took place, even though cities are not supposed to gamble with taxpayers' dollars (ibid., xvi). Indeed, during that time period, successive mayors Edward I. Koch and Rudolph Giuliani were hostile to planning and showed a distinct preference for entrepreneurial deal making (ibid., xii). Sagalyn asks: What public good did the project represent? Fainstein also examined the Times Square case in detail and, like Sagalyn, could not call its transformation "planning." In her view, the project was overreliant on property-led development and growth and avoided planning (2001b, 218, 219). The result was poor use of the site for which "better practical alternatives were possible" (ibid., 210). Good development is not just concerned with economics but also with using a site well, she says. Sagalyn and Fainstein indicate the limits of what can be called planning. Interestingly, one implied feature of planning is using a site well. In urbanism, surely that means paying attention to both the principles of building in context and socioeconomic matters.

Fainstein's point about using a site well can form a bridge to two other property-led projects, both of them largely residential, in New York (Battery Park City) and Toronto (the Kings).[7] Both sites were reshaped primarily via urban-form guidelines instead of the models of social well-being that have been used in a succession of neighbourhood unit models, garden cities, new towns, and suburban developments generally and, specifically, for the 42nd Street–Times Square and Yonge-Dundas redevelopments.

The design principles that structured Battery Park City (later echoed in the Kings) were described by its design consultant as "solving complex urban design problems" (Eckstut 1986). There were four of them: think smaller – plan small, viable increments; learn from what exists – include and even highlight existing structures or other visual elements to provide a sense of place; integrate – at the edges; and design streets, not buildings – because, as the oldest and most basic unit of urban life, the street can be manipulated to achieve the aforementioned goals. For David Gordon (1997), as for many others, Battery Park City is an admirable project that is well connected to the urban fabric in the ways the design consultants intended. Fainstein agrees and has concluded that although the project is separated from the city grid, it nonetheless works well for both residents and the city at large. She says that while Battery Park City is "the antithesis of the naturally developing, heterogeneous urban district prescribed by Jane Jacobs, ... it incorporates many of her lessons nevertheless. It is dense and has multiple uses, short blocks, buildings along the street line, and small accessible parks" (2001a, 172-73). Fainstein expresses a notion of urbanism that engages with physical space as a generator of activity.

Those who conceptualized the Kings – those who worked on behalf of Toronto's city planning department, including Jane Jacobs – insisted that site features be established first, rather than the land use and zoning regulations, which are based on socioeconomic considerations. Developers would then be invited to make proposals. The Kings was the first and largest contemporary market-led neighbourhood development project in Canada. At 500 acres (just over 200 hectares), the site is over five times the size of Battery Park City. It is on land that had been held for employment uses until it was clear that neither the area nor the buildings would be needed exclusively for those purposes. As described by two members of the team, the redevelopment concept emerged from a few urbanistic principles that were similar to those described above and to the following: any use – buildings could be put to any use except a few toxic industries; use change – an owner could change a building's use because the market had changed or for some other reason; and building envelope – rules for new building would be about height, daylight penetration, and the relationship to the street (Greenberg and Lewinberg 1996, 26-27). Social issues would be dealt with as needed. Fashioned for Toronto's use, the concept was called a "reinvestment area." Its next application after the Kings was in the Yonge-Dundas regeneration plan (see Chapter 3 and Appendix 1).

These cases illustrate different ways cities have recently used land to advance their development interests (Yonge-Dundas and Times Square) and repair ruptures in central urban areas (London Docklands, Battery Park City, and the Kings). There are many more examples. These ones starkly illustrate that thinking about urbanism through spatial principles is not the same as thinking about it through a prism in which space is constructed through social relations. The London Docklands case is a reminder that planning contributes to a structurally effective city. And Yonge-Dundas and Times Square show the controlling intent of a utopian model, one that is unrelieved by delivering much, if anything, in the interests of the public. Using a site well, perforce, engages urbanism. Ideally, it draws together the best intelligence that actors can bring to bear on the technical-aesthetic and socioeconomic construction of space. Contributions that planning activities can make within urbanism remain those long associated with the field, particularly helping to create an overall vision to guide individual decisions, supporting public objectives, and thinking ahead to ensure that infrastructure and other needs are in place. But these cases also highlight the need for innovative planning as urban areas change.

Concerns were raised in the planning and development literature that property-led approaches spelled the end of planning because planning could no longer get the job done. These concerns were unfounded. Rather, the new approaches marked the end of being able to mistake planning for a leftist, or centrist, political practice. Property-led development has helped break apart the nearly monolithic view that planning is a regulatory tool with a curative orientation, one that is expected to deliver social benefits. This view is interlocked with the claim that planning began as a social welfare activity in industrializing cities, a supposition that hides traces of planning for urbanism that go back centuries. Instead, we witness a multiple-styled activity that may be used by a variety of people, not just planners, to pursue whatever goals can be successfully argued to be in the public interest. This is a useful, if perhaps unsettling, realization. It is a forceful reminder that social well-being will not necessarily be delivered by any particular style of planning: it is, as always, the result of specific, explicit actions.

On Trying to See a Little Better

Theor, from the Greek, refers to seeing or viewing. In its simplest form, a theory is a mental view of phenomena; in more complex forms, a theory becomes either a system of ideas or statements that are held to explain or account for a group of facts or phenomena or a systematic statement of rules or principles to be followed (see, e.g., the *Oxford English Dictionary*). I do not propose a new theory; that would overreach this case study research. Rather, I make observations based on the research that, in my view, challenge contemporary theorizing about what planners, planning activities, and planning frameworks contribute to urbanism. In that sense, then, what is the mental view of phenomena reflected in the practices witnessed in this case?

First, the practices in this case had to do with urbanism, a matrix of space, time, people, and phenomena that actors seek to influence. It was in the language of urbanism that issues were presented, discussed, and decided – that is, via normative ideas, data, and practicable actions concerning urbanism. Regardless of whether a lawyer, developer, public or private planner, or politician spoke, he or she used an urbanistic context to situate the argument. Rules and policies were applied by using ideas about urbanism to gauge their probable effect. Even if they were called planning principles, they were more accurately urbanism principles because they were specific to urban matters, with the inevitable mix of social, spatial, economic, political, and historical conditions. Planning was not exercised as if it was a generic practice but rather as if it was a specific one, the subject of which was urbanism. Planning was one of various tools in the service of urbanism.

Second, if urban planning is about urbanism and not just about planning (that is, about itself) then the space that urban planners conceptualize must be urbanistic space. How that space is understood is critical. The current theoretical convention in planning is to assume that space is produced through socioeconomic relations. That view leaves the technical-aesthetic facets of space that play a role in urbanistic space unaccounted for. The convention is arrived at through a chain of assumptions: first, the substance of planning is described as "urban theory"; second, the definition of urban theory identifies it only with the social sciences (especially geography, politics, economics, and sociology); and third, the thesis developed by social scientists that holds that space is socially constructed is applied to the substance. While space may certainly be viewed advantageously as socially produced, it is more than that. The argument that space is socially constructed serves an analogue function in this chain of assumptions, one that ties planning to the social sciences. Essentially, it tells planners that one way to understand space is the way social scientists do – as having been produced through social relations. That is fine as long as one does not forget that the analogue is just that: the comparison of two unlike phenomena – urban planning and social science – to show that it is a benefit to understanding to see the first in light of the second. The work of an analogue is similar to that of a metaphor: to see one thing in terms of another along some dimension, not to reduce one to the other by forgetting all the ways in which the two are not alike. But that analogue, whose status has been long forgotten, is now the habitual point of departure for theorizing about planning. The effect is to structure planning as if the technical-aesthetic facets of space have no effect or could and should be explained entirely by the social production of space thesis. Planning structured in such a way does not accord with the case data. After all, broadly speaking, technological changes in communication and transportation were factors in the creation of the spatial problem that Yonge-Dundas became. More specifically, the technical-aesthetic facets of space in the regeneration plan were central to the planning recommendation about what to do with the area. Not every relevant aspect of urban space is properly understood as a social construction. Perspective, height, depth, light, movement, smell, sound, colour, scale, pattern, proximity, containment, and so on are partly experiential and able to be explained apart from social constructionism via techno-scientific or aesthetic theories. Experiential phenomena carry meaning even if they are not constructs of contemporary society and economy. They constitute other ways of relating to facets of "the urban."

Third, the case study area was conceptualized metaphorically, first as a generator of possibilities and later as a platform on which to realize socioeconomic ambitions. The direction for change was captured in phrases and images such as "the sky is not falling" and the rotting heart. Urbanistic terminology, ratios, quantities, heights, and so on were invoked to support each of the images. The graphic rotten heart image, which was often associated with the word "blight," may seem like an aberrant use of language in a relatively sophisticated city at the end of the twentieth century. Not necessarily. There is always a metaphor, or its extension as a model or analogue, at work, regardless of whether it is verbalized or whether planners or others have devised the image. And metaphors are not simply rhetorical flourishes that if purged would leave behind a nonmetaphorical, business-like, nonliterary assessment of the situation. Metaphors are essential to Western thinking. Because the details of every intervention differ, the selection of metaphors will be local, but they will not be absent. If imagery helps shape how planners do their urbanistic work, as is shown in this case, what should its connection be to planning theories?

Fourth, not just any imagery was at work. For urbanism, there appear to be three root images, which Françoise Choay has isolated and called the enduring figures of urbanism – the rule, the model, and the theory of urbanism. Between them they capture the basic paths and outcomes that are argued for when it comes to urbanism. Each plan in this case employed and combined the enduring figures of urbanistic discourse differently. If, as this case seems to confirm, the figures really have endured and can literally be identified in planners' everyday statements, then they ought to be helpful in analyzing urbanists' proposals. It would be valuable to do this work because the figures would help spot excesses and warn about the dangers of falling into one trap or the other when grappling with proposals. Choay points out that both the rule and model approaches propose positive conceptions of building – but they also propose negative ones: the rule approach exalts building in the image of ourselves, for our own pleasure, while the model approach, with its totalitarian tendency, which is "alien to desire and pleasure," claims to convert and heal us ([1980] 1997, 274). Contemporary urbanism is in far greater danger of developing a creeping totalitarianism from abundant and overeager utopian models than it is of being smothered by a surfeit of aesthetic pleasure from excessive use of generative rules. Witness how the redevelopment model in the Yonge-Dundas case was designed, argued for, widely accepted, and implemented as a cure. Planners and planning activities can stagnate and become irrelevant to urbanism if they get stuck in the utopian stage of making mirror models that propose an ideal set of qualities that are simply the inverse of the actual. Currently, the strongest feed line into theorizing about planning is from the social sciences, whose specialty is theorizing about how space is socially produced to better control how it is used in the interests of healing society (from poverty, injustice, and so on). We would do well to keep in mind that the social science knowledge attached to utopian models is not necessarily beneficent. Overreliance on social science theories reduces the oxygen flowing into planning.

Fifth, neither the data from this case nor logic suggests a reason why continuous tension between the process and substance of planning would ever go away. Both contribute to reaching a planning recommendation. Planning theorists seem to agree on this fundamental point. If the tension is inevitable, and if recommendations are preferably reached by going back and forth, why are process and substance not in a side-by-side, rather than hierarchical, relationship? Would that not better reflect good practice?

Sixth, practitioners in the case study fashioned their image of themselves and the work they did as participants in urbanism along with many others, not as the only or even the main actors. It is important to note that their relationships with others were unlike those found in various forms of consensual planning theory, in which the planner is the neutral, centre person charged with finding a solution out of the middle. In the regeneration phase, planners used consultation as just one element to shape the options. They also used their own expertise with the planning framework and understanding of urbanism. In the redevelopment phase, the contract development consultant played the role of idiosyncratic visionary, the building hero, but with a cast of supporting players from business, the professions, and politics.

Seventh, planners working for public, as compared to private, employers can differ on what constitutes the public interest. The problem at its most basic is that a municipality's (or other government body's) interest and the public interest are supposed to be approximately the same. By contrast, a private firm has its own interests, and the planner's ethical responsibility is to respect his or her employer's private interest alongside the putative public interest. A further complication is that planners employed by private-sector clients usually work within shorter time horizons and smaller scales, for instance, a project site and its immediate surroundings. There is at least as much planning expertise for hire to private-sector developers, lawyers, financiers, and various property interests as there is to municipalities, regions, and other public bodies. Challenges to public-sector projects will be brought by private-sector development companies that employ fully qualified and experienced planners. Contemporary theories make no distinctions between public and private, which suggests that these theories are intended to guide a planner working in any capacity. Should these distinctions be somehow captured in planning theories?

Eighth, the planning framework mattered. In the regeneration plan for the Yonge-Dundas area, planners used the publicly vetted and adopted official plan to back up their recommendations. One particularly important element of the newly adopted official plan of 1993 was that the low height of buildings on Yonge Street was bravely reconfirmed as being in the public interest (to control shadowing in conjunction with the street's character). The few extra metres in height added as a result of the regeneration plan were not boosted by the more radical redevelopment plan before it was approved. An official plan (or its equivalent) presents a general vision and shapes the range of foreseen actions. As a significant part of the planning framework, the official plan is expected to establish public interests, to stand against fragmented and disorganized cities that are unprepared for growth and decline, and to provide a modicum of support when the law is called on to settle development disputes. The content of an official plan matters precisely because it is part of a larger framework. A municipality with a well-developed official plan in which its urbanistic interests are stated as policies that are backed by strategies for implementing them has at least a reasonable chance of being able to defend its interests when necessary because they are formal confirmation of the city's intended direction. An official plan sounds like an archaic device in these fast-moving times, but for urbanism it is like the commons – valuable as a kind of social contract by which players in urbanistic endeavours agree to abide, at least for a specified period of time, willingly or by force of law.

Finally, if the substance of urbanism is to be linked nonhierarchically to process, as the case research proposes would be realistic, then process would have to be rethought too. Procedural planning theory has mainly taken a model form since it was first spelled out as survey-analysis-plan in the late nineteenth century and in subsequent variations on the theme of problem-solution. To conceptualize planning activities as curative is but one of several options, as many of the researchers discussed earlier observed. Procedural theory needs more scope, which could be achieved by incorporating and validating elements that generate innovative new openings, not only cures. Using the enduring figures of urbanism to interpret the processes associated with the two plans described in this book would show that the regeneration plan exhibited a process that was a reasonably balanced combination of rule and model developed within a pragmatic concept of urbanism. Ultimately, however, that plan did not (perhaps could not) realize the potential for innovation offered by the generative rules of the reinvestment area designation in the short time before the ward councillor took planning out of the department's hands. The process he fostered for the redevelopment plan was his attempt at innovation, which ironically was more controlling than the one it replaced. The redevelopment plan did not harness the reinvestment area's potential but instead was quintessentially utopian, a copy of a model devised to cure spaces of perceived socioeconomic ills.

The Yonge-Dundas case, as I have interpreted it, urges renewed attention to old debates in the planning field in light of changes to what is construed as "the urban." One of the debates concerns the origin of the field itself, which has not been much of a debate because the view that planning began in the nineteenth century as a response to the Industrial Revolution, a view that is widely, if unreflectively, adopted, especially in Canada and the United States. Sometimes "modern" is placed before "planning" to suggest that non-modern planning preceded it. However, the common view infers that prior discourse about urbanism did not invoke notions of planning sufficient to carry that name and that planning was born with the apparently "natural" objective of responding to the effects of the Industrial Revolution and relieving its worst effects through attention to land and building. Now that the Industrial Revolution has matured and ebbed in Western industrial countries, leaving behind a landscape that is being shaped by new technologies and socioeconomic-ecological conditions, some key land use assumptions of the past cease to be apt. This calls for rethinking planning's origins and mission.

Meanwhile, a second debate centres on whether planning practitioners who are on the front lines of this shift from an industrial to a postindustrial urbanity are helped by theorizing in their field. This case study shows that space has largely been dropped from theorizing on the assumption that space is a construction that results from socioeconomic-political relations. Thus, theorists have proposed that those relations should be the focus of planners' actions, and they posit that appropriate spatial solutions will follow. This orientation to space has so captured the field's theorists that there was no theory from the planning field to help the very experienced planners in this study articulate and defend their view of urban regeneration, which was based partly on spatial principles. They did not have the vocabulary, the concepts, or the examples to form a persuasive argument to counter the utopian, curative proposal, which was backed by political and financial leaders, that displaced the regeneration plan. The tendency to split space off from process derails efforts to connect planning and urban design. Their common matrix is urbanism. The search for a generic theory of planning focuses on the procedures of planning and gives a second and residual place to "the urban."

A third, often boring and esoteric debate concerns what planning is. It is worth revisiting this debate because a significant, rarely mentioned point emerged from this study: planners, planning activities, and the planning framework are distinguishable elements that should not be blended together in research or commentaries as if planning were a cream soup. The planning framework of a jurisdiction can be used by anyone and, indeed, must be paid attention to by everyone who participates in the land use and built-form game, but this does not mean that all those participants are planners, because non-planners may also carry out planning activities. The framework has been arrived at through processes that were answerable to democratic challenges;

it was constructed within the zeitgeist of the Industrial Revolution. The framework presents a structure of regulations and penalties regarding land use that are intended to protect against the worst excesses while being mindful of private-property rights. It is not held in place only, or even primarily, by planners but rather by the entire development industry and government. The framework does not require planners to make it function. When planners are indistinguishable from planning activities and the framework, planners can be scapegoated, accused of actions governed by the planning framework and not within their professional capacity to determine. Indeed, one of the storylines in this case traces how the city council took planning activities out of the hands of its own planners and gave the task it wanted done to a development consultant who had the backing of a lawyer who specialized in expropriation law. City council's actions led it toward a legal confrontation that would be adjudicated within the framework. What began as a discussion about urbanism became, once it was transferred into the legal system, a discussion about property rights. Outside of the legal system, however, the discussion can be "thicker," in the sense of involving built-form principles, ethics, and public-interest preferences that are hard to fully capture in a local official plan. In addition, if planners think they are a part of the framework, or buried under it, they may forget their professional obligations regarding independence and courage – that is, that their role is to be not only accurate but also creative and innovative in land use and built-form matters.

Finally, there is debate about how best to research planning. Most often, researchers use socioeconomic theories of how phenomena are related to one another to structure their investigations. Using the historically derived insights of Françoise Choay, I have shown the discourse of urbanism as it was carried out in a contemporary planned intervention for a small area in a large city. Based on the case material, the discussion about the area was framed first and foremost in terms of urbanism, although economics, politics, and social concerns were also vital components of the discussion. The three root figures that Choay identified – the rule, the model, and the theory of urbanism – were evident and shaped discussions about what to do about the area and the eventual plans. These enduring figures of urbanism show that a multidimensional approach to space can inform investigations of planned interventions.

Planners should recognize that the broad scope of urbanism – its long trajectory, not just its past focus on industrialization – is a resource that can help them generate and argue persuasively for a creative postindustrial urbanity.

APPENDIX 1
Selected elements of the planning framework

This appendix is for those who want a fuller elaboration of the planning framework pertinent to this case. Following a very brief outline of how urban and regional planning responsibilities are allocated in Canada, the principal elements of the framework discussed in the book are described.

Overview of Planning in Canada

Since Canada was founded, specific powers have been assigned either to the federal or provincial governments and, more recently, the three territories. Powers related to land-use planning are delegated to the provinces. In turn, provinces derogate some of their power over land-use planning to municipalities, regions, and other subprovincial jurisdictions. A tiered or nested approach to planning results. For instance, a municipal plan must fit within the plan of the metropolitan area or region, and that plan must, in turn, fit within provincial rules and stated interests. In Canada urban and regional planning is fully integrated into virtually all jurisdictions and is accepted as a responsibility of subprovincial governments by the general public, even if its scope is not widely understood.

Municipal and regional planning in Canada has a strong land use orientation. Other closely associated functions that have to do with the economy, health, education, and social services, for example, are dealt with separately via other provincial legislation or local-level institutional structures, but they must be given attention when plans are created.

Many of the elements seen in this case study will be familiar because planning practices have been widely diffused over the decades, mainly from Britain and the United States to other countries (Ward 1997a, 1999, 2000, 2003). It is common for statutory rules to provide the basic articulation of the process and participants in planning activities, while a municipality or other jurisdiction builds on those basic minimums to meet its wishes. For example, a level of consultation beyond that mandated by legislation is often expected by the public. Some statutory planning activities are common across the country, such as zoning and municipal land use plans; others may or may not be used, and their purposes may vary widely – for instance, appeal bodies and site-plan review provisions. For a comparison of land-use planning terminology used across the country, see David Gordon and Tasha Elliott (2007).

A planning process for reaching a recommendation will incorporate statutory requirements within an approach that is locally designed for a given situation. For instance, Hodge and Gordon (2008, 176) depict a classic problem-solution planning process. It might be used for a project undertaken within the context of an existing official plan.

Some Ontario-Specific Elements

The Planning Act

Official Plans (Part 3 of the Planning Act)
The province's *Planning Act* requires every city (as well as other defined jurisdictions) to prepare an official plan. Its purpose is to describe the policies of the jurisdiction with respect to how land will be used. This includes where uses will be located, the utilities and other services that will be needed, where growth and change will be urged to occur, and the forms it should take. Official plans must contain goals, objectives, and policies for managing and directing "physical change and the effects on the social, economic and natural environment" (*Planning Act*, s. 16[1][a]). They may also contain the measures for attaining the goals. Importantly, all public works and bylaws of the municipality must conform to the official plan (ibid., s. 24).

These plans must be revised at least every five years, and the public must be informed about changes being made at that time or at any other time. Detailed requirements are laid out for amending the plan.

The content of official plans is determined by the city itself, not by the province; however, the plan must be developed in discussion with the relevant ministry, and most jurisdictions must have their plans approved by the ministry. If a city wants to take advantage of certain options offered in the *Planning Act*, then its official plan must specify this. For example, in order to make use of the provisions regarding a community improvement project area, as players attempted to do in this case, there must be appropriate statements in the official plan to recognize this possibility.

The official plan was used extensively in this case to ground many different arguments that were put forward to come to grips with Yonge Street's problem. It was used by the city to argue in favour of keeping retail and entertainment as principal uses in this section of the street and against the proposal for office and residential redevelopment at the corner of Yonge and Elm. Later in the Ontario Municipal Board (OMB) hearing, the official plan would be used again to argue against office and residential uses. It was also used as an initial bargaining position in discussions with Eaton's in which the latter brought considerable clout to the table. Even though Eaton's eventually won concessions, the damage to the public direction of city development would have been much greater had there been a weaker official plan – or none at all – as a starting point of discussions, or had there been a weaker cadre of planners. On the other hand, the official plan was modified to slightly increase site coverage so that small-format urban box retailing could develop and to increase the allowable height while keeping similar street shadowing prohibitions. The official plan wore well through this tussle by anchoring a firm, if not universally accepted, vision. Even appellants at the OMB were uncritical of the set of changes associated with the regeneration plan.

Community Improvement Plan and Project (s. 28)
A section of the *Planning Act* gives municipalities the opportunity to designate areas within their jurisdiction as areas in need of improvement. They can then use a special set of tools within those areas as they fix it up. In the Toronto case, section 28 of the *Planning Act* was used to designate the area around Yonge and Dundas as a community improvement project (CIP), which enabled the city to take steps such as offering grants and loans to property owners and acquiring land via expropriation. The CIP area was established near the start of the regeneration phase, although its boundaries were later changed. When the initiative turned into a redevelopment project, it was debated whether a CIP was the right tool or if a body separate from the city should be set up, as had been done in many European cities and in the United States: for instance, the New York State Urban Development Corporation drove the 42nd Street Development Project. It was decided that the CIP was adequate for the task.

Section 28 of the Act defines community improvement as "the planning or replanning, design or redesign, resubdivision, clearance, development or redevelopment, reconstruction and rehabilitation, or any of them, of a community project area, and the provision of such residential, commercial, industrial, public, recreational, institutional, religious, charitable or other uses, buildings, works, improvements or facilities, or spaces therefor, as may be appropriate or necessary" (s. 28[1]). Plans produced under this section must be approved by the ministry.

A vital question that arose in this case was: How does one know when an area needs that sort of improvement? The answer depends on what a city council asserts (and, if called to do so, successfully defends) is a problem. This is discussed at length in Chapter 5. The Act defines a community improvement project area as "an area within a municipality, the community improvement of which in the opinion of the council is desirable because of age, dilapidation, overcrowding, faulty arrangement, unsuitability of buildings or for any other reason" (s. 28[1]). The phrase "or for any other reason" became the interpretive linchpin of the case. Opponents were sure that the city was overstepping the bounds of the definition of a community improvement project because the buildings were not decrepit; the city's lawyer, by contrast, illustrated why so-called social blight could be covered by the phrase "or for any other reason" found in the definition of the Act.

The "Community improvement" section of the Act replaced a previous section that dealt with urban renewal and focused on "curing blighted areas, in other words, how bad things were" (Joint Board 1998e, 20[a]). The city claimed that the new section 28 was intended to be "more flexible and emphasize improvement and economic and social issues ... [and] not limited to curing physical blight" (ibid.), and that was how it has used this tool.

Opinion was divided over how to interpret the section. One respected planner in private practice with decades of experience who testified for the appellants said section 28 was overused in this case because the economic conditions did not call for it. Another planner said that, in this case, section 28 was being used to advance economic goals and that this was inappropriate. The lawyer for the appellants, in his closing submission, said that it was still necessary under the new section of the Act to show blight in some form to use section 28. He said that despite his efforts to have the city produce evidence of blight, serious decline, or "decline for several decades," the planner "could not refer the Board to any report" (Joint Board 1998d, 12-13). The city itself strenuously argued that "community improvement" had to be broadly interpreted to encompass much more than physical structures and to embrace flexibility and exercise of council discretion, which the "ordinary meaning of the words" does not suggest.

Given that the city produced neither factually convincing economic nor social evidence as grounds for its request to expropriate under section 28, and given that there were said to be no prior cases on point, this test case at the OMB has left as its legacy the possibility that other cities in the future can claim that social blight is hindering their development.

Grants and Loans (section 28[7])

One feature of a CIP is that a city can make grants or loans toward the cost of rehabilitating land and buildings to property owners within the area. Under ordinary circumstances the grants and loans would be considered unacceptable. Toronto moved ahead with a facade improvement program at an early point in the regeneration phase, and it was extremely successful (see Chapter 3).

Bonus Zoning (s. 37)

A municipality can come to an agreement to allow more height and density on a site than is allowed as of right in its zoning bylaw. However, to do so, it must have passed a bylaw to this effect in the manner required under the land use provisions of the Act. Consequently, using this provision of the Act becomes voluntary on the part of a city, and agreement to use it is deemed to have the support of its voting public because the city had to execute the required public notification procedures before adopting it. Ordinarily, this provision is part of an omnibus zoning bylaw, so it is not as if citizens had a good look at it and said yes. Yet, in a "representative democracy sense," citizens have agreed to its use, given the public notice requirements for introducing it. Indeed, bonus zoning may seem like a bad idea because it smacks of the bureaucracy saying, "Let's make a deal" (Sewell 2003). This approach is used in many other jurisdictions, where it carries different names – for example, "planning gain" in Britain (Healey, Purdue, and Ennis 1995), "exactions" in the United States, and, in some places, "density bonusing." Some jurisdictions expressly do not use it.

Bonus zoning is a trade-off tool because increased profit to a developer from a project is made possible in exchange for benefits the city wants. The "deal" is cemented in one or more development agreements and registered against the land to which it applies. Thereafter, the municipality is entitled to ensure that the provisions are met by the original and subsequent owners and to use other provincial legislation, such as the *Registry Act* and the *Land Titles Act,* in support of its claims.

If bonus zoning is going to be used, the trick is to use it well. That requires expertise and experience estimating development profitability in cases where the buildings are large and costly, when the timeline is only a best estimate, where the future of the economy is uncertain, and where making the best deal from a position of strength or weakness depends on whether one's "side" is in the better or worse bargaining position. Acuity is likewise needed to estimate the costs of the civic benefit that the city wants to have in return. A recent estimate of financial gains from bonus zoning showed that Toronto was obtaining very low gains in comparison to Vancouver (Porter 2005). A 1988 study of a series of buildings in New York for which bonuses were exchanged for benefits estimated "that the market value of the benefits received by the developers was $108 million, while the cost of the amenities they provided was about $5 million" (cited in Fainstein 2001a, 247n144). More skill on the side of municipalities is needed, which was one of the main points made by Healey, Purdue, and Ennis (1995). Agreements can be appealed to the OMB, and even the failure on the part of a city to have arrangements in place to make deals can be a subject of appeal by an individual.

Healey, Purdue, and Ennis' work (1995) stands out among the few studies that have explored this arcane practice. Based on their research in England, their book describes why development impacts, compensation, and agreements came to have a large role from the mid-1980s into the 1990s. They describe the legal and planning mechanisms and how they worked in five cases. In Ontario, Krushelnicki (2007) says that compensation had a way of creeping into municipal practices before any legislation was in place. For him, the appropriate question is not whether it should happen but rather, if it is going to happen, whether it should be controlled by legislation. If bonus zoning is public and registered, the benefits are at least more likely to reach the agreed upon destination.

In the Yonge-Dundas redevelopment phase, agreements entered into under section 37 worked in two directions: to capture benefits from the Metropolis UEC and other buildings in the redevelopment project and to capture benefits from buildings outside the project to put toward finishing the square.

Ontario Municipal Board and the Ontario Municipal Board Act

The Ontario Municipal Board is governed by the *Ontario Municipal Board Act (OMBA)*. It is a quasi-judicial administrative board that deals primarily with disputes having to do with land use that arise in conjunction with the application of the *Planning Act*. Thus, the *Planning Act* is one of the board's areas of jurisdiction, and it is its most important in terms of workload. The board also has jurisdiction in other nonplanning areas that are tied to land development. Some of these areas (such as parts of the *Municipal Act,* the *Ontario Heritage Act,* the *Expropriations Act,* and the *Consolidated Hearings Act*) played a role in this case; others (such as the *Aggregate Resources Act* and the *Development Charges Act*) did not (see Krushelnicki 2007 for a practical description of all facets of the board).

The board is quasi-judicial in that it functions partly like a court: it calls witnesses and evidence, uses an adversarial structure in its hearings, and has hearing officers that serve as adjudicators. It is only "quasi" judicial, however, because its decisions are administrative in the sense that they interpret local plans and government policies on behalf of the minister in charge of municipalities and land use. There are no identical bodies in other Canadian provinces, the United States, or Britain, although there are other forms of appeal boards. Appeals may also go to regular courts. People appointed to the Ontario board as members to hear and adjudicate cases are drawn from fields such as law, planning, engineering, accounting, surveying, and municipal politics and with some attention being paid to geographical representation from across the province. A hearing panel may have one to three members who may or may not have expertise in the subject matter of the case or know the geographical area well.

The board has had a very long and often contentious history (Chipman 2002), and while there are periodic calls for its abolition, it seems very unlikely that it will disappear because it is fully implicated in the planning framework. Of course, its structure and responsibilities are modified from time to time. Everyone with an interest in land development has a stake in its survival. Members of city council make their decisions fully aware of, and in light of, the possibility that a decision could be appealed to the OMB by any interested party – a developer, a development lobby organization, a business, an ordinary citizen, or the province itself. Therefore, city councils are sometimes suspected of making planning decisions for political reasons, for reasons they know full well will be overturned at the board, but they make the decisions anyway because they may save them from political heat. On the other hand, the business of cities has also been held up or reversed through appeals to passages of official plans, which cities see as their policy statements of direction. Most cases that go to the board require lawyers for the various interests involved, and lawyers are likely involved in deciding whether to appeal a decision in the first instance. The board's existence tends to make planners very careful that their recommendations to councils and the development industry can be rationalized within the legal framework of the planning function.

Joint Board Hearings

Occasionally disputes involve more than one statute; therefore, a hearing is held under the *Consolidated Hearings Act (CHA)*. The reason for the Joint Board hearing is to avoid conflicting decisions arising from hearings under separate statutes. Indeed, it is one's right to have a comprehensive hearing if one's dispute straddles different statutes that one board, acting alone, is unable to rule on. The *CHA* applies to a specific list of statutes, and the *Planning Act* is one of them. A frequent union for a joint board hearing is that of the OMB and the Environmental Review Tribunal. In the case at hand, a joint board heard a case that involved both the *Planning Act* and sections of the *Expropriations Act*.

In these cases, the hearing panel may have a member from each of the applicable boards. Any decision carries the authority of the *CHA* rather than the tribunals individually. Both members of the panel in the case study were from the OMB.

The Expropriations Act

Certain public bodies are designated as expropriating authorities, and municipalities are one of them. (There are also a few quasi-private bodies, like hospitals, that can have that authority.) If the expropriation is deemed appropriate via an inquiry, then the municipal council is the approving authority. That is, the ultimate decision to carry out an expropriation once its appropriateness has been documented and appeals have been settled lies with the municipal council with whatever political consequences it may engender.

A municipality that intends to expropriate property must signal this with published notifications (*Expropriations Act*, s. 6[1]). If a landowner who is the subject of an intention to expropriate wants a hearing on the matter, then he or she must inform the municipal council (s. 6[2]). This is what nine of the ten Yonge Street property owners did. This may be called a hearing of necessity. Then an inquiry board must be set up with an inquiry officer who is not from the OMB. The task of the inquiry is to decide if the expropriation of land is "fair, sound and reasonably necessary in the achievement of the objectives of the expropriating authority" (s. 7[5]).

However, another section of the Act (s. 6[3]) allows the expropriating authority to petition the province to forego the inquiry, which is what the City of Toronto did in the Yonge-Dundas case. Under special circumstances, it may be "necessary or expedient" and "in the public interest" to proceed straight to expropriation without having an inquiry. The city tried to use this argument in its favour but failed to persuade the province that its case met the conditions. Consequently, an inquiry was held, the expropriation was deemed to meet the not very strenuous condition of being reasonably necessary, and the property owners moved to appeal the inquiry officer's finding.

An appeal, such as the one examined here against the City of Toronto, goes to the OMB because that body has jurisdiction to deal with sections 6, 7, and 8 of the *Expropriations Act* (see schedule attached to the *Consolidated Hearings Act*). And it was at the OMB where the appeal against the expropriations joined with appeals against certain planning actions in a joint board hearing under the *Consolidated Hearings Act* (see Chapter 5).

The Municipal Act

In a political structure like Canada's, where provinces are given specific responsibilities and devolve some of them to subordinate bodies, including municipalities, this devolution is handled via legislation that sets out precisely what those delegated responsibilities are and how they must be handled. That is what Ontario's *Municipal Act* does. It describes the general powers of the different levels of municipalities and regions (single and two-tier arrangements, wherein local municipalities are generally referred to as lower tier while regional governments are upper tier) and their relationships to other levels of government. The Act describes each level's specific powers and areas of responsibility, such as transportation, waste management, public utilities, flood control, economic development, health and safety, and so on; it outlines how the levels are to conduct the licensing and registration of various services and facilities (from taxicabs to group homes); it defines what form municipal organization and reorganization is to take; it clarifies how councils are to proceed; it sets out how finances of a municipality are to be administered and how taxation, fees, debt, and investment are to be managed; it defines the permitted means of enforcement of responsibilities; and it describes how and in what ways a municipality is liable for damages that result from its actions or inactions. Therefore, the Act is an encompassing contractual arrangement between completely unequal participants.

Three provisions of the Act stood out in the Yonge-Dundas case, but in reality its entire content lay behind all actions because the Act determines intergovernmental actions, the tasks of city councils, and the financial leverage a city has (or, mostly, does not have).

Municipal Code

The Municipal Code is simply a device for gathering together a municipality's bylaws within a single compilation. For example, all of the rules and regulations about what one can and cannot do in a public park or square appear in a section of the *Municipal Code*. The power to determine those actions is devolved from the province via the *Municipal Act* and is then regulated via bylaws established at the municipal level, which are codified there in a form approved by the province, that is the *Municipal Code*. Section 248 of the *Municipal Act* describes *the Municipal Code* as a "comprehensive general by-law." It was also the *Municipal Code* that had to be revised when the sign size and wattage for Yonge-Dundas were changed, but like control over behaviour in public squares, the right to control signage begins higher up with the province. For example, a newspaper notice that advised the public of a meeting about the sign bylaw identified it as a meeting to request an amendment to the *Municipal Code* that would be held in compliance with the *Municipal Act*. One can readily see that cities in Ontario (and elsewhere in Canada) are kept in a dependent state. Control is almost as draconian in British-influenced systems like Australia and, indeed, in Britain itself.

Business Improvement Areas (ss. 204-15)

In Ontario a business improvement area (BIA) is mandated to improve, beautify, and maintain public lands and buildings within the area beyond the levels provided by the municipality at large and to promote the area as a business and shopping district. Sections 204 to 215 of the *Municipal Act* set out the rules for establishing, maintaining, and winding down BIAs. The city oversees the proper conduct of the rules but, in effect, does not have the capacity to deny their emergence. Cities do have options regarding how they interact with BIAs, however. For example, a city can help BIAs take on more activities by offering money for studies and projects, establishing a central liaison office at city hall, or supporting an umbrella BIA group that lobbies the city and gives members the opportunity to exchange experiences (see Chapter 6). The first organization of the BIA type in any Western country appears to have been formed in 1971 in Toronto in the area called Bloor West Village.

A BIA in the Ontario context can be a powerful body. By contrast to the situation of a business association like the Yonge Street Business and Residents Association, membership in a BIA is not voluntary for companies located within the area. Through a process that is specified by the province and monitored by the city, the willingness of business owners to form a BIA is assessed through polling in the area. Once a decision is made that a BIA will be created, then all businesses and property owners in the area are automatically members. None can stand aside and reap free rider benefits. Thus, boundaries can become contentious. Furthermore, the levy on a business is calculated by using the realty assessment, so a BIA like Downtown Yonge can generate a substantial annual budget quite easily and have considerable effect (Symes and Steel 2003).

However, as Hoyt (2004, 379) notes, a municipality does not coordinate where the BIAs are located. In Ontario the city does not have that role. Therefore, what occurs in the interstitial areas becomes an issue for cities.

Public-Private Partnerships (s. 203)
"Same bed, different dreams" is said to be the English translation of a Chinese description of public-private partnerships (PPPs). In 1996, when the Yonge-Dundas Redevelopment Project was designed, the right to establish a PPP was not accorded to municipalities. The revised *Municipal Act* assigned power to municipalities to establish corporations of the PPP form in 2003. The Conservative government had begun a process for making municipalities more like corporations in 1995. But it took until 2001 to pass the legislation, and it was not implemented until 2003. Section 203 is simply a general statement announcing that municipalities will be able to establish and own corporations and that the regulations have not yet been determined. On its own, the section provides no hope of ensuring equity in the distribution of risks and

benefits between public and private partners or of public accountability for the PPPs' actions. Those are two of the key issues repeatedly raised in the literature, whether in Canada, the United States, Britain, or Europe (see, e.g., Nelson 2001; Siemiatycki 2007; Vining and Boardman 2008).

Impetus for PPPs has come not only from Ontarian neoconservative ideology and the fact that PPPs are so widely used elsewhere but also from the fact that being able to form a PPP is now the quid pro quo for gaining access to some types of federal funding administered by the Federation of Canadian Municipalities (Warson 2004). Although there is general agreement in the first instance that the US model of PPPs was imported to other countries in the 1970s and 1980s, recent developments show that relationships are now likely to be based on the forms of joint labour between the public and private sectors that existed before the turn to US-style PPPs.

In the Yonge-Dundas case, what was sometimes called a PPP was renamed a collaboration model, and even that began to lose its shape after December 1996, when the whole intervention began to look more like the "same bed, same dream."

Toronto's Three Lenses Approach to Planning

In November 1995 Toronto City Council adopted a new conceptual way of thinking about planning in the city, which it called the three lenses approach. As an approach it sought to recognize that different areas of the city should receive different planning treatment to achieve local and city-wide goals (Toronto 1995c). This initiative echoes efforts described by Brindley, Rydin, and Stoker (1989) and Healey et al. (1988) to make planning in Britain more flexible. In the Toronto case, the impetus for introducing flexibility came from municipal rather than more senior government sources.

One of the three lenses, or categories of designation for a city area, was "reinvestment," which indicated that an area needed revitalizing. In February 1996 the planning commissioner recommended this reinvestment designation for Yonge-Dundas. This meant removing density numbers from the official plan, specifying planning objectives and built-form principles, and removing some parking restrictions (Toronto 1995c). It was said that the planning objectives would give more importance to built form, to maintaining a high degree of pedestrian comfort on the street, and to community benefits such as parking and open public space. These changes were in addition to an increase in nonresidential density permission from 2.0 to 4.0 times the lot area as of right for the area between Gerrard and Dundas streets and an increase in the height limit on Yonge Street from eighteen to twenty metres, while maintaining the existing five-hour sun angle provisions.

The goal of the three lenses approach was to introduce varied descriptions and regulatory tools to suit the various needs of districts in the city – for example, "to direct growth to key strategic districts, and protect others from major physical change. A zoning by-law that describes and prescribes the existing site standards in great detail can be a very useful tool for conserving the established physical form of residential neighbourhoods, but is a genuine roadblock where transformational change is desirable" (Toronto 2000b, 27). The three lenses were (1) areas designated for major reinvestment and development – such as the downtown core, the waterfront, brownfields, and greenfields – which would have new tools available, such as tax increment financing, as incentives; (2) established, relatively stable areas where major change was not desirable, which would have policies to protect their character yet improve amenities; and (3) areas where gradual change was both expected and desirable, such as along the major arteries of the city (ibid., 27-36).

One can see from this example that innovation in planning style was possible, even in a formal way, within the centralized provincial planning legislation and regulations.

APPENDIX 2
Chronology

March 1953	Subway line on Yonge Street opens.
1977	The Eaton Centre opens.
1992	Application for redevelopment submitted for site at 350 Yonge Street, corner of Elm: 16-storey commercial-residential, with retail at grade and first basement; unspecified commercial uses on second floor, one level of parking; 71 residential units; 47.75 metres, including mechanical penthouse; overall density, 9.24 times the lot area with 2.0 times commercial and 7.24 times residential. Request is well over allowable envelope. Holding bylaw applied to the property until new official plan completed.
July 1993	City council adopts new official plan (Cityplan '91) on 20 July.
September 1993	City of Toronto Land Use Committee requests a study of the planning controls affecting the Yonge Street Strip between Gerrard and Dundas streets to reply to the Yonge and Elm redevelopment application.
April, May 1994	Public meeting held 5 April regarding Yonge-Dundas Improvement Plan. A community committee established at the meeting met 3 times (25 April, 9 May, and 24 May 1994) and represented the Eaton Centre, the Yonge Street Association, Ryerson University, local retail property owners, street vendors, street portrait artists, street musicians and buskers, students, the ward councillor, and three city departments: Metro Transportation, Planning and Development, and Public

	Works and the Environment. Meetings were open to the public.
26 May 1994	Report from Planning and Development to Land Use Committee on the subject of recommended amendments to Part 1 of the official plan to address concerns raised by the referral request filed by the T. Eaton Company Limited.
27, 28 June 1994	City council approves official plan amendments. Sends them to the Ontario Municipal Board (OMB) for approval.
8 September 1994	Official plan approved by the OMB.
26, 27 September 1994	City council approves Yonge Street Improvement Committee.
November 1994	Municipal election; Barbara Hall replaces June Rowlands as Toronto mayor.
March 1995	Yonge Street Business and Residents Association (YSBRA) launched.
31 March 1995	Planning and Development Department completes *Yonge Street between Dundas and Gerrard: Urban design discussion paper* for in-house use.
June 1995	Planning and Development Department completes *Downtown Yonge Street Improvement Plan* for public discussion.
July 1995	YSBRA incorporates as a nonprofit organization.
24 July 1995	City council approves *Downtown Yonge Street improvement plan*.
16 October 1995	City council passes bylaw No. 1995-0630, designating the Downtown Yonge Street Improvement Area as a community improvement project area for the purpose of implementing a range of public and private property improvement projects. Passed under s. 28 of the *Planning Act* of Ontario.
3 November 1995	Planning and Development Department issues *Downtown Yonge Street community improvement plan*.
6, 7 November 1995	City council adopts Planning and Development Department report *New directions for physical planning: The three lenses*.
December 1995	Neighbourhoods Committee reviews the *Community improvement plan for the Downtown Yonge Street Community Improvement Area*.

1996	Bicentennial of Yonge Street. Celebrations all year under the banner "200 Years Yonge."
22 January 1996	City council approves the *Community improvement plan for the Downtown Yonge Street Community Improvement Area*.
24 January 1996	Private consultant presents his report, *Downtown Yonge: Program to promote the regeneration of Toronto's main street*, at a meeting of YSBRA.
20 February 1996	Economic Development Committee approves proposal by YSBRA for collaborative revitalization of the Yonge-Dundas area with the city.
March 1996	Planning and Development Department issues *New planning amendments for Downtown Yonge Street*. Report responds to 23 September 1993 request from Land Use Committee for a study of the planning controls affecting the Yonge Street Strip between Gerrard and Dundas streets. The study was triggered by an application for official plan and zoning bylaw amendments for 350 Yonge Street. The commissioner of planning and development said, "I have not reported on the study until this time, to allow for a general direction on Yonge Street revitalization initiatives to emerge" (1).
4 March 1996	City council adopts *New planning amendments* (from Planning and Development Department); *Downtown Yonge Street regeneration program* (from private consultant); and bylaw No. 1996-0420, which lays out a community improvement plan covering Queen to Gerrard *within* the larger Queen to College Community Improvement Project Area, which had been approved on 16 October 1995 (as bylaw No. 1995-0630).
11 March 1996	City and YSBRA establish a steering committee (sometimes called a public-private partnership) to carry out Yonge Street programs.
1996	Jazz Place, a parkette between Yonge and Victoria streets, opens.
13 June 1996	Land Use Committee adopts *Final report: New planning amendments for DTYS*.

24 June 1996	Steering committee for the Downtown Yonge regeneration program establishes a four-person subcommittee to work secretly on the redevelopment plan.
September 1996	Administrative reorganization at the city. A Board of Management made up of four "super" commissioners replaces the former structure of ten commissioners. Commissioner of planning and development, under whom the regeneration planning had proceeded, leaves city employment. Planning and Development Department now headed by a chief planner who reports to a commissioner who has no background in planning. Department renamed Urban Development Services (UDS).
September 1996	Ward councillor meets with Ontario's deputy minister of the ministry of municipal affairs and housing (MMAH) to ask for approval to expropriate properties without going through a hearing of necessity. Request turned down.
9 December 1996	UDS presents report secretly developed over previous six months to city council sitting in camera: *DTYS regeneration program: DTYS Redevelopment Project – Project plan. A City of Toronto/Yonge Street Business and Residents Association Inc. initiative.* City council approves it and requests continuation of feasibility studies.
February 1997	Public meeting on Downtown Yonge Street Community Improvement Project (CIP) amendments.
19 June 1997	MMAH approves official plan and CIP amendments.
22 September 1997	Notice of Application for Approval to Expropriate is served on landowners.
16 February 1998	Joint Board hearing begins; ends 15 May 1998.
5 June 1998	Joint Board issues its decision and reasons for decision.

APPENDIX 3

Basic characteristics of the planning area

Land Uses and Built Form

The area's land use is mixed. Retail, restaurant, and entertainment uses dominate Yonge Street from Queen north to College/Carlton. Residential uses are mainly at the western edge of the orbit, on Bay Street. Ryerson University, with 25,000 full-time and 65,000 part-time students, sits one block north and east of the intersection and occupies the majority of eight city blocks. Commercial offices are spread throughout the area but are most heavily concentrated at the three subway nodes at College/Carlton, Dundas, and Queen streets. Three hotels in the immediate area furnish about 2,300 rooms. Four live theatres – Massey Hall, the Elgin and Winter Garden, and the Canon – lie between Dundas and Queen streets, with a total of about 7,500 seats. All of them are heritage performance venues. At the southwest corner of Yonge and Dundas is the enormous Eaton Centre, which sits on a 5.7-hectare site. Its glass-ceilinged, vaulted interior is thirty-nine metres high. Some say its design is reminiscent of the 1878 Victor Emmanuel galleria in Milan, others say it evokes the 1851 Crystal Palace in Brighton (Glancey 1998, 290). There are 1.6 million square feet for 300 stores, of which 900,000 square feet were dedicated to the Eaton's store alone.

The built form in the area is characterized by two primary typologies that, because of their placement, create a saucer effect. First, there are the older, smaller-scale, street-oriented retail and office structures, dating from 1889 onward. These buildings characterize Gerrard Street south to Queen. The properties are about forty metres deep on the east side and shallower on the west; they have narrow frontages, ranging from as little as six and up to thirty-two metres; and they are mainly two to three storeys high. Nineteen buildings are listed and six are designated as heritage buildings by the Toronto Historical Board, which provides different degrees of conservation protection. In what is often referred to as "the strip," the three-block area of Yonge Street between Dundas Square and Gerrard, the land parcels are held mainly by separate owners who have tenants occupying their properties.

The second typology is characterized by newer, large-scale high-rises in commercial, hotel, and condominium uses. These are found north of Gerrard Street, south of Queen, and off Yonge. They typically occupy most of a city block and are controlled by a corporation that rents space to retailers in off-street, off-grade shopping concourses. A study presented at the Joint Board hearing showed that 80 percent of retail on Yonge Street between College/Carlton and Queen is off-street. This format is found in the Eaton Centre, College Park, and the Atrium on Bay (which also has an entrance on Yonge). The city's planner noted in his evidence to the Joint Board hearing that the creation of the saucer effect from these two built forms was intended to favour street-oriented retail and entertainment activities in the dip of the saucer.

The official plan states that retail and entertainment are the uses for the redevelopment section of Yonge Street (Toronto 1990b, ss. 1.4, 3, 9, and 13). Part of the rationale for the designated uses derived from historical and contemporary uses, but part also came from the geometry of the land parcels. They are generally narrow and shallow, with large structures such as Ryerson University, the Delta Chelsea Hotel, the Atrium on Bay (a high-rise office and shopping mall) bordering Yonge Street, and heritage buildings to the south of Dundas. The configuration makes it difficult to achieve large land assemblies and structures that do not shadow the street.

From at least 1976, various studies noted either that a public square in the Yonge-Dundas vicinity would be appropriate or that public open space would help address the needs of the street (Joint Board 1998e, 31[6]). Three hard-surface public spaces have been added to the orbit since then, although not precisely at the Yonge-Dundas intersection. Yet Cityplan '91 described the orbit as being deficient in terms of parks and open space, and designated it a priority area for open-space acquisition (Toronto 1994c).

Movement

The Yonge-Dundas intersection can be easily reached. For public transit users, two subway stations sit below the Eaton Centre on the north-south line. The second north-south line is less than 700 metres away, and from there two more stations can be reached by walking or by streetcar. A frequent east-west streetcar service is provided on both Dundas and Queen streets (it runs along the north and south ends of the Eaton Centre) as well as along the next main street north, College/Carlton. A limited bus service is also provided on Yonge Street. The intercity bus terminal is one block to the west of the intersection, at Bay and Dundas streets. Regional commuter trains (GO Transit) and the national passenger train service (VIA Rail) converge at Union Station, which is located less than one and a half kilometres to the southwest. These rail stations can be directly reached by using the north-south subway line that runs down Yonge Street.

For motorists, both Yonge and Dundas streets connect to the regional expressway network within two kilometres. The streets are also relatively easy to use because they are part of Toronto's orthogonal grid system of main streets. There are over 2,000 parking spaces in the immediate vicinity, with an additional 4,000 within less than a 750-metre radius (Joint Board 1998b, Exhibit 69, 12).

The Yonge and Dundas area is also a major pedestrian node. Throughout the afternoon and evening, the sidewalks of Yonge Street along the strip are usually crowded with pedestrians, even during the winter. Sidewalks are generally 3.7 metres wide, and streets have a 20-metre right-of-way. Access to the underground pedestrian system, which runs beneath the central core, is provided through the Eaton Centre and the Atrium on Bay complexes on the west side of Yonge Street.

APPENDIX 4
Socioeconomic information about the planning area
reported in city and noncity statements 1994 to 1996

People and their use of the Yonge-Dundas area:
- "Some indications suggest that Toronto area residents are visiting downtown less often than in the past" (Toronto 1994a, 95).
- "The general public's use of the downtown has not been systematically addressed in recent years" (ibid.).
- "The general public's use of the downtown is critically important to the economic vitality of its retail space, restaurants, and entertainment facilities" (ibid.).
- Two analyses conducted by noncity researchers estimated that more than half of downtown retail sales were made to people who lived in the Greater Toronto Area and did not work downtown (ibid.).
- There are "insufficient customers with adequate spending power to patronize" the kind of establishments that should be here if the area is to compete with other parts of the city (Dennis L.M. Harrs, chair, YSBRA, to Toronto Mayor Barbara Hall, 8 February 1996).
- "Most Toronto area residents shop downtown less often than they did five years ago" (Toronto 1994a, 97).
- "There has been an increase in negative comments made about the downtown on attitudinal surveys" (ibid.).

Economic activity in the Yonge-Dundas area:
- Information about downtown revitalization in other cities indicates that a strong retail sector is important for safety, tourism, and conventions (Toronto 1994a, 95).
- Statistics for retail jobs in properties outside the three large retail malls of College Park, the Atrium on Bay, and the Eaton Centre – that is for about 20 percent of total retail jobs on Yonge between Bloor and Queen – for 1983-1992 were as follows. The number of retail jobs on Yonge stayed about

the same from 1983 to 1992, while retail jobs in the central core generally went down about 25 percent over the period. Although Yonge's share of the overall Metropolitan Toronto market slid a bit, it was modest, especially when compared to the 25 percent drop for the rest of the central core (ibid., 92). Thus, the Yonge stores with addresses on the street itself were doing rather well compared to the rest of the core.
- The issues for Yonge were "not so much a decrease in market share as more qualitative issues ... the type of activity, social problems, safety concerns, and physical amenity and appearance" (ibid., 91).
- "Research undertaken by Eaton's indicates that the downtown's share of the Toronto area consumer goods market had dropped to a mere 6% by 1992, down from about 25% in 1971" (ibid., 97).
- "Our own [the city's] analysis indicates that 42,000 jobs were lost in the Central Core between 1989 and 1993. The retail sector accounted for 4,500 of the lost jobs, a 20% contraction. However, all other sectors of the downtown economy also have contracted – offices, hotels, institutions, factories and warehouses and services" (ibid., 97).
- There is "insufficient diversity in the range and quality of retail and entertainment facilities to compete with other districts in the city" (Dennis L.M. Harrs, chair, YSBRA, to Toronto Mayor Barbara Hall, 8 February 1996).
- "Most of the new stores which have recently located on the street [Yonge] are of the short-term and discount variety, but there have been a few encouraging instances of longer term investment and commitment by innovative merchants in major destination stores, with one or two others rumored to be in the wings" (ibid.).
- "One of the strongest trends in retailing in recent years has been the emergence of large scale (20,000 to 75,000 square feet) superstores. These stores specialize in particular categories of merchandise and offer a combination of choice, value and service in a contemporary environment, often interlaced with recreational or entertainment elements ... They can be successful in dense urban areas which are well served by transportation ... The urban prototype generally has its main entrance on a major street rather than a mall ... [They provide] better local choice; they increase local market share and stem the out-migration of spending power to suburban locations. The trend appears to be accelerating in Canada among local retailers as well as American retailers who are seeking to enter the market and are interested in doing so via Toronto. The challenge is to entice as many of them as possible to downtown Yonge Street" (ibid.).
- The current state of the street discourages potential investors. Aside from the usual safety and appearance issues, there is "a lack of well located buildings which are of sufficient dimension to accommodate many of these

stores without substantial redevelopment. There are a handful of larger structures which could be adapted, but most of them are currently divided into smaller tenancies. Most of the properties on the street are small and land assembly is complex" (ibid.).

APPENDIX 5
Seven development options
Yonge and Dundas area, December 1996

Development Options

The following briefly describes seven development options available to the City pursuant to the legislative parameters established by the Municipal Act, the Planning Act (Community Improvement Provisions Section 28) and the Community Economic Development Act. One or a combination of these options provide the mechanism to achieve the Redevelopment Project.

Private Developer Assembles Land

This is the conventional scenario under which most development activity occurs. In this case, the City would provide encouragement to potential developers by announcing Official Plan and Zoning By-law amendments for a specific redevelopment within the Community Improvement Project Area. It presumes that a developer would then take the initiative to assemble the required sites. The City could then, using its Section 28 powers, expropriate any remaining parcels and sell them to the developer.

Generally, this option poses the least financial risk and the least expenditure of funds to the City.

City Expropriates Land

The City could expropriate targeted sites within the project area and sell the land to a developer as required, in pieces or a block. This option may take several forms including calling for Expressions of Interest to identify exactly what land is required and how the project financing would work.

This option requires a cash flow commitment from the City for a period of time and risks associated with costs and undetermined revenue from sale.

City Obtains Options to Purchase

The City could obtain options to purchase property, purchase the land and then sell to a developer. Alternatively the City could transfer options to third party developers and not acquire the land itself.

This option requires a cash flow commitment from the City for the options and the requirement which could increase substantially if the City has to finalize the options and acquire the properties.

City Expropriates Land for Square Only
The City could acquire land for a public square only and through this action, encourage revitalization indirectly around the square.

This option entails property acquisition costs but no assurance that redevelopment will take place nor assurance that municipal benefits outlined in Section 2.3 [titled "Municipal benefits"] will be achieved.

Expressions of Interest – Joint Ventures
The City could propose the project and call for expressions of interest from developers. This is a mechanism which could be used in conjunction with other options.

Public Private Partnership – Creation of a Municipal Capital Facility
The City could enter into agreements with respect to the provision of municipal capital facilities including facilities used for cultural, recreational, tourist and certain parking facilities. Under the provisions of the Municipal Act, a tax exemption could then be granted under certain conditions. This may provide a financial incentive for a portion of the development. This option requires a competitive bidding process.

This option limits the City's financial risk and facilitates development of portions of the proposal.

Redevelopment Incentive Program
The City could provide inducements for core tenants or developers in the project. An incentive program could be established under Section 28 of the Planning Act which would have the net effect of lowering operating costs for the start-up years has been investigated [sic]. Under the program, Council would have the authority, should it be considered necessary during negotiations with developers and tenants, to forgo, for a limited period, the revenue that would result from increased taxes paid after a reassessment. Based on a City of London, Ontario model, it is a program to entice development without requiring "up front" money from the municipality. The new tax level would be gradually increased over a period of time after which the City would be receiving taxes at the fully reassessed rate.

Source: Joint Board (1998b, Exhibit 53, 12-13), verbatim extract.

APPENDIX 6
Financial plan and costing scenarios
Yonge and Dundas area, December 1996

Financial Plan

Detailed financial plans are shown on two attached Executive Summary sheets. Two scenarios have been put forward – an optimistic scenario which assumes that negotiated land purchases can be made with a majority of owners and a pessimistic scenario which assumes all properties are expropriated.

The cash flow projections were prepared by KPMG Management Consulting based on land appraisal work undertaken by Stewart, Young, Hillesheim and Atlin Limited, business valuation and disturbance analysis undertaken by Price Waterhouse Chartered Accountants and hotel pre-feasibility analysis undertaken by Horwath Consultants.

The cash flow projections assume that the City will acquire all the land either through purchase or expropriation. Development options discussed in the Summary Report may reduce the amount of land the City would acquire. This would be finalized in the Stage Two process.

Project Costs

Net expenditures which need to be financed by the City are in the range of $13.4 to $17.1 million. Long term financing for this will not be required until the end of 1998 after all properties have been sold. We are recommending that the City determine, at that time, the optimal means of funding. The sources may range from using reserves such as the Parking Authority reserves, capital funds from assets sold, a debenturing or a combination of all of these options. Completion of the project is too far in the distance to determine at this time what the best mechanism for long term funding would be.

Short Term Financing

Under the option where the City chooses to expropriate, maximum cash requirements at any one time, up until the project completion would be up to

$30 million. This is the cash flow requirement after all properties have been acquired, but not yet sold.

We are proposing that all short term financing be from working capital, namely the reserve from uncollected taxes. This working capital would be used until the project completion at which time the working capital fund would be reimbursed, with interest.

Project Financing from December 10, 1996, to April 30, 1997

As the Stage Two Feasibility and Approvals process is undertaken, additional project legal and consulting work needs to be done prior to Council making a final decision on the project. We are recommending that these costs be funded by working capital as well. If the project is given approval by Council in May 1997, short term financing will continue until the completion of the project.

To commence Stage Two work, approval is required for up to $750,000 to cover the expenses needed to carry the project to its next decision point. This amount is broken down as follows:

Option Costs:	$400,000
Legal Fees related to Stage Two	$100,000
Appraisal and Project Planning e.g. RFQ Process	$150,000
Project Management	$100,000

If Council terminates the project in May 1997, we will find a permanent source of financing at that time. If the project continues, working capital will continue to be used until the end of the project. In short, the maximum expenditure required until the next decision point is $750,000.

Prepared by the City Treasurer

YONGE STREET PRIVILEGED AND CONFIDENTIAL – NOT FOR DISTRIBUTION
DEVELOPMENT   DRAFT – FOR DISCUSSION PURPOSES

Development: complete
Scenario: optimistic

Total Cash Expenses	($millions)
(a) Commercial land assembly costs (cash expenses)	(15.5)
(b) Public Square land assembly costs (cash expenses)	(12.6)
(c) Sub-total land assembly costs = (a) + (b)	(28.0)
(d) Interest costs	(1.2)
(e) Replacement of 277 Victoria	(4.0)
(f) Move costs and improvements for 277 Victoria	(3.5)
(g) Sub-total other costs = (d) + (e) + (f)	(8.7)
(h) Total cash expenses = (c) + (g)	*(36.7)*

Total Sale Revenues

(i) Revenue from the sale of commercial land and rights   23.4

Total Cash Outlay to be Financed

(j) Total cash expenses net of revenues = (h) + (i)	*(13.3)*
(k) Direct project tax revenue arising from an increased assessment base – present value @ 8%; and residential and commercial levies for the Public Square	5.5
(l) Spin-off tax revenue arising from an increased assessment base –present value @ 9%	19.9
(m) Foregone City land value for right of way	(0.4)
(n) Public Square improvement costs	(1.5)

Totals may not add due to rounding.
All numbers are based on preliminary information received from the City, Messrs. Stuart, Young, Hillesheim & Atlin Limited, Price Waterhouse, and Horwath Consultants.
No due diligence on this information has been undertaken by KPMG and no opinion is offered by KPMG with respect to the appropriateness or completeness of the information presented herein.
Hotel options assume a viable development potential exists.
Land sale revenue assumes a transfer of density from the public square lands.
Assume no interest on City-owned assets (except for costs relating to 277 Victoria) and hence no associated revenues.
Land purchase cost estimated in contemplation of litigation.

Draft printed 12/9/96 11:18 AM
File: City Cash Flow Worksheet

YONGE STREET DEVELOPMENT

PRIVILEGED AND CONFIDENTIAL – NOT FOR DISTRIBUTION
DRAFT – FOR DISCUSSION PURPOSES

Development: complete
Scenario: pessimistic

Total Cash Expenses	($millions)
(a) Commercial land assembly costs (cash expenses)	(17.5)
(b) Public Square land assembly costs (cash expenses)	(14.2)
(c) Sub-total land assembly costs = (a) + (b)	(31.7)
(d) Interest costs	(1.3)
(e) Replacement of 277 Victoria	(4.0)
(f) Move costs and improvements for 277 Victoria	(3.5)
(g) Sub-total other costs = (d) + (e) + (f)	(8.8)
(h) Total cash expenses = (c) + (g)	(40.5)
Total Sale Revenues	
(i) Revenue from the sale of commercial land and rights	23.4
Total Cash Outlay to be Financed	
(j) Total cash expenses net of revenues = (h) + (i)	(17.1)
(k) Direct project tax revenue arising from an increased assessment base – present value @ 8%; and residential and commercial levies for the Public Square	5.5
(l) Spin-off tax revenue arising from an increased assessment base – present value @ 9%	19.9
(m) Foregone City land value for right of way	(0.4)
(n) Public Square improvement costs	(1.5)

Totals may not add due to rounding.
All numbers are based on preliminary information received from the City, Messrs. Stuart, Young, Hillesheim & Atlin Limited, Price Waterhouse, and Horwath Consultants.
No due diligence on this information has been undertaken by KPMG and no opinion is offered by KPMG with respect to the appropriateness or completeness of the information presented herein.
Hotel options assume a viable development potential exists.
Land sale revenue assumes a transfer of density from the public square lands.
Assume no interest on City-owned assets (except for costs relating to 277 Victoria) and hence no associated revenues.
Land purchase cost estimated in contemplation of litigation.

Draft printed 12/9/96 11:19 AM
File: City Cash Flow Worksheet

Source: Joint Board (1998b, Exhibit 53, Appendix 1, 19-20 and two unnumbered pages), verbatim extract.

APPENDIX 7

Issues raised at public meetings and via correspondence
regarding the redevelopment scheme, spring 1997

6.3 Matters Raised at Public Meetings

Public meetings were held by Land Use Committee on February 27 and Planning Advisory Committee on March 17th, with both Committees recommending approval of the draft Official Plan, Zoning By-law and Community Improvement Plan amendments. The following addresses issues raised at those meetings and in correspondence received by the City to date:

a   Proposed public square:
    The proposed public square is clearly supportable from a planning point of view by virtue of its location within a Parks Acquisition Priority Area designated in the Official Plan. The new square would serve many purposes including changing the perception of Yonge and Dundas Streets as a retail environment, providing an improved visual presence for Ryerson Polytechnic University and serving the increasing population of residents and workers in the Central Core and east Downtown communities.

    While the specific process has not yet been defined, the planning and design for the proposed public square will involve both technical advice and community advice, including consultation with the Safe City Committee as recommended by the Planning Advisory Committee. Other groups such as the Yonge Street Business and Resident Association, TEDRA and Ryerson will be included in the process.

b   Issue of "down zoning" lands between Dundas Street and Dundas Square:
    The site-specific provisions of the proposed Zoning By-law which relate to the Redevelopment Project permit only public open space on these lands. The general by-law provisions, however, have not been amended and continue to permit commercial and residential uses up to 3.0 times the area of the lot. It was stated in the February 11, 1997 report of the

Commissioner of Urban Development Services that it would be inconsistent to upzone these lands to 4.0 times given City Council's direction to approve the Redevelopment Project in-principle in December 1996. As is the case with the structure of most site-specific by-laws, the by-law amendment would allow two options for development – the new site-specific permission or the permission afforded by the general provisions of the underlying by-law.

c Concerns about redevelopment incentives:
   It is appropriate to reiterate from the February 11, 1997 report that the Reinvestment Area approach for Downtown Yonge Street would have to be re-evaluated if the Redevelopment Project does not proceed. This is based on experience gained from understanding the economics of the street and land speculation which have prevented assembly and redevelopment and discouraged long term tenancies. The Redevelopment Project is an effort to break the speculative cycle which has contributed to the decline of the street as Toronto's main shopping street. Zoning By-law changes which have been proposed for the Street increase the non-residential density permission; in the absence of significant change, represented by the Redevelopment Project, zoning changes may actually be counter productive if they contribute to increased speculation instead of tangible improvement.

d Tax and employment benefits:
   The Redevelopment Project is estimated to have a net tax benefit of $9.6 million (net present value of City and Metro share of direct project tax revenue) and $11.1 million (net present value of City and Metro share of spin-off tax revenue). Net retail employment growth is estimated to be between 700 and 1,100 jobs with potential for up to 1,500 construction jobs.
   The Canadian Centre for the Study of Retail Activity at Ryerson has advised that the Redevelopment Project will increase retail employment in the downtown and contribute to maintaining the downtown retail core's current market share which is estimated at seven percent of the Metro retail market.

e Issue of continuity of retail on Yonge Street:
   The introduction of a public square does not violate the principle of continuous retail; the square will create a new sense of place at Yonge and Dundas, increasing the retail frontage from 50 to 225 [sic] in a continuous fashion around the square, improving linkages to Ryerson and surrounding areas.

f   Permission for interactive electronic games establishment:
Concern has been raised by the owner and/or tenant at 334 Yonge and 315 Yonge Street, both storefront pinball and electronic game establishments. The Redevelopment Project includes permission for a larger scale establishment for interactive electronic games. The intent of permitting such a use in association with the Project is to implement the proposed Official Plan objective for the Reinvestment Area which is to increase the proportion and range of residents of the region and visitors who use Downtown Yonge Street. In order to achieve this, entertainment uses such as a large format, interactive electronic game establishment which typically involve personal and group entertainment, food and beverage service and other features will have a broader appeal than smaller, storefront establishments. The size requirement of a minimum of 21 machines is consistent with the City's general Zoning By-law provisions which permit establishments with up to 20 machines only in certain areas.

It should be noted that the existing establishments on Yonge Street are not prejudiced in that they currently enjoy legal non-conforming status. The Planning Act provides a means for these uses to renovate or expand should the owner desire.

Source: Toronto (1997a, 6-7), verbatim extract.

APPENDIX 8
Bylaws before the Joint Board

Nature of the Applications before the Board

Having unanimously approved, in principle, the regeneration project and publicly announcing it on December 10, 1996, Council, on May 6, 1997, enacted an amendment to its Official Plan, an amendment to the CIP and a zoning by-law to implement the regeneration project and two specific by-laws related to parking. At a public meeting October 6 and 7, 1997, Council further amended the documents to reflect further refinements of the various block proposals.

By-law 1997-0193, Tab 1 of Ex. 56, is OPA 92. It deletes Section 11.7(b), the former policies affecting the area, and replaces it with Section 18.355 to incorporate policies governing the "Downtown Yonge Street Reinvestment Area," and provides for specific "Built Form Principles."

By-law 1997-0194, Tab 2, Ex. 56, as modified by Exhibit 30, does two things. Part I of the by-law incorporates the provisions of Section 37 of the *Planning Act* and increases the density of those properties previously limited to a 2x commercial to a 4x and increases the height limits. This follows from [the Program Manager's] evidence that the City is replacing some of its more rigid restrictions by adherence to specific built form provisions in OPA 92. Part II of the by-law applies specifically to the parcels A through D of the regeneration project to implement the project described earlier in this decision.

By-law 1997-0195 (Tab 3, Ex. 56) is a site specific by-law for 207 and 209 Yonge Street and sets a parking standard for those properties. This by-law was not contested.

By-law 1997-0196 (Tab 4, Ex. 56) amends the CIP to "incorporate the Regeneration Program into the Plan in order to facilitate implementation of regeneration strategies developed under the Regeneration Program." In compliance with Section 15 of Cityplan, S. 3.0, Rationale for Regeneration, it implements the objectives by providing as follows:

The regeneration of Yonge Street as a main shopping street with new retail and entertainment premises and the improvement of the environment of the street with improved public amenities is a key to maintaining the economic and social well-being of the downtown and the region.

By-law 1997-0361 (Tab 5, Ex. 56) passed July 14, 1997 amends By-law 1997-0194 which is site specific to the 4 parcels in the Regeneration Project. It fine tunes various aspects of the by-law.

Source: Joint Board (1998k, 21-22), verbatim extract.

APPENDIX 9
Decision of the Joint Board
Jurisdiction, conclusions and findings, decision and conditions, and obiter dicta

Jurisdiction

The Board was exercising two different functions in these proceedings, hence the establishment of the Joint Board of the Ontario Municipal Board, to deal with matters arising pursuant to the provisions of the *Planning Act,* R.S.O. 1990, c.P.13, and the Board of Inquiry, pursuant to Section 7 of the *Expropriations Act,* R.S.O. 1990, c.E.26 and this affects the jurisdictional issues that the Board must address.

The standard test of the Board in assessing matters arising pursuant to the provisions of the *Planning Act* is whether the proposal represents good planning and is in the public interest. The ability of the Board to make this determination and its power to approve, reject or modify the Official Plan Amendments and its power in a zoning by-law to dismiss an appeal, allow an appeal, in whole or in part, or amend the by-law or direct its amendment were not questioned by any party. The jurisdictional issue that did arise, in the planning context, related to Section 28 of the *Planning Act.* In this respect, there were three issues arising from the meaning and applicability of Section 28. The first was whether the use of Section 28 was limited to being used in areas which were in such a state of physical dilapidation and deterioration to require the intervention of the municipality. The second issue was whether the section can be used, especially the acquisition (expropriation) right, to promote and further the economic and social growth and benefits of a "community improvement project area" and is not restricted to curing blight. The third issue was the ability of the municipality to assemble and acquire and transfer some of the assembled lands to a third party private development interest.

Section 28 of the *Planning Act*, and its predecessors, has had a long history dating back to 1952 which introduced the concept of a redevelopment area.

The *Planning Act* was amended in order to introduce Section 16a to the Act. By its terms, a municipality which had an Official Plan, could designate an area within the municipality as a redevelopment area. It was to be redeveloped through the adoption of a redevelopment plan for the redevelopment area, which redevelopment plan required the approval of the Ontario Municipal Board. The provisions of the Act remained virtually unchanged until the adoption of the "new" *Planning Act* in 1983. With the 1983 Act, came the new nomenclature. As well, it was made a Part, Part IV, of the Act and given the title of "Community Improvement." Although the words found in the definitions under the old and new Acts were virtually the same, the old provisions, by the use of the term "redevelopment" had focussed activities on the physical redevelopment of areas suffering from blight. The new Act now referred to the entire process as " community improvement" to reflect a broader range of activities than commonly associated with the term "redevelopment."

The 1983 Act also saw the introduction of a list of matters of provincial interest to which the Minister, in carrying out his responsibilities under the Act, was to have regard to. Under the provisions of the *Planning Act* now in force, and which applies to these proceedings, not only the Minister, but the Council of a municipality, a local board, a planning board, and the Municipal Board, in carrying out their responsibilities under the Act, shall have regard to matters of provincial interest such as the orderly development of safe and healthy communities (Section 2[h] *Planning Act*), the resolution of planning conflicts involving public and private interests (Section 2[n]) and the appropriate location of growth and development (Section 2[p]).

Another major change brought about by the 1983 *Planning Act* was the change in definition of an "official plan." Prior definitions required it to deal solely with the physical development of the municipality. The 1983 Act expanded that definition by providing that it was to contain objectives and policies established primarily to provide guidance for the physical development of a municipality while having regard to relevant social, economic and environmental matters. The present Act, while repealing the definition of "Official Plan," now provides in Section 16 that an Official Plan shall contain goals, objectives and policies established primarily to manage and direct physical change and the effects on the social, economic and natural environment of the municipality.

Section 28(2) of the *Planning Act* requires that a municipality's Official Plan contain provisions relating to community improvement in the municipality and when it does, Council may, by by-law, designate the whole or any part of an area covered by such an Official Plan as a community improvement project area. Once passed, Council may provide for the preparation of a plan suitable for adoption as a community improvement plan (CIP) for the community improvement project area. The Act makes the procedures to be followed the same as those employed in the adoption of an Official Plan or an Official Plan amendment (Section 17[15] to [50] of the *Planning Act*). So, although not adopted as an amendment to the Official Plan, the Official Plan and its policies are a prerequisite to the adoption of the CIP. Therefore, the Board must look at the legislative description given to an Official Plan to determine whether or not the CIP is to deal solely with physical deterioration. In this regard, pages 13 to 16 of this decision, set out in detail the various Official Plan policies that govern the use of Section 28 in this City. The findings on that section must be read in conjunction with this analysis. Taken together, it is clear to the Board that there is sufficient jurisdiction to accomplish the City's project as proposed and with acquisition by expropriation.

The definition found in section 28(1) for a community improvement project area is as follows:

> "community improvement project area" means an area within a municipality, the community improvement of which in the opinion of the Council is desirable because of age, dilapidation, overcrowding, faulty arrangement, unsuitability of buildings or for any other reason.

The Board finds on the analysis of the legislative framework of the Official Plan and particularly the matters to which it is to have regard, that the use of the terms "age, dilapidation, overcrowding, faulty arrangement, unsuitability of buildings or for any other reason" are not to be narrowly restricted to the physical condition found on the street. However, the Board finds that because of age, faulty arrangement and unsuitability of buildings, the properties, individually, do not have the ability to respond to the demands of today to be able to effect a major change at Yonge and Dundas as is occurring in downtown urban areas throughout North America. The fact that those in opposition were not satisfied with the status quo, and had alternative development proposals that they presented to the Board, is confirmation of the recognition that these properties are in need of improvement which cannot be achieved on a property by property basis.

Additionally, the Board finds that the City's proposal comes within the terminology of "for any other reason." The City's proposal is intended to attain the economic and social benefits that will come with the creation of the catalyst which is intended to lead to the "improvement" of the community so delineated in the CIP and the community improvement project area.

As a result, the Board finds that all of the above, taken together, cumulatively results in the appropriate use by the City of the provisions of Section 28 of the *Planning Act*.

Mr. Waqué, in his argument to the Board, stated the following in his written submissions:

> The new legislative approach was to be more flexible and emphasize improvement and economic and social issues. Thus, Section 28 was to become understood as a tool for community improvements which was not limited to curing physical blight.

The Board agrees.

The Board has, in coming to these conclusions, given an interpretation to the words of the section that does not require it to employ the *ejusdem generis* rule of statutory interpretation in that it has looked at and applied the ordinary meaning of the words used in the section. The Board finds that the use of the adjectives "other" and "any" in the phrase "for any other reason" indicates that a broad interpretation was to be maintained and that, in any event, the proposal meets both, some of the "physical" criteria and the social and economic criteria delineated in the section as reasons for undertaking a CIP in a community improvement project area.

The Board, in arriving at this conclusion, has also applied the principle recently stated in *Periz (Litigation Guardian of) v. Salvation Army* (1998), 37 O.R.(3d) Part 6, p. 447. at p. 452, where Chapnik, J. states the following:

> Every statute shall receive such fair, large and liberal construction and interpretation as will best ensure the attainment of its object according to its true intent, meaning and spirit: Interpretations Act, R.S.O. 1990, c.I.11.

The issue of whether the municipality can acquire (expropriate) private interests and, in turn, sell or lease those interests to a private developer arose in both the context of Section 28 of the *Planning Act* and Section 7 of the *Expropriations Act* and will be dealt with in the following consideration by the Board of the provisions of the *Expropriations Act*.

The second test which the Board was required to examine in these proceedings is that found in Section 7(5) of the *Expropriations Act* whereby the Inquiry Officers are required to make a recommendation concerning whether a taking is "fair, sound and reasonably necessary in the achievement of the objectives of the expropriating authority." The Board has carefully considered the submissions it heard and makes the following findings:

1 The objectives of the public authority is [sic] not to be questioned by the Inquiry Officers. The objectives are presumed to have been appropriately

determined by elected officials and the remedy for any complaint is to replace the policy-making elected officials at the ballot box.

The Board, in these proceedings, is in the unique position of being the final decision-maker on the planning objectives of the City through its determination of all the planning documents before it.

Walters v. Essex County Board of Education, [1971] 3 O.R. 346 at 347-348.

2   The decided cases on the interpretation of these words have found that the question to be determined by the Inquiry Officer is whether the expropriation is "reasonably defensible" in light of the objectives of the expropriating authority.

Walters v. Essex County Board of Education, ibid., at p. 349

Re Parkins and the Queen (1977), 13 L.C.R. 306 (Ont. H.C.J.) at p. 315, aff'd. O.C.A. 1978, 19 O.R. (2d) 473 at 477.

3   Once the expropriating authority's objectives are placed beyond review, the question of whether there should be an expropriation is generally replaced with, where is the best location for the proposal.

Karn v. Ontario Hydro (1977), 11 L.C.R. 1(Ont. C.A.) at 8.

Re Grey County Hydro v. Ontario Hydro, 12 L.C.R. 193 (Ont. H.C.J.) at 195.

4   The Inquiry Officer only makes a recommendation to the approving authority and the ultimate responsibility for a proceeding, that is for accepting or rejecting the recommendation of the Inquiry Officer, lies with the approving authority, in this instance the City of Toronto.

Section 6, 7, 8 *Expropriations Act.*

5   Four of the ten properties to be acquired are required for the public square beneath which there will be underground parking open to the public for short term use. Section 191 of the *Municipal Act* permits assembly for municipal purposes, which would include a public square, and, permits acquisition or expropriation as the reasons for carrying out the assembly. The City did not proceed on this basis because the evidence was that the City concluded that a public square without the development adjoining it on Parcel A, the northern block, might, in the current circumstances, have a negative, rather than a positive, impact on the area. Section 191 of the *Municipal Act* refers to acquisition and expropriation as alternatives without distinction. Section 28(3) of the *Planning Act* speaks of authority for land acquisition but does not expressly state expropriation. The Board

finds that expropriation is an implementing tool which can be used for land acquisition which is governed by the *Expropriations Act* and its policies, which are the fair, sound and reasonably necessary policies, that is, reasonably defensible. The *Planning Act,* by its terms, is not directly concerned with the method by which land acquisition takes place.

In his argument, Mr. Waqué made the following submission:

> The possibility of expropriation is always present. It is an element of land ownership. What is protected under our law is not freedom from expropriation, but the presumption is that if public acquisition takes place, full compensation is required.

The Board agrees and would add that full compensation is "required" by the provisions of the *Expropriations Act.*

6   The Board finds that both with respect to the *Expropriations Act* and Section 28 of the *Planning Act* that there is no prohibition to properties being acquired or expropriated by the municipality and then re-sold or leased to private interests. There is a history of development by private interests in a redevelopment plan, the predecessor of the CIP, and there is precedent for an expropriating authority to expropriate property which is ultimately to be used for commercial purposes.
Legoyeau Holdings Limited v. Windsor, [1994] O.J. 1350 (Ont. C.A.)

Conclusions and Findings

The Board finds that OPA 92, the CIP amendment and zoning by-laws before it represent good planning and are in the public interest as they will allow the development of the public square, parking facility and UEC at Yonge/Dundas. The Board finds that the development of the project will act as a catalyst in improving the economic and social conditions of the CIP area in specific but of all of Toronto in general. Although the Board is not able to say categorically that the media tower at the Atrium, the announcement of the Livent development at Shuter and the commencement of the extensive renovations of the Eaton Centre, which will see the "popping out" of retail stores and restaurants onto the west sidewalk on Yonge, are directly related to the December 10th, 1996 announcement of the subject project, the Board can find that the timing of all these projects, including the subject's, is critical to the economic well being of Toronto. The Board will then dismiss the appeals and approve the documents subject to conditions which follow.

The Board finds that 6 properties are necessary for the achievement of a proper development of Parcel A.

The Board finds that it is critical to this project that the newly formed City of Toronto Council fully endorse its commitment and funding of the project. To that end, counsel for the City advised that the Board's Order should be withheld until August 31, 1998 to allow for such endorsement and the fulfilment of conditions and should such endorsement not be forthcoming by that date, the Board should dismiss the City's applications.

The Board finds that it is essential that YSBRA continue its efforts to ensure that the principles expressed in the CIP are fully realized. In this regard, the Board encourages its active participation in the maintaining of the area as a safe and clean environment which attracts the tourists and visitors and citizens of Toronto to Yonge and Dundas as has been accomplished by the BID in Times Square.

The Board finds, on the evidence, that the street entrance to the subway on the northeast corner of Dundas should be relocated to an internal access to the project and have an on-street access on the south side of Dundas as part of the public square. This was recommended by the Architect Franklin and the Board agrees. The Board also finds that the suggestions made by Mr. Pellow, with regard to the project, should be seriously considered and incorporated, if feasible.

The Board finds that expropriation is in the public interest to achieve the project that the Board has approved. In this regard and acting in its role as Inquiry Officers, the Board finds that "the taking of the lands is fair, sound and reasonably necessary in the achievement of the objectives" of the City. The Board makes this finding based on the commitments made by City officials in evidence that the expropriated owners will receive full and fair compensation for the properties taken. By this decision, the Board, as Inquiry Officers, reports to the approving authority, in this case, the City of Toronto, that the application for approval has merit and should proceed.

Decision and Conditions

The Board, based on all of the above, dismisses all of the appeals, approves OPA 92 and the amendment to the CIP, By-law 1997-0196 as modified in Tab 1 and Tab 4 of Exhibit 56, and amends the by-laws as found in Tabs 2, 3 and 5 of Exhibit 56 as further amended by Exhibit 30. The Board's Order will not issue until the following conditions are met and the Board is so advised:

1   That the newly formed City of Toronto Council endorse the commitment to proceed with the project put before this Board and commit the necessary funding and confirm its intent to proceed with the expropriation. The Board imposes Mr. Waqué's timing that such commitment be made by

June 30, 1998, and that plans of expropriation be filed within the first two weeks of July.
2   The formal lease between AMC and PenEquity and the terms of the agreements between PenEquity and the City be finalized and confirmed by July 15, 1998.
3   That the planning conditions filed as Exhibit 296 and attached as Schedule "C" shall be fulfilled on or before August 30, 1998.

Obiter Dicta

The Board offers the following observations and suggestions that arise out of hearing the matter. The Board was impressed with the comprehensive approach taken in Times Square with the co-ordinated efforts of the City, the police, the BID and the social agencies, to reclaim the streets so that they can be enjoyed by the general public in a safe, clean and unobstructed manner. The Board heard a great deal of evidence and complaints by the general public about panhandling, vagrancy and drug dealing and the need for the City of Toronto to take corrective action. The evidence of Detective McDonald and a representative of one of the social agencies actively involved in this area was very persuasive and convincing. Both support the project but advised that many of the street people have adopted panhandling as an occupation to gain easy money to support their habits and [panhandling] is not essential to survival. Both recommended to the Board that the City should undertake an active program to educate the general public to say "no" to these people and, in the alternative, to buy them a coffee or a hot meal. In addition, the City could pass legislation modelled on the Winnipeg By-law and the City of Kingston By-law and the experience in New York, to take action to prevent undesirable uses of City streets that act as a deterrent to economic vitality. Having said this, the Board is cognizant of the fact that the Winnipeg By-law has yet to face a court challenge, expected in the fall.

With the exception of Mr. Illion, who represented Lick's, no representatives of tenants unassociated with landlords, appeared before the Board. The Board believes that the reason for this is the fact that tenants have greater rights under an expropriation scenario than under a development scenario if their landlord has a demolition clause in the lease.

The Board well appreciates the sentiment of the landowners whose properties are to be expropriated. Part of that reticence is the underlying fear and suspicion of not receiving compensation that reflects their perception of the market rise or increase in value as a result of the project which requires their land but will benefit adjacent lands not taken. These perceptions may have hindered a negotiated acquisition. The Board, as part of the services it provides, can offer mediation on request, either by this panel or other Board members, to assist in trying to achieve a negotiated settlement, obviating the need for a protracted and expensive arbitration to determine the compensation payable to the owners.

The Board was asked to determine cost awards in favour of the appellants against the City. The Board will set time for a motion on costs, on request. However, the City may wish to consider this aspect in its pending negotiations with property owners in an attempt to settle the acquisitions and achieve a more timely resolution of all outstanding matters related to this project. In this regard, the Board may be spoken to.

The Board was reminded that since its proceedings were subject to the provisions of the *Consolidated Hearings Act,* a petition to the Lieutenant Governor in Council (Cabinet) is possible. As well, the likelihood of this decision being appealed to court by some or all of the appellants was put forcefully to the Board in argument. The parties are always entitled to exercise the rights given to them by statute. The Board, however, is confident that it has carefully considered and given full and proper weight and attention to all of the evidence proffered and all arguments advanced and is confident in its findings and in its decision and report.

Source: Joint Board (1998k, 37-47), verbatim extract.

APPENDIX 10

Sample calendar of events at Nathan Phillips Square
January to July 2000

Jan. Feed the Hungry; Al-Quds Day; NHL All-Star hockey game

Feb. Winterfest; Flag Day

Mar. Kids Millennium Mosaic; Chechnya Rally

Apr. World Vision thirty-hour famine sit-in; International Noise Awareness Day; Ashura Day procession; Ithaca High School Jazz Band; Enviro Festival; Moose Project unveiling; Ecumenical Good Friday Walk; Earth Day; safe and responsible driving campaign; bazaar for visible minority women; Khalsa Day celebrations

May Canadian Hearing Society 60th anniversary celebration; taxi appreciation kickoff; Heart and Stroke Foundation Expressway Breakfast; homelessness march; marijuana march; Ontario Police Memorial – marshalling location only; Clean Slate (tile display) unveiling ceremony; Crohn's and Colitis charity BBQ; Youth Week 2000 event; Ethnomusic Gospelfest (Festival of Praise); Police Week – community BBQ; Toronto Bus Wrap media launch; Walk against Male Violence; Partnership Walk BBQ; National Tap Dance Day; Flock of Flyers performance; Schizophrenia Walkathon; Israel Walk; Bike Week pancake breakfast and launch of bicycle ride; National Kids Day kickoff

June Seniors Safety Fair; Mundelein High School Banc Concert; Universal Peace Festival 2000; Camp Jumoke Walk; Professional Marketing Research Launch (Giant Scrabble Game); D-Day Ceremony; farmers' market – every Wednesday until early October; Hire-a-Student Day; Clean Air Commute launch; Philippine Independence Day Celebration; Victim Recognition Day; Floyd County Youth Orchestra; Busker Festival; Dragon Boat Parade; Caravan Opening Ceremonies;

	First Nations City Celebration; National Aboriginal Day Concert; Jazz Festival
July	Canada Day Celebration; Philippine Ambassador's Chair; Day Star Men's Chorus; Harmuss Brazil; Toronto Outdoor Art Exhibition; Finn Grand Fest 2000; Sounds in the City concerts every Wednesday afternoon throughout July and August; Large Truck Safety Awareness; Festival of Praise – Historical Fashion Show; Toronto Classico Concert; Kids Tuesday (four in July and August); Scottish Bag Pipe Band; Caribana Official Launch; United Pentecostal Assembly; Latin American Folk Lore Show; Trans Canada Trail Relay 2000 Media Launch; United Way Walkathon News Conference; Canadian Organic Growers; Friends for Life Bike Rally; Mosport Festival

Source: Toronto (2000a).

Notes

Chapter 1: Opening

1 Notable exceptions include Castells (1989) on the socioeconomic-technical matrix of factors changing cities, regions, and societies; Corey and Wilson (2006) on planning in a networked society; and Graham and Marvin (2001) on the processes behind historical and contemporary infrastructure networks.
2 I owe this usage and definition of urbanity to Françoise Choay (1994, 28), who says one could call urbanity "l'ajustement réciproque d'une forme de tissu urbain et d'une forme de convivialité."
3 Use of the term "entrepreneurial" in this context derives from David Harvey's (1989a) concept of entrepreneurial urban governance. He used the concept to describe the process by which managerialism was already giving way to entrepreneurial governance in some cities by the 1970s and 1980s. He related the change to deindustrialization, structural unemployment, and fiscal austerity, which were fuelled partly by neoconservatism, although heightened appeals to market rationality and privatization also crossed political ideologies and national boundaries. With this shift toward entrepreneurialism, cities became places to be marketed to generate revenue rather than institutions for managing public affairs. However, there was no single model of realignment. Toronto was late to see signs of such a shift, perhaps because, as David Clark (2002) suggests, neoliberal reforms were first filtered through the national level "by political stealth" and each province in due course responded differently. The ground shifted but in highly variable ways. See Wendy Larner (2003) for a discussion of the varied conditions to which the term "neoliberal" is applied.
4 See Mitchell and Staeheli (2006) for a case study on the connections among homelessness, other street people, redevelopment, and public space.
5 Thanks to Brendan Cormier for bringing these particular Dundas Square events to my attention.
6 For a discussion of privatization and privatism as social dynamics in cities that are similar and complementary but separable, see Lyn Lofland (1998). For another account selected from a substantial literature, see Loukaitou-Sideris and Banerjee (1998).
7 Research has suggested that this was the intention in many downtown projects that tried to revive flagging cores by creating tourist bubbles, places safe from any disturbing scenes that could discourage tourists from arriving, staying, and spending. See, for example, Corcoran (1998), Fainstein and Stokes (1998), Levine (1987), Newman (2002), and Reichl (1999).
8 The public interest is a much-disputed concept. It refers to the normative injunction that actions by or under the guidance of governments should serve the good of all.

Thus, the concept is an ideal of fields like public-sector planning, although its embodiment in a planned intervention will not be entirely the responsibility of planners but also of elected and appointed officials. The definition of "public interest" is elusive, to say the least. The literature on the topic is plentiful. Practical places to start investigating it in a planning context are Alexander (2002), Campbell and Marshall (2002), Moroni (2004), and Grant (2005). It may be taken as a given that the public interest and good planning are intimately connected. However, even though this connection has been recognized and disputes about both concepts have been heard for decades, neither term is clearly defined in the decisions of the Ontario Municipal Board, the tribunal that hears land use conflict cases such as Yonge-Dundas (see Chipman 2002, especially chap. 4).

9 In Britain and Australia, the term "planning system" is often used to refer to both planning legislation and policy (see, e.g., Gilg 2005; Healey et al. 1988), although the term "framework of planning policy and legislation" has also been used (Brindley, Rydin, and Stoker 1989, 1). When they are discussed in the context of institutionalist analysis, system and practices are tied together as the hard and the soft elements (Healey 1997). In Canada the term "planning system" is used very little, although by 2008 it began to appear in Ontario to describe activities associated with legislation and implementation but not policy. Thanks to Luigi Mazza and Marcia Wallace for discussions about framework versus system.

10 For a discussion of planning rights, including property rights, see the special issue of *Planning Theory* on land use, planning, and the law. Articles by Alexander (2007) and Booth (2007) are especially relevant to the points made here.

11 The national planning body is called the Canadian Institute of Planners or Institut canadien des urbanistes. The names of its provincial affiliates vary the usage – for example, the Ontario Professional Planners Institute is Institut des planificateurs professionnels de l'Ontario while the Atlantic provinces affiliate, which includes the officially bilingual province of New Brunswick, is Institut des urbanistes de l'Atlantique. The Quebec affiliate, L'Ordre des urbanistes du Quebec, is not translated into English, and the other affiliates have not translated their names into French.

12 Exceptions in English usage are Louis Wirth's phrase "urbanism as a way of life," which was widely used from the 1930s, although it is now rare, and "new urbanism," which is a restricted use of "urbanism" that denotes a style of residential greenfield development found mainly in the United States.

13 Evelyn Ruppert (2006), who studied the same Yonge-Dundas project and used many of the same data sources, focuses on the redevelopment. She does not mention the regeneration plan. Thus, our conclusions about the planning activities differ considerably. Furthermore, she is interested in how a moral economy is created by professionals, whom she lists as including urban planners, architects, urban designers, and marketing analysts (2006, 11). The general categorization of professionals is later made specific when she lists by name exactly who qualified. Her list excludes significant actors who used moralistic arguments to drive the agenda to clean up this area. In particular, the list omits the local ward councillor and business owners, although it does include these people elsewhere in the discussion. Those left out are so significant, and their interrelationships with the "professionals" were so important to what was done, that I question Ruppert's findings on the role of planners – both those on the city's planning staff and those who testified against the city's proposal – in creating a moral economy. Notwithstanding our different findings, her analysis of the data provides a complement to the one offered here.

14 For an example of how theories are distinguished as either "planning" or "urban," see the complementary volumes on planning theory (Campbell and Fainstein 2003) and urban theory (Fainstein and Campbell 2002).

15 An excellent review of the evolution of planning theory from 1945 is presented by Nigel Taylor (1998). For an equally fine overview of the procedural-substantive typology and its inadequacies, one that proposes an alternative, see Yiftachel (1989).
16 Whether procedural planning theories are prescriptive or normative is disputed. See, for example, Forester (2000) and Yiftachel and Huxley (2000) on the distinctions between "prescriptive" and "normative" as they are applied to planning theory.
17 I do not wish to be reductive by describing only two main lines. At any given moment, several procedural planning theories are under development or are experiencing ascending or descending influence, and there is never agreement about how many or which theories are actually in use. My choice of these two reflects my judgment that most contemporary practising planners are likely aware of these composites and some of their variations but perhaps not others.
18 Two useful exegeses on rationality in planning contexts are Reade (1985) and Alexander (2000).
19 For descriptions of these processes see, for example, Allmendinger (2002); Nigel Taylor (1998); Forester (1989); Healey (1997), (2003); Innes (1996), (2004).
20 Choay associates this approach to city building with Leon Battista Alberti, specifically his book *De re aedificatoria,* published in 1452. The title is significant, Choay argues: it can be translated as "The art of edification" or as "On building" but not as "On architecture" because the book is about city-building issues that extend beyond architecture. Alberti described edification as having to satisfy necessity, commodity, and aesthetic pleasure. Alberti defined rules and principles to achieve edification that were based on sources that included mathematics, perspective, music, and physics. Necessity had to do with natural laws, technical and scientific rules of construction, and the fulfillment of basic human needs. Commodity referred to desires and demands, and this was where a potentially inexhaustible list of present and future desires, desires that could hardly even be guessed at, lay. For Alberti, building to accommodate that range required dialogues between the builder and his client, peers, and workers, as well as background knowledge of exemplary structures. Aesthetic pleasure is the ultimate aim. It is realized when a work calls forth appreciation: the "greater the praise, the more rigorously the work will conform to ... the 'principle of economy,' according to which it should be impossible to add or subtract anything from the work without damaging it" (Choay [1980] 1997, 68).
21 Choay uses Thomas More's *Utopia* (1516) as the paradigmatic text in this instance. After analyzing the many ways that the utopian concept was described both before and after Thomas More, Choay concluded that More had created a unique genre. In the true utopia, "the model society is supported by *a model space which is an integral, necessary part of it* (Choay [1980] 1997, 34).
22 Concinnitas has to do with skilfully fitting parts together, creating harmonious combinations.
23 Hyperspatialization is the attachment of a utopian model to a space that is designed in detail to correct or avoid social ills. Hyperspatialization goes beyond utopian space as Thomas More described it in his original work. See, for example, the detail concerning dwellings, institutions, and public space in the nineteenth-century utopias of Robert Owen (Owen and Cole [1813] 1966) or Charles Fourier (1975).
24 Cerdá's work, first published in 1867, only came to the general attention of planners outside of Spain a hundred years or more afterward. For a summary of his contribution, see Soria y Puig (1995).
25 One who has expressed the political salience of his poststructural approach is Michel Foucault. He argued that the very purpose of his approach was to challenge what is taken to fall within the realm of politics and to be of interest to politics. Not all questions arise through politics, and indeed politics, because of its structure, can inhibit

questions. Therefore, it is important to have other ways to get at questions. Foucault makes this point eloquently in an interview with Paul Rabinow (Rabinow 1984, 384-86).
26 A large part of the problem in the assessment of poststructuralism, especially in anglophone contexts, has been the tendency to confuse it with postmodernism, to reduce the one to the other. In the field of urbanism, the analytic capacity of "postmodern" and "postmodernism" is unclear. They remain descriptive terms that characterize the temper of the times, the period in which Westerners live that differs in specific ways from other times because of new conditions. This period is described as being marked by capitalism moving "from being an economic and cultural system based upon the discipline necessary for production to one centred on the pleasures of consumption" (Payne et al. 1996, 429). I prefer the terms "structural" and "poststructural" to name two multifaceted, analytic approaches to living in and building urban regions.

Chapter 2: History
1 Ann Forsyth (1999, especially chap. 3) explores the use of metaphor to discuss the type of solution to move toward in a planned development case in which images of Los Angeles, Toronto, and Canberra were proposed as alternatives for a new suburb in Australia. It is impossible not to use some sort of metaphor (or its extension as a model or an analogue) when, in Donald Schön's terms, one is problem setting or problem solving. Scholars of metaphors have long provided advice on how to use them productively without being used by them (see, e.g., Max Black 1962; Turbayne 1971).
2 For information regarding construction of the new city hall and the Eaton Centre, respectively, see Sewell (1993, 119-22, 139-44) and McQueen (1999, 163-64, 193-96). John Sewell tells an amusing story about himself: as a member of City Council, and before his election as mayor, he asked Eberhard Zeidler what the Eaton Centre would look like. Zeidler replied, "Opaque." Sewell said he ought to have had his dictionary with him because he mixed up "opaque" with "transparent" and therefore missed a chance to try to get it changed.
3 The College Street store was permanently closed in 1977 and sold off to a consortium that redeveloped the site into a shopping-residential complex called College Park. The retail component has not fared well: there are frequent vacancies within its elegant concourses. The redevelopment also included the creation of large open spaces, both paved and grassed, that are underused most of the time, despite being near the high-pedestrian areas of Yonge Street. The auditorium and other spaces on the top floors of the former College Street store were renovated recently and reopened in spring 2003. Those spaces have been named the Carlu, after Jacques Carlu, the architect who designed the restaurant and concert auditorium, which included murals by his wife, Natasha. He was a professor of design at MIT and had designed Eaton's ninth-floor restaurant in Montreal (which has also been preserved) and dining salons on the luxury French liner *Île de France* (McQueen 1999, 62).
4 A floor space index, or FSI, is a standard measure of density of built form. The FSI refers to bulk, the relationship between a built structure and its land site. An FSI of 1.0 describes a one-storey building built to the edges of the land parcel on which it sits. An FSI of 3.0 describes a three-storey building built to its parcel edges. Alternatively, a building may cover only part of the site. For example, an FSI of 2.0 offers the possibility of a four-storey structure occupying half the property. The floor space index is also called floor area index (FAI) or floor area ratio (FAR), and it is not the only measure of density. Another measure of density is the number of units on a given unit of land, for example, fifteen dwelling units per hectare or acre.
5 Planners tend to be more wary than merchants and others about designating pedestrian-only streets, given their past experiences and current research that shows the conditions

needed to make the closing off of streets to motorized vehicles a success. See, especially, Gehl (1996, 2000) and Gehl and Gemzøe (1996).
6 It is interesting to note that, in the 1970s, the Metropolitan Toronto government was also alarmed by the decline of Yonge Street and proposed a two-phase open-space development on the northeast corner of Yonge and Dundas. It approached Ryerson Polytechnical Institute, as the university was then called and which owned part of the site, with the following suggestion: If Ryerson developed the vacant property into a park with an underground parking garage, Metro would expropriate properties along the east side of Yonge Street, from Dundas one block north to Gould. This would have generated a much larger open space than the current redevelopment is creating at the southeast corner of Yonge and Dundas. The scheme was reported to us by the former head of the university's architectural and buildings services. Of course, it did not come to fruition (George Hume 1999).
7 At the time, "designated" meant the building had been designated under the *Ontario Heritage Act,* while "listed" referred to an action by the Toronto Historical Board.
8 The north-south arm of Dundas, which leads south to Queen Street, was renamed Ossington Avenue, and several old Toronto streets were eliminated or truncated. Based on a 1910 plan of the city of Toronto, this included Arthur Street, from Ossington to Bathurst; St. Patrick Street, truncated from Bathurst to McCaul; Anderson Street, from McCaul to University; Agnes Street, from University to Yonge; Wilton Avenue, from Yonge to the Don Valley; and Elliott Street, east of the Don Valley.
9 Subsequent realignment of streets in the 1920s extended Dundas Street eastward across the Don River, where city development had followed a more haphazard pattern (Lemon 1985, 45).
10 The properties demolished were 303 to 309 Yonge and 270 to 290 Victoria.
11 See Lakoff and Johnson (1980) for an illustrative discussion of types and uses of metaphors. See Culler (1983) and Gutting (2001) on the pervasiveness of metaphor in Western thought. Turbayne (1971) discusses the similarities between metaphors and models and the difference between using metaphors and being used by them. For a discussion of metaphor in the context of public policy, see Reddy (1979), and also Schön (1979), who connects metaphor to problem setting.

Chapter 3: Regenerating
1 My declaration that the urban design and the street survey are the only studies that underpinned this project is based on (1) finding no others, (2) not learning of others during interviews with key actors, (3) assuming that the city, if it had it, would have mentioned any other solid evidence that supported its decisions in one or another of its reports, and (4) assuming that if other evidence had been raised orally in the OMB hearing, it would have been used in the written arguments of the counsel for either the proponents or the appellants, depending on which it benefited.

Chapter 4: Redeveloping
1 Version B of the minutes is slightly different in Point 3: "Ron, *in collaboration with the City,* recommends Stephen Waqué of Borden & Elliott [sic]" (my emphasis).
2 A few comments about the background of the program director, Ron Soskolne, are in order because he had a history with the city and in large-scale redevelopment. Soskolne was trained as an architect in Johannesburg and Toronto and was employed in the 1970s by the City of Toronto, where he worked mainly on central core and waterfront plans. But most of his career was spent in private development. He had been with the developer Olympia & York from 1979 and was its senior vice-president, planning and development when it went bankrupt in 1991. He was then executive vice-president of development for Reichmann International Development Corporation until 1995, when he set up his own consulting firm in Toronto. With Olympia & York, Soskolne had

worked on London's Canary Wharf, New York's World Financial Center, San Francisco's Yerba Buena Gardens redevelopment, and on projects in Mexico; at the time of the Yonge-Dundas assignment, he was working as a consultant for the Disney Corporation on a development in Anaheim, California (Joint Board 1998b, Exhibit 55A).
3 PATH is the name given to the way-finding program in the underground pedestrian system. The term is usually used to refer to the underground pedestrian system itself.
4 The developer chosen for Parcel A called his UECs "power entertainment centres" (Joint Board 1998b, Exhibit 42).
5 At that time "Metro" referred to the six cities of metropolitan Toronto: three older inner cities and three newer suburban cities. Beyond these cities stretched a rapidly urbanizing part of the Greater Toronto Area in which a far greater proportion of new retail sales space was being located.
6 The other planning issues, which are mentioned briefly in the feasibility study, are urban design and site planning, loading and servicing, infrastructure implications, and the Parking Authority of Toronto lot at 25 Dundas Street East.
7 In fact, according to a report by the PPP subcommittee that was delivered to city council on 9-10 December 1996, two of the in-process applications for facade funds were for properties that would be slated for purchase or expropriation by the city. When city council approved the report in principle, these two properties were immediately made ineligible for facade funds. During the 1998 OMB hearing, counsel for the property on the southeast corner of Yonge and Dundas, the World's Biggest Jean Store, argued that this was an act of injustice toward his client, who was attempting to engage with the city's plans to revitalize the area. See also Moloney (1997).
8 These were as follows: 27 February 1997, Land Use Committee; 17 March 1997, Planning Advisory Committee; and 5 June 1997, Land Use Committee.
9 In his "Notes for final argument," counsel for the appellants Bohdan Onyschuk wrote that Councillor Rae – who had been the project's instigator, the chair of the steering committee, and a member of the confidential subcommittee – had said to the board's hearing officers when he was being questioned

> that he did not know about AMC's offer or interest until February or May 1997. He then recalled that he knew about the discussions with Cineplex prior to the December 1996 meeting; but he indicated that neither the AMC nor the Cineplex expressions of interest were mentioned to City Council at the meeting of December 9th. This is completely contrary to the evidence of Mr. Soskolne, who indicated that he had kept Mr. Rae informed at all steps along the way, and that the discussions and expressions of interest by both AMC and Cineplex had been presented before City Council at its in camera meeting of December 9, 1996. (Joint Board 1998d, 19[7])

Another example of contrary evidence about the AMC–City of Toronto agreement (and by implication the developer of Parcel A) appears in an exchange of letters between the counsel for the appellants, Onyschuk, and the counsel for the respondents, Waqué, prior to the hearing. Onyschuk asked Waqué for a copy of the letter from AMC to the city dated 2 December 1996, a letter that had been referred to by AMC when it confirmed its obligations to the city regarding the cinema complex on 17 November 1997 (Joint Board 1998h, Tab 16, Onyschuk to Waqué, 14 January 1998). In reply, Waqué said, "I am advised as follows: Although the November 17th, 1997 Agreement between AMC and the City of Toronto refers to a pre-existing Agreement dated December 2nd, 1996, no such pre-existing Agreement actually exists. There is no other Agreement between the City of Toronto and AMC" (ibid., Tab 17, Waqué to Onyschuk, 26 January 1998). Waqué changed one word: he wrote that there was no "agreement," but the AMC letter refers to a "letter," not an agreement, and AMC was making the point that that its letter of November 1997 superseded the letter of December 1996. This 17 November 1997 letter on AMC letterhead was signed and countersigned by no fewer than four people: the head of AMC in Canada; a city solicitor who "approved as to form"; the assistant city clerk; and a member (the chair) of the city's Executive Committee/ Board of Management who had been dealing with the Yonge-Dundas matter for at least sixteen months.

10 In the original arrangement, the steering committee hired consultants and was supposed to pay them from the funds for the project. That the consultant reported in this case to a city employee – not to the steering committee's program director, who was supposed to have been in charge of this part of the task – suggests that the authority of the steering committee had begun to change. It was less in charge than had been intended in early 1996. This observation is supported by a report presented to city council on 24 March 1997 that asks for a new grant agreement with YSBRA to be drawn up to cover a new allocation of $154,000 from the city. The report recommends that "the Program *continue to be administered* by the Commissioner of Urban Development Services and that the existing Steering committee *continue to oversee* the program and the account" (Toronto 1997e, 62, my emphasis).

11 The explanation for the expunged figures came out during preparations for the OMB hearing, when the appellants' lawyer, Onyschuk, demanded these figures from counsel for the city, Waqué. The city's lawyer said that the figures had not been disclosed in compliance with the OMB's order to keep financial arrangements between AMC and PenEquity secret (Joint Board 1998i, Tab 8). Onyschuk wrote back: "The Board did not order the 'non disclosure of the financial arrangements between AMC and PenEquity,' as you allege in your letter. The Board simply did not order the production of the PenEquity-AMC Agreement to Lease. Therefore the portions of the document that have been whited out should *not* have been whited out. We require the production of the full January 22, 1997 document without any adjustments or deletions forthwith" (Joint Board 1998i, Tab 8a). Four days later, the report, with all its numbers in place, was sent to Onyschuk. A copy of the AMC-PenEquity Agreement was also sent to him because PenEquity had authorized its limited disclosure. The numbers, however, were not publicly revealed through the hearing process.

12 Neither a request for qualifications (RFQ) nor a request for proposals (RFP) falls under bidding and tendering law, even though they both seek sellers of services who are willing to match a buyer's needs. In RFQs and RFPs, the buyer tries to keep all the elements of choice in its own hands and to leave the doors as wide open as possible to negotiate terms with any party or parties whose proposal seems potentially suitable. Documents announcing an RFQ or an RFP can be written in a way that implies that no contract will necessarily result from the process, or they can make no mention of a contract whatsoever. The RFQ is an initial and optional weeding-out phase that checks the background and experience of companies interested in a future call for proposals. If it alone is used, the RFP may seek expressions of interest or preliminary proposals without incurring obligations. By using careful disclaimer language, the buyer can avoid claims if it does not proceed with the project or if it chooses a proponent whose bid is not the lowest (Sandori and Pigott 2000, 239-40). A seller of services who responds to an RFP must be aware that all costs incurred are its own responsibility and that the deck is stacked entirely in the buyer's favour.

13 This Ontario ministry had responsibility at that time for the OMB, the hearings under the *Expropriations Act,* and planning matters, among other things. See Appendix 1.

14 A second meeting with the deputy minister was held on 24 January 1997, after city council had approved the project in principle. That meeting included the program manager as well as the program director, ward councillor, and contract lawyer for the city (Rae n.d.).

15 The main categories were assault, robbery, shoplifting, fraud, theft from motor vehicle, break and entry, prostitution-related offences, gaming and betting, arson, drugs, drinking and driving, and failure to remain. I am using the data made available at the

OMB hearing. Concerns could certainly be raised about the quality of the crime figures and therefore the quality of the data being used to make decisions.
16 Vancouver's bylaw to regulate panhandling was enacted on 30 April 1998, and no charges had been laid under it when the solicitor was writing his memo in June 1998. The Winnipeg bylaw was passed on 26 January 1995. It became the subject of a legal challenge on 22 January 1998 on the following grounds: "(a) It violates the *Charter of Rights and Freedoms* as follows: – denial of equality rights (s. 15[1]); – denial of right to liberty and fundamental justice (s. 7); – denial of freedom of expression (s. 2[b]). (b) It is beyond the jurisdiction of the City to enact as there is no legislative authority under the *City of Winnipeg Act* to pass the by-law as framed. (c) It is beyond the jurisdiction of the City of Winnipeg to enact as the by-law is in essence a regulation in relation to criminal law, which is an area of Federal jurisdiction" (Toronto 1998b, 6).

Chapter 5: Defending

1 The city's presentation on the matter of blight was clarified during the course of the hearing. Its use of the term "blight" was in reference to social blight, not the condition of the buildings. The city decided it could not establish that the buildings in the area were blighted to justify expropriation; therefore, it was careful to specify that it meant that the area was afflicted by social blight.
2 Trickle-down economics is "the proposition that economic development benefits the poorest members of society mainly through the effects of increased national income on the demand for labour, rather than through explicit measures to assist them" (Black 1997, 478). At the municipal level, the application of trickle-down theory assumes that increased income within its jurisdiction translates into fewer jobless, homeless, and otherwise impoverished people. As so many have pointed out, the actual permeability of economic regions is not accounted for in basic trickle-down theory.
3 Bryant Park is a square behind the New York Public Library that is tranquil and grassy. It is heavily patrolled. It is a subsidiary of the Bryant Park Business Improvement District and is financed and managed by a private organization whose members are large and small corporations. It does the work ordinarily associated with a public authority, providing, maintaining, and redesigning amenities and redesigning the park, as needed, by raising money from its private members. It is an example of the privatization of a public park that had become derelict. Thus, a choice was made not to use government policies to deal with the problem of poverty and homelessness and bring everyone within common public institutions; instead, the choice was made to "buy protection" against the problem while simultaneously fostering the growth of the private-security industry (Zukin 1995, 39, and chap. 1 in general).
4 This interpretation was corroborated by interviews.
5 This statement was bolstered by statements made by Rebecca Robertson, an urban planner who testified at the hearing. Born and educated in Toronto, she was vice-president of real estate and special projects for the Schubert Organization, but she had also been president of the 42nd Street Development Project in New York. She gave free consulting to the Toronto redevelopment project and said that cinemas, not theatres, were the key to invigorating the street because they were cheaper, played all day, and therefore could attract a larger, steadier stream of people. (For her witness statement, see Joint Board 1998b, Exhibit 34, Tab 15, 258-60.)
6 Compare the program director's description of UECs to that of the principal industry manual, which was published by the Urban Land Institute with financial support from several companies, including Walt Disney Imagineering, AMC Theatres, and Trizec-Hahn, and which was one of the exhibits at the OMB hearing (Beyard et al. 1998). The publisher, the Urban Land Institute, thanked several companies (including Walt Disney Imagineering, AMC Theatres, TrizecHahn, and others) for their generous

financial support in the production of the book, and it thanked the president of Walt Disney Imagineering especially "for coordinating the sponsorship effort" (iii).

7 One description of the arcane and often cutthroat practices that surround movie distribution is found in Drabinsky (1995, chap. 3 and elsewhere).

8 Two witnesses for the appellants pointed out this problem. The discontinuity in the retail rhythm that would be caused by the west side of the square abutting Yonge Street would be harmful because retailing operates rather like the keys on a piano: a full set is needed to keep the rhythm going.

9 On borrowing and adapting in urban planning in general, and with specific reference to Canada and the United States, see Ward (2000, 1999).

10 "City building" as a rallying cry began appearing in reports in December 1996, when council approved the redevelopment plan in principle. It appears in several of the reports prepared for the Joint Board hearing in 1998, particularly in Exhibit 184. Is the call to city build *the cri de l'entrepreneur de la ville*, the slogan of the city builder in the new economy? It was championed by an internationally successful Canadian planning consultant who was a frequent consultant to the City of Toronto. It was, however, by no means an original term created for this generation. It was used in Barcelona by Cerdà in 1859, although he replaced it less than two years later with "urbanization" (see Soria y Puig 1999, chap. 2). It was also used in Austria and Germany by the early planner Camillo Sitte in 1889 and by Stübben in 1890 (Collins and Collins 1965). Compare the rhetorical use of "city building" to that of "urbanism" as discussed in Chapter 1.

11 See Kayden's (2000) extensive discussion of privately owned public space in New York, especially the history of zoning in the 1960s and 1970s for these spaces, 11-13.

12 Nathan Phillips Square is the civic apron in front of the City of Toronto's city hall. In terms of managing the new public square, information given at the hearing and to the press always suggested that it and Dundas Square were essentially alike and, therefore, the management could be essentially the same. For example, one of the city's witnesses, who was herself involved in programming Nathan Phillips Square, "described the types of programming activities coordinated by the City of Toronto on Nathan Phillips Square, and indicated that many of these activities could be replicated at Dundas Square, and that there is demand for same; a code such as Municipal Code 237 ... could be implemented for the management of Dundas Square" (Joint Board 1998h, 11). "Programming," she said, "can be used to create a certain ambience during the day and night, and the experience at Nathan Phillips Square is that programming minimizes undesirable and criminal activity" (ibid.). She noted, too, that she had had discussions with representatives of the Toronto Police Service and that YSBRA was interested in "assisting with programming and regulating Dundas Square" (ibid.). See note 3 for more on Bryant Park.

13 However, that was an exception. The city had previously expropriated to obtain open space, build socially assisted housing, and create an edge for the residential neighbourhood of St. Lawrence when it was being planned.

14 The *ejusdem generis* rule states that where "general words follow an enumeration of particular persons or things having a specific meaning, the general words are constructed as being limited to all other persons or articles of a like class or nature" (*Canadian Law Dictionary*, 3rd ed., 77). If that was the end of the rule, then it might be argued that the city's lawyer had used the rule incorrectly because a "like class or nature" was evident in the sense that all the items in the list referred to *physical* conditions. However, the law dictionary definition states that interpretation "must give way to the general intent of the enactment or document under consideration. This is true where the specific words exhaust the category or genus and the general words would be meaningless if governed by the rule of *ejusdem generis*."

15 For the view of the city's counsel on this case, presented in a different forum, see Waqué (2000).
16 An *obiter dictum* is a passing or incidental statement. In a court it is a decision reached that is not essential for disposition of the case (*Canadian Law Dictionary*, 3rd ed.).
17 A BID, the designation used in the United States, is equivalent to a BIA (business improvement area) in Canada. See Chapter 6 and Appendix 1.
18 Over 300 people are said to have attended the public meeting, of which twenty-eight individuals spoke, including two former Toronto mayors and the architect of the Eaton Centre. Two speakers opposed the development.
19 After a five-year constitutional battle, the National Anti-Poverty Organization forced the City of Winnipeg to repeal its begging bylaw in January 2001. In a court-filed settlement of the case, the City of Winnipeg "acknowledged 'the social condition of poverty' in Winnipeg, and the entitlement of poor people to be 'present,' 'visible' and 'participating' in public spaces, and that freedom of expression and equality are 'fundamental rights'" (Hermer 2001).

Chapter 6: Implementing

1 The media tower exceeded the height limit of 30 metres; the building exceeded the overall gross floor area by 9,000 square feet or 880 square metres.
2 The observations and quotes that follow are from the author's personal notes, 27 September 2000.
3 Olympic Spirit Toronto was licensed, in cooperation with the Canadian Olympic Committee, by the International Olympic Committee through the International Spirit Development Organization.
4 The first phase of the design competition was launched on 21 September 1998 and concluded on 5 October with the submission of qualification documents. Forty-eight proposals were submitted. Six proposals were carried into the second, juried phase. Designs were due by mid-November. The winner was selected from those six proposals, and the decision was announced on 1 December 1998 (Toronto 1998d, 4).
5 Chapter 636 of the *Municipal Code* replaced the temporary chapter 270, which had been developed in late 1998 to comply with the Joint Board decision. Chapter 270 was deleted.
6 Compare ch. 237 of the old City of Toronto's *Municipal Code* with ch. 270 and the current ch. 636, art. 3.
7 However, the Joint Board decision notes that the Eaton Centre developments and two other projects discussed elsewhere – the Atrium Media Tower and the Livent developments a block south at Shuter – may not have been outcomes of or dependent on the city's redevelopment plans. According to one report, Cadillac-Fairview had already renovated an urban shopping centre in Victoria, BC, according to the then new trend in "urban retailing to bring the action back to the street" (Barber 1997). To the OMB's list of improvements that were likely independent of the redevelopment plan but related to the regeneration plan, we could also add Gap. And one that was certainly independent of it was the renovation of the elegant Ryrie Building by the Cheung family, which was completed in 1996 and leased by the end of the year to a new-to-Toronto US retailer, Urban Outfitters.
8 Telephone communication, March 2004.
9 These are discussed briefly in Appendix 1.
10 The historical background on this property is from N.W. Leduke, coordinator of public relations/programs, Ontario Central Divisional Headquarters, Salvation Army. E-mail communication to author, 9 February 2004.
11 Contrary to media reports, this shelter was not part of the Out of the Cold program (Leduke, e-mail communication to author, 9 February 2004).

12 For a case with some parallels regarding deciders and their advisors, see Leo (1995).

Chapter 7: Closing

1 A reinvestment area designation meant that built-form principles would be used to achieve objectives such as maintaining pedestrian comfort on the street. See Appendix 1.
2 Allan Jacobs (1978) described in detail his experiences as director of planning for San Francisco, and his book remains relevant. One of his messages was that the best "politics" for a planner is "top professional work, forcefully presented and defended" (313).
3 If something other than urbanism is the subject of one's planning, then the process should be attached to it instead. That would be the subject of a different book.
4 See Healey et al. 1988; Foster 1993; Fainstein 2001a. Peter Foster, who studied O&Y for about ten years, believed that "the problem with Canary Wharf was that they'd done it back-to-front. O&Y had put up the buildings in advance of the transportation corridors" (Foster 1993, 236). However, he also attributed the collapse to (1) O&Y's vision for Canary Wharf, which was far more ambitious than the one the British government had for the area; (2) how differently land development was done in the London area compared to the United States or Canada, where O&Y had been active; and (3) the series of business decisions made in the previous three years or so that left the company without cash or leverage when the property market turned down.
5 Using their matrix of planning styles, the Yonge-Dundas redevelopment phase would fall under the market-positive (and market-led) category and, more specifically, shows characteristics of leverage planning with a dose of private-management planning.
6 See Brownill's (1999) extensive description of the shift by the British government from antiplanning to a more moderate stance on planning that took place during the LDDC project. The cost of learning those lessons was enormous. See also Imrie and Thomas (1993); Moulaert, Rodriguez, and Swyngedouw (2002); Turok (1992).
7 Battery Park City is located at the southern tip of Manhattan, and the land has had several uses, an early one being a military fortification. Prior to development, the site was mainly a ruin. King-Spadina and King-Parliament – generally known as the Kings, after their main thoroughfare, King Street – are two large parcels of land in south central Toronto that became available for redevelopment because most of their industrial occupants had gradually left over a period of many years.

References

Joint Board Hearing Documents
The Yonge Street Regeneration Project Hearing was conducted by a panel constituted as a Joint Board acting for the Consolidated Hearings Office under the *Consolidated Hearings Act* to hear matters related to the *Planning Act* and the *Expropriations Act*. Ontario Municipal Board File Numbers R97 0179; O97 0146; O97 0149. Joint Board File Number: CH-97-01.

Joint Board. 1998a. Answers to the board's questions.
Joint Board. 1998b. Exhibit list to the Joint Board in regard to the Yonge Street Regeneration Project.
  15, Tab E: Fiona McCall, communication to Kyle Rae, fax, 5 May.
  21: Pictorial representation of Yonge/Dundas redevelopment project.
  34: Respondent City of Toronto's brief of witness statements.
  34, Tab 1A: Healing the neighbourhood. Report of the jobs Ontario Community Action (jOCA) and the Toronto East Downtown Residents Association (TEDRA) project to identify new community development initiatives in Toronto East Downtown, 3 October 1996.
  34, Tab 6: Statement of Detective Colin McDonald, 8 January.
  34, Tab 10: Statement of Renée Auer, 14 January 1998.
  34, Tab 12: Statement of Michael Thomas, 14 January 1998.
  34, Tab 15: Witness statement of Rebecca Robertson, 14 January 1998.
  37: Incident Report. Metropolitan Toronto Police, 30-I/CAD, address analysis report and criminal stats, 1-2.
  39: A. Heisey to S. Waqué, 13 February 1998, and S. Waqué to A. Heisey, 15 February 1998, regarding production from Eamon Kelly.
  42: Glenn Miller, witness statement, 15 January.
  49A, Tab C: Millward report.
  53: Downtown Yonge Street Regeneration Program: Yonge and Dundas redevelopment project. Summary report from commissioner of urban development services to city council (in camera), 9 December 1996.
  53, Appendix 1: Financial plan and executive summaries for two-year cash flow – Pessimistic and optimistic scenarios.
  55A: Appendix A to witness statement, Ron Soskolne.
  69: Expert report, Gregg Lintern.

75: Minutes (various) of the steering committee for the Yonge Street Regeneration Program.
83: Memorandum dated 29 October 1996 from Gary Wright to Board of Management et al.
90: Memorandum dated 26 March 1997 from Cho Khong to Gary Wright.
96: Executive Committee report No. 17, adopted by city council (1987), re: Colonial Tavern – 201 Yonge Street.
106: Buildings and their relationship to Yonge Street. Report by Littlewood Hesse, Berridge Lewinberg Greenberg, et al. 1986-87.
126: Yonge Street between Dundas and Gerrard – Urban design discussion paper. By Robert Glover, 31 March 1995.
151: Expert report of Cam Watson [C.N. Watson and Associates, Ltd., economists], 15 January, Appendix B.
157: Competitive evaluation matrix – RFQ.
162: Agra Environmental, Phase 1 report, 18 September 1997.
184: Expert report of Joe Berridge.
192: Downtown Yonge Street briefing background material. Memorandum, 19 July 1996, from G. Lintern to J. Morand.
206: Pellow scheme.
207A: Expert report, Gary Stamm.
216: Newsletter, YSBRA, November 1995.
233: Amendment reports/additional tables. Package of Gary Stamm.
247: Report, 17 September 1997, from commissioner of urban development services to the City of Toronto Land Use Committee.
259: Addendum to section 2 of MacDougall witness statement, 17 April 1998.

Joint Board. 1998c. Financial productions. Tab 8: Arthur H. Peckham III to Gary Wright, 17 November 1997.

Joint Board. 1998d. Notes for final argument, Yonge and Dundas, 14-15 May 1998 (B.S. Onyschuk, counsel for four appellants).

Joint Board. 1998e. Notes on argument in chief by the City of Toronto (Stephen Waqué, counsel for the City of Toronto).

Joint Board. 1998f. OMB production order – Listing of documents.
  Tab 16: Request for proposals – June 1997.
  Tab 22: City of Toronto Land Use Committee Report re: Recommended amendments to Part I official plan to address concerns raised by the referral request filed by the T. Eaton Company Limited – 26 May 1994.

Joint Board. 1998g. Respondent City of Toronto's closing submissions reference brief.
  Tab 5: Admissions by appellants' witnesses.

Joint Board. 1998h. Summary of evidence from all city witnesses and public session witnesses.

Joint Board. 1998i. Supplemental productions in addition to productions set out in document list produced by the city, Vol. 1.
  Tab 8: Letter dated 10 December 1997 addressed to All Who Signed Confidential Undertaking, with copy of KPMG report of 22 January 1997 re: financial analysis of cinema proposals.
  Tab 8A: Smith Lyons to Borden & Elliot, 15 December 1997.
  Tab 16: Smith Lyons to Borden & Elliot, 14 January 1998.
  Tab 17: Borden & Elliot to Smith Lyons, 26 January 1998.

Joint Board. 1998j. Yonge Street Regeneration Project: Board decision on costs and order of the board, November.

Joint Board. 1998k. Yonge Street Regeneration Project: Decision and reasons for decision, 5 June.

Municipal Documents

Toronto city council records before amalgamation are titled Proceedings of Toronto City Council. From 1998, following amalgamation, the title changed to City of Toronto Council Minutes.

Toronto. 1934. Committee to Enquire into Housing Conditions in the Several Areas of the City of Toronto. *Report* (Bruce Report). Toronto: Press of the Hunter-Rose Company.

Toronto. 1959. Planning Board. *The changing city: Planning issues for the city of Toronto, 1956-1980.* Toronto: Planning Board.

Toronto. 1963. Planning Board. *Plan for downtown Toronto.* Toronto: Planning Board.

Toronto. 1971. Planning Board. Letter from Dennis A. Barker, chief planner, City Planning Board, to George Bruce, chairman, Sub-Committee of the Transportation Technical Advisory Committee, Metropolitan Toronto Roads and Traffic Department, 16 June.

Toronto. 1974. Development Department. Fairview-Eaton's, Trinity Church development. March.

Toronto. 1975. Planning Board. Central Area Plan review, part 2: Area plan for downtown. October.

Toronto. 1987. Toronto Transit Commission. *Transit in Toronto.* Toronto: Toronto Transit Commission.

Toronto. 1990a. Planning Board. *Window on Toronto.* Toronto: Planning Board.

Toronto. 1990b. Planning and Development Department. *Cityplan '91: Central Area Trends Report.* Toronto: Planning and Development Department.

Toronto. 1992. Planning and Development Department. *City patterns: An analysis of Toronto's structure and form.* Report 29. October. Toronto: Planning and Development Department.

Toronto. 1994a. Establishment of downtown task force, 15 August. Proceedings of City Council, meeting no. 12, 26 September, Executive Committee report 21, clause 25, pp. 87-97.

Toronto. 1994b. Yonge Street, Dundas Street West, and Queen Street West: Establishment of city public highway and removal zones adjacent to Eaton Centre to control unauthorized vending and other undesirable activities. Proceedings of City Council, meeting no. 11, 29 August, Executive Committee report 18, clause 36, pp. 85-89. (Report from commissioner of public works and environment.)

Toronto. 1994c. Planning and Development Department. *Cityplan '91.* Toronto: Planning and Development Department.

Toronto. 1995a. Planning and Development Department. *Downtown Yonge Street community improvement plan.* Toronto: Planning and Development Department.

Toronto. 1995b. Planning and Development Department. *Downtown Yonge Street improvement plan.* June. Toronto: Planning and Development Department.

Toronto. 1995c. Planning and Development Department. *New directions for physical planning: The three lenses.* October. Toronto: Planning and Development Department.

Toronto. 1996a. Downtown Yonge: A program to promote the regeneration of Toronto's main street (Ward 6). Minutes of City Council, meeting no. 14, 10 June, minute 14.53, communication no. 31, n.p.

Toronto. 1996b. Downtown Yonge: A program to promote the regeneration of Toronto's main street (Ward 6). Proceedings of Toronto City Council, meeting no. 8, 4 March, Executive Committee report 9, clause 28, pp. 86-91.

Toronto. 1996c. Downtown Yonge Street community improvement plan (Ward 6), 3 November 1995. Proceedings of Toronto City Council, meeting no. 5, 22 January, Executive Committee report 6, clause 35, pp. 133-39.

Toronto. 1996d. Progress report – Downtown Yonge Street Commercial Façade Improvement Grant and Loan Program – Downtown Yonge Street community improvement area. Proceedings of City Council, meeting no. 17, 16 September, Executive Committee report 26, clause 18, pp. 37-39.

Toronto. 1996e. Planning and Development Program. *New planning amendments for Downtown Yonge Street*. March. Toronto: Planning and Development Department.

Toronto. 1996f. Urban Development Services. *Downtown Yonge Street Regeneration Program – Yonge Dundas redevelopment project – Project plan*. Toronto: Urban Development Services.

Toronto. 1997a. Land Use Committee report 5, clause 1: Draft zoning by-law, official plan amendment and proposed community improvement plan amendment for Downtown Yonge Street reinvestment area (Ward 6). Proceedings of City Council, special meeting no. S16, 6 May, section 16.2., pp. 1-20.

Toronto. 1997b. Motion (Councillor Kyle Rae) re: Executive Committee report 17, clause 42, Yonge Dundas Redevelopment Project. Proceedings of City Council, meeting no. 18, June 23-24, Communication no. 17, n.p.

Toronto. 1997c. Motion 1 (Councillor Kyle Rae): Amendment to Executive Committee report 17, clause 12, June 23-24 1997: Street involved youth engaged in the "squeegee" trade. Proceedings of City Council, meeting no. 21, 21 August, n.p.

Toronto. 1997e. Request for 1997 funding – Downtown Yonge Street Regeneration Program. Proceedings of City Council, meeting no. 10, 24 March, Executive Committee report 10, clause 23, pp. 61-63.

Toronto. 1997f. Yonge-Dundas Redevelopment Project – Status and direction report. [Clause discussed in camera. Commissioner's report of 3 October 1997 included in minutes.] Proceedings of City Council, meeting no. 24, 6 October, minute no. 24.6, re: Executive Committee report 23, clause 4, pp. 18-27.

Toronto. 1997g. Yonge-Dundas Redevelopment Project (Ward 6). Proceedings of City Council, meeting no. 24, 21 August, Executive Committee report 19, clause 16, pp. 66-67.

Toronto. 1997h. Planning and Development Department. *Yonge Dundas Redevelopment Project report*. November. Toronto: Planning and Development Department.

Toronto. 1998a. Downtown Yonge Street update. News release, 10 June.

Toronto. 1998b. Emergency and Protective Services Committee report 8, clause 1: Proposed by-laws to regulate panhandling and squeegee activities – 8567-8580. City Council Minutes, 29 July.

Toronto. 1998c. Strategic policies and priorities, Committee of City Council, 30 June. Research assistant's notes of discussion.

Toronto. 1998d. Community and Neighbourhood Services Department. *Diversion options for youth involved in the squeegee trade*. 9 July. Toronto: Community and Neighbourhood Services Department.

Toronto. 1998e. Urban Planning and Development Services. Proposed Municipal Code amendment (Ward 24 – Downtown). Memorandum from commissioner of urban planning and development services to Corporate Services Committee, 22 October.

Toronto. 2000a. Economic Development, Culture and Tourism Department. Monthly planner for Nathan Phillips Square. Special Events Office.

Toronto. 2000b. Urban Development Services. *Toronto at the crossroads: Shaping our future – Toronto plan directions report*. Toronto: City Planning Division, Urban Development Services, 2000.

Toronto. 2001a. Yonge-Dundas Square – Operations resulting from Urban Development Services capital project and governance model (Ward 27 – Toronto-Centre). City Council Minutes, meeting no. 10, December 4-6, Policy and Finance Committee report 16, clause 27, pp. 1-19.

Toronto. 2001b. Yonge-Dundas Square Board of Management. City of Toronto Municipal Code, chapter 636, article 2. 12 June.
Toronto. 2003. Economic Development, Culture and Tourism Department. News release, 30 May.

Books, Articles, and Other Publications

Albrechts, Louis. 2000. From traditional land use planning to strategic spatial planning: The case of Flanders. In *The changing institutional landscape of planning,* ed. Louis Albrechts, Jeremy Alden, and Artur da Rosa Pires, 83-108. Aldershot, UK: Ashgate.
Alexander, Ernest. Rationality revisited: Planning paradigms in a post-postmodernist perspective. *Journal of Planning Education and Research* 19, 3: 242-56.
–. 2002. The public interest in planning: From legitimation to substantive plan evaluation. *Planning Theory* 1, 3: 226-49.
–. 2007. Planning rights and their implications. *Planning Theory* 6, 2: 112-26.
Allmendinger, Philip. 2002. *Planning theory.* Hampshire: Palgrave.
Architecture. 2000. 89 (March): 138-39.
Armstrong, F.H. 1988. *A City in the making: Progress, people and perils in Victorian Toronto.* Toronto: Dundurn Press.
Arthur, Eric. 1978. *Toronto: No mean city.* Toronto: University of Toronto Press.
Ascher, François. 2001. *Les nouveaux principes de l'urbanisme.* Paris: Éditions de l'Aube.
Barber, John. 1997. Eaton Centre planning face lift. *Globe and Mail,* 23 January.
Bartley, Brendan, and Kasey Treadwell Shine. 2003. Competitive city: Governance and the changing dynamics of urban regeneration in Dublin. In *The globalized city: Economic restructuring and social polarization in European cities,* ed. Frank Moulaert, Arantxa Rodriguez, and Erik Swyngedouw, 145-66. Oxford: Oxford University Press.
Bassin, Arthur. 1990. Does capitalist planning need some *glasnost? Journal of the American Planning Association* 56, 2: 216-18.
Beauregard, Robert A. 1990. Bringing the city back in. *Journal of the American Planning Association* 56, 2: 210-15.
–. 1993. *Voices of decline: The postwar fate of US cities.* Cambridge, MA: Blackwell.
Benali, Kenza. 2006. La ville à l'ère actuelle: Vers une nouvelle définition? *Canadian Journal of Urban Research* 15, 1: S79-S98.
Beyard, Michael D., Raymond E. Braun, Herbert McLaughlin, Patrick L. Phillips, and Michael S. Rubin. 1998. *Developing urban entertainment centers.* Washington, DC: Urban Land Institute.
Black, John. 1997. *A dictionary of economics.* Oxford: Oxford University Press.
Black, Max. 1962. *Models and metaphors.* Ithaca, NY: Cornell University Press.
Bone, James. 2001. Gap shuts New York shops. *The Times* (London), 10 April.
Booth, Philip. 2007. The control of discretion: Planning and the common-law tradition. *Planning Theory* 6, 2: 127-45.
Bordreuil, Jean-Samuel. 2000. La ville desserrée. In *La ville et l'urbain: L'état des savoirs,* ed. Thierry Paquot, Michel Lussault, and Sophie Body-Gendrot, 169-82. Paris: Éditions La Découverte.
Bourette, Susan. 2000. Critics, panhandlers plan next moves as province's squeegee law takes effect. *Globe and Mail,* 1 February.
Brindley, Tim, Yvonne Rydin, and Gerry Stoker. 1989. *Remaking planning: The politics of urban change in the Thatcher years.* London: Unwin Hyman.
Brooks, Michael P. 1990. The city may be back in, but where is the planner? *Journal of the American Planning Association* 56, 2: 218-20.
Brownill, Sue. 1990. *Developing London's docklands: Another great planning disaster?* London: Paul Chapman Publishing.

–. 1999. Turning the East End into the West End: The lessons and legacies of the London Docklands Development Corporation. In *British urban policy: An evaluation of the urban development corporations,* ed. Rob Imrie and Huw Thomas, 43-63. 2nd ed. London: Sage.

Campbell, Heather, and Robert Marshall. 2002. Utilitarianism's bad breath? A reevaluation of the public interest justification for planning. *Planning Theory* 1, 2: 163-87.

Campbell, Scott, and Susan S. Fainstein, eds. 2003. *Readings in planning theory.* 2nd ed. Oxford: Blackwell.

Canadian Architect. 1999. Award of excellence: Dundas Square. 44, 12: 28-29.

Canadian Olympic Committee. 2003. Olympic Spirit Toronto makes its mark at Yonge and Dundas Square. 19 June. http://www.olympic.ca/EN/organization/news/2003/0619.shtml.

Careless, J.M.S. 1984. *Toronto to 1918: An illustrated history.* Toronto: James Lorimer.

Castells, Manuel. 1989. *The informational city: Information technology, economic restructuring, and the urban-regional process.* Oxford: Basil Blackwell.

–. 1996. *The information age: Economy, society and culture.* Vol. 1 of *The rise of the network society.* Oxford: Blackwell.

Cerdá, Ildefons. [1867] 1999. *The five bases of the general theory of urbanization.* Ed. Arturo Soria y Puig. Trans. Bernard Miller and Mary Fons i Fleming. Barcelona: Electa. Published in 1867 as *Teoría general de la urbanización y aplicación de sus principios y doctrinas a la reforma y ensanche de Barcelona.* French translation, *La théorie générale de l'urbanisation,* 1979.

Chipeniuk, Raymond. 2005. Planning for rural amenity migration. *Plan Canada* 45, 1: 15-17.

Chipman, John G. 2002. *A law unto itself: How the Ontario Municipal Board has developed and applied land use planning policy.* Toronto: Institute of Public Administration of Canada/University of Toronto Press.

Choay, Françoise. [1980] 1997. *The rule and the model: On the theory of architecture and urbanism.* Cambridge, MA: MIT Press. Published in 1980 as *La règle et le modèle: Sur la théorie de l'architecture et de l'urbanisme.* Paris: Éditions du Seuil.

–. 1994. Le règne de l'urbain et la mort de la ville. In *La ville, art et architecture en Europe, 1870-1993,* ed. Jean Dethier and Alain Guiheux, 26-35. Paris: Éditions du Centre Pompidou.

–. 1999. De la ville à l'urbain: Entretien avec Thierry Paquot. *Urbanisme* 309: 6-8.

City People Community Planning and Research. 1974. *The Yonge Street Mall: A feasibility study.* Toronto: City People.

Clark, David. 2002. Neoliberalism and public service reform: Canada in comparative perspective. *Canadian Journal of Political Science* 35, 4: 771-93.

Collins, George R., and Christiane Crasemann Collins. 1965. *Camillo Sitte and the birth of modern city planning.* New York: Random House.

Corcoran, Mary. 1998. The re-enchantment of Temple Bar. In *Encounters with modern Ireland,* ed. Michel Peillon and Eamon Slater, 9-24. Dublin: Institute of Public Administration.

Corey, Kenneth E., and Mark I. Wilson. 2006. *Urban and regional technology planning: Planning practice in the global knowledge economy.* London: Routledge.

Courchene, Thomas J., and Colin R. Telmer. 1998. *From heartland to North American region state: The social, fiscal and federal evolution of Ontario.* Toronto: Faculty of Management, University of Toronto.

Courcier, Sabine. 2005. Vers une définition du projet urbain: La planification du réaménagement du Vieux-Port de Montréal. *Revue canadienne de recherche urbain/Canadian Journal of Urban Research* 14, 1: S57-S80.

Culler, Jonathan. 1983. *On deconstruction: Theory and criticism after structuralism.* Ithaca, NY: Cornell University Press.

Curtler, Hugh M. 2004. *Ethical argument: Critical thinking in ethics.* 2nd ed. New York: Oxford University Press.

Daily Star. 1921. Plan for cross-town car line. 8 October.

Dault, Gary Michael. 1999. The brash face of a new pop-culture palace. *Globe and Mail,* 15 May.

Deas, Iain, Brian Robson, and Michael Bradford. 2000. Re-thinking the urban development corporation "experiment": The case of central Manchester, Leeds and Bristol. *Progress in Planning* 54, Pt. 1: 1-72.

DeFilippis, James. 1997. From a public re-creation to private recreation: The transformation of public space in South Street Seaport. *Journal of Urban Affairs* 19, 4: 405-17.

Dendy, William. 1986. *Toronto observed: Its architecture, patrons, and history.* Toronto: Oxford University Press.

—. 1993. *Lost Toronto: Images of the city's past.* Rev. ed. Toronto: McClelland and Stewart.

Dennison, Barry. 2003. Tempest around a teacup: Dealing with the problems Yonge gave to Church. *Eye Magazine,* 5 June. http://www.eye/net/issue_06.06.03/news/church.html.

Deutsche, Rosalyn. 1996. *Evictions: Art and spatial politics.* Cambridge, MA: MIT Press.

Ditchett, S.H. 1923. *Eaton's of Canada: A unique institution of extraordinary magnitude.* New York: Dry Goods Economist (239 Thirty-Ninth Street).

Dixon, Guy. 2005. Big screen losing its magic in Canada. *Globe and Mail,* 29 June.

Donald, Betsy. 2002a. The permeable city: Toronto's spatial shift at the turn of the millennium. *Professional Geographer* 54, 2: 190-203.

—. 2002b. Spinning Toronto's golden age: The making of a "city that worked." *Environment and Planning A* 34, 12: 2127-54.

Drabinsky, Garth. 1995. *Closer to the sun: An autobiography.* Toronto: McClelland and Stewart.

Eckstut, Stanton. 1986. Solving complex urban design problems. In *Waterfront planning and development,* ed. A. Ruth Fitzgerald, 54-56. New York: ASCE.

Educon Marketing and Research Systems. 2003. A literature review to identify approaches and "really good examples" for dealing with social and physical disorder conditions in business improvement areas. Prepared for Wellesley Central Health Corporation and the Downtown Yonge B.I.A. Toronto. May.

Eisinger, Peter. 2000. The politics of bread and circuses: Building the city for the visitor class. *Urban Affairs Review* 35, 3: 316-33.

Fainstein, Susan S. 2001a. *The city builders: Property development in New York and London, 1980-2000.* Lawrence: University Press of Kansas.

—. 2001b. Inequality in global city-regions. In *Global City-Regions,* ed. Allen J. Scott, 285-98. Oxford: Oxford University Press.

—. 2005. Planning theory and the city. *Journal of Planning Education and Research* 25, 2: 121-30.

Fainstein, Susan S., and Scott Campbell, eds. 2002. *Readings in urban theory.* 2nd ed. Oxford: Blackwell.

Fainstein, Susan S., and Robert James Stokes. 1998. Spaces for play: The impacts of entertainment development on New York City. *Economic Development Quarterly* 12, 2: 150-65.

Faludi, Andreas. 1973. *Planning Theory.* Oxford: Pergamon.

Filey, Mike. 1986. *Not a one-horse town: 125 years of Toronto and its streetcars.* Toronto: Mike Filey.

Filion, Pierre, Heidi Hoernig, Trudi Bunting, and Gary Sands. 2004. The successful few: Healthy downtowns of small metropolitan regions. *Journal of American Planning Association* 70, 3: 328-43.

Fischler, Raphaël. 1995. Planning theory as culture and experience. *Journal of Planning Education and Research* 14, 3: 173-78.

—. 1998. Toward a genealogy of planning: Zoning and the welfare state. *Planning Perspectives* 13, 4: 389-410.
Fleming, R.B. 1996. Yonge at 200. *The Beaver*. August-September: 29-33.
Flyvbjerg, Bent. 1998. *Rationality and power: Democracy in practice*. Chicago: University of Chicago Press.
Foglesong, Richard E. 1990. Planning for social democracy. *Journal of the American Planning Association* 56, 2: 215-16.
Forester, John. 1989. *Planning in the face of power*. Berkeley: University of California Press.
—. 2000. Conservative epistemology, reductive ethics, far too narrrow politics: Some clarifications in response to Yiftachel and Huxley. *International Journal of Urban and Regional Research* 24, 4: 914-16.
Forsyth, Ann. 1999. *Constructing suburbs: Competing voices in a debate over urban growth*. Amsterdam: Gordon and Breach Publishers.
Foster, Peter. 1993. *Towers of debt: The rise and fall of the Reichmanns*. Toronto: Key Porter Books.
Fourier, Charles. 1975. *The utopian vision of Charles Fourier*. Trans. and ed. Jonathan Beecher and Richard Bienvenu. London: Jonathan Cape.
Friedmann, John. 1969. Notes on societal action. *Journal of the American Institute of Planners* 35: 311-18.
Frisken, Frances. 2008. *The public metropolis: The political dynamics of urban expansion in the Toronto region, 1924-2003*. Toronto: Canadian Scholars' Press.
Gallant, Thomas. 2004. Interview by Andy Barrie, CBC Radio, 22 October. http://www.cbc.ca. File name: 20041022GREoct.ram.
Gandhi, Unnati. 2005. Torontonians adapt to frightening "routine." *Globe and Mail*, 28 December.
Garden District Residents Association. The Garden District Residents Association. http://www.gardendistrict.ca.
Gehl, Jan. 1996. *Life between buildings: Using public space*. Copenhagen: Arkitektens Forlag.
—. 2000. *New city spaces*. Copenhagen: Danish Architectural Press.
Gehl, Jan, and L. Gemzøe. 1996. *Public spaces, public life*. Copenhagen: Arkitektens Forlag.
Gertler, Meric S. 2001. Flows of people, capital and ideas. *Canadian Journal of Policy Research* 2, 3: 119-30.
Gertler, Meric S., Yael Levitte, Denise Moylan, and Greg Spencer. 2000. *A region in transition: The changing structure of Toronto's regional economy*. Toronto: Neptis Foundation/Department of Geography, University of Toronto.
Gilg, Andrew W. 2005. *Planning in Britain: Understanding and evaluating the postwar wystem*. London: Sage.
Glancey, Jonathan. 1998. *Twentieth-century architecture: The structures that shaped the century*. London: Carlton Books.
Gleeson, Brendan. 2003. The difference that planning makes. *Environment and Planning A* 35, 5: 765-70.
Globe and Mail. 1974. Yonge Street is wrong place for a mall, report says. 4 June.
—. 1999. Corner stories. Photographs by Patti Gower. 11 September.
—. 2001. Notice of public meeting: Request to amend the Municipal Code, chapter 297. 16 January.
Godfrey, Stephen. 1983. Wintergarden plan would give Toronto mini "Times Square." *Globe and Mail*, 24 February.
Goheen, Peter. 1993. The ritual of the streets in mid-19th-century Toronto. *Environment and Planning D: Society and Space* 11, 2: 127-45.

Gómez, María V. 1998. Reflective images: The case of urban regeneration in Glasgow and Bilbao. *International Journal of Urban and Regional Research* 22, 1: 106-21.

Gómez, María V., and Sara González. 2001. A reply to Beatriz Plaza's "The Guggenheim-Bilbao Museum effect." *International Journal of Urban and Regional Research* 25, 4: 898-900.

Gordon, David L.A. 1997. *Battery Park City: Politics and planning on the New York waterfront.* Amsterdam: Gordon and Breach.

Gordon, David L.A., and Tasha Elliott. 2007. Lost in translation: A brief comparison of Canadian land use planning terminology. *Plan Canada* 47, 1: 28-31. Updated at Planning Canadian Communities. http://www.PlanningCanadianCommunities.ca.

Gordon, Todd. 2004. The return of vagrancy law and the politics of poverty in Canada. *Revue canadienne de politique social/Canadian Review of Social Policy* 54: 34-57.

Graham, Stephen, and Simon Marvin. 2001. *Splintering urbanism: Networked infrastructures, technological mobilities and the urban condition.* London: Routledge.

Grant, Jill. 2005. Rethinking the public interest as a planning concept. *Plan Canada* 45, 2: 48-50.

Graser, Dina. 2000. Panhandling for change in Canadian law. *Journal of Law and Social Policy* 15: 45-91.

Greenberg, Kenneth. 1991. Toronto: Streets revived. In *Public streets for public use,* ed. Anne Vernez Moudon, 189-202. New York: Columbia University Press.

Greenberg, Kenneth, and Frank Lewinberg. 1996. Reinventing planning in Toronto. *Plan Canada* 36, 3: 26-27.

Gutting, Gary. 2001. *French philosophy in the twentieth century.* Cambridge: Cambridge University Press.

Hagen Hodgson, Petra. 1997. Centro Oberhausen: Les choses vont mal pour la véritable ville. *BauDoc-Bulletin* (April): 5-13.

Hall, Peter G. 2002. *Cities of tomorrow: An intellectual history of urban planning and design in the twentieth century.* 3rd ed. Oxford: Blackwell.

Hall, Peter G., and Kathy Pain, eds. 2006. *The polycentric metropolis: Learning from mega-city regions in Europe.* London: Earthscan Publications.

Hanna, Kevin S., and Margaret Walton-Roberts. 2004. Quality of place and the rescaling of urban governance: The case of Toronto. *Journal of Canadian Studies* 38, 3: 37-67.

Harrold, David, Frances Mathers, Richard Schachow, Alison Will, and Kenneth Wong. 1971. The Mall Project. Student class project, Ryerson Polytechnical Institute, funded by an Opportunities for Youth Program grant.

Harvey, David. 1989a. From managerialism to entrepreneurialism: The transformation in urban governance in late capitalism. *Geografiska Annaler* 71 B, 1: 3-17.

–. 1989b. *The urban experience.* Baltimore: Johns Hopkins University Press.

Healey, Patsy. 1983. *Local plans in British land use planning.* Oxford: Pergamon.

–. 1997. *Collaborative planning: Shaping places in fragmented societies.* London: Macmillan.

–. 2003. Collaborative planning in perspective. *Planning Theory* 2, 2: 101-23.

–. 2007. *Urban complexity and spatial strategies: Towards a relational planning for our times.* London: Routledge, RTPI Library Series.

Healey, Patsy, Simin Davoudi, Mo O'Toole, Solmaz Tavsanoglu, and David Usher. 1992. *Rebuilding the city: Property-led urban regeneration.* London: E. and F.N. Spon.

Healey, Patsy, Paul McNamara, Martin Elson, and Andrew Doak. 1988. *Land use planning and the mediation of urban change: The British planning system in practice.* Cambridge: Cambridge University Press.

Healey, Patsy, Michael Purdue, and Frank Ennis. 1995. *Negotiating development rationales and practice for development obligations and planning gain.* London: E. and F.N. Spon.

Hebbert, Michael. 2006. Town planning versus *urbanismo*. *Planning Pespectives* 21, 3: 233-51.

Hermer, Joe. 2001. Streets Act an excuse to outlaw tender hearts. *Globe and Mail*, 27 February.

Hodge, Gerald, and David L.A. Gordon. 2008. *Planning Canadian communities: An introduction to the principles, practice, and participants.* 5th ed. Toronto: Thomson Nelson.

Hoyt, Lorlene M. 2003. The Business Improvement District: An internationally diffused approach to revitalization. Paper presented at ACSP/AESOP conference, Leuven, Belgium, July 2003. http://www.urbanrevitalization.net.

–. 2004. Collecting private funds for safer public spaces: An empirical examination of the business improvement district concept. *Environment and Planning B: Planning and Design* 31, 3: 367-80.

Hume, Christopher. 1998a. "Big Urban Room" a Winner. *Toronto Star*, 2 December.

–. 1998b. Dundas Square could set Yonge Free. *Toronto Star*, 12 September.

–. 1999a. Dundas Square "Torch" getting ready for liftoff. *Toronto Star*, 11 September.

–. 1999b. The Tower of Babel rises over Toronto. *Toronto Star*, 30 October.

–. 2000a. Dundas Square sets the stage for innovation. *Toronto Star*, 20 December.

–. 2000b. Pleasure palace still on deck. *Toronto Star*, 12 December.

–. 2002. Dundas Square already inspiring. *Toronto Star*, 28 March.

–. 2003. Eaton Centre's unfolding rebirth. *Toronto Star*, 26 August.

Hume, George. 1999. Interview by the author and Nik Luka. Tape recording. 5 February. Toronto.

Hurst, Lynda. 1994. The trouble with Yonge Street. *Toronto Star*, 6 August.

Ibbitson, John. 1997. *Promised land: Inside the Mike Harris revolution.* Toronto: Prentice Hall.

Immen, Wallace. 1998a. A date with the wrecker's ball: Urban renewal strikes at the heart of Yonge Street's seedy "strip." *Globe and Mail*, 19 November.

–. 1998b. Toronto duo awarded Dundas Square contract. *Globe and Mail*, 2 December.

–. 1999. Downtown facelift starts with wrecking ball. *Globe and Mail*, 23 March.

–. 2001a. Project breathes life into Yonge. *Globe and Mail*, 21 May.

–. 2001b. Times Square goes north. *Globe and Mail*, 7 August.

Imrie, Rob, and Huw Thomas. 1993. The limits of property-led regeneration. *Environment and Planning C: Government and Policy* 11, 1: 87-102.

–. 1999. *British urban policy: An evaluation of the urban development corporations.* 2nd ed. London: Sage.

Innes, Judith E. 1996. Planning through consensus building: A new view of the comprehensive planning ideal. *Journal of the American Planning Association* 62, 4: 460-72.

–. 2004. Consensus building: Clarifications for the critics. *Planning Theory* 3, 1: 5-20.

Israelson, David. 1997. New Gap dresses up Yonge Street. *Toronto Star*, 26 September.

Jacobs, Allan B. 1978. *Making city planning work.* Chicago: American Society of Planning Officials.

James, Natalie. 1998. Business complaints shut down Salvation Army's 50-bed hostel. *Toronto Star*, 27 May.

Jonas, Andrew E.G., and Kevin Ward. 2007. Introduction to a debate on city-regions: New geographies of governance, democracy and social reproduction. *International Journal of Urban and Regional Research* 31, 1: 169-78.

Kastner, Susan. 1997. Taking the fight to the streets. *Toronto Star*, 13 September.

Kayden, Jerold S. 2000. *Privately owned public space: The New York experience.* New York: Wiley.

Kilbourn, William. 1984. *Toronto remembered: A celebration of the city.* Toronto: Stoddart.

Kipfer, Stefan, and Roger Keil. 2002. Toronto Inc? Planning the competitive city in the new Toronto. *Antipode* 34, 2: 227-64.
Kluckner, Michael. 1988. *Toronto: The way it was*. Toronto: Whitecap.
Krushelnicki, Bruce W. 2007. *A practical guide to the Ontario municipal board*. 2nd ed. Markham, ON: LexisNexis.
Kuitenbrouwer, Peter. 2001a. Chaos reigns in parking garage. *National Post*, 10 September.
–. 2001b. It's the pits – More woes at Yonge-Dundas. *National Post*, 22 May.
Lakoff, George, and Mark Johnson. 1980. *Metaphors we live by*. Chicago: University of Chicago Press.
Larner, Wendy. 2003. Neoliberalism? *Environment and Planning D: Society and Space* 21, 5: 509-12.
Lauria, Mickey, and Robert K. Whelan. 1995. Planning theory and political economy: The need for reintegration. *Planning Theory* 14 (Winter): 8-33.
Laxer, James. 1995. Rise of new capitalism doomed Rae government. *Toronto Star*, 11 June.
Lemon, James T. 1985. *Toronto since 1918*. Toronto: James Lorimer.
–. 1996. *Liberal dreams and nature's limits: Great cities of North America since 1600*. Toronto: Oxford University Press.
Leo, Christopher. 1995. Global change and local politics: Economic decline and the local regime in Edmonton. *Journal of Urban Affairs* 17, 3: 277-99.
Lester, Lee. 2001. Dundas Square retail development edges forward. *Toronto Business Journal*, 1 (October): 5.
Levine, Marc. 1987. Downtown redevelopment as an urban growth strategy: A critical appraisal of the Baltimore renaissance. *Journal of Urban Affairs* 9, 2: 103-23.
Lofland, Lyn H. 1998. *The public realm: Exploring the city's quintessential social territory*. New York: Aldine de Gruyter.
Lord, Ian. 1998. Marvin Hertzman Holdings Inc. et al. v. City of Toronto, Corbett J., Toronto Court file No. 427-98, September 28, 1998 (Divisional Court). *Municipal and Planning Law Today* [Newsletter, Weir and Foulds LLP, Toronto] (October): 2493.
Loukaitou-Sideris, Anastasia, and Tridib Banerjee. 1998. *Urban design downtown: Poetics and politics of form*. Berkeley: University of California Press.
Lowry, Hollie. 1996. The Yonge Street subway. In *Researching Yonge Street*, ed. S.J. Brown, 62-67. Toronto: Ontario Genealogical Society/Toronto Historical Board.
Lyon, N. Barry. 1978. *Yonge Street Revitalization Project*. Toronto: N. Barry Lyon Consulting.
MacDonald, Gayle, and Paul Waldie. 1998. Livent: A real-life drama unfolds. *Globe and Mail*, 21 November.
Mathers, Debra, and Imtyaz Mohamed. 2004. 381 Yonge Street: 100 years of shared life. *Urban Lights* 6, 1: 1-2.
Mays, John Bentley. 1994. *Emerald City: Toronto revisited*. Toronto: Penguin.
McGuirk, Pauline M., and Andrew MacLaran. 2001. Changing approaches to urban planning in an "entrepreneurial city": The case of Dublin. *European Planning Studies* 9, 4: 437-57.
McQueen, Rod. 1999. *The Eatons: The rise and fall of Canada's royal family*. Rev. ed. Toronto: Stoddart.
Merlin, Pierre, and Françoise Choay. 2000. *Dictionnaire de l'urbanisme et de l'aménagement*. 3rd ed. Paris: Presses universitaires de France.
Milroy, Beth Moore. 1989. Constructing and deconstructing plausibility. *Environment and Planning D: Society and Space* 7, 3: 313-26.
Mirvish Productions. Our theatres – The Canon. Mirvish Productions. http://www.mirvish.com/OurTheatres/Canon.html.

Mitchell, Don, and Lynn A. Staeheli. 2006. Clean and safe? Property redevelopment, public space, and homelessness in downtown San Diego. In *The politics of public space,* ed. Setha Low and Neil Smith, 143-75. New York: Routledge.

Moloney, Paul. 1997. Yonge Street shops to fight plan. *Toronto Star,* 29 February.

—. 1998a. Spirit of renewal hits Yonge: Project draws calls from retailers, brokers. *Toronto Star,* 10 July.

—. 1998b. Yonge-Dundas plan may curb drug deals. *Toronto Star,* 18 February.

—. 2002. Downtown project still on: Councillor. *Toronto Star,* 28 March.

Moroni, Stefano. 2004. Towards a reconstruction of the public interest criterion. *Planning Theory* 3, 2: 151-71.

Moulaert, Frank, Arantxa Rodriguez, and Erik Swyngedouw. 2002. *The globalized city: Economic restructuring and social polarization in European cities.* Oxford: Oxford University Press.

Myers, Dowell, and Tridib Banerjee. 2005. Toward greater heights for planning: Reconciling the differences between profession, practice, and academic field. *Journal of the American Planning Association* 71, 2: 121-29.

Myers, J. 1977. *The great Canadian road: A history of Yonge Street.* Toronto: Red Rock.

Nelson, Suzy. 2001. The nature of partnership in urban renewal in Paris and London. *European Planning Studies* 9, 4: 483-502.

Newman, Harvey K. 2002. Race and the tourist bubble in downtown Atlanta. *Urban Affairs Review* 37, 3: 301-21.

Ontario Heritage Foundation. Elgin and Winter Garden theatres. Ontario Heritage Foundation. http://www.heritagefdn.on.ca/userfiles/HTML/nts_1_2374_1.html.

Owen, Robert, and G.D.H. Cole. [1813] 1966. *A new view of society and other writings.* Introduction by G.D.H. Cole. Everyman's Library. London: Dent.

Payne, Michael, Meenakshi Ponnuswami, and Jennifer Payne. 1996. *A dictionary of cultural and critical theory.* Oxford: Blackwell.

Pendakur, Manjunath. 1998. Drabinsky always dreamed the big dream. *Toronto Star,* 14 August.

Phillips, Rhys. 2000. The circus comes to town. *Globe and Mail,* 23 May.

Piccinato, Giorgio. 1987. Las teorias del urbanismo: Un intento de analisis. *Urbana* 7: 9-14.

Pine, B. Joseph, II, and James H. Gilmore. 1999. *The experience economy: Work is theatre and every business a stage.* Boston: Harvard Business School Press.

Plaza, Beatriz. 1999. The Guggenheim-Bilbao Museum effect: A reply to María V. Gómez's "Reflective images: The case of urban regeneration in Glasgow and Bilbao." *International Journal of Urban and Regional Research* 23, 3: 589-92.

—. 2008. On some challenges and conditions for the Guggenheim Museum Bilbao to be an effective economic re-activator. *International Journal of Urban and Regional Research* 32, 2: 506-17.

Porter, Catherine. 2005. Inside the Vancouver advantage: The price to put up paradise. *Toronto Star,* 14 May.

Powell, Betsy. 2000. No sign of curtain rising on Metropolis. *Toronto Star,* 6 October.

—. 2001a. Eaton Centre Cineplex suddenly fades to black. *Toronto Star,* 13 March.

—. 2001b. Movie chain sticking with Metropolis. *Toronto Star,* 26 January.

Rabinow, Paul. 1984. *Foucault reader.* New York: Pantheon Books.

—. 1989. *French modern: Norms and forms of the social environment.* Cambridge, MA: MIT Press.

Rae, Kyle. n.d. Personal agenda of Yonge-Dundas meetings. In possession of author.

Reade, Eric. 1985. An analysis of the use of the concept of rationality in the literature of planning. In *Rationality and planning: Essays on the role of rationality in urban and regional planning,* ed. M. Breheny and A. Hooper, 77-97. London: Pion.

Reddy, Michael. 1979. The conduit metaphor – A case of frame conflict in our language about language. In *Metaphor and thought,* ed. Andrew Ortony, 284-324. Cambridge: Cambridge University Press.

Reichl, Alexander J. 1999. *Reconstructing Times Square: Politics and culture in urban development.* Lawrence: University Press of Kansas.

Rochon, Lisa. 2003. There's no there there. *Globe and Mail,* 22 May.

Rowe, Peter G. 1997. *Civic realism.* Cambridge, MA: MIT Press.

Ruppert, Evelyn. 2006. *The moral economy of cities: Shaping good citizens.* Toronto: University of Toronto Press.

Sagalyn, Lynne B. 2001. *Times Square roulette: Remaking the city icon.* Cambridge, MA: MIT Press.

Sancton, Andrew. 2000. Amalgamations, service realignment, and property taxes: Did the Harris government have a plan for Ontario's municipalities? *Canadian Journal of Regional Science* 23, 1: 135-56.

Sandori, Paul, and William M. Pigott. 2000. *Bidding and tendering: What is the law?* 2nd ed. Toronto: Butterworths.

Sassen, Saskia. 2001. Impacts of information technologies on urban economies and politics. *International Journal of Urban and Regional Research* 25, 2: 411-18.

Scadding, Henry. [1873] 1966. *Toronto of old.* Abridged and edited by F.H. Armstrong. Toronto: Oxford University Press.

Schön, Donald A. 1979. Generative metaphor: A perspective on problem-setting in social policy. In *Metaphor and thought,* ed. Andrew Ortony, 254-83. Cambridge: Cambridge University Press.

Scott, Allen J., and Michael Storper. 2003. Regions, globalization, development. *Regional Studies* 37, 6-7: 579-93.

Sewell, John. 1993. *The shape of the city: Toronto struggles with modern planning.* Toronto: University of Toronto Press.

–. 2003. Let's make a deal planning. *Eye Magazine,* 20 February.

Sewing, Werner. 2000. Heart, artificial heart or theme park? Trying to make sense of Potsdamer Platz. In *Potsdamer Platz: Urban architecture for a new Berlin,* ed. Yamin von Rauch and Jochen Visscher, 47-58. Berlin: Jovis.

Sharpe, L.J. 1996. Is there a case for metropolitan government? In *Urban regions in a global context: Directions for the Greater Toronto Area,* ed. Judith K. Bell and Steven Webber, 83-102. Toronto: Centre for Urban and Community Studies/Program in Planning, University of Toronto.

Siemiatycki, Matti. 2007. What's the secret? Confidentiality in planning and infrastructure using public/private partnerships. *Journal of the American Planning Association* 73, 4: 388-404.

Slinger, Joey. 1998. More Outfitters than you can shake a paddle at. *Toronto Star,* 19 November.

Soria y Puig, Arturo. 1995. Ildefonso Cerdà's general theory of "urbanización." *Town Planning Review* 66, 1: 15-39.

–. 1999. *Cerdà: The five bases of the general theory of urbanization.* Madrid: Electa.

Soskolne, Ronald L. 1996. *Downtown Yonge: A program to promote the regeneration of Toronto's main street.* Report submitted to YSBRA. January.

Stagg, Ronald. 1998. *Serving society's needs: A history of Ryerson Polytechnic University.* Toronto: Ryerson Polytechnic University.

Steed, Judy. 2002. Dundas Square coming to life. *Toronto Star,* 18 March.

Stein, David Lewis. 1996. Let's give Yonge St. a piazza. *Toronto Star,* 3 March.

Stone, Clarence N. 1989. *Regime politics: Governing Atlanta, 1956-88.* Lawrence: University Press of Kansas.

–. 1993. Urban regimes and the capacity to govern: A political economy approach. *Journal of Urban Affairs* 15, 1: 1-28.

Strauss, Marina. 1999. Hudson's Bay to close Outfitters store. *Globe and Mail,* 13 May.

Symes, Martin, and Mark Steel. 2003. Lessons from America: The role of business improvement districts as an agent of urban regeneration. *Town Planning Review* 74, 3: 301-13.

Taylor, Bill. 1998. Curtain about to rise on Pantages Tower condos. *Toronto Star,* 29 August.

Taylor, Nigel. 1998. *Urban planning theory since 1945.* London: Sage.

Theobald, Steven. 1999. Building a new icon in Toronto's heart. *Toronto Star,* 23 March.

–. 2000. Lanes and pool hall anchor Yonge and Dundas complex. *Toronto Star,* 16 March.

Tiesdell, Steve, and Philip Allmendinger. 2005. Planning tools and markets: Towards an extended conceptualisation. In *Planning, public policy and property markets,* ed. David Adams, Craig Watkins, and Michael White, 56-76. Oxford: Blackwell.

Tompkins, Jeremy. 2003. Square to nowhere. *Now Magazine,* 24-30 April. http://www.nowtoronto.com/issues/2003-04-24/news_feature_p.html.

Turbayne, Colin Murray. 1971. *The myth of metaphor.* Rev. ed. Columbia: University of South Carolina Press.

Turok, I. 1992. Property-led urban regeneration: Panacea or placebo? *Environment and Planning A* 24, 3: 361-79.

Vaughan, Colin. 1998. Planning for the new social order. *Toronto Star,* 6 July. http://www.thestar.com/back_issues/EDI...06/opinio/980706NEW02_OP-VAUGHAN.html.

Vining, Aidan R., and Anthony E. Boardman. 2008. Public-private partnerships in Canada: Theory and evidence. *Canadian Public Administration* 51, 1: 9-44.

Waitt, Gordon. 1999. Playing games with Sydney: Marketing Sydney for the 2000 Olympics. *Urban Studies* 36, 7: 1055-77.

Wanagas, Don. 2003. Developer's dream: Kyle Rae was a three-storey man – Now he promotes tall towers. *Now Magazine,* 6 March. http://www.nowtoronto.com/issues/2003-03-06/news_feature.php.

Waqué, Stephen. 2000. The role of expropriation in city centre revitalization. Speech to the spring meeting of the Ontario Expropriation Association, 1 June. The Expropriation Law Centre. http://www.expropriation.ca.

Ward, Stephen V. 1997a. A paradoxical persistence? British influences on Canadian and Australian urban planning. In *Old institutions – New images,* ed. J.M. Barker, 51-60. Perth: Curtin University.

–. 1997b. *Selling places: The marketing and promotion of towns and cities, 1850-2000.* London: E. and F.N. Spon.

–. 1999. The international diffusion of planning: A review and a Canadian case study. *International Planning Studies* 4, 1: 53-77.

–. 2000. Re-examining the international diffusion of planning. In *Urban planning in a changing world,* ed. Robert Freestone, 40-60. London: E. and F.N. Spon.

–. 2003. Learning from the US: The Americanisation of Western urban planning. In *Urbanism imported or exported?* ed. Joe Nasr and Mercedes Volait, 83-106. Chichester: Wiley.

Warson, Albert. 2004. P3s get broader role in infrastructure. *Globe and Mail,* 25 May.

White, N. 1999. The great divide. *Toronto Star,* 30 October.

Whyte, William H. 1980. *The social life of small urban spaces.* Washington, DC: Conservation Foundation.

–. 1988. *City: Rediscovering the center.* New York: Doubleday.

Williams, Gwyndaf. 2003. *The enterprising city centre: Manchester's development challenge.* London: Spon Press.

Winter, I., and T. Brooke. 1993. Urban planning and the entrepreneurial state: The view from Victoria, Australia. *Environment and Planning C: Government and Policy* 11, 3: 263-78.

Wirth, Louis. [1938] 1969. Urbanism as a way of life. In *Classic essays on the culture of cities,* ed. Richard Sennett, 143-64. New York: Meredith Corporation.

Wolfe, Jeanne M. 1989. Theory, hypothesis, explanation and action: The example of urban planning. In *Remaking human geography,* ed. Suzanne MacKenzie and Audrey Kobyashi, 62-77. London: Unwin Hyman.

Woltjer, Johan. 2000. *Consensus planning.* Aldershot, UK: Ashgate.

Wong, Tony. 1997. Square dealings on Yonge. *Toronto Star,* 23 February.

Yiftachel, Oren. 1989. Towards a new typology of urban planning theories. *Environment and Planning B* 16, 1: 23-39.

Yiftachel, Oren, and Margo Huxley. 2000. Debating dominance and relevance: Notes on planning theory. *International Journal of Urban and Regional Research* 24, 4: 907-23.

Young, Pamela. 1999. Street of dreams. *Azure* (September-October): 75.

Zukin, Sharon. 1995. *The cultures of cities.* Cambridge, MA: Blackwell.

Index

Note: "(f)" after a page number indicates a figure

Alberti, Leon Battista, 284*n*20
Albrechts, Louis, 226
Alexander, Christopher, 33
Alexander, Ernest, 26, 283*n*8, 283*n*10, 284*n*18
Allmendinger, Philip, 17, 27, 284*n*19
amalgamation, 195; of Metropolitan Toronto, 12-13
AMC, 136, 175, 181-82; as anchor tenant, 121-25, 172, 222, 287*n*9, 288*n*11
analogue (between planning and urban social science), 22-24, 225, 232-33, 285*n*1. *See also* metaphor; models, utopian
architectural treatise, 31, 220
Architecture, 190
argument: forms of, 138-40
Armstrong, F.H., 62
Arthur, Eric, 46
Ascher, François, 14
Atrium, The, 72, 130, 131, 186, 207, 291*n*7

Banerjee, Tridib, 9, 17, 282*n*6
Barber, John, 291*n*7
Barberian, Arron, 86, 87
Barberian's Steak House, 86
Bartley, Brendan, 22
Bassin, Arthur, 27
Bata, 208
Battery Park City (NY), 229-30, 292*n*7
Beauregard, Robert, 26-27, 42

Benali, Kenza, 14
Beyard, Michael D., 181, 289*n*6
Black, John, 289*n*2
Black, Max, 285*n*1
blight, 233; physical, 158-59, 173; social, 143-47, 150, 159, 173, 177
Board of Management (City of Toronto), 135; on land negotiations, 123, 129, 288*n*9; on redevelopment, 104, 106-7, 128
Board of Trade building, 47
Boardman, Anthony E., 248
Bone, James, 208
bonus zoning, 125, 127, 191, 242-43
Booth, Philip, 283*n*10
Bordreuil, Jean-Samuel, 14
Bourette, Susan, 135
Bradford, Michael, 22
Branson, Sir Richard, 11
Brindley, Tim, 9, 224, 226-27, 248, 283*n*9
broken window theory, 146
Brooke, T., 10
Brooks, Michael P., 27
Brown Derby restaurant, 51
Brown + Storey Architects, 189, 190
Brownill, Sue, 227, 292*n*6
Bruce Report, 63
Bryant Park (NY), 145, 168, 179
business improvement area (BIA), 10, 196-97, 246-47
business improvement district (BID), 176, 177

Cadillac-Fairview, 86, 122, 291n7
Campbell, Heather, 283n8
Campbell, Scott, 22, 283n14
Canadian Architect, 190
Canadian Centre for the Study of Retail Activity, 114
Canadian Charter of Rights and Freedoms, 134, 289n16
Canadian Institute of Planners, 283n11
Canadian Law Dictionary, 290n14, 291n16
Canadian Music Hall of Fame, 183
Canadian Olympic Committee, 189
Canary Wharf, 179, 227, 228, 287n2, 292n4. *See also* Docklands, The (London); London Docklands Development Corporation (LDDC)
Canon Theatre, 61
Careless, J.M.S., 62
Castells, Manuel, 282n1
Cerdà, Ildefons, 32
Chipeniuk, Raymond, 14
Chipman, John, 18, 244, 283n8
Choay, Françoise, 225, 237, 282n2; on enduring figures of urbanism, 24, 31-33, 215, 220-21, 233
Church-Wellesley BIA, 212
cinemas, 45, 61, 159-60, 174, 182; as anchor, 107, 121-22, 125; megaplex format, 111-12, 154, 172, 175, 181-82; multiplex format, 121, 181, 182, 186, 199. *See also* AMC; Cineplex Odeon; Famous Players; Festival Hall; playdium
Cineplex Odeon, 61, 86, 91; bankruptcy of, 172, 199; bid to anchor PenEquity development, 121-22, 124, 287n9
City People Community Planning and Research, 51
Cityplan '91, 61, 57, 255
Clark, David, 282n3
ClearChannel, 136, 207
closed-circuit television (CCTV), 203, 215
College Park. *See* Eaton's (T. Eaton Company Limited), College Street store
Collins, George R. and C.C., 290n10
Colonial Tavern, 60
commissioner of planning and development (R. Millward), 70, 73, 89-90, 135; planning style, 218; and regeneration planning, 76-85, 94-96, 105-6, 248;
commissioner of urban development services (J. Morand), 123, 126, 127
community improvement project (CIP), 79, 97, 240-42; actions permitted under, 74, 79, 128, 170-72; boundaries of, 80(f); grants and loans program, 74, 79, 81, 106, 241-42; relationship to blight, 171-72, 173-74, 240-41
concinnitas, 284n22
constructionism. *See* space, social construction of
conviviality, 2, 226
Corcoran, Mary, 282n7
Corey, Kenneth, 282n1
Cormier, Brendan, 282n5
Courchene, Thomas J., 9, 12
Courcier, Sabine, 22, 226
criminal activities, 5, 55, 64, 131-33; clash with economic interests, 70, 124, 165-68; displacement of, 12, 91-92, 212-13; and DYBIA, 201-4
Crombie, David, 87, 95
Culler, Jonathan, 286n11
Curtler, Hugh M., 139

Daily Star, 63
Dault, Gary Michael, 113
David Bitton Buffalo, 208
Deas, Iain, 22
DeFilippis, James, 10
Dendy, William, 49, 57, 59, 63, 64
Dennison, Barry, 213
density bonusing. *See* bonus zoning
Derrida, Jacques, 36
Deutsche, Rosalyn, 10
discourse on urbanism. *See* urbanism, discourse on
Disney, 106, 121, 136, 287n2; Imagineering, 289n6; Quest, 182; World, 186
displacement, 175, 179, 209-13
Ditchett, S.H., 48
Dixon, Guy, 182
Docklands, The (London), 227-28, 230. *See also* Canary Wharf; London Docklands Development Corporation (LDDC)
Donald, Betsy, 16
Downtown Yonge Business Improvement Area (DYBIA), 201-4, 212, 215. *See also* Yonge Street Business and Residents Association
Drabinsky, Garth, 60-61, 199, 209, 290n7. *See also* Livent

drug dealing. *See* criminal activities
Dundas Square (Parcel D), 62, 64, 189-99, 205; board of management for, 195-99, 204, 207, 215; as catalyst for renewal, 43, 115-16, 163, 171-72; commercial use of, 10-11, 20, 153, 195-97; construction of, 91, 191-92; design of, 120, 189-91, 184; early proposal for, 286*n*6; opening of, 192-93, 197; as part of redevelopment package, 124, 150, 158, 160, 167; public features of, 174, 179, 193-99; siting of, 115, 189, 190, 223
Dundas Square Street, 75
Dykstra, Gretchen, 176

eatertainment, 148, 154
Eaton Centre, 4, 29, 42-43, 82, 90; as complement to Urban Entertainment Centre (UEC), 112, 121, 172, 181; and crime, 165-68; exterior changes to, 106, 199-201, 206; and loitering, 156, 215; and official plan, 61, 67-70, 218; property interests of, 71-73, 157-58; and Yonge Street Business and Residents Association (YSBRA), 86. *See also* Cadillac-Fairview
Eaton's (T. Eaton Company Limited): bankruptcy of, 199; College Street store, 49-50, 285*n*3; historical connection to downtown Toronto, 45-50, 63
Eckstut, Stanton, 229
ecological fallacy, 151
Economic Development, Culture and Tourism Department (Toronto), 195-97
Eisinger, Peter, 10
ejusdem generis rule, 171, 290*n*14
Elgin and Winter Garden theatres, 60-61
entertainment district (Toronto), 112-13, 142, 180, 202-3, 214
environmental determinism, 85
Evergreen. *See* Yonge Street Mission (YSM)
exactions. *See* bonus zoning
expropriation, 102-3, 119-21, 174; appeal of, 178; appropriate use of, 158, 160, 164; and property owners, 113-14, 128-30; and social blight, 168-70
Expropriations Act, 169-70, 173-74, 245

facade grants and loan program. *See* community improvement project (CIP), grants and loans program

Fainstein, Susan S.: and Campbell, 283*n*14; on income disparities, 15, 228; on planning theories, 27-28; on property development, 22, 228, 229, 242, 292*n*4; and Stokes, 282*n*7
Faludi, Andreas, 24
Famous Players, 60-61, 113, 121
feasibility studies, 98, 114, 117, 118-21, 223
Festival Hall, 113, 172, 182
Filey, Mike, 62
Filion, Pierre, 15
filter-down economic theory. *See* trickle-down economic theory
Fischler, Raphaël, 30-31, 39
Fleming, R.B., 44
floor space index, 59, 285*n*4
Flyvbjerg, Bent, 10, 223
Foglesong, Richard E., 27
Forester, John, 284*n*16, 284*n*19
Forsyth, Ann, 285*n*1
Foster, Peter, 292*n*4
Foucault, Michel, 32, 36, 284*n*25
Fourier, Charles, 284*n*23
Friedmann, John, 37
Friends of Old City Hall, 57
Frisken, Frances, 13

Gallant, Thomas, 44
Gandhi, Unnati, 203
Gap, 208
Garden District Residents Association (GDRA), 205-6
Garnier, Tony, 32
Gauvreau, Mike, 192
Gehl, Jan, 286*n*5
Gemzøe, L., 286*n*5
gentrification, 76, 96, 219
Gertler, Meric S., 16
Gilg, Andrew W., 283*n*9
Gilmore, James H., 181
Glancey, Jonathan, 254
Gleeson, Brendan, 16
Globe and Mail, 55, 192, 197
Glover, Robert. *See* urban design study
Godfrey, Stephen, 60
Goheen, Peter, 44
Gómez, María V., 10
González, Sara, 10
Gordon, David L.A., 22, 219, 220, 229, 239
Gordon, Todd, 9
Graham, Stephen, 282*n*1

Grant, Jill, 283*n*8
Graser, Dina, 10
Greenberg, Kenneth, 51, 56, 59, 230
Guess Jeans, 208
Gutting, Gary, 286*n*11

H&M, 199, 208
Hagen Hodgson, Petra, 10
Hall, Peter G., 9, 15, 30
Hanna, Kevin S., 9
Hard Rock Cafe, 154, 203, 208
Harrold, David, 55
Harvey, David, 30, 282*n*3
Healey, Patsy: on planning gain, 242, 243; on planning system, 17, 248, 283*n*9; on planning theory, 28, 284*n*19; on property-led development, 22, 228, 292*n*4
Hebbert, Michael, 19
Heintzman building, 60, 208
Henderson Development, 122
Hennes & Mauritz. *See* H&M
Hermant building, 208
Hermer, Joe, 291*n*19
highest and best use, 71, 77, 78
Hodge, Gerald, 219, 220, 239
Holy Trinity Church, 56-57
homeless, 212, 225, 289*n*2; and public space, 282*n*4, 289*n*3; as a Yonge-Dundas area issue, 5, 74, 133, 141, 144-46. *See also* hostels
hostels, 5, 69, 205; displacement of, 94, 109, 184, 209-10, 213. *See also* homeless
House of Industry, 64
Howard, Ebenezer, 32
Hoyt, Lorlene M., 10, 247
Hudson's Bay Company, 52, 208
Hume, Christopher, 91; on advertising media, 181, 199, 207, 208; on Dundas Square, 190, 192, 193, 201; on Metropolis, 183; on the Torch, 184, 186
Hume, George, 49, 286*n*6
Hurst, Lynda, 89, 90
Huxley, Margo, 284*n*16
hyperspatialization, 284*n*23

Ibbitson, John, 12
imagery, 42, 82, 233; fall-and-redemption, 65; rotting heart, 42-45, 51, 232; sky is not falling, 219, 232; Toronto's heart, 153, 175, 179, 214, 225. *See also* urbanism, enduring figures of

Immen, Wallace, 43, 91, 183, 189-90, 208, 212
Imrie, Rob, 226, 292*n*6
incremental change, 95, 98, 128, 224; as inadequate, 111, 164, 142-43, 152-53; as intention of regeneration, 74-77, 84, 158-59; support from studies for, 85, 96, 118, 214
Industrial Revolution, 13, 15
industrial-era cities, 14
Innes, Judith, 284*n*19
innovation, 2, 31-43, 235; and planning, 16, 30, 237, 249
Institut canadien des urbanistes, 283*n*11
International Gap Inc. *See* Gap
Irigaray, Luce, 36
Israelson, David, 208

Jacobs, Allan B., 292*n*2
Jacobs, Jane, 229, 230
James, Natalie, 210
Jewellery Exchange, 86
Johnson, Mark, 286*n*11
Joint Board, 38, 244; decision, 173-77, 271-79; hearing arguments and evidence: by appellants, 155-62; by city's contract lawyer, 162-73; by city's program planner, 140-53; by consulting program director, 153-55. *See also* Ontario Municipal Board (OMB)
Jonas, Andrew E.G., 15

Kastner, Susan, 93
Kayden, Jerold S., 290*n*11
Keil, Roger, 9
Kerim, Vahe, 86
KFC, 87, 166
Kilbourn, William, 55
Kings, The (Toronto), 149, 229-30, 292*n*7
Kipfer, Stefan, 9
Kirkland, Michael, 113
Kluckner, Michael, 46, 47, 62, 63, 64
KPMG, 102, 122, 123, 124, 127
Krushelnicki, Bruce W., 176, 243
Kuitenbrouwer, Peter, 91, 192

Lakoff, George, 286*n*11
Lamb, Thomas, 60-61
land assembly, 107-11, 108(f), 147-48, 156, 160
land speculation, 120, 143
Larner, Wendy, 282*n*3
Lauria, Mickey, 27

Laxer, James, 9
Le Corbusier (Charles-Édouard Jeanneret), 32
Leduke, N.W., 291n10, 291n11
Leicester Square (London), 1, 136
Lemon, James, 13, 63; on Toronto's downtown streets, 44, 47, 49, 57, 286n9
Leo, Christopher, 292n12
Lester, Lee, 183
leveraging, 222, 227, 292nn4-5
Levine, Marc, 282n7
Lewinberg, Frank, 230
Lintern, Gregg. See program planner
Livent, 61, 209, 291n7. See also Drabinsky, Garth
Loews Cineplex, 182
Lofland, Lyn H., 10, 282n6
London Docklands Development Corporation (LDDC), 227-28, 292n6. See also Canary Wharf; Docklands, The (London)
Loukaitou-Sideris, Anastasia, 9, 282n6
Lowe, Herbert, 51
Lowry, Hollie, 50, 51
Luka, Nik, 38, 39
Lynch, Kevin, 33
Lyon, N. Barry, 47, 59

MacDonald, Gayle, 209
Mackenzie, William Lyon, 43
MacLaran, Andrew, 10, 226
Maple Leaf Gardens, 51
market synergy, 112, 181, 189
Marshall, Robert, 283n8
Marvin, Simon, 282n1
Massey Hall, 52, 60
Mathers, Debra, 64
Mays, John Bentley, 44
Mazza, Luigi, 283n9
McGill-Granby Residents' Association, 93, 94, 206-7
McGuirk, Pauline M., 10, 226
McQueen, Rod, 47, 49-50, 56-57, 285n2
megaplex. See cinemas
Merlin, Pierre, 19
metaphor, 36, 66, 232-33, 285n1, 286n11. See also analogue; models, utopian
Metropolis (Parcel A), 121, 175-76, 180-84, 209; renamed, 183
Millennium Partners, 122
Millward, Robert. See commissioner of planning and development

Milroy, Beth Moore, 37
Mirvish Productions, 60, 61
Mitchell, Don, 282n4
models, utopian, 31-33, 38, 215, 222-24, 230-33. See also urbanism, enduring figures of
Mohamed, Imtyaz, 64
Moloney, Paul, 91, 119, 131, 174, 183, 287n7
More, Thomas, 284n21
Moroni, Stefano, 283n8
Moulaert, Frank, 22, 228, 292n6
multiplex. See cinemas
municipal reorganization, 135, 136
Municipal Act, 158, 201, 245-48
Municipal Code, 194, 195, 201, 246
Myers, Dowell, 17
Myers, J., 53, 54, 55

Nathan Phillips Square (Toronto), 168, 170, 193-97, 280-81, 290n12
Nathanson, Nathan L., 60
National Anti-Poverty Organization, 291n19
Nelson, Suzy, 248
neoconservatism, 12, 282n3
neoliberal, 282n3
Newman, Harvey K., 282n7
Normal School, The, 64

obiter dicta, 176-77, 291n16
Oceanic Adventures International Corporation, 122-23, 126
official plan, 34, 96-97, 105, 220, 234-35, 239-43; arguments about, at Joint Board hearing, 150-51, 156-58, 160, 163; Eaton's challenge of, 61, 67-70, 218
O'Keefe Brewing Co. Ltd., 64
Old City Hall, 56-57
Olympia & York, 227, 286n2, 292n4
Olympic Spirit Toronto. See Torch, The (Parcel C)
Ontario Coalition Against Poverty (OCAP), 93, 212
Ontario Heritage Act, 286n7
Ontario Heritage Foundation, 60-61
Ontario Human Rights Code, 194
Ontario Municipal Board (OMB), 38, 42, 243-44; as a locus of debates about urbanism, 18-19, 30, 283n8. See also Joint Board
Onyschuk, Bohdan, 287n9, 288n11

Owen, Robert, 284*n*23

Pain, Kathy, 15
panhandling, 5, 56, 74, 124, 176-77; confusion with criminal activity, 144, 225; displacement of, 175; regulation of, 10, 134, 201, 289*n*16, 291*n*19. *See also* squeegeeing
Pantages, Pericles Alexander, 60
Pantages Theatre, 60-61, 86, 209
Pantages Tower, 209
parking. *See* Yonge-Dundas area, parking
Payne, Michael, 285*n*26
pedestrian counts, 55, 111, 151
pedestrian mall, 54-56
Pendakur, Manjunath, 209
PenEquity Management Corporation, 121-25, 127, 174, 182-83, 288*n*11
Phillips, Rhys, 186
Piccinato, Giorgio, 19
Pigott, William M., 288*n*12
Pine, B. Joseph, II, 181
planners, 17; scapegoating of, 34, 226, 237
planning: in Canada, 238-39; entrepreneurial approach to, 218, 227, 229, 282*n*3; entrepreneurial approach to: and Toronto, 9, 86, 97, 179, 215; as field of practice, 16, 29-30; as marketing, 87-89, 103, 222; in Ontario, 239-48; origins of, 235-36; three lenses approach to, 81, 94, 97, 105, 230, 248-49
Planning Act (ON), 239-43
planning activity, 34, 226, 236-37; as catalyst, 218; as curative, 33, 231, 235; customary practices associated with, 219-21, 224
planning and development department (Toronto). *See* Urban Development Services department (Toronto)
planning framework, 17-18, 31, 34, 283*n*9; demands of, 219, 222, 225-26, 234-37; use of, 23, 30, 197, 198, 224. *See also* official plan
planning gain. *See* bonus zoning
planning methods. *See* planning activity, customary practices associated with
planning theories, 21-34, 35, 37, 217-26, 235-36, 284*n*15
playdium, 112, 113, 214
Plaza, Beatriz, 10

policing: displacement of criminal activity, 91-92, 212-13; Joint Board on, 176, 177; and regeneration project, 69, 73-74, 149; sub-station in the Eaton Centre, 73, 131, 199, 201; testimony at Joint Board hearing, 131-33, 146, 160-61, 166-67. *See also* criminal activities
Porter, Catherine, 242
postindustrial city, 15
poststructuralism, 36-38, 284*n*26
Potsdamer Platz, 42
Powell, Betsy, 182, 199
program director, 99-104, 106, 129-30, 136, 174-75; and small property owners, 113-14, 143. *See also* Joint Board, hearing arguments and evidence; Soskolne, Ron
program manager, 103-4, 107, 130, 183
program planner, 103, 106, 158, 159. *See also* Joint Board, hearing arguments and evidence
property owners: small, 114, 128-30, 177, 223; as speculators, 143, 168
property-led development, 22, 218, 227, 229-31
public interest, 168-70, 282*n*8; locus of, 18, 177, 235; and property-led redevelopment, 179, 228-31, 118; in relation to private interest, 12, 34, 37, 127, 155
public space, 10-11
public-private partnership (PPP), 86, 227; characteristics of, 89-90, 99-105, 179, 222; in *Municipal Act*, 247-48; Toronto's use of, 10, 118, 128; YSBRA/Toronto PPP, 86-87, 95

Rabinow, Paul, 31, 285*n*25
Rae, Kyle, 89, 90-91, 129, 134, 287*n*9, 288*n*14. *See also* ward councillor
Reade, Eric, 284*n*18
Realrationalität, 10, 137, 223
Reddy, Michael, 286*n*11
regime theory, 23, 27, 36
Reichl, Alexander J., 22, 42, 282*n*7
request for proposals (RFP), 125-28, 288*n*12
request for qualifications (RFQ), 113, 120, 122-25, 288*n*12
retail, 77, 114, 120, 267; and capital investment, 12, 23, 101, 149, 156-58; changed patterns of, 15, 20, 45, 47, 51,

52, 56; and Eaton's, 4, 61, 67-69, 131, 141, 165; and entertainment synergy, 180-81, 189; new type of, 91, 98, 103, 208-9; off-street, 52, 68, 255; street-oriented, 50-51; and Yonge-Dundas area redevelopment, 115-17, 147-48, 150, 151-55; and Yonge-Dundas area regeneration, 79, 105, 221. *See also* urban box format
rhetoric, 65-66, 85, 163-67, 178; of city-building, 104, 163-64, 172, 225, 290n10. *See also* imagery
RKO Pictures. *See* Famous Players
Robert Simpson Company, The, 46-47, 49-50
Robertson, Rebecca, 106, 176, 289n5
Robson, Brian, 22
Rochon, Lisa, 193
Rodriguez, Arantxa, 22, 228, 292n6
Rowe, Peter, 11
Roy Thomson Hall, 52
Royal Alexandra Theatre, 52
Ruppert, Evelyn, 283n1
Rydin, Yvonne, 9, 224, 226-27, 248, 283n9
Ryerson Polytechnical Institute. *See* Ryerson University
Ryerson University, 5, 64, 196, 209, 218; air rights negotiation, 115, 175, 181; involvement in regeneration, 73, 95
Ryrie Building, 47, 106, 291n7

Safe Streets Act (Ontario), 135
Sagalyn, Lynne B., 22, 228-29
Salvation Army, 94, 109-10, 127, 184, 209-10
Sam the Record Man, 131, 208-9, 210-11
Sancton, Andrew, 13
Sandori, Paul, 288n12
Sassen, Saskia, 15
Scadding, Henry, 46
scapegoating. *See* planners, scape-goating of
Scéno Plus Inc., 186
Schön, Donald, 285n1, 286n11
scientism, 33, 224
Scott, Allen J., 15
Sears, 199
Senator Restaurants, 86, 122, 127, 184, 209, 210
Sewell, John, 242, 285n2
Sewing, Werner, 42

SFX/ClearChannel Entertainment, 61. *See also* ClearChannel
Sharpe, L.J., 13
shelters. *See* hostels
shoppertainment, 20
Siemiatycki, Matti, 248
signage: as feature of regeneration, 76-77, 97, 130-31; sign features, 183, 184, 187(f), 188(f), 207-8. *See also* ClearChannel; Skyemedia
Silver Rail restaurant, 51, 208
Simcoe, John Graves, 46
Sitte, Camillo, 32, 290n10
SkyeMedia, 208
Slinger, Joey, 208
Sniderman, Robert, 86, 87, 104, 184, 189
social construction of space. *See* space, social construction of
Society for Working Boys, 64
Soleri, Paolo, 32-33
Soria y Mata, Arturo, 32
Soria y Puig, Arturo, 284n24, 290n10
Soskolne, Ron, 87, 124, 286n2; as consultant to YSBRA, 87, 90, 94, 96. *See also* Joint Board, hearing arguments and evidence; program director
space: conceptualizations of, 2, 11, 33, 221, 229-30; and planning theories, 226, 230-33, 236; social construction of, 23-24, 36
Spadina Expressway, 44
spectacularization of public space, 11, 204, 215
speculation. *See* land speculation
squeegeeing, 133-35. *See also* panhandling
St. James Square, 64
Staehli, Lynn A., 282n4
Stagg, Ronald, 64
statutory planning requirements. *See* planning framework
Steed, Judy, 190, 193
Steel, Mark, 247
steering committee. *See* public-private partnership (PPP)
Stein, David Lewis, 55
Stoker, Gerry, 9, 224, 226-27, 248, 283n9
Stone, Clarence N., 23
Storper, Michael, 15
Strachan, Bishop John, 43
Strauss, Marina, 208
street survey, 77, 84

Strip, The. *See* Yonge Street Strip
structuralism, 35-36
Stübben, Joseph, 290n10
suburbanization, 16
super commissioners, 104, 115, 135
Swisscan Developments, 122
Swyngedouw, Erik, 22, 228, 292n6
Symes, Martin, 247

Taylor, Bill, 209
Taylor, Nigel, 22, 24, 284n15, 284n19
Telmer, Colin R., 9, 12
Theobald, Steven, 182, 207, 208
theory of urbanism, 32
Thomas, Huw, 226, 292n6
350 Yonge Street development application, 70-71, 76, 81, 148, 161
three lenses planning approach. *See* planning, three lenses approach to
Tiesdell, Steve, 17
Times Square (New York City), 42, 183, 186; Business Improvement District for, 176-77, 195; and expropriation, 100, 128; as inspiring two features of regeneration, 76, 96; as model for core area redevelopment, 1, 60, 106, 136, 185; Tompkins, Jeremy, 91, 183; as utopist model, 175, 228-29, 230
Torch, The (Parcel C), 184-89, 209
Toronto: urban form of, 16, 45, 50-51, 66, 226
Toronto Association of Business Improvement Areas (TABIA), 201
Toronto East Downtown Neighbourhood Alliance (TEDNA), 205
Toronto East Downtown Neighbourhood Association (TEDNA), 204-5, 207
Toronto East Downtown Residents Association (TEDRA), 91-93, 95, 204-7, 210
Toronto Historical Board, 60, 286n7
Toronto Life Square, 183
Toronto Parking Authority, 197
Toronto Theatre Alliance, 196
Toronto Transit Commission (TTC), 50-51, 71, 91, 182
tourism, 82, 112, 181; and local economy, 12, 101-2, 170; safe-and-clean environment for, 87, 176, 210, 282n7
Treadwell Shine, Kasey, 22
trickle-down economic theory, 145, 228, 289n2

Turbayne, Colin Murray, 285n1, 286n11
Turok, I., 292n6

underground pedestrian system (PATH), 71, 287n3
urban box format, 71, 72(f), 77, 97, 221. *See also* retail
urban design study, 71, 74-77, 84, 89; use in clarifying direction for Yonge Street, 148-49, 219, 221
urban development corporation (UDC), 22, 176, 227, 240, 292n6. *See also* London Docklands Development Corporation (LDDC)
urban development project (UDP), 22, 227
Urban Development Services department (Toronto), 8, 69-70
urban entertainment centre (UEC), 91, 111-13, 153, 154-55, 289n6; defence of, 148, 150, 163, 167, 175-76; implementation of, 180-84
Urban Outfitters, 291n7
urban theory, 23, 27, 35
urbanism, 13, 19-20, 23, 228-37; discourse on, 29-33, 220-21, 224-25, 228, 236-37; enduring figures of, 24, 31, 215, 220-21, 224, 233-37; long trajectory of, 31-33, 237. *See also* models, utopian
Urbanism, New, 283n12
urbanity, 2, 15, 60, 226, 236
urbanization, 13-14, 226

Vaughan, Colin, 175
Vining, Aidan R., 248
Virgin Entertainment Group Inc., 11, 182-83

Waitt, Gordon, 10
Waldie, Paul, 209
Wallace, Marcia, 283n9
Walton-Roberts, Margaret, 9
Wanagas, Don, 91
Waqué, Stephen, 102, 286n1, 287n9, 288n11, 291n15
Ward, Kevin, 15
Ward, Stephen V., 42, 238, 290n9
ward councillor, 73, 90-91, 129, 175; characterizations of others 91, 114, 143, 182, 184-86; distrust of planning by, 95-97, 222-23, 235; power of, 85, 117, 213-14, 215; and PPP, 86, 99,

103-4, 179; and resident associations, 205-7; and Salvation Army property, 209-10; and squeegee youth, 134; and UECs, 106, 113, 121. *See also* Rae, Kyle
Warson, Albert, 248
Webb & Knapp, 50
Whelan, Robert K., 27
White, N., 46
Wickson, Ted, 50
Williams, Gwyndaf, 10
Wilson, Mark I., 282*n*1
Winter, I., 10
Wirth, Louis, 14, 283*n*12
Wolfe, Jeanne M., 17
Woltjer, Johan, 26, 28
Wong, Tony, 91
World's Biggest Jean Store, 6(f), 11, 130, 287*n*7
Wright, Frank Lloyd, 32
Wright, Gary. *See* program manager

Yiftachel, Oren, 284*n*15, 284*n*16
Yonge, Sir George, 46
Yonge Street Business and Residents Association (YSBRA), 69, 85-90, 176, 212; consultant's report to city council, 94-95; conversion to BIA, 201; public-private partnership with City of Toronto, 99-103, 128. *See also* Downtown Yonge Business Improvement Area (DYBIA); public-private partnership (PPP)
Yonge Street Mission (YSM), 64, 91, 93, 196, 207
Yonge Street Strip, 5, 51-54, 59, 77, 165; and development controls, 67, 70-71, 82, 156-58
Yonge-Dundas area, 3-8; built form and land use, 64-65, 76, 82, 83(f), 146-48, 254-56; knitting of east and west, 92, 110, 152, 219; parking, 105, 110, 115, 150, 191-92
Yonge-Dundas Square Board of Management, 195-99, 204
Young, Pamela, 91, 190

Zeckendorf, William, 50
Zeidler, Eberhard, 57, 285*n*2
Zukin, Sharon, 289*n*3

Printed and bound in Canada by Friesens

Set in Myriad and Garamond by Artegraphica Design Co. Ltd.

Copy editor: Lesley Erickson

Proofreader: Stephanie VanderMeulen